TENTH ANNUAL EDITION

THE
DAILY PLANET
ALMANAC

1985

Terry Reim, Editor

 AVON
PUBLISHERS OF BARD, CAMELOT, DISCUS AND FLARE BOOKS

STAFF Art/Production Director . . . . .Kim Long
Science Editor .Christopher Richard
Astrologer . . . . .Nan De Grove
Gardener . . . . .Liz Caile
Meteorologist . . . . .Ed Pearl
Copy Editing . . . Sally Furgeson, Tom Auer, Jim Atherton
Proofreading . . . Louis Gregory, Bonnie Zee, Barbara Platz,
Gabrielle Zeiss-Zeplezauer

TYPESETTING	Argent Typesetting, Boulder, Colorado
	Typo/Graphics Dixon, California
CAMERA	Eight Days A Week, Boulder, Colorado
	The Stat House, Denver
	Holt Graphics, Oakland, California
PRINTING & BINDING	Offset Paperback, Dallas, PA
ASTRONOMICAL DATA	LeRoy E. Doggett, Nautical Almanac Office
	U.S. Naval Observatory, Washington, D.C.
TECHNICAL CONSULTANTS	Dr. Robert McFarland, M.D.
	Irving Kerner
	Larry Sessions
NETWORKING SUPPORT	Network Resources, Denver, Colorado
RESEARCH	Kathleen Cain, Library of the Community College
	of Denver, North Campus
SOFTWARE PROGRAMMING	Leif Smith
DATA STORAGE	Gathers Software, Denver, Colorado

The *Daily Planet Almanac* is written, edited, and composed on Eagle PC II's from
EAGLE COMPUTER COMPANY, Los Gatos, California.

LITERARY AGENT   Peter Livingston Associates, Boulder, Colo

AVON BOOKS   Copyright© 1984 by Daily Planet Almanac, Inc.
A division of   Published by arrangement with Daily Planet Almanac, Inc.
The Hearst Corporation
1790 Broadway   **ISBN:** 0-380-88344-9
New York, New York 10019   **ISSN:** 0148-5369

Avon Books are available at special quantity discounts
for bulk purchases for sales promotions, premiums,
fund raising or educational use. Special books, or
book excerpts, can also be created to fit specific
needs.

For details, write or telephone the office of the
Director of Special Markets, Avon Books, 1790
Broadway, New York, New York 10019. 212-399-1357.

Through rain or shine, or dark of night . . . . *The Daily Planet Almanac*
is available through the mail. Order additional copies
from the address below. Please make checks payable to: **AVON BOOKS**

$3.95 plus $1.00 postage and handling . . . $4.95 total   No C.O.D.'s, please.

The Daily Planet Almanac (Title No. 88344-9)
AVON BOOKS, DEPT. DP1
Order Entry
Route 2 Box 767
Dresden, TN 38225

Table of Contents
Calendar begins on page 17

HOLIDAYS

Dec. 25	**Christmas Day (*)** ...... **Tue**	May 05	Cinco De Mayo .... Sun
Dec. 26	Boxing Day* .... Wed	May 12	Mother's Day .... Sun
Jan. 01	**New Year's Day** .... **Tue**	May 15	Armed Forces Day ..... Wed
Jan. 06	Epiphany .... Sun	May 16	Ascension Day .... Thu
Jan. 11	John McDonald's B'day* . Fri	May 18	Peace Day .... Sat
Jan. 15	Martin Luther King Day . Tue	May 20	Victoria Day* .... Mon
Jan. 20	Inauguration Day .... Sun	May 21	1st Day of Ramadan .... Tue
	Super Bowl Sunday ..... Sun	**May 27**	**Memorial Day** .... **Mon**
Feb. 02	Ground Hog Day .... Sat	June 09	Children's Day .... Sun
Feb. 11	Inventor's Day .... Mon	June 14	Flag Day .... Fri
Feb. 12	Lincoln's Birthday .... Tue	June 16	Father's Day .... Sun
Feb. 15	Susan B. Anthony Day ... Fri	June 24	St. John Baptist Day* ... Mon
Feb. 18	**President's Day** .... **Mon**		Discovery Day* .... Mon
Feb. 19	Mardis Gras .... Tue	July 01	Dominion Day* .... Mon
Feb. 20	Ash Wednesday .... Wed	**July 04**	**Independence Day** ..... **Thu**
Feb. 22	Washington's Birthday ... Fri	July 15	Orangemen's Day* .... Mon
Feb. 24	First Sunday in Lent ..... Sun	Aug. 05	Civic Holiday* .... Mon
Mar. 08	Int'l Women's Day ...... Fri	Aug. 19	Discovery Day* .... Mon
Mar. 11	Johnny Appleseed Day . Mon	**Sep. 02**	**Labor Day (*)** .... **Mon**
Mar. 15	Ides of March .... Fri	Sep. 16	Rosh Hashanah .... Mon
Mar. 17	St. Patrick's Day .... Sun	Sep. 24	Native American Day ... Tue
Mar. 18	St. Patrick's Day* ...... Mon	Sep. 25	Yom Kippur .... Wed
Mar. 31	Palm Sunday .... Sun	Oct. 09	Leif Erickson Day ..... Wed
Apr. 01	All Fool's Day .... Mon	Oct. 12	Columbus Day .... Sat
Apr. 05	Good Friday (*) .... Fri	**Oct. 14**	**Columbus Day (obs.)** ... **Mon**
Apr. 06	1st day of Passover .... Sat		Canadian Thanksgiving . Mon
Apr. 07	**Easter Sunday** .... **Sun**	Oct. 24	United Nation's Day .... Thu
	World Health Day ..... Sun	Oct. 27	Daylight Time Ends ..... Sun
Apr. 08	Easter Monday* .... Mon	Oct. 31	Halloween .... Thu
Apr. 15	Income Tax Deadline .. Mon	Nov. 01	All Saints' Day .... Fri
Apr. 19	Patriots' Day .... Fri	Nov. 05	Election Day .... Tue
Apr. 23	St. George's Day* ...... Mon	Nov. 11	Remembrance Day* ... Mon
Apr. 24	Arbor Day .... Wed		Veteran's Day .... Mon
Apr. 28	Daylight Time Begins ... Sun	**Nov. 28**	**Thanksgiving** .... **Thu**
May 01	May Day .... Wed	Dec. 08	Hanukkah .... Sun
May 03	National Sun Day .... Fri	Dec. 17	Wright Brothers' Day ... Tue

* Denotes Canadian Holiday; **Bold** denotes U.S. Federal Holiday.

Seasons

Winter Solstice: 08:23 PST; 12/21/84
Vernal Equinox: 08:14 PST; 3/20/85
Summer Solstice: 03:44 PDT; 6/21/85
Autumnal Equinox: 19:08 PDT; 9/22/85
Winter Solstice: 14:08 PST; 12/21/85

Cycles and Eras

Gregorian	1985	Jan. 01
Japanese	2645	Jan. 01
Julian	6698	Jan. 14
Roman	2738	Jan. 14
Chinese (Ox)	4683	Feb. 20
Indian (Saka)	1907	Mar. 22
Nabonassar	2734	Apr. 27
Diocletian	1702	Sep. 11
Grecian	2297	Sep. 14
Byzantine	7494	Sep. 14
Islamic (Hegira)	1406	Sep. 15
Jewish	5746	Sep. 16

Meteor Showers

Showers	Maximum	per hour
Quadrantid*	Jan. 03	50
Lyrid	Apr. 21	15
Eta Aquarid*	May 05	20
Delta Aquarid*	July 30	20
Perseid*	Aug. 10-13	50
Draconid	Oct. 09	10
Orionid	Oct. 20	20
Taurid	Nov. 09	16
Leonid	Nov. 16	15
Andromedid	Nov. 25-27	10
Geminid*	Dec. 13	50

* most intense

HOOLIGANS

At Home And Abroad

A Tale From Ken Kesey

There was this guy stopped by here, he was my translator from Czechoslovakia — his name was Jraslav. He was also the translator of Vonnegut and had a great big moustache like Vonnegut. He had traveled across the country on a bus to meet me.

So we got to talking, smoking dope, drinking Canadian Club, and he says how when he got back to Czechoslovakia, he wouldn't see any more good booze or dope for years.

"Have you thought about defecting?" I asked.

"Of course I've thought about defecting . . . but it's my land, I gotta fight for it," he said. "I did 19 months in jail; I'm a hero to many of these people."

"What'd you do 19 months for?"

"Hooliganism," he says.

"You mean that's what they called it?"

"Yes, hooliganism," he says.

I looked it up. It goes back to a family — the Hooligans — they were a bad, fightin', brawlin' bunch of guys who came over to the United States, and the word stuck, both in the U.S. and Europe. So in Czechoslovakia you can be busted for acting like a Hooligan.

"Well what'd you actually do?" I asked Jraslav.

"Oh, me and some friends were at a coffeehouse," he says. "We'd been drinking and my friends were talking aloud about the Soviet Union. You know how you Americans hate the government? Well imagine how you'd hate the government if they were the Russians!

"Anyway, this guy suddenly tells us

we better shut up about that because he's a member of the KGB. But we keep talking anyway. So he calls somebody else over, then they call some soldiers. I went to the toilet. I thought I could get out the window, but two soldiers came with me and escorted me out. I realized I was going to jail.

"I was about three-quarters drunk and, as I was escorted back to our table, there's this KGB agent standing with his back to me. So I blind-sided the motherfucker! Put him in the hospital for five months!

"When the judge sentenced me he said, 'You know you'd have only got nine months if you hadn't hit him? For hitting him you get ten months more.' But, by god, every extra month was worth it!"

When I let Jraslav off down at the bus station, where he took a bus to catch the plane back to Czechoslovakia, we looked in each other's eyes. We both knew everything about each other, and that we were some kind of allies in this worldwide struggle going on. He was a big warm-eyed good guy, kind of worthless, just like *everybody* we know. Tears came to our eyes, and we embraced.

"The reason they let *Cuckoo's Nest* be translated in Czechoslovakia was because they think it's an anti-American novel," he told me before boarding the bus.

"This is a joke over there — everyone knows it's not anti-American, it's anti-totalitarian!" Jraslav chuckled. "This is the flaw with the government's thinking — they never really know what's going on."

HOW TO USE THE ALMANAC

All Calendar Times are PACIFIC TIME
(00:00 = midnight   12:00 = noon)

THE DAILY PLANET ALMANAC uses a seasonal calendar beginning with the first day of winter, the Winter Solstice, which occurs this year on December 21, 1984 (page 17). This is the time when, from the northern hemisphere, the Sun appears at its lowest point in the southern sky; it is thus the shortest day of the year. This Almanac divides the year into twelve seasonal months, named for the twelve portions of the heavens through which the Sun, Moon, and planets all appear to travel.

WEATHER FORECASTS

Ten pages of monthly weather predictions for all regions of the U.S. begin on page 112, with a large map defining these regions. A professional meteorologist provides these forecasts exclusively for the *Daily Planet Almanac*. The predictions are computed with scientific data derived from advanced instrumentation, using pioneering techniques of forecasting.

THE CALENDAR

The *Daily Calendar* (pages 17 - 169) provides a box for each day, which always appears on the right hand page. There are six calendar pages in each month. Each calendar box gives the Sunrise/Sunset and Moonrise/Moonset which vary somewhat with latitude and longitude. If you live far from the San Francisco area, you can determine exact times for these phenomena at your location by consulting the tables on p. 196, for the Sun, and p. 192, for the Moon; and then applying corrections found on page 8.

The calendar box also depicts the lunar phase for each day, and gives the moonsign and the times of its changes, planetary aspects, and other important astronomical information. The times of these events do not vary with terrestrial co-ordinates.

For instance, the Full or New Moon occurs at one instant, regardless of your location. If it happens to be noon, Pacific Time, readers outside the Pacific Time Zone need only add the hourly correction necessary for their time zone. Consult page 12 and inside covers for any questions regarding time.

Capricorn, the first month of Winter, begins at the point in the Earth's orbit called the Winter Solstice (page 17), and continues until the Earth has travelled 1/12th (30°) of its distance around the Sun. The next 1/12th of the journey is the second month of Winter, Aquarius (pages 29-40) and so on.

Throughout this almanac, various astronomical terms are used to describe planetary positions and times. For further explanation see **About Time**, page 8 and the **Glossary**, pages 219-221.

Within the calendar section for each month, the first three left-hand pages always contain the recurring monthly **Growing**, **Celestial Events**, and **Forecast**, in this order.

GROWING

This monthly kitchen and garden guide provides suggestions for various gardening activities through the cycle of the seasons, and offers information on topics of particular interest relating to food production.

Application of this information can vary slightly depending on the length of the growing season at your location. Growing seasons will vary with latitude, altitude, local climatic conditions and seasonal weather anomalies.

CELESTIAL EVENTS

The DPA also features a monthly star map (second left-hand page each month) which depicts the relative position of the stars at the beginning of each month for 40° N. latitude at 22:00. These maps should require no adjustment to local time, or to time zones, since variance here is negligible.

They will vary, however, depending on the time of the night, and the time of the month you are viewing.

The information listed in the corners of the Star Maps refers you to the most accurate map for your particular hour of viewing. For viewing at times other than 22:00, it will prove a handy reference. Locations at great variance from 40° N. latitude will exhibit more or less of the northern and southern stars.

The text at the bottom of each page lists times when the planets are visible, occultations, and other astronomical events.

FORECASTS

The DPA also provides a monthly astrological forecast (third left hand page each month) and a planetary map which shows the relative positions of all the planets at month's beginning, and depicts their motion through the month.

If you are confused about which planets and signs are represented by which symbols, see **Glossary** (page 219).

This map can also serve as a guide for viewing the planets, since their relative positions are depicted accurately.

It is important to remember, however, that the zodiacal symbols on this map represent the signs, or the seasonal months, and NOT the zodiacal constellations. The relationship betwen the signs and the constellations is continually changing because of the precessional movement of the Earth. The Signs represent a measure of distance East from our reference point, the Vernal Equinox, which is presently located about two degrees in the Constellation of Pisces.

For an accurate picture of the planetary positions in relation to the Constellations of the Zodiac, imagine the map with the planets stationary in their same relationship, the 12 segments rotated counterclockwise 28° (about one whole segment).

TABLES AND CHARTS

An abundant selections of Tables, Charts and Maps begin on page 183 with a directory to this section.

INDEX

For the location of any subject not immediately apparent in the Table of Contents (page 5), refer to the handy **Index**, page 222.

Aspects

Planets are said to be in **conjunction** when they occupy the same celestial longitude, or Right Ascension.

CONJUNCTION

They are in **opposition** when they are on exact opposite sides of the sky as we view them from the Earth, or at opposite Celestial Longitudes (180° apart) or opposite Right Ascensions (12 hours apart).

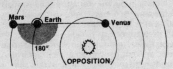

OPPOSITION

Syzygy is a configuration of any three or more celestial objects lined up as in conjunction or opposition.

Trine occurs when two planets are 120° apart.

TRINE

Square occurs when two planets are 90° or 270° from each other.

By extension all of these terms are used to describe a close approximation of any such configuration. In astronomy, the terms *at conjunction* or *at opposition* refer to a planetary alignment with the Sun.

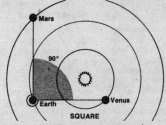

SQUARE

The Inner Planets, Mercury and Venus, cannot be at opposition. The term **Inferior Conjunction** describes the alignment where the inner planet is directly between the Sun and the Earth. **Superior Conjunction** occurs when the inner planet is directly beyond the Sun.

INFERIOR CONJUNCTION

SUPERIOR CONJUNCTION

ABOUT TIME

All times in the calendar section of the Daily Planet Almanac are computed for San Francisco, California (122°28′ W. longitude; 37°48′ N. latitude). Calendar times are expressed in Pacific Standard Time (Dec. 21 to April 2, and October 27 to December 21) or Pacific Daylight Time (April 28 to October 26).

For locations outside of the *Pacific Time Zone*, obtain *clock times* of phenomena other than risings and settings, by adding the PST correction for your time zone from the map, inside front cover, to the time given on the daily square. If your location does not observe *daylight time*, you must subtract one hour between April 24 and October 29.

For most locations in the U.S. and southern Canada, times of rising and setting of the sun and moon given for San Francisco will be within one hour of *clock time* in your location. Since the elevation of the observer and the horizon can easily produce variations in rising and setting times of at least one hour, greater accuracy is seldom necessary. However, to obtain exact times for your location, given a flat horizon, see the corrections given below.

SUN RISE and SET — Obtain the *local mean time* of rise or set at your latitude from the table, page 196. Next, find the *time zone meridian* of longitude for your time zone on the map, inside front cover. If you are west of the *time zone meridian*, add four minutes for every degree west. If you are east, subtract 4 minutes for every degree. Add one hour if *daylight time* is in effect.

MOON RISE and SET — Obtain the *local mean time* at the *meridian of Greenwich* of rise or set at your latitude from the table, page 192. Subtract this time from the time given on the following day. Multiply these minutes by four times the number of degrees in your longitude and divide by 24. Add this number of minutes to the *local mean time* at the *meridian of Greenwich* for your day. This gives your *local mean time*. To find your *clock time*, find the *time zone meridian* of longitude for your time zone on the map, inside front cover. If you are west of the *time zone meridian*, add four minutes for every degree west. If you are east, subtract 4 minutes for every degree east. Add one hour if daylight time is in effect.

Sidereal Time. Time based on the rotation of the earth relative to the vernal equinox. Used for stellar and planetary calculations.
Ephemeris Time. Sidereal time corrected for variations in the Earth's rotational velocity.
Apparent Solar Time. Time based on the rotation of the Earth relative to the Sun.

Because the rates of the earth's rotation and revolution are not constant, the sun's speed across the sky varies. The sun is sometimes either fast or slow.

Local Apparent Time. Sundial time; *apparent solar time* with noon established each day as the sun's crossing of the observers meridian of longitude.
Mean Solar Time. Apparent solar time corrected for variations in the Earth's rotational and orbital velocities. Hence average *apparent solar time*. This is the basis of most systems of time encountered in life and this almanac.
Local Mean Time. *Mean solar time* with noon established as the mean time of the sun's crossing of the observers meridian of longitude.
Time Zone Meridian. One of a series of meridians of longitude spaced every 15° from the *meridian of Greenwich* used to establish the *zone time* kept within a time zone.
Meridian of Greenwich. The meridian passing through the observatory in Greenwich, England, serving as the prime meridian i.e. 0° longitude, and the *time zone meridian* for Greenwich Time.
Greenwich Mean Time. *Local mean time* at the *meridian of Greenwich*.
Zone Time. *Local mean time* at a *time zone meridian* kept over an area enclosed within meridians of longitude 7½° on either side of the *time zone meridian*, or within a similar area defined by convention or law. See time zone maps on the inside covers.
Standard Time. *Zone time* adopted in a legally defined time zone, especially on or near land.
Daylight time. *Standard time* plus one hour.
Pacific Standard Time. *Standard* time in the Pacific time zone based on the 120° *time zone meridian* and used as the major time reference in this almanac.
Clock Time. *Standard* or *daylight time* kept at the appropriate times of the year on your clock.
Universal Time. *Greenwich Mean Time*.

FISHING PREDICTIONS FOR 1985

Sometimes when you go fishing, it seems that there is no substitute for luck. However, in the long run, skill and experience result in more and bigger fish caught. The days indicated can help you be more successful when you fish by choosing days when fish are more active and hungrier. These days have been predicted in advance using lunar and solar movements in relation to the earth. Good Luck!

	01	02	03	04	05	06	07	08	09	10	11	12	13	14	15	16	17	18	19	20	21	22	23	24	25	26	27	28	29	30	31
JAN				🐟	🐟	🐟	🐟	🐟	🐟	🐟						🐟	🐟	🐟	🐟	🐟	🐟										
FEB			🐟	🐟	🐟	🐟	🐟	🐟							🐟	🐟	🐟														
MAR			🐟	🐟	🐟	🐟	🐟	🐟								🐟	🐟	🐟													🐟
APR	🐟	🐟	🐟				🐟	🐟	🐟	🐟																					
MAY					🐟	🐟	🐟	🐟	🐟											🐟	🐟	🐟	🐟								
JUN			🐟	🐟	🐟	🐟														🐟	🐟	🐟					🐟	🐟			
JUL			🐟	🐟	🐟	🐟	🐟	🐟	🐟																		🐟	🐟	🐟		
AUG	🐟	🐟														🐟	🐟	🐟										🐟	🐟	🐟	
SEP													🐟	🐟	🐟																
OCT																	🐟	🐟	🐟	🐟	🐟										
NOV													🐟	🐟	🐟	🐟											🐟	🐟	🐟	🐟	
DEC											🐟	🐟	🐟	🐟	🐟	🐟											🐟	🐟	🐟	🐟	

Factors Influencing Results:
1) **Time of Day.** It is usually best to fish within 2 hours after sunrise and 2 hours before sunset.
2) **Weather.** Steady or rising barometer indicates time of increased feeding. Never fish during a thunderstorm; but light steady rain can prompt some kinds of fish to feed.
3) **Traffic.** Lots of other people fishing can cause enough commotion to keep fish from biting, but it can also indicate that a lot of people have discovered that the fish are biting.
4) **Time of Year.** Later spring and early fall are almost always the best times of year to fish. However, some kinds of fish don't follow this rule, and anyway, most people cannot always adjust their lives to the fishing season.

Lunar Gardening

The Lunar Gardening chart below is based on the age-old tradition that the most beneficial results are obtained if each specific gardening task is performed when the Moon is in both the appropriate phase (vertical columns) and appropriate sign of the zodiac (horizontal rows). Discretion must be exercised, however, since this chart is designed to indicate only the most propitious times for the gardening chores listed in the Legend below, providing other conditions are favorable. These other conditions will vary with each locality depending on the length of the **growing season, latitude, altitude, local climatic conditions, seasonal weather patterns,** and the **individual life cycle** of the fruits and vegetables being nurtured.

LEGEND

1 PLANT for Leaf	7 PLANT for Trees	13 HARVEST and Can	19 PRUNE to Lessen
2 PLANT Grains	8 PLANT for Winter	14 HARVEST and Dry	20 CULTIVATE
3 PLANT for Vine	9 HARVEST	15 FERTILIZE Quickacting	21 CONTROL Pests
4 PLANT to Fruit	10 HARVEST Leaf	16 FERTILIZE Slowacting	22 COMPOST
5 PLANT for Root	11 HARVEST Fruits	17 PRUNE to Set	23 IRRIGATE
6 PLANT for Seeds	12 HARVEST and Store	18 PRUNE to Limit	24 FERMENT

	NEW MOON → FIRST QUARTER	FIRST QUARTER → FULL MOON	FULL MOON → LAST QUARTER	LAST QUARTER → NEW MOON
ARIES	9 17 18 20	3 8 10 11	12 18 20	7 14 19
TAURUS	1 15	8	5 13 16	23
GEMINI	2 17	3 4 8	12	6
CANCER	1 2 15 23	3 4 8 10	5 13 16	6 7 22 23 24
LEO	18	11 21	12 13 20	14 19
VIRGO	9 20	21	9	22 23 24
LIBRA	2 23	4		
SCORPIO	1 2 9 15 17 23	3 4 10	5 13	6 7 22 23 24
SAGITT	9 17 18 20	11	12 16 18 20	7 14 19
CAPRIC	15	8 21	5 16	7
AQUAR	17 20	3 11	12 13 18	
PISCES	1 9 15 20 23	10	5 13 16	6 7 22 23 24

→WAXING MOON→ →WANING MOON→

EXAMPLE: Let's say it's May 22, 1985. What gardening tasks can you perform according to the lunar gardening tradition? ① Consult the Calendar box for this day (page 77). ② Determine lunar phase for this day (between New and 1st Quarter) ③ Determine Lunar Sign for this day (Cancer). ④ Consult chart above for phase (left hand vertical column) and the sign of Cancer (fourth row). ⑤ Consult Legend above for the gardening activity defined by each number in this box: *1= plant for leaf; 2= Plant for grains; 15= Fertilize with quick acting nutrients; 23= Irrigate.* Perform any or all of these tasks providing weather conditions are appropriate.

EXAMPLE: Let's say you want to schedule a week's vacation in August to can some garden vegetables. ① Scan the chart above, find the number which represents Canning (13= Harvest and can). ② Scan the chart above for appearances of the number 13: It appears in the right middle column (lunar phase between Full and Last Quarter) when the Moon is in the signs of Taurus, Cancer, Leo, Scorpio, Aquarius, and Pisces. ③ Turn to the calendar section for the month of August, and locate the day of the Full Moon (July 31 — page 103). ④ Find the days between Full and Last Quarter Moon when the Moon is in any of the signs above (August 3, 4, 9, 10). Schedule your vacation accordingly and can away.

On January 21, 1984, Jed Kesey, the youngest son of Faye and Ken Kesey, was fatally injured when the van in which he was a passenger, plummeted from an icy road into a ravine near Spokane, Washington. Jed was 20 years old. Another passenger, Lorenzo West, also died in the accident.

Both were members of the University of Oregon wrestling team. At the time, they were traveling, along with seven others, to a wrestling meet. Upon receiving news of the accident, the Keseys traveled to Spokane. There they anguished for two days, standing watch over their son, who was attached to a life support system in the intensive care unit.

Their tragic vigil ended finally, when a solitary tear rolled down Jed's cheek. It was the only response he had made since receiving the severe head injuries two days before. The family ordered the necessary surgery for organ donations and the discontinuation of the life support system.

On Friday, January 27, Jed was buried on the family farm outside Springfield, Oregon.

It was from those same sad and soggy fringes of the Willamette Valley that this almanac was born fifteen years ago. On St. Patrick's Day, 1984, I began a pilgrimage, taking a sentimental journey back, after an absence of twelve years.

I arrived at the Kesey farm late on a drizzly Saturday night. The cherry and apple and plum trees were already blossomed; daffodils and jonquils bloomed eagerly about the family home.

Faye and Ken were still in the midst of their grief over the loss of their youngest son. During the next three days, I shared their grief and their hospitality and their farm chores, while recording the following conversation. Some fifty feet behind the home, a fresh mound of earth reveals Jed's gravesite, marked by a simple stone. It is inscribed with a 5-pointed star and the words:

Jed Kesey
July 5, 1963
January 23, 1984
Aw Right!

— Terry Reim, Editor

A Conversation With
KEN KESEY

At the memorial ceremony for Jed and Lorenzo over at the Mac Court, all the speakers — the coaches and the kids — said good, true stuff . . . until the preacher got up. We called him Reverend Mellow. It was all mellowspeak, devoid of spirit or even magic. For instance, when he read the "Twenty-Third Psalm," it was from something like the *Modern American Bible:*

The Lord is my busdriver I shal!
not wait.
He gives me a nice pad to lay
back in.
I can groove on the vibes.
And even when it gets heavy,
I know he's there with his stick
to straighten me out.
And surely He'll be around for
the rest of the week.

Now Shakespeare helped King James translate that book, and when you go in and begin to change it, when you start second guessing the *Old Testament* and William Shakespeare, you gotta be damn sure you're coming up with something better.

When you come in there as a preacher, and you start trying to teach poetry for the sake of making God more accessible to the so-called contemporary public, you forego magic for hucksterism, and all your reverent mellifluous intonation is just some kind of celestial ass-kissing.

God doesn't want his ass kissed. He wants his kids safe and cared for. When you do that, magic takes place. When you do something so that kids that might have suffered don't, that's a magical act.

The most important thing we learned in the sixties, was that we were not able to insulate ourselves, that when people in Vietnam were being napalmed, we couldn't enjoy the high anymore.

You can't take acid and do napalm at the same time. It bums you out.

People *feel* other people's losses . . . this is the real power. When there's somebody blown up in Lebanon, when the media shows these weeping old guys carrying these pitiful little wrapped-up baggages, it hurts me. And I know I'm not different from anybody else, any other father who's been hurt, anywhere. That which hurts anybody, hurts *everybody*.

We're going to link up until finally we're going to overwhelm this flaw that has crept into our society — this military flaw. We're going to overwhelm it by the inescapable power of shared grief.

The job of the writer, the job of the magician, is to illuminate this worldwide grief. To give it a handle so other people can grab hold of that handle and use the tool to halt the hurting in their own communities and countries.

Besides losing my youngest son, I lost a good farmhand and an upstanding citizen in what Martin Buber calls the "Nation of Community." That hurts.

LOVE AND GRIEF ★ ★ ★ ★ ★ ★ ★ ★ ★ ★ ★ ★ ★ ★ ★ ★ ★

This whole thing has been a real slap in the face — WHAP! WHAP! It wakes you up to a lot of stuff that's real and true and beautiful, and has been there and not been noticed.

I realized that women, by giving birth, have a better understanding of death than men. Most men don't know this — that birth is, by its nature, connected with death.

I also realized that love is connected with grief. You don't grieve unless you love, and as soon as you love, you grieve. When you try to disconnect the two, what you get is love without grief; it's a one-sided love, it's a shallow love. It's like saying, "Oh, I only want all the good stuff, the *better*." But unless you go, "for *better or worse*, in sickness and health," you don't really get love. You get . . . disco!

As I grieved for Jed, I felt a comradeship with fathers that went back thousands and thousands of years.

Doesn't make any difference whether your son is being fried by a nuclear bomb or shot by an M-1 or has a spear sticking in him in Rome 2,000 years ago.

Since this loss, I've watched videos of these Lebanese families weeping over the death of their kids. And I couldn't tell whether they were Muslim or Druse, Communists or Christians, Arabs or Jews. They were just parents, fathers like me who were hurting — that's a more ancient nation than all these other minor league nations.

Hurting people can reach across the planet and form a power that we're only just beginning to recognize.

All of a sudden this violence you see on TV isn't just some border war. It's *your* war. It's *your* flesh. Agony is absolutely personal: it extends out to the people who love you, who recognize that agony. *That* is the main nation.

When you care about someone so much that you would do ANYTHING — ANYTHING to trade places, ANYTHING to die for that person who has died, ANYTHING — you would kiss Satan on the tip of his dick to change places — when you care that much for somebody, then you belong to that main nation.

You're thinking of your kids when
you're thinking of nuclear waste.
You're thinking of your family and
their families in the centuries to come.
That's civilization.

You think that you're vulnerable now — wait till your kids have kids. And if those kids get hurt, your kids are hurt and you're hurt even more. That kind of vulnerability makes you civilized. It makes you want to stop spraying herbicides; it makes you go out there and protect them against nuclear warheads. It makes you suddenly move outside yourself. Suddenly there's a lot you care for more than you do your own ass.

SPIRIT ★

It's better to get out there and try to do a thing, and fail at it than to
realize you're going to fail and not try. Always go for the blue ribbon.

The whole notion of family is connected with spirit.

Spirit is a real thing. Sometimes a school will have it, sometimes a family will have it, or a nation will have it. And that's what carries them. When it's broken everything begins to fall apart.

You *know* that spirit exists because you can feel it when it's breaking. You can see what happens to people when their spirit is injured. They quit doing anything. They quit accomplishing anything. They quit.

All of my kids are wrestlers, going

through the same wrestling program that I went through. We know the sport, but I begin to wonder, why do this? Why do we go through this agony of winning and losing? And then watching the people in Lebanon, I began to get an idea of why. It's because when you put something out on a "win-lose" basis, you have to pull and cheer and root and lift and pray for somebody. And care — so that when they lose, you hurt, and when they win, you celebrate. That is how spirit is strengthened.

It's more important to do something good by yourself than to do
something bad with Ghandi, Hitler, and Buffalo Bill.

LIBERTY AND JUSTICE ★ ★ ★ ★ ★ ★ ★ ★ ★ ★ ★ ★ ★ ★ ★

My father, Fred Kesey, used to say: "I may not know what is right, but
I know what is fair."

This land really *is* the last hope for freedom, just like those Woody Guthrie songs all sing. But we haven't taken responsibility for keeping the torch burning. When you know what America means, when you begin to believe it, you realize, good God, what a task.

We are the people who create justice. We keep expecting our elders to come up with it — "here's justice, honey love, on a platter" — give us righteousness. But if we don't do it, our kids will have to do it, or their kids.

Justice was never given — but the ground has been left open for us to cultivate it.

This is what the Egyptians and Greeks and intelligent people of the past labored thousands of years at, and we're expected to do it before the whole thing blows at the end of the century.

If you don't know the difference
between Bach and Barry Manilow,
you'll never be free, and you'll never
know why.

We're expected to get it together and do it, and we *can* do it. Just like Bucky Fuller says, we *have* the capability. It's all within our grasp. If we fail, we can't point our finger at Reagan. *It's us. We, we're it; we're the last hope for this globe.*

We hear more music, we see more of other people from other lands, we have more knowledge than anybody ever did in history. We're also going to be older than anybody who has ever lived. We could all live to be 100. We *can* do it.
The trouble is, if you can't remember, you can't be free. Your freedom is connected to your memory.

If you don't remember, they can put you in a box and say, "Hey, you got it better than ever before in your life. You're livin' in this nice box — it's warm." And you think "Yeah, that's true."

If the memory can be attacked — how we lived yesterday, and how we lived twenty years ago, and a hundred years ago — if that can be washed out, they got us. And they're attacking us through our memory right now. The bad guys.

RELIGION ★ ★ ★ ★ ★ ★ ★ ★ ★ ★ ★ ★ ★ ★ ★ ★ ★

The reason people talk about crap like school prayer is because they don't want to deal with true, hard life.

It's nice to have a good spiritual underpinning, so you believe in something.

I mean when you're hooked on something that counts, like when you suddenly have a kid that's died and you hear people talking about whether they should pray or not in school, you think: "What bullshit! Dumb shit coming from both sides; we got more important stuff to talk about."

It's like when they put "One nation under God," in the Pledge of Allegiance instead of just "One nation, indivisible, with liberty and justice for all." It not only kills the meter, it indicates that someone thought they knew more than we did.

I pray as much as anybody I know, and as constantly. I've delivered the same prayer every night steadily, for as long as I can remember. It goes:
> Bless this house,
> Bless this place,
> Bless these people.
> Bless these plants
> And these animals.
> Bless this action,
> And bless these spirits
> That abide nearby.
> Protect us all,
> And help us in Your way.
> Amen.

You can learn to pray, but you can't be taught to pray. That's the thing — you've got to *want to learn* to pray.

It's like you'll be outside alone someplace — say you're peein'. And your mind comes free, and you think, *"Hey, I like this place and I like these people! Bless them."* And I've done it just as steady as I can.

POLITICS ★ ★ ★ ★ ★ ★ ★ ★ ★ ★ ★ ★ ★ ★ ★ ★ ★

The Pentagon belief that national defense is directly related to a gun is, I think, Republican thinking.

Reagan is not the villain. You know *exactly* what Reagan is. Reagan may even be a tool of God — God may be trying to speak to us: "Hey, the President doesn't really run things fools. Things are run by big oil and big money around the world, big banking money, big insurance money. That's why I put an *actor* in the job. Get it?"
Our job is to realize that none of the people are the villains. None of us is a villain. The villain is something bigger than us . . . badder than we'll ever be, but people *can* fall into its grip and do its work.

If you were a villian and wanted to attack people on earth, one of the best ways to do it would be to fool with the food and the water and the air. Fool with the most basic things that make it all go.

Everybody says there's just not enough money to adequately take care of all these kids — seat belts in school buses, budgets, etc. There is six billion dollars less federal aid for education this year than last year — and there's just not enough money in communities, everybody says. But there's *plenty* of money in the communities; it's just that the bulk of it is going for national defense.

So something gradually became obvious to me. I thought, you guys want to be in charge of national defense? Okay, defend us. Defend us where we are truly vulnerable, in the streets, in the hospitals, in the schools. And this means you got to see to getting seat belts on school buses. National defense doesn't just mean you need a gun.

Once you think that spirit's just bullshit, then you drop back to the seventeenth century. As though all this ache and effort didn't mean anything. But it does. A lot of damn people fought and worked and died for it. Just like all the songs say.

The thing is, very few of them were ever Republicans. They were usually the ones that got us into wars, all right, but it was the Democrats who usually did the dyin'.

Republicans think of the villain as being somewhere outside the gate, beyond the moat, over the stone fence, in the ghetto, in El Salvador, in Lebanon. Whereas, the Democrat thinks that the villain is faulty wiring in the nuke plant, or dead-end illiterates knocking over a *7-11*, or asbestos in the ceiling of the second grade. Fight these villains and we have a chance for victory at home, not glory overseas.

WAR AND PEACE ★ ★ ★ ★ ★ ★ ★ ★ ★ ★ ★ ★ ★ ★ ★

That is the real difference now: we all have our asses on the line. The idea that nuclear war is more awful than the old-fashioned kind is dumb.

When we're lobbing shells into Lebanon, we're losing the war. We're not conscious of how to fight the war anymore. We're fighting it without that old American pizzazz. Where are the crazy Americans, the ones with spirit? We went to the moon. We put together labor unions and built bridges. Sometimes they fell down, but it was the spirit that put them up again.

We have 5,000 times more firepower now than we had in World War II. That means that if we go to a national war, all our asses are on the line. Not just the "Gook's" asses, or the "Jap's" asses, or the asses of the poor kids who enlisted because there was no other way out of the ghetto.

Previously, it has always been the rich who could sequester themselves from war behind their borders, their lands, their walls, their guards. They could wage war without being jeopardized. Not so anymore. Even the richest do not want nuclear war. All have to cool it or lose it all.

As Einstein said when he completed his formula with Niels Bohr, "This means we've either got to end war completely, or end civilization." That's fair.

MAGIC ★ ★ ★ ★ ★ ★ ★ ★ ★ ★ ★ ★ ★ ★ ★ ★ ★ ★ ★

We must realize that every time we turn a switch on to get electricity, it's a magical act; it's important.

How do we solve these problems? Magic. We've got to have magic. Every act that we perform must become a magical act, important to God, to America and to the planet Earth.

You can be shown by example, but you can't teach people to recite a litany and have the magic work. Otherwise, what you've got is voodoo, zombies, and weird shit.

We can learn about magic from all the magicians, the great magicians, everybody knows who they are. Bach, Beethoven, Shakespeare, Martin Buber — all the people who've dealt with the deep problems as hard as they could, who've sent us all the messages on how to perform these rites, these rituals.

When you go out on the highway and put on your seat belt, that's a magical act against misfortune. If you put smoke alerts in your house, that's a magical act. If you go to school board meetings and help with decisions in your local school system, that's a magical act. I worked to get the blinking yellow lights up on the highway that goes past the school — this has saved people's lives. That's a magical act. Yet this is an act that goes through the customary system.

But if you don't know that this involves your heart and your soul, everything you care for, if you're doing it because you're going to try to run for mayor of Pleasant Hill, then that's a dumb act. If you're doing it because it's a magical act, it becomes a magical act.

Here's the main magical act we have to perform: we have to stop this world on its way to a bad war. And here's the way I think we ought to do it: through the ritual of art, and song, and poetry, and theatrical activism like the good ol' Bread and Puppet Theatre uses.

The high school's our gathering fire. places left where we can still exercise our magic in our communities, where we can still get together and I can talk with my neighbors and say, "Hey, I don't know about this new highway; should it go through here or not?" "Well, I don't think so, it's going to cut through old man so-and-so's place, and we don't need it anyway."

Without that kind of contact between neighbors occurring naturally, we can't be free. Someone could come in and say, "We'll put the highway through here, we don't care what you guys think because you can't get it together to oppose us."

The high schools's our gathering fire. Those sporting events are our tribal rituals. They are as magical today as they were around the campfire, tens of thousands of years ago.

POWER ★ ★ ★ ★ ★ ★ ★ ★ ★ ★ ★ ★ ★ ★ ★ ★ ★ ★

Power doesn't happen because everybody likes you, or everybody votes for you. Power happens when you perform the fair act at the crucial time and make the right thing happen.

We're down to the elements of what makes things go. What makes things go is power. Power does not corrupt. Power purifies.

What corrupts is a false sense of power. What corrupts is *thinking* you have power and really knowing you don't.

I knew I was never going to be student body president. I know I'm not going to be a senator, but I know what power is. Why relinquish power and have to go down to D.C. and kiss asses?

Everybody knows when the power card falls into their hands. Sometimes you can play it well, and sometimes you can't. But play it you must.

When Lt. Calley said, "Oh, I did this because the higher command told me to do it," he relinquished power. When *you* say, "It's not gonna' work, because the government, etc. will just stop it," then you relinquish power.

When poets who sometimes come by, talk about how the Administration is doing this and doing that, bringing about all the badness in the world, it seems to me they are being just like Lt. Calley. And if the poets don't have the power to lead, who does . . . the FTC?

Your force may get bigger, but your power goes down. Force is what a man uses when he is bereft of power. He rapes. A man with power doesn't have to rape. He can court.

Who's had the power in this country when you really finally get down and start giving people grades? Woody Guthrie is way out above most politicians, for instance.

It's like when I was up there at the Spokane hospital, watching this intensive care unit — the way it was run, the way these nurses moved, the way they dealt with each other — and I thought, boy, they're right down to the nitty-gritty stuff. This is *keep 'em alive or don't keep 'em alive.* And I saw the nurses as soldiers. Fighting the battle against the real enemies — against death and disease.

DECEMBER

CAPRICORN

December 21 – January 18

FRIDAY — DEC. 21

Sun Rises 07:23
Sun Sets 16:53
Moon Rises 06:41
Moon Sets 16:14

MOON IN SAGITTARIUS

moon conj uranus-00:01. moon conj mercury-01:12.
uranus at desc node-12:00.

Sun Enters Capricorn 08:23
WINTER SOLSTICE

Heinrich Boll 1917	Kurt Waldheim 1918
Alicia Alonso 1921	Phil Donahue 1935
Jane Fonda 1937	Frank Zappa 1940

1940: *F. Scott Fitzgerald dies.* **1967:** *Louis Washkansky, age 55, dies of double pneumonia in hospital in Capetown, South Africa—he had lived for 18 days with first transplanted heart.*

It is better to die alongside a wise man than live in a house with an idiot.
Chinese Proverb

SATURDAY — DEC. 22

Sun Rises 07:23
Sun Sets 16:54
Moon Rises 07:47
Moon Sets 17:10

MOON ENTERS CAPRICORN 02:20

sun conj moon-03:47. moon conj neptune-04:18.
sun conj neptune-11:14.

NEW MOON 03:47

Andre Kostelanetz 1901	Kenneth Rexroth 1905
Lady Bird Johnson 1912	Steve Garvey 1948

1877: *American Bicycling Journal published.* **1956:** *First gorilla born in captivity (Columbus, Ohio).* **1972:** *Bach Mai Hospital in Hanoi is bombed for the 2nd time—is completely destroyed.*

I want people with compassion, and people who feel, and people who care around me, just as much as I want people who think.
Lyndon Johnson

SUNDAY — DEC. 23

Sun Rises 07:23
Sun Sets 16:54
Moon Rises 08:45
Moon Sets 18:12

MOON IN CAPRICORN

moon conj jupiter-12:55.

John Jay 1745	Helmut Schmidt 1918
Jose Greco 1918	Floyd Kalber 1924
Harry Guardino 1925	Robert Bly 1926
Prince Akihito 1933	Paul Hornung 1935
Jorma Kaukonen 1940	Elizabeth Hartman 1941

1972: *Earthquake devastates Managua, Nicaragua.* **1975:** *Most deaths from single lightning strike—21 die inside shed in Rhodesia.*

You're born in pain. Pain is what we are in most of the time, and I think that the bigger the pain, the more God you look for.
John Lennon

MONDAY — DEC. 24

Sun Rises 07:23
Sun Sets 16:55
Moon Rises 09:34
Moon Sets 19:16

MOON ENTERS AQUARIUS 07:47

mercury directs-08:05. moon conj pluto-15:30.
MARS ENTERS PISCES-22:38.

Howard Hughes 1905	I.F. Stone 1907
Ava Gardner 1922	John Matuszak 1950

1889: *Pedal brake for bicycle patented.* **1914:** *Naturalist John Muir dies.*

CHRISTMAS EVE

GROWING
BY LIZ CAILE

NOW'S THE TIME—Northeast, Midwest, Mountain States: Keep your thumb green by gardening indoors. Start by sprouting trays of sunflower, buckwheat, and wheatgrass for winter salads. Send for garden catalogues. Begin to map out the coming season's garden plot. **Northwest:** Garden soil can be improved with manure and mulch. Bring switches of forsythia and other Spring blooming shrubs indoors; warm in lukewarm water, then bring to blossom in a vase. **Southeast, South:** Cool season veggies, including onions, can be started outdoors now. **Southwest:** Weather may be mild, but is still frost-prone. Start cool weather crops; set out hardy bedding plants in southern portion of the region.

Theme Variations

There are as many variations on the theme of growing as there are people, places, plants and seasons. Growing offers a way to improve our lives, homes and planet that is available to every willing person.

On fertile plains and in lush temperate valleys, the elements seem to bless every effort to grow crops. If one has land, the only limits are how much time and energy one wants to devote to growing.

In other locations, soil itself is rare, or warm days or water is in short supply. Ancient Peruvians carried dirt up to their mountain fastnesses, load-by-human-load to overcome one obstacle, and created an agriculture behind terraced rock walls. They clothed steep and barren hillsides with their crops.

In tropical and semi-tropical regions growers have defeated plagues of insects by intermixtures of useful wild and domestic plants.

In the arid southwest, the Native American learned to plant seeds deep in the protective sand. **Every environment provides plants that are useful and nourishing and adjusted to its conditions.**

Tomatoes and peppers, herbs, and lettuce may be grown by a sunny window or may be crops covering acres of land. At any level, growing offers us a way to produce something for ourselves, from ourselves, out of inexpensive and sometimes cost-free materials.

Providing the oxygen we breath, plants cleanse, feed, and decorate our world; some even produce fuels, lubricants and medicines. If our efforts at growing involve nothing more than respecting the natural mantle of plants around us, the quality of our lives will still be enriched.

Growing is an adventure offering insight into the unique chemistry of the life process. At the same time it provides an alternative to the toxic contamination of our land and our food. It is within our own means to contribute to our own healthful growth with the nutritious fruits of our labors.

Plotting

Gardeners have lately been wandering more and more from straight and narrow garden paths. Disadvantages to the single-row, single-crop approach include the fact that too much space is wasted between the rows.

Intensive gardening plots make use of wide beds and deeply cultivated soil, so that root growth reaches down instead of spreading out to soil nutrients. The result: less soil is exposed to the drying air; and closely planted crops leave little room for weeds.

Two or more species may be planted together when they are mutually beneficial. For instance, summer savory enhances the growth and flavor of onions and beets. Combined plantings of marigolds, beans, and potatoes have been shown to reduce the number of potato beetles on spud plants, not because of an effective chemical repellent, but because foraging insects can't munch their way right down the line of favored potatoes.

Row planting *does* have the advantage of easier crop-plant recognition; and in the case of large plantings, easier routes for watering and cultivation. But heavy traffic on these roots will compact the soil, damaging root access.

However you map your garden, remember that some plants act as growth inhibitors to others, and that close plantings of certain species increase potential for plant diseases. Potatoes and apples don't make it together. Rotate potatoes, tomatoes and eggplants, all members of the *Solanaceae* family, to thwart virus infections. That is, don't grow any of these crops on the same ground more than once every three years.

What to Grow

Historic and prehistoric crops in your region provide clues as to what to plant for the greatest amount of sustenance from your garden. In northern latitudes, potatoes, corn, pumpkin, beans, wheat, beets, and apples provide a basis for year-round nutrition.

In southern latitudes, sweet potatoes, cowpeas, citrus fruits, soybeans, rice and peanuts do the same. A diet combining a rich variety of garden vegetables, can assure your nutritional needs.

TUESDAY — DEC. 25
Sun Rises 07:24
Sun Sets 16:55
Moon Rises 10:14
Moon Sets 20:21

MOON IN AQUARIUS
moon conj venus-20:41.

Isaac Newton 1642
Rebecca West 1892
Nellie Fox 1927
Barbara Mandrell 1948

Louis Joseph Chevrolet 1878
Humphrey Bogart 1893
Jimmy Buffett 1946
Sissy Spacek 1949

1758: Comet appears as predicted by astronomer Edmund Halley. 1946: W.C. Fields, comedian and juggler, dies from effects of excessive drinking at his home (Hollywood).

CHRISTMAS DAY

WEDNESDAY — DEC. 26
Sun Rises 07:24
Sun Sets 16:56
Moon Rises 10:47
Moon Sets 21:23

MOON ENTERS PISCES 16:18
moon square saturn-05:07. moon conj mars-19:03.

George Dewey 1837
Steve Allen 1921
Donald Moffat 1930

Henry Miller 1891
Alan King 1927
Phil Spector 1940

1865: Coffee percolator patented. 1972: Harry Truman, 33rd Pres. of U.S., dies at age 88 years and 232 days (Independence, Mo.)—he had minor lung congestion at time, and cause of death was determined to be collapse of his cardiovascular system, along with other system failures.

We must remember who is in charge: Language comes first; the method of communication comes second.
William Safire

BOXING DAY

THURSDAY — DEC. 27
Sun Rises 07:25
Sun Sets 16:57
Moon Rises 11:16
Moon Sets 22:23

MOON IN PISCES
moon trine pluto-00:36. mercury conj uranus-04:42.
moon square uranus-22:03. moon square mercury-22:38.

Johannes Kepler 1571
Marlene Dietrich 1904

Sydney Greenstreet 1879
William H. Masters 1915

1722: James Bradley measures Venus through a telescope. 1836: Avalanche in England kills 8. 1927: Showboat opens (New York City). 1941: Howdy and Double Doody born in Doodyville, Texas. 1947: First Howdy Doody Show. 1965: Ken Kesey and Merry Pranksters stage first "Acid Test" (Longshoreman's Hall, San Francisco). 1969: Reports from Zambia list deaths of 9 people after their boats were overturned by rampaging hippopotamuses on Namwala River.

A book is like a garden carried in the pocket.
Chinese Proverb

FRIDAY — DEC. 28
Sun Rises 07:25
Sun Sets 16:57
Moon Rises 11:41
Moon Sets 23:21

MOON IN PISCES
moon trine saturn-16:38.

Woodrow Wilson 1856
Sam Levenson 1911

Charley Weaver 1905
Maggie Smith 1934

1895: Roentgen demonstrates X-rays. 1912: San Francisco begins streetcar operation. 1974: Pakistan earthquake kills 5,000.

Formlessness and chaos lead to new forms. And new order. Closer to, probably, what the real order is. When you break down the old orders and the old forms and leave them broken and shattered, you suddenly find yourself a new space with new form and new order which are more like the way it is.
Jerry Garcia

SATURDAY — DEC. 29
Sun Rises 07:26
Sun Sets 16:58
Moon Rises 12:04
Moon Sets ----

MOON ENTERS ARIES 03:49
moon square neptune-06:39. sun square moon-21:27.

FIRST QUARTER MOON 21:27

William Gladstone 1809
Pablo Casals 1876
Thomas Bradley 1917
Tom Jarriel 1934
Jon Voight 1938

John Ingalls 1833
Robert Ruark 1915
Ed Flanders 1934
Mary Tyler Moore 1937
Gelsey Kirkland 1952

1782: First nautical almanac published. 1975: Terrorist bomb at La Guardia Airport in New York kills 11 and wounds 58.

Don't count your chickens until the check has cleared the bank.
Lawyers' Proverb

SUNDAY — DEC. 30
Sun Rises 07:26
Sun Sets 16:58
Moon Rises 12:27
Moon Sets 00:18

MOON IN ARIES
venus square saturn-02:07. moon at apogee-04:00.
moon trine uranus-10:49. moon trine mercury-14:32.
mars trine pluto-15:00. moon square jupiter-22:59.

Rudyard Kipling 1865
Del Shannon 1939

Stephen Leacock 1869
Vladimir Bukovsky 1942

1854: First oil company incorporated. 1873: American Meteorological Society formed. 1922: U.S.S.R. formed. 1965: Ferdinand Marcos inaugurated as President of Philippines.

TOO TRUE

Distance, n. The only thing that the rich are willing for the poor to call theirs and keep.
The Devil's Dictionary

CELESTIAL EVENTS

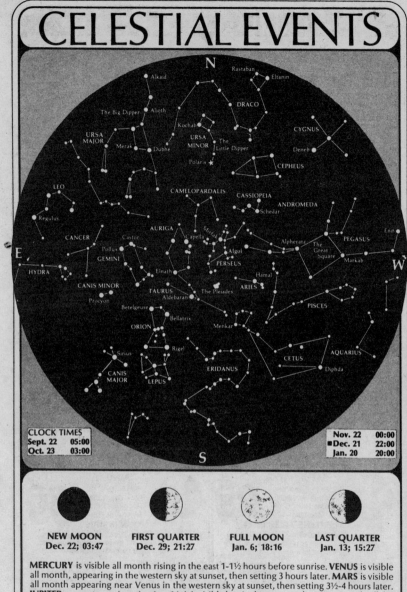

N

Rastaban
Eltanin
Alkaid
DRACO
The Big Dipper Alioth
Kochab
CYGNUS
URSA
MAJOR URSA
Merak Dubhe MINOR The
Little Dipper Deneb
Polaris ★ CEPHEUS
LEO CAMELOPARDALIS CASSIOPEIA
ANDROMEDA
Regulus Schedar Enif
CANCER AURIGA Mirfak Alpheratz PEGASUS
Castor Capella The
Great Markab
Pollux Algol Square
E GEMINI PERSEUS
HYDRA Elnath Hamal W
Canis Minor ARIES PISCES
TAURUS The Pleiades
Procyon Aldebaran
Betelgeuse Bellatrix Menkar
ORION CETUS AQUARIUS
Sirius Rigel Diphda
CANIS ERIDANUS
MAJOR LEPUS

S

CLOCK TIMES
Sept. 22   05:00
Oct. 23   03:00

Nov. 22   00:00
■Dec. 21   22:00
Jan. 20   20:00

NEW MOON	FIRST QUARTER	FULL MOON	LAST QUARTER
Dec. 22; 03:47	Dec. 29; 21:27	Jan. 6; 18:16	Jan. 13; 15:27

MERCURY is visible all month rising in the east 1-1½ hours before sunrise. **VENUS** is visible all month, appearing in the western sky at sunset, then setting 3 hours later. **MARS** is visible all month appearing near Venus in the western sky at sunset, then setting 3½-4 hours later. **JUPITER** comes to conjunction Jan. 14; it is visible low in the western sky at sunset only till the first of the year, then is too close to the sun for viewing the rest of the month. **SATURN** is visible all month, rising in the east 2-4 hours before sunrise. **Dec. 21:** WINTER SOLSTICE, first day of Winter. **Dec. 23:** Jupiter 4° N. waxing crescent Moon (evening sky). **Dec. 25:** Venus 3° N. of waxing crescent Moon (evening sky). **Dec. 26:** Mars 4° N. of waxing crescent Moon (evening sky). **Jan. 03:** Mercury at gr. elong. W.(23°) ; EARTH AT PERIHELION. **Jan. 16:** Saturn 2° N. of waning crescent Moon (morning sky).

MONDAY DEC. 31

Sun Rises 07:26
Sun Sets 16:59
Moon Rises 12:50
Moon Sets 01:14

MOON ENTERS TAURUS 16:36

moon trine neptune-19:37.

Elizabeth Arden 1884
Pola Negri 1894
Odetta 1930
Anthony Hopkins 1937
Andy Summers 1942
John Denver 1943
Ben Kingsley 1943
Patti Smith 1946

1775: Washington' authorizes enlistment of free blacks into Continental Army. 1965: Involvement by U.S. in Vietnamese War to date—180,000 troops, 1,365 deaths, 5,300 wounded, 148 missing in action. (This compares to 1964 involvement—23,000 troops with 146 dead). 1972: Roberto Clemente, baseball player, dies at age 38 in plane crash near San Juan, Puerto Rico—he was accompanying supplies being flown to victims of earthquake in Nicaragua.

One picture is worth a thousand miles.
NBC News

NEW YEAR'S EVE

TUESDAY JAN. 01

Sun Rises 07:26
Sun Sets 16:59
Moon Rises 13:15
Moon Sets 02:12

MOON IN TAURUS

moon oppos pluto-01:24. sun trine moon-15:43.

Lorenzo de Medici 1448
Anthony Wayne 1745
Roxas y Acuna 1892
J. Edgar Hoover 1895
Barry Goldwater 1909
Eliot Janeway 1913
J.D. Salinger 1919
Ernest Hollings 1922

1801: Piazzi discovers the first asteriod, Ceres. 1808: African slave trade banned by Congress. 1816: U.S. public debt exceeds $100 million for first time. 1821: Missouri begins taxing bachelors. 1840: First bowling match played—Knickerbocker Alleys (New York City). 1863: Lincoln signs *Emancipation Proclamation*. 1950: *Hopalong Cassidy* first heard on radio. 1953: Hank Williams, singer and composer, suffers a heart attack and dies in back seat of his Cadillac (W. Vir.). 1955: U.S. begins financial aid to South Vietnam.

NEW YEAR'S DAY
JAPANESE NEW YEAR

WEDNESDAY JAN. 02

Sun Rises 07:26
Sun Sets 17:00
Moon Rises 13:44
Moon Sets 03:12

MOON IN TAURUS

moon trine jupiter-12:12. moon oppos saturn-18:09.

James Wolfe 1727
Sally Rand 1902
Isaac Asimov 1920
Renata Tebaldi 1922
Michael Blumenthal 1926
Julius La Rosa 1930

1777: John Rosbrugh is first chaplain to be killed in action—2nd Battle of Trenton (N.J.). 1975: Elizabeth Domitien named first female premier, Central African Republic. 1980: Bert Parks canned as Miss America host.

Z-Z-Z-Z

THURSDAY JAN. 03

Sun Rises 07:27
Sun Sets 17:01
Moon Rises 14:18
Moon Sets 04:14

MOON ENTERS GEMINI 04:00

moon square venus-02:11.
EARTH AT PERIHELION-12:00.
moon square mars-18:24. moon at asc node-21:22.
VENUS ENTERS PISCES-22:23

Marion Davies 1897
Zasu Pitts 1898
Victor Borge 1909
Maxene Andrews 1918
Bobby Hull 1939
Victoria Principal 1945

1882: Oscar Wilde shocks customs officials by declaring "nothing but my genius" on arriving in U.S. 1888: Moscow University closed because of student unrest. 1938: March of Dimes organized. 1961: U.S. severs diplomatic relations with Cuba. Eisenhower says, "There's a limit to what the U.S. can endure in self-respect." 1961: Atomic reactor blows up in Idaho Falls, Idaho. 1965: New Univ. of Calif. Berkeley Chancellor relents, opening Sproul Plaza for political activity—Free Speech Movement wins, 1960's student movement is born.

FRIDAY JAN. 04

Sun Rises 07:27
Sun Sets 17:02
Moon Rises 14:59
Moon Sets 05:17

MOON IN GEMINI

moon oppos uranus-09:39. moon oppos mercury-21:50.

Jacob Grimm 1785
Louis Braille 1806
Everett Dirksen 1896
Jane Wyman 1914
Dyan Cannon 1937
John McLaughlin 1942

1885: First appendectomy. 1924: Automobile completes trip across Sahara Desert in 3 days—end of 9 day camel trip. 1941: Charlie Chaplin refuses Film Critics Award because he seeks "only to please the public." 1965: T. S. Eliot, poet, dies at age 76 (London). 1975: Robyn Smith is first female jockey to win a stake's race. 1979: In an out-of-court settlement, parents of Kent State students killed and injured in 1970 receive $600,000. 1983: Spiro Agnew repays Maryland $268,482—alleged kickback money plus interest.

Don't spit in the soup. We've all got to eat.
Lyndon Johnson

SATURDAY JAN. 05

Sun Rises 07:27
Sun Sets 17:03
Moon Rises 15:48
Moon Sets 06:20

MOON ENTERS CANCER 12:17

moon oppos neptune-15:20. moon trine venus-15:45.
moon trine pluto-20:23.

Konrad Adenauer 1876
Walter Mondale 1928
Alvin Ailey 1931
Robert Duvall 1931
Prince Juan Carlos 1938
Diane Keaton 1946

1928: First woman sworn in as governor, Nellie T. Ross (Wyo.). 1933: Calvin Coolidge, 29th Pres. of U.S., suffers a heart attack and dies on floor of his bedroom (Northampton, Mass.). 1943: George Washington Carver dies. 1949: Harry S. Truman labels his administration "Fair Deal." 1964: Leaders of Roman Catholic and Orthodox churches meet for first time since 1400s. 1970: Joseph Yablonski, United Mine Workers Union, is shot to death along with his wife and daughter at their home (Clarksville, Penn.).

Happiness is an occasional occasion.
Tennessee Williams

FORECAST
BY NAN DE GROVE

CAPRICORN

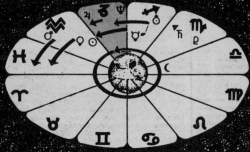

LONGITUDE OF THE PLANETS
08:23 PST; 12/21/84

Sun	00°00′ **Capricorn**
Moon	19°35′ **Sagittarius**
Merc	15°17′ **Aquarius R**
Venus	14°36′ **Aquarius**
Mars	27°15′ **Aquarius**
Jupiter	19°05′ **Capricorn**
Saturn	23°42′ **Scorpio**
Uranus	14°45′ **Sagittarius**
Neptune	01°06′ **Capricorn**
Pluto	04°07′ **Scorpio**

The Sun joins Neptune in Capricorn on the Winter Solstice, the New Moon occurring the following morning. Coming on the heels of the November 22nd solar eclipse, this pattern suggests major changes in government and social institutions, including redistribution of power at many levels.

Traditionally, solar eclipses herald the advent of a new order and a challenge to established power. In medieval times, the Sun was symbolic of the ruling principle, therefore, eclipses were thought to portend the downfall of kings and the disruption of order. As the influence of an eclipse extends for several months before and after the actual event, we are likely to see the effects of the November eclipse throughout the winter quarter.

A deep restlessness and an urge to be more than we are is pervasive, but we may express these expansive urges in more practical ways than we have in the past. Now that many of us are growing up, assuming greater responsibility, and getting into "the system," this is a favorable time for reconciling youthful idealism with the responsibilities of maturity.

EARTH SIGNS now have special opportunities relating to travel, finance, education, and the pursuit of enlightenment.

Taurus: complete your long cycle of effort. Work in harmony with opposition rather than meeting it head-on. Take time to unwind around the second week of January.

Virgo: confusion and frustration will result if you expect everything to be perfect and on schedule. Hold off on decisions, judgments, and commitments until after December 25th. Heart and head may disagree in the second and third weeks of January.

Capricorn: you are vitalized and inspired, philosophically or mystically inclined. Pitfalls include martyrdom and paranoia. Stay in touch with your feelings and watch the tide turn around the 7th.

AIR SIGNS are sought out now for their fairness, objectivity, and wit.

Gemini: you may be renegotiating an agreement or mediating a dispute. Avoid final decisions until after December 25th, and make practical adjustments after January 12th.

Libra: focus attention on matters of finance, real estate, and domestic concerns. Look for creative and educational opportunities as well. Efficient use of time and resources may be a key issue.

Aquarius: charisma and charm, can furthur your special impassioned cause. But avoid sacrificing ethics for expediency.

FIRE SIGNS could be smoldering, chafing at restrictions and delays.

Aries: you are ready for a new cycle of professional explorations caused by disenchantment with present work conditions. But this is a period of waiting, refining, and making contacts. Don't leap before looking.

Leo: it's time to rebound from those past disappointments. Gather momentum and find new sources of inspiration; but take it easy and be aware of emotional undercurrents around the 7th.

Sagittarius: you have much to be thankful for; long-term efforts are now bearing fruit. Watch nerves and avoid taking on too many new projects now. Decisions are best delayed until after December 25th.

WATER SIGNS are are inclined to be elusive and enigmatic, conserving energy and concealing their motives, even from themselves.

Cancer: don't get overconcerned with matters of security and social status; be open to receiving inspiration and support from others. A turning point comes with the Full Moon on the 7th.

Scorpio: brooding won't help. Harvest the fruits of past efforts, face the consequences of past failures, or both. Reflect.

Pisces: work to materialize visions, sharpen focuses, define perspectives. Practical idealism is the key concept now.

JANUARY

SUNDAY — JAN. 06

Sun Rises 07:27
Sun Sets 17:04
Moon Rises 16:47
Moon Sets 07:20

MOON IN CANCER

moon trine mars-05:12. sun oppos moon-18:16.

FULL MOON 18:16

Alexander Scriabin 1872
Kahlil Gibran 1883
Earl Scruggs 1924
E.L. Doctorow 1931

Carl Sandburg 1878
John Lilly 1914
John De Lorean 1925
Bonnie Franklin 1944

1918: Passenger in WWI airplane falls out of plane and back in again at a lower altitude. 1919: Theodore Roosevelt, 26th Pres. of U.S., dies from inflammatory rheumatism at age 60 years and 71 days (Oyster Bay, N.Y.) —his last words were, "Please put out the light." 1927: American Marines sent to Nicaragua to protect American interests. 1930: Sherlock Holmes dies (according to fan club). 1945: Alexander Calder, sculptor, dies at age 74 (New York City).

EPIPHANY

TUESDAY — JAN. 08

Sun Rises 07:27
Sun Sets 17:06
Moon Rises 19:03
Moon Sets 09:01

MOON IN LEO

venus trine pluto-00:34. moon square pluto-01:15.
moon trine uranus-20:37.

Kiplinger 1891
Peter Arno 1904
Hanae Mori 1926
Elvis Presley 1935
Little Anthony 1940

Sherman Adams 1899
Butterfly McQueen 1911
Bill Graham 1931
Shirley Bassey 1937
David Bowie 1947

1642: Galileo Galilei, astronomer, dies. 1916: British forces evacuate Gallipoli. 1925: Texas appoints all-woman state Supreme Court. 1963: Mona Lisa's first U.S. showing. 1977: U.S. Census Bureau announces that for the first time a majority of Americans live in the Sunbelt states of the South and West.

You have to have courage to be a creator.
Rube Goldberg

THURSDAY — JAN. 10

Sun Rises 07:27
Sun Sets 17:08
Moon Rises 21:26
Moon Sets 10:15

MOON IN VIRGO

moon oppos venus-08:32. moon oppos mars-18:19.
moon square uranus-23:31.

Michel Ney 1769
Robinson Jeffers 1887
Paul Henreid 1908
Johnnie Ray 1927
Willie McCovey 1938
Jim Croce 1942

Francis X. Bushman 1883
Ray Bolger 1904
Max Roach 1926
Ronnie Hawkins 1935
Sal Mineo 1939
George Foreman 1949

1776: Thomas Paine publishes Common Sense. 1870: John D. Rockefeller incorporates Standard Oil with capital of one million dollars. 1882: Barbed wire patented. 1911: First aerial photograph from an airplane. 1928: Leon Trotsky ordered into exile. 1951: A 6-foot long piece of ice falls from sky and spears a carpenter on roof of a house, killing him (Dusseldorf, W. Germany). 1951: Sinclair Lewis, writer, dies in a sanitarium (Rome, Italy) in the presence of nuns.

MONDAY — JAN. 07

Sun Rises 07:27
Sun Sets 17:05
Moon Rises 17:53
Moon Sets 08:14

MOON ENTERS LEO 17:28

moon oppos jupiter-05:15. moon trine saturn-09:23.

Saint Bernadette 1844
Orval Faubus 1910
Vincent Gardenia 1922

Adolf Zukor 1873
Charles Addams 1912
Douglas Kiker 1930

1610: Galileo discovers 4 moons of Jupiter. 1926: George Burns and Gracie Allen get married. 1927: Transatlantic phone service begins between N.Y. and London. 1943: Nikola Tesla, creative genius, dies. 1973: Six killed and 15 wounded in New Orleans sniper attack. 1980: Nun elected mayor of Dubuque, Iowa.

I see no end to progress so long as there is freedom for every voice to be heard and every idea to compete.
Spiro Agnew

WEDNESDAY — JAN. 09

Sun Rises 07:27
Sun Sets 17:07
Moon Rises 20:15
Moon Sets 09:40

MOON ENTERS VIRGO 20:39

moon square saturn-13:06. moon trine mercury-16:55.
moon trine neptune-23:45.

Carrie Chapman Catt 1859
Gracie Fields 1898
Simone de Beauvoir 1908
Gypsy Rose Lee 1914
Joan Baez 1941

Karel Capek 1890
George Balanchine 1904
Richard Nixon 1913
Fernando Lamas 1915
Susannah York 1941

1793: First balloon ascent in America—J.Blanchard rises 5,812 feet (N.J.). 1894: First telephone switch board in operation. 1923: Katherine Mansfield, writer, dies (Fontaine- bleau, France).

FRIDAY — JAN. 11

Sun Rises 07:27
Sun Sets 17:09
Moon Rises 22:36
Moon Sets 10:45

MOON ENTERS LIBRA 23:13

sun trine moon-08:45.
MERCURY ENTERS CAPRICORN-10:25.
moon trine jupiter-13:06. moon at perigee-19:00.

William James 1842
Eva Le Gallienne 1899
Juanita Kreps 1921

Alice Paul 1885
Alan Paton 1903
Mary Rodgers 1931

49bc: Caesar crosses the Rubicon. 1770: Rhubarb shipped to the U.S. for the first time. 1928: Thomas Hardy, writer, dies (Dorset, England). 1935: Amelia Earhart flies solo across the Pacific Ocean.

I never unpack and I never want to get there. I always want the journey to last forever.
Sting

SIR JOHN MacDONALD'S BIRTHDAY

1965 Retrospective

by Paul Krassner

What was it like twenty years ago? How did mainstream America help nurture the development of a counter-culture? Why did young people across the country begin to build their lives upon the notion that it was more important to trust your friends than the government?

There was a cold war then. Agents of the United States had managed to apply a substance to Cuban sugar being shipped to the Soviet Union that would spoil its taste and usefulness. Alvin Dark, manager of the San Francisco Giants, declared that "Any pitcher who throws at a batter and deliberately tries to hit him is a Communist."

Veteran black reporter William Worthy wrote: "When social historians review the crucial year of 1965, they may well conclude that the non-violent civil rights movement in the U.S. effectively collapsed in the blood-stained streets of Los Angeles. The greatest irony may be that the Reverend Martin Luther King, chief spokesman of the Ghandian approach, may have discredited his own philosophy by publicly blessing the use of governmental forces to repress the spontaneous upheaval in the ghetto of Watts."

On the other hand, it was Dr. King whose leadership inspired the non-violent voter registration in Selma, Alabama, that year. Terry Southern claims that it was the Beat Generation that provided "the source or origin of the great wave of Civil Rights action. White participation...gave the movement its real center of momentum, in terms of scope, vastness of scope — Martin Luther King stressed this time and again, the necessity of not alienating the whites who were part of it — and this participation can be traced directly to the spirit first engendered by books like On the Road — that kind of personal, impulsive, do-something-crazy-and-impossible spirit — setting out for California with only three gallons of gas, or

walking through Georgia armed with nothing but a beard and a guitar." And, of course, the Beats served as the roots of the Hippie Generation.

Ethnic jokes were running rampant. "Why don't Polacks get a fifteen-minute coffee break? Because if they're away from the job for ten minutes you have to retrain them." There were also Tom Swifties: " 'Me a homosexual?' said Tom, half in Ernest."

The Tallahassee Police Department was paying ten dollars to each Florida State University student who reported being approached by a gay person at the local bus station. A report by the Committee on Public Health of the New York Academy of Medicine cited the suggestion that homosexuality is the answer to the population explosion.

Vogue magazine had criticized the Beatles' first movie, A Hard Day's Night for being "viciously pro-youth." Hundreds of fans showed up for an auction of Beatles' eating utensils, unwashed towels, and bed linens, which were cut up into two-inch squares.

Pope Paul visited the United States, and a band at JFK Airport played "Hello, Dolly." This was not even done for the Dalai Lama, for whom it might have been more appropriate. A street vendor sold out his entire supply of Pope lapel buttons and went to the wholesaler to get resupplied, but there were no more. Instead, the distributor gave him a few hundred "I Love Paul" buttons, referring to Paul McCartney. The vendor took them to Yankee Stadium where the Pope was speaking and sold out in half an hour.

The Ku Klux Klan opened its membership to Catholics. The Mafia tried to take over the kosher meat business on Long Island. American Nazi Party leader George Lincoln Rockwell snuck into Canada unrecognized

SATURDAY — JAN. 12

Sun Rises 07:26
Sun Sets 17:09
Moon Rises 23:46
Moon Sets 11:14

MOON IN LIBRA

moon square mercury-00:31. moon square neptune-02:27. mercury conj neptune-21:41.

Ray Price 1926   Bernadine Dohrn 1942

1932: *Ed Sullivan Show* premieres on radio. **1933:** First U.S. woman Senator, Hattie W. Carraway. **1966:** *Batman* on TV for first time. **1971:** *All in the Family* seen for first time on TV . **1976:** Agatha Christie, mystery writer, dies.

SUNDAY — JAN. 13

Sun Rises 07:26
Sun Sets 17:10
Moon Rises ----
Moon Sets 11:42

MOON IN LIBRA

sun square moon-15:27. moon square jupiter-16:44.

LAST QUARTER MOON 15:27

Horatio Alger 1834   Charlotte E. Ray 1850
G.I. Gurjieff 1877   Sophie Tucker 1884
Gwen Verdon 1925   Brock Adams 1927

1864: Stephen Foster, composer, dies in a hospital (New York City), a few days after being found naked on floor of his rented room in the Bowery—he left these words written on a scrap of paper, "Dear friends and gentle hearts." **1885:** Schuyler Colfax, former vice-pres., died in Minnesota after walking about a mile between 2 railroad stations in -30 deg. weather. **1898:** Theosophical Society founded. **1979:** Donny Hathaway, singer and arranger, commits suicide by jumping from roof of Essex House Hotel (New York City).

MONDAY — JAN. 14

Sun Rises 07:26
Sun Sets 17:11
Moon Rises 00:55
Moon Sets 12:12

MOON ENTERS SCORPIO 02:07

moon conj pluto-10:00. sun conj jupiter-14:20. moon trine venus-22:37.

Benedict Arnold 1741   Hugh Lofting 1886
Hal Roach 1892   John Dos Passos 1896
William Bendix 1906   Julian Bond 1940
Faye Dunaway 1941   Marjoe Gortner 1944

1863: First publication on paper made from wood pulp in U.S. **1952:** *The Today Show* premieres. **1957:** Humphrey Bogart, actor, dies. **1967:** First Human Be-In, "Pow-Wow," organized by Berkeley political activists and Haight-Ashbury members of "Love Generation", held in Golden Gate Park (San Francisco). **1969:** Explosions kill 10 sailors on **USS Enterprise**. **1977:** Peter Finch, actor, dies.

Americans like fat books and thin women.
Russell Baker

TUESDAY — JAN. 15

Sun Rises 07:25
Sun Sets 17:12
Moon Rises 02:05
Moon Sets 12:44

MOON IN SCORPIO

mars square uranus-02:25. moon trine mars-06:01. moon conj saturn-22:58.

Moliere 1622   Sonya Kovalevski 1850
Pierre Samuel Du Pont 1870   Goodman Ace 1899
Edward Teller 1908   Gamal Abdel Nasser 1918
Joao Figueiredo 1918   Maria Schell 1926
Martin Luther King, Jr. 1929   Margaret O'Brien 1937

1867: In London, ice on a lake in Regent's Park gives way under a crowd of people, more than 40 drown. **1870:** Cartoon donkey first appears, symbolizing Democratic Party. **1919:** The Great Boston Molasses Flood—a huge holding tank containing over 2 million gallons of molasses bursts open, flooding a large area of Boston with a heavy sea of molasses, 20 to 30 feet high. Twenty-one people die. **1922:** Irish Free State established.

MARTIN LUTHER KING DAY

WEDNESDAY — JAN. 16

Sun Rises 07:25
Sun Sets 17:14
Moon Rises 03:16
Moon Sets 13:22

MOON ENTERS SAGITTARIUS 05:48

moon at desc node-22:29.

Andre Michelin 1853   Robert Service 1874
Ethel Merman 1908   Dizzy Dean 1911
Allard Lowenstein 1929   Marilyn Horne 1934
A.J. Foyt 1935   Ronnie Milsap 1944

1874: Chang and Eng, Siamese twins, die (Mount Airy, N. Car.)—Chang died first, followed about 3 hours later by Eng. **1920:** Prohibition begins era of the speakeasy. **1932:** Duke Ellington records *It Don't Mean a Thing*. **1935:** Ma Barker, outlaw gang leader, dies of a gunshot wound after a 4 hour gun battle with police (Lake Weir, Fl.). **1942:** Carole Lombard dies at age 34 in crash of TWA flight #3 bound for Los Angeles from Indianapolis, Indiana—plane crashed in Table Rock Mountains, southeast of Las Vegas, Nevada, killing all 22 passsengers, including Carole's mother. **1965:** Sheriff, deputy, and 16 others are arrested in Neshoba County Miss. for murder of 3 civil rights workers in June 1964.

THURSDAY — JAN. 17

Sun Rises 07:25
Sun Sets 17:15
Moon Rises 04:26
Moon Sets 14:06

MOON IN SAGITTARIUS

mercury at desc node-01:00. moon square venus-06:59. moon conj uranus-10:13. moon square mars-13:17.

Leonhard Fuchs 1501   Benjamin Franklin 1706
Anne Bronte 1820   Anton Chekhov 1860
Mack Sennett 1880   Al Capone 1899
Betty White 1922   Moira Shearer 1926
James Earl Jones 1931   Muhammad Ali 1942

1893: Rutherford B. Hayes, 19th Pres. of U.S., dies from heart disease at age 70 years and 105 days. **1961:** Patrice Lumumba murdered. **1963:** Ten contestants on rigged quiz shows receive suspended sentences for perjury. **1977:** Capital punishment resumes in the U.S. with the execution of Gary Gilmore by firing squad at Utah State Prison .

Once a boy, always a boy.
Mrs. Ward (June) Cleaver

— by disguising himself as an orthodox Jewish rabbi.

In South Africa, a brassiere holster was put on the market. In America, traces of radioactive Strontium 90 were found in mothers' milk. Tranquilizers in the form of suppositories were being manufactured in order to make it more difficult for a citizen to commit suicide.

In France, Jean-Paul Sartre refused the Nobel Prize and the $53,000 that accompanied the award. In the U.S., Senator George Murphy — song-and-dance film star turned politician — declared that "You have to remember that Americans can't do that kind of work (picking fruits and vegetables). It's too hard. Mexicans are really good at that. They are built low to the ground, you see, so it is easier for them to stoop."

Conspiracy theories about the assassination of John F. Kennedy increased. Lyndon B. Johnson continued to escalate the war in Southeast Asia.

In Berkeley, the Free Speech Movement was transformed by the media into the Filthy Speech Movement when a lone University of California student was arrested for carrying a protest placard that stated, simply, "Fuck." Meanwhile, the latest James Bond flick featured a character named Pussy Galore.

Norman Mailer spoke out: "I believe our present situation in Vietnam is so irrational that any attempt to deal with it logically, is illogical in the way surrealism is illogical, and rational political discussion of Adolf Hitler's motives was illogical and then obscene. Bombing a country at the same time you are offering it aid is as morally repulsive as beating up a kid in an alley and stopping to ask for a kiss."

Draft boards were punishing young men who had been protesting U.S. policy in Vietnam by drafting them into the armed services. Representative Paul Fino introduced a bill to provide for drafting individuals with criminal records. He suggested special "Junkie battalions" for those with narcotics records.

Meanwhile, in in the privacy of their homes, women with unwanted pregnancies were continuing to pray for the decriminalization of abortion. for the decriminalization of abortion.

LSD was not yet illegal. The psychedelic served millions of Americans as a catalyst for realizing the arbitrariness of institutions. A spiritual revolution was blossoming. The push to get prayer into the public schools became a puerile joke.

On December 31, 1965, a psychedelic press conference was held in San Francisco — without LSD, psilocybin, DMT, mescalin, hashish, or marijuana — to announce the advent of the infamous Trips Festivals.

One of the organizers, Ken Kesey — novelist, Merry Prankster, and acid tester extraordiniarre — was a fugitive from a pot bust at the time. Meetings with his participation had to be held in secret.

Another organizer was Stewart Brand, who founded the America Needs Indians movement and would later publish The Whole Earth Catalog. In his faded red Volkswagen bus, armed with a loudspeaker system, he rode around explaining, "Hey, look! It's a parade! We're all in it, folks! The whole city's a parade!" People were tossing the pages of their memo calendars out the windows of office buildings in keeping with that New Year's tradition. "They're like big, beautiful snow flakes. It's snowing in San Francisco!"

Brand was heralding a series of events that led to the Fillmore Auditorium and the Family Dog, with light shows accompanying rock music — the Grateful Dead, Jefferson Airplane, Big Brother and the Holding Company with Janis Joplin, Quicksilver Messenger Service, Anonymous Artists of America — along with the satirical Committee, the Ann Halprin Dance Workshop, freelance belly dancers. It was like a convention of the underground.

The Haight-Asbury love generation was spawned. Built into their value system was the concept of positive change. Before long, bird-watchers became environmental activists. The year 1965 represented an evolutionary leap in consciousness. The seeds planted then are finally about ready for harvest now. This gives me a tremendous sense of optimism. Of course, that may just be due to damaged chromosomes.

FRIDAY   **JAN.**

Sun Rises 07:24
Sun Sets 17:16
Moon Rises 05:33
Moon Sets 14:58

18

MOON ENTERS CAPRICORN 10:29
moon conj neptune-14:17.

Montesquieu 1689   Peter Roget 1779
Daniel Webster 1782   A.A. Milne 1882
Cary Grant 1904   Danny Kaye 1913

1778: *Captain Cook first sights Hawaii.* **1862:** *John Tyler, 10th Pres. of U.S., dies from "bilious fever" at age 71 years and 295 days—his last words were, "Doctor, I am going...perhaps it is best."* **1911:** *First launch and landing of an airplane from a ship (San Francisco Bay).* **1945:** *Burma Road re-opens.*

I'm willing to run for anything, including dogcatcher, for peace.

Dr. Benjamin Spock

Your Analysis
by Robert McFarland, M.D.

Urine tests to detect the presence of marijuana are becoming more popular these days. These moderately inexpensive tests first became available in the 1980s, and are now widely used by private industry to screen prospective employees and by the government to detect drug use by personnel in the Armed Forces and other sensitive branches of government, such as the Supreme Court.

The tests detect metabolites of delta-9-tetrahydrocannibinol. They will show a positive result for two days after the test subject has smoked one marijuana cigarette. Chronic pot users can show positive urine tests for two weeks after they stop smoking because the drug accumulates in the fatty tissue and is only slowly excreted.

Because the tests are sometimes carelessly conducted, experts and test kit manufacturers suggest conducting a second test — one using a more reliable detection method — to confirm positive results. The Center for Disease Control recently checked sixty-four laboratories and found that the tests were reliable 95 percent of the time, but were also

falsely positive 4 percent of the time. This might be accurate enough for screening tests conducted in large numbers, but not good enough for many purposes. For example, if someone is fired from their job because of a false positive test, they might have good cause for a lawsuit.

The military services test 3 million GIs a year. Colonel William Manders of the Armed Forces Institute of Pathology, was chief quality control officer for this program until he testified at a court-martial in which the defendant was accused of marijuana use. Colonel Manders was also one of the individuals responsible for developing the confirmatory lab test using gas chromatography.

When the defendant in the marijuana case was acquitted because of the good doctor's expert testimony, he was transferred to another post. Apparently Colonel Manders confused honesty and duty, for he was unable to testify with certainty that the urine tests were reliable enough to establish the defendant's guilt.

Word Magic by Linda Hogan

The knowledge that words have power is not new. Orpheus, through songs, could move stones and charm animals. The songs of the sirens could turn men into swine. Traditional healers in all cultures use the magic of language to its fullest extent. They know how to fuse the power of repetition, of image and symbol with their own subliminal message.

Ritual language and poetry have always been associated with magic and medicine. It is through language as prayer or incantation that people reach states of mind — where the soul enters the land of spirits and the spirits are called to the human realm.

For the Cherokee, certain formulae enable healing to take place. Swimmer, a medicine man, wrote down many of the formulae at the turn of the century. An excerpt from the song for curing children of constant crying is: "With the noise as of thunder, he (the Red Man spirit) has taken it (the crying) to the Night Land to stay, never to look back. Relief will be caused constantly."

And for a sore throat: "Now then! Brown Frog, in the great lake in the direction of the Sun land thou art staying. Quickly thou has arisen, facing us. It is Pain that has put the important thing under him. But now thou has come and caused him to relinquish his grasp. Relief has been caused. Sharply!"

With the spoken word, the pain releases. Saying makes it so. When we speak healing, we create healing. Ruth Underhill documented Papago songs for healing:

Then did the moisture that lies above
begin to fall,
And all together did destroy the
sickness.
Thus you also always think, all you my
kinsmen.

The "correct words" usually derive from a religious tradition, and have been tested and empowered by years of use. In Christian tradition, examples of prayers that hold power are The Lord's Prayer and the 23rd Psalm, which could be described as rituals dispersing fear and attracting good: "Yea, though I walk through the valley of the shadow of death, I will fear no evil. . . ."

The argument that these magical incantations relieve only psycho-somatic maladies has been refuted, since the ritual use of words has been known to heal animals who do not speak the human language, and to assist food crops in their growth, as in this excerpt of a Papago song for "Singing up the Corn":

The corn comes up;
It comes up green;
Here upon our fields
White tassels unfold.

Word magic usually comes about through images that are visualized, and via metaphors that illuminate relationships otherwise not apprehended by the person. Language concentrates energy that heals the hearer and radiates into the world. It changes the broken balance of the environment to one of harmony and renewed unity. The songs heal what is broken.

For the non-traditional contemporary world, therapy is used as a substitute for ritual language. Talking therapy removes layer after layer of what covers the core reality of an individual. A patient knows when the magic words are spoken, for they feel whole, right, and true.

However, contemporary therapies often overlook the key element which traditional healing ceremonies embody: the necessity of connecting the individual with the larger community of life, the earth, and the universe. Our identification with all life is necessary for true spiritual health. Language is the living magical form which creates this union.

A traditional Navajo healing ceremony called the "Night Chant" is one of the best examples of a ritual healing song for creating balance in the world:

Happily may I walk.
Happily, with abundant dark clouds,
    may I walk.

Happily, with abundant
    showers, may I walk.

Happily, with abundant plants,
    may I walk.

Happily, on trail of pollen, may I walk.
Happily, may I walk.

May it be beautiful before me.
May it be beautiful behind me.
May it be beautiful below me.
May it be beautiful above me.
May it be beautiful all around me.
In beauty it is finished.

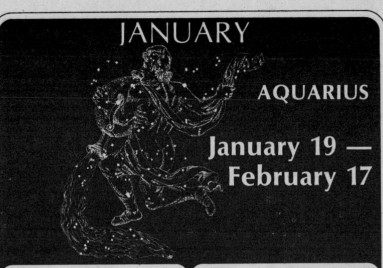

JANUARY

AQUARIUS

January 19 — February 17

SATURDAY JAN. 19
Sun Rises 07:24
Sun Sets 17:18
Moon Rises 06:34
Moon Sets 15:57

MOON IN CAPRICORN

venus square uranus-03:15. moon conj mercury-05:38.

Sun Enters Aquarius 18:58

Robert E. Lee 1807 — Edgar Allan Poe 1809
Alexander Woollcott 1887 — Jean Stapleton 1923
Robert MacNeil 1931 — Tippi Hedren 1931
Phil Everly 1939 — Janis Joplin 1943
Shelley Fabares 1944 — Dolly Parton 1946

1937: Howard Hughes flies across U.S. in 7 hrs., 28 mins. and 25 secs., a new record. **1955:** First Presidential news conference covered by movie and television cameras. **1977:** Astronomers discover presence of water outside the earth's galaxy (on the edge of galaxy 1 C 133, 2.2 million light years away), indicating for the first time the possibility of life in distant parts of the universe **1977:** Tokyo Rose pardoned by President Ford.

SUNDAY JAN. 20
Sun Rises 07:23
Sun Sets 17:18
Moon Rises 07:26
Moon Sets 17:00

MOON ENTERS AQUARIUS 16:38

moon conj jupiter-09:26. sun conj moon-18:28.

NEW MOON 18:28

Andre Ampere 1775 — Huddie "Leadbelly" Ledbetter 1888
George Burns 1896 — Federico Fellini 1920
Patricia Neal 1926 — Robert Denard 1929
Arte Johnson 1934 — Anatoly Shcharansky 1948

1892: First official basketball game. **1964:** Wisconsin Cheese Foundation starts making the "World's Largest Cheese"— 34,591 pound cheddar. **1965:** Lyndon Johnson inaugurated as Pres. of U.S. **1965:** Alan Freed, rock 'n roll disc jockey, dies of uremia (Palm Springs, Fl.). **1975:** Schoolteacher Harriet Wardlaw transferred to a librarian's job because she is pregnant and unmarried—she was denied reinstatement to a classroom by a Texas judge.

INAUGURATION DAY

MONDAY JAN. 21
Sun Rises 07:23
Sun Sets 17:19
Moon Rises 08:09
Moon Sets 18:05

MOON IN AQUARIUS

moon square pluto-01:16.

John Fremont 1813 — Christian Dior 1905
Paul Scofield 1922 — Jack Nicklaus 1940
Richie Havens 1941 — Placido Domingo 1941
Mac Davis 1942 — Robby Benson 1956

1793: Louis XIV guillotined. **1908:** New York City enacts Sullivan Ordinance, making smoking by women illegal. **1924:** Lenin dies near Moscow at age 58. **1930:** First Buck Rogers comic strip appears. **1950:** Alger Hiss found guilty of perjury. **1954:** Nautilus, first atom-powered sub, launched. **1966:** Stewart Brand's 3-day "Trips Festival," begins (San Francisco). **1977:** President Carter pardons Vietnam-era draft evaders who did not commit violent acts.

Action is the antidote to despair.

Joan Baez

TUESDAY JAN. 22
Sun Rises 07:23
Sun Sets 17:20
Moon Rises 08:45
Moon Sets 19:08

MOON IN AQUARIUS

moon square saturn-18:26. venus at asc node-04:00.

Ivan The Great 1440 — Lord Byron 1788
August Strindberg 1849 — D.W. Griffith 1875
Rosa Ponselle 1897 — Ann Sothern 1909
Piper Laurie 1932 — Sam Cooke 1935
Joseph Wambaugh 1937 — Linda Blair 1959

1444: Johannes Gutenberg listed as eligible for military service. **1789:** The Power of Sympathy, first American novel, published in Boston. **1879:** With only spears as weapons, Zulu warriors kill 1,745 British troops in battle of Isandhlwana in southeast Africa. **1901:** Queen Victoria dies in her 82nd year. **1967:** George P. Metesky arrested for 32 bombings of utilities in New York City over the previous 16 years. **1973:** Supreme Court legalizes abortion. **1973:** Lyndon Johnson, 36th Pres. of U.S., dies at San Antonio International Airport in Texas—he was being transported from his ranch to a hospital after suffering a heart attack.

GROWING
BY LIZ CAILE

NOW'S THE TIME—Northern Regions can improve soils with top dressing of manure. Start cool weather plants indoors (cabbage, broccoli, leeks, lettuce); prune grape vines. **Northeast, Midwest, Mountain States:** Test seed viability by sprouting in moist paper towels; 80 percent of last summer's purchased or gathered seeds should sprout if they are to be sown in the garden. Collect and clean containers for indoor seedlings. Fill out mail orders. **Southeast:** Transplant greens from the cold frame into the garden. Start rhubarb in rich soil if far enough north for cool, dormant period. **South:** Set out tomatoes, sweet potatoes—you can sprout sets indoors. Plant blackberries. **Southwest:** Use debris from winter crops in compost. For kitchen gardens sow chard, lettuce, parsley, radishes, onion sets or plants, and carrots.

Plots & Strategies

Weather and soil conditions can suggest the path of least resistance for productive growing. Ideally, a garden site should be well drained, with a slight slope to the south so the sun's rays will warm the soil most effectively.

In cool, damp locations, cabbages won't be at a disadvantage. But cucumbers, squash, melons, pumpkins — all *Cucurbitae* family members — and beans, corn, eggplant and tomato must have warm, dry soil.

Lush growth in a yard or field will indicate a good site, and dandelions will be found blossoming in sweet soil. In temperate regions, avoid cold air drainages; a south-facing wall or overhanging eave will help protect tender crops from frost in the fall. In the south, choose a site with good air circulation.

Plant garden perennials to take advantage of microenvironments — for example, plant spearmint near a leaky faucet, no special soil preparation needed. Rhubard needs a well fertilized bed, but can adapt to landscaping needs.

Brambles & Berries

Small fruits can be established in low-maintenance beds. Strawberries, raspberries or blackberries will produce generous amounts of fruit in a small plot at one end of the garden. Try mulching strawberry beds with pine needles, or interplanting them with chives, or border them with shallots. A critical step in establishing strawberries is setting the plants out at the right depth in the soil. Plant so that soil comes up against the short central stem, or crown, just above the roots.

Don't expect to eat raspberries or blackberries from your first year's planting. Establish them in partial shade — be careful they don't shade a portion of the vegetable garden. The first year's efforts will establish plants that will bear for up to ten years. Keep black and red varieties of raspberries well apart from one another, as the black are very

susceptible to viruses the red may carry.

Space Savers

Plants that are tall and bushy at lower elevations and temperate latitudes are found in miniature on the alpine and northern tundra. There, tiny yarrows and alpine forget-me-nots a few inches in height are miniature replicas of common garden plants that grow several feet tall. These miniatures have adapted to harsh conditions and short seasons.

Like their alpine counterparts, miniature garden plants that have been developed as space-savers can be counted on to mature early. Fruit and plant size are one-fourth to one-half the size of regular garden varieties. For example, Golden Midget corn has four inch ears on a 30 inch stalk and matures in 60 days. Some miniatures, such as watermelon, don't do well indoors or in containers, however.

Other plant varieties, including the tomato strains of Patio, Pixie and Small Fry, have been developed especially for containers. They have compact roots and vegetation, but produce standard size fruits and flowers.

Many suitable varieties of the cucurbits — squash, cucumbers and cantalopes — don't prosper indoors, but will thrive on an apartment porch or small-yard patio.

Miniature fruit trees bear full-sized fruit and can be container grown, but are rather expensive and must be managed for a cold dormant period, without being exposed to strong winter blasts.

Herbs of small growth habit include: chamomile, 3 to 6 inches; chervil, 6 to 12 inches; cumin, 6 inches; marjoram, 8 to 12 inches; parsley, 12 inches; pennyroyal, 4 to 6 inches; shallots, 12 inches; thyme, 4 to 10 inches.

JANUARY

WEDNESDAY JAN. 23
Sun Rises 07:22
Sun Sets 17:22
Moon Rises 09:15
Moon Sets 20:10

MOON ENTERS PISCES 01:02.
moon trine pluto-10:07.

Stendahl 1783
Edith Wharton 1862
Potter Stewart 1915
Jeanne Moreau 1928
Edouard Manet 1832
Dan Duryea 1907
Ernie Kovacs 1919
Chita Rivera 1933

1849: Elizabeth Blackwell first woman to receive medical degree in U.S.. **1899:** Humphrey Bogart born—Warner Brothers changed date to Dec. 25. **1968:** U.S. spy ship Pueblo seized in North Korean waters. **1978:** Terry Kath, member of rock group Chicago, dies attempting to prove a gun wasn't loaded by pointing it at his head and pulling trigger. **1980:** Topless dancers banned from U.S. Army service clubs worldwide.

The truth brings with it a great measure of absolution, always.

R.D. Laing

THURSDAY JAN. 24
Sun Rises 07:22
Sun Sets 17:23
Moon Rises 09:41
Moon Sets 21.09

MOON IN PISCES
moon square uranus-09:23. sun square pluto-10:00. moon conj venus-20:24. moon conj mars-23:22.

Emperor Hadrian 76
Oral Roberts 1918
Desmond Morris 1928
Sharon Tate 1943
John Belushi 1949
Maria Tallchief 1925
Neil Diamond 1941
Warren Zevon 1947

1888: Typewriter ribbon patented. **1922:** Eskimo Pie patented. **1931:** Anna Pavlova, ballerina, dies of pleurisy of lungs in The Hague, Holland—her last words were, "Get my swan costume ready." **1965:** Winston Churchill, British statesman, dies at age 90 from cerebral thrombosis in his home in London.

FRIDAY JAN. 25

Sun Rises 07:21
Sun Sets 17:24
Moon Rises 10:05
Moon Sets 22:07

MOON ENTERS ARIES 12:05
moon trine saturn-05:32. moon square neptune-16:52.

Robert Boyle 1627
W. Somerset Maugham 1874
Edwin Newman 1919
Robert Burns 1759
Virginia Woolf 1882
Anita Pallenberg 1943

1856: Indians led by Yakima war chief, Kamiakin, attack Seattle, but are defeated by a U.S. battleship sent to guard the city. **1890:** Trying to outdo Jules Verne's hero in Around the World in 80 Days, Nellie Bly returns, having completed a tour around the world in 72 days, 6 hours and 11 minutes. **1915:** Transcontinental telephone service inaugurated by Alexander Graham Bell. **1947:** Alphonse "Scarface" Capone dies (Miami Beach, Fla.)—it is generally believed he died from an untreated advanced case of syphillis.

I'm not infatuated with frivolousness. We're just good friends.

Tom Robbins

SATURDAY JAN. 26

Sun Rises 07:20
Sun Sets 17:25
Moon Rises 10:28
Moon Sets 23:03

MOON IN ARIES
moon trine uranus-21:52.

Frank Costello 1893
Paul Newman 1925
Jules Feiffer 1929
Cora Baird 1912
Eartha Kitt 1928
Angela Davis 1944

1885: Khartoum falls. **1886:** Internal combustion motorcar patented by Karl Benz. **1965:** South Africa refuses television on the grounds that it would be mainly dependent on British and American films which are drenched with liberalistic and demoralizing propaganda. **1979:** Nelson Rockefeller, ex-Vice-Pres. of U.S., dies of cardiac arrest at age 70 in New York City.

Blest is that nation whose silent course of happiness furnishes nothing for history to say.

Thomas Jefferson

SUNDAY JAN. 27

Sun Rises 07:20
Sun Sets 17:26
Moon Rises 10:51
Moon Sets ----

MOON IN ARIES
moon at apogee-02:00. moon square mercury-10:28. moon square jupiter-20:26.

Wolfgang Amadeus Mozart 1756
Hyman Rickover 1900
Donna Reed 1921
Troy Donahue 1936
Lewis Carroll 1832
William Randolph Hearst, Jr. 1908
Edith Cresson 1934
Mikhail Baryshnikov 1948

1302: Dante expelled from Florence, even though he had left the year before. **1888:** National Geographic Society founded. **1965:** South Vietnamese military leaders oust U.S.-supported civilian government of Tran Van Huong. **1973:** Cease-fire agreement in Vietnam.

MONDAY JAN. 28

Sun Rises 07:19
Sun Sets 17:27
Moon Rises 11:15
Moon Sets 00:00

MOON ENTERS TAURUS 00:53
moon trine neptune-05:53. moon oppos pluto-10:29. sun square moon-19:29.

FIRST QUARTER MOON 19:29

Auguste Piccard 1884
Claes Oldenburg 1929
Nicholas Pryor 1935
Susan Howard 1943
Jackson Pollock 1912
Susan Sontag 1933
Alan Alda 1936
Corky Laing 1948

1829: William Burke, body-snatcher, executed in Edinburgh. **1948:** First Emmy Awards presented.

CRUISE

Speedy—Efficient—Economical | Makeshift—Unreliable—Costly | Slow—Uncertain—Costly

CELESTIAL EVENTS

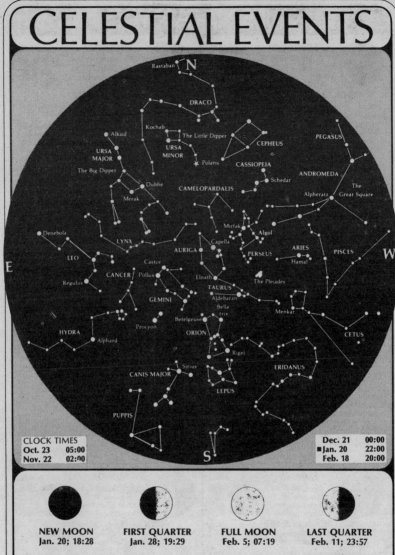

CLOCK TIMES
Oct. 23 05:00
Nov. 22 02:00

Dec. 21 00:00
■Jan. 20 22:00
Feb. 18 20:00

NEW MOON
Jan. 20; 18:28

FIRST QUARTER
Jan. 28; 19:29

FULL MOON
Feb. 5; 07:19

LAST QUARTER
Feb. 11; 23:57

MERCURY is visible till Feb. 6 rising in the east about 1 hour before sunrise; thereafter it is too close to the sun for viewing. **VENUS** is visible all month appearing in the western sky at sunset, then setting about 3 hours later. **MARS** is visible all month appearing near Venus in the western sky at sunset, then setting 3 hours later. **JUPITER** is visible after Feb. 1, rising in the east 1-2 hours before sunrise. **SATURN** is visible all month rising in the east 4-6 hours before sunrise, then fading near midsky with morning twilight. **Jan. 19:** Mercury 3° N. waning crescent Moon (morning sky). **Jan. 21:** Venus at gr. elong. E.(47°).**Jan. 24:** Venus 5° N. of waxing crescent Moon (evening sky); Mars 4° N. of waxing crescent Moon (evening sky). **Jan. 30:** Mercury 1.3° S. of Jupiter (morning sky). **Feb. 07:** Venus 3° N. of Mars (evening sky). **Feb. 12:** Saturn 3° N. of last quarter Moon (morning sky). **Feb. 15:** Venus 4° N. of Mars (evening sky). **Feb. 17:** Jupiter 4° N. of waning crescent Moon (morning sky).

32

JANUARY—FEBRUARY

TUESDAY   JAN.
29
Sun Rises 07:18
Sun Sets 17:29
Moon Rises 11:42
Moon Sets 00:59

MOON IN TAURUS

mars trine saturn-09:39. venus trine saturn-20:11.

Daniel Bernoulli 1700   Thomas Paine 1737
Romain Rolland 1866   W.C. Fields 1880
Victor Mature 1916   Paddy Chayefsky 1923
Noel Harrison 1936   Germaine Greer 1939
Katherine Ross 1943   Tom Selleck 1945

1933: Scraps of clothes and tiny skeleton of a child missing since 1931 are discovered in nest of eagle on farm in eastern Finland. **1975:** Weather Underground bombs U.S. State Department (Washington, D.C.). **1977:** Freddie Prinze, comedian and actor, dies at age 23 in Los Angeles hospital 36 hours after he had shot himself in head with a revolver—note found in his apartment said, "I cannot go on any longer."

For a while, you can kind of get off on being complex and broody; it's cool.

Tim Hutton

WEDNESDAY   JAN.
30
Sun Rises 07:17
Sun Sets 17:30
Moon Rises 12:13
Moon Sets 01.59

MOON ENTERS GEMINI 13:00

moon oppos saturn-07:12. moon trine mercury-07:52. moon trine jupiter-09:53.

Franklin D. Roosevelt 1882   Saul Alinsky 1909
Dorothy Malone 1925   Shirley Hazzard 1931
Tammy Grimes 1934   Vanessa Redgrave 1937
Boris Spassky 1937   Marty Balin 1943

1838: Seminole chief Osceola dies in prison—he never surrendered and his people as a nation were never conquered. **1862:** USS Monitor launched. **1900:** William Goebel, Governor of Kentucky, is assassinated. **1933:** First radio broadcast of *The Lone Ranger*. **1933:** Hitler named Chancellor of the German Reich. **1948:** Gandhi assassinated. **1948:** Orville Wright, co-inventor of airplane, dies of natural causes at age 76 in Dayton, Ohio,—on same day, 3 separate U.S. airplane crashes kill 50 people.

THURSDAY   JAN.
31
Sun Rises 07:16
Sun Sets 17:31
Moon Rises 12:50
Moon Sets 03:01

MOON IN GEMINI

moon at asc node-01:22. mercury conj jupiter-01:52.
venus conj mars-10:39. sun trine moon-12:06.
moon oppos uranus-21:38.
MERCURY ENTERS AQUARIUS-23:44.

Rudolph Wurlitzer 1831   Zane Grey 1875
Eddie Cantor 1892   Alva Myrdal 1902
John Agar 1921   Carol Channing 1921
Norman Mailer 1923   James Franciscus 1934
James Watt 1938   Johnny Rotten 1956

1606: Guy Fawkes and others executed in London for conspiracy. **1615:** Cape Horn discovered. **1956:** A.A. Milne, creator of Winnie the Pooh, dies (Hartfield, Sussex, England). **1958:** First U.S. satellite, **Explorer I**, launched. **1961:** Chimpanzee rocketed into space.

Even a pig can be flattered into climbing a tree.   *Chinese Proverb*

FRIDAY   FEB.
01
Sun Rises 07:15
Sun Sets 17:32
Moon Rises 13:35
Moon Sets 04:03

MOON ENTERS CANCER 21:59

moon square mars-21:17. moon square venus-21:47.

John Ford 1895   Clark Gable 1901
S.J. Perelman 1904   Muriel Spark 1918
Don Everly 1937   Garrett Morris 1937
Rick James 1952   Elsa The Lion 1956

1790: First Supreme Court meeting. **1893:** Thomas Edison builds first motion picture studio. **1949:** Mount Palomar begins using its 200-inch telescope. **1965:** Martin Luther King and 770 blacks arrested in Selma, Ala. while demonstrating against voter registration restrictions.

SATURDAY   FEB.
02
Sun Rises 07:14
Sun Sets 17:33
Moon Rises 14:29
Moon Sets 05:04

MOON IN CANCER

VENUS ENTERS ARIES-00:29.
moon oppos neptune-02:45. moon trine pluto-06:38.
MARS ENTERS ARIES-09:19.

Charles de Talleyrand 1754   Havelock Ellis 1859
James Joyce 1882   George Halas 1895
Ayn Rand 1905   Abba Eban 1915
James Dickey 1923   Valery Giscard D'Estaing 1926
Stan Getz 1927   Herb Kaplow 1927
Farrah Fawcett 1947

1870: Cardiff Giant revealed as a hoax. **1892:** Bottle cap patented. **1893:** First close-up movie taken (of a sneeze). **1970:** Bertrand Russell dies. **1979:** Patricia Hearst released from federal prison after serving 22 months of a 7-year sentence. **1979:** Sid Vicious, punk rocker, dies of heroin overdose (New York City).

GROUND HOG DAY

SUNDAY   FEB.
03
Sun Rises 07:14
Sun Sets 17:34
Moon Rises 15:32
Moon Sets 06:01

MOON IN CANCER

moon trine saturn-22:24. mercury square pluto-22:57.

Felix Mendelssohn 1809   Gertrude Stein 1874
Norman Rockwell 1894   James Michener 1907
Melanie 1947   Morgan Fairchild 1950

1882: P.T. Barnum buys Jumbo the Elephant. **1913:** 16th Amendment on income tax takes effect. **1924:** Woodrow Wilson, 27th Pres. of U.S., dies of "apoplexy paralysis" at age 67 years and 36 days (Washington, D.C.). **1933:** Nine woman patients at mental institution in Cleveland, Ohio, die in fire—after being led outside to escape flames, they ran back inside to get warm. **1959:** Ritchie Valens, The Big Bopper, and Buddy Holly die near Mason City, Iowa in airplane crash. **1965:** Selma, Ala. police arrest 1,000 black children who are protesting voter registration requirements.

All happiness depends on a leisurely breakfast.   *John Gunther*

FORECAST

BY NAN DE GROVE

AQUARIUS

LONGITUDE OF THE PLANETS
18:58 PST; 01/19/85

Sun 00°00′ Aquarius
Moon 18°06′ Capricorn
Mercury 11°31′ Capricorn
Venus 17°01′ Pisces
Mars 19°42′ Pisces
Jupiter 25°55′ Capricorn
Saturn 26°21′ Scorpio
Uranus 16°22′ Sagittarius
Neptune 02°11′ Capricorn
Pluto 04°40′ Scorpio

Change is in the air as Aquarius blows in. The theme of power reorganization that emerged with the November eclipse is intensifying now. The Water Bearer's purpose is to awaken us from our somnambulent conformity and scatter the seeds of creative thought in our minds. Tolerance and flexibility are needed to avoid the reactionary extremes of this sign, where the urge to reform often becomes fanaticism.

The last transit through Aquarius in 1973 coincided with the rise of the feminist movement, the legalization of abortion, and the Watergate scandal, among other things. This year the expansive, visionary nature of Jupiter in Aquarius is certain to generate change and controversy in the political and social arenas.

Jupiter in Aquarius may provide us with a vision of a better, more hopeful world, but responsibility for actualizing that vision begins on an individual level. In essence, Aquarius is the light of consciousness, illuminating the dark recesses of the psyche.

AIR SIGNS experience the expansive, uplifting influence of Jupiter most directly. Everything is taking on greater meaning and purpose, even if details are initially a bit fuzzy.

Gemini: opportunities arise for travel, education, and personal growth. Consolidate efforts, and be open to new activities.

Libra: concentrate on your creative potentials waiting to be developed; but gain self-esteem through using developed talents. Relationships will intensify around the first week of February.

Aquarius: you may feel a little ahead of the crowd now, sensing change in the wind. Your life is on an upswing and opportunities abound in education, travel, group involvement, politics, and personal growth.

WATER SIGNS moving with the tide, may be pulled this way and that by shifting emotional currents. Strive for an objective overview.

Cancer: you can reap benefits by being more trusting in relationships now. Look for returns on material, intellectual, and emotional investments this month.

Scorpio: time for you to emerge from that intense period of mental exertion. Recognize the change percolating in the depths and be prepared for an ending which will pave the way for a new beginning.

Pisces: simultaneous urges to connect and retreat may make you appear elusive and magnetic at the same time. Affairs of the heart are favored, but a new relationship needs time to develop.

EARTH SIGNS are finishing old projects and striving to put new plans into effect.

Taurus: review and revise in many areas. You may need to take risks in order to expand professionally and gain much deserved recognition.

Virgo: there is a danger of being swept away emotionally; avoid playing a martyr or savior role. Opportunities are present to become free of burdens in many areas.

Capricorn: in beginning a new cycle of financial growth, you may be inclined to loosen the purse strings a bit while considering what constitutes security in life. Over-generosity to self or others could be dangerous.

FIRE SIGNS may be in a muddle early in Aquarius, but inspiration and direction will return around the first week of February.

Aries: you should experience some dramatic new beginnings in both relationships and self-awareness this month. Energy peaks the first week of February.

Leo: you are also ready to begin a new cycle now, balancing personal needs with the requirements of relationships. Cooperation with others is a key issue. Energy peaks around the 5th.

Sagittarius: you are lightening up, feeling a new sense of freedom and an urge to be on the move. Travel, communication, learning, and friendship are favored.

FEBRUARY

MONDAY — FEB. 04

Sun Rises 07:13
Sun Sets 17:35
Moon Rises 16:42
Moon Sets 06:51

MOON ENTERS LEO 03:02

moon oppos jupiter-02:09. moon trine mars-05:23. moon trine venus-06:31. moon square pluto-11:07. moon oppos mercury-12:42.

Nigel Bruce 1895	Charles Lindbergh 1902
Joan Payson 1903	Byron Nelson 1912
Agha Khan 1917	Ida Lupino 1918
Betty Friedan 1921	Isabel Peron 1931
David Brenner 1945	Alice Cooper 1948

1861: Confederate congress organized (Montgomery, Ala.). **1913:** Demountable automobile tire patented. **1965:** Air Force Academy officials announce resignation of 15 cadets in wake of cheating scandal. **1968:** Neal Cassady found "dead on the tracks" (San Miguel Allende, Mexico). **1974:** Patricia Hearst is kidnapped by the Symbionese Liberation Army.

UNLIKELY

TUESDAY — FEB. 05

Sun Rises 07:13
Sun Sets 17:36
Moon Rises 17:56
Moon Sets 07:35

MOON IN LEO

venus square neptune-00:02. sun oppos moon-07:19. moon trine uranus-07:50. pluto retrogrades-16:05.

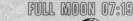

Adlai Stevenson 1900	John Carradine 1906
William Burroughs 1914	Red Buttons 1919
Hank Aaron 1934	Bernard Kalb 1922
Charlotte Rampling 1946	Al Kooper 1944

WEDNESDAY — FEB. 06

Sun Rises 07:12
Sun Sets 17:37
Moon Rises 19:10
Moon Sets 08:12

MOON ENTERS VIRGO 05:09

mars square neptune-00:24. moon square saturn-00:53. JUPITER ENTERS AQUARIUS-07:35. moon trine neptune-09:39.

Christopher Marlowe 1564	Aaron Burr 1756
Charles Wheatstone 1802	Henry Irving 1838
Babe Ruth 1895	Ronald Reagan 1911
Zsa Zsa Gabor 1919	Gerald K. O'Neill 1927
Rip Torn 1931	Francois Truffaut 1932
Walter Fauntroy 1933	Mike Farrell 1939
Tom Brokaw 1940	Fabian 1943

1933: Highest wave ever recorded on open sea—112 feet (Pacific Ocean). **1971:** Alan Shepard hits 3 golf balls on the moon.

They are fresh out of heroes in the eighties.
Joan Baez

THURSDAY — FEB. 07

Sun Rises 07:11
Sun Sets 17:38
Moon Rises 20:23
Moon Sets 08:45

MOON IN VIRGO

moon square uranus-09:14. moon at perigee-20:00.

Charles Dickens 1812	Mendeleev 1834
Alfred Adler 1870	Sinclair Lewis 1885
Buster Crabbe 1908	Elizabeth Taylor 1932
Ralph Nader 1934	Huey Newton 1942

1894: Adolphe Sax, (Paris). **1965:** George out. — inventor of saxophone, dies **1964:** Beatles come to the U.S. Harrison has his tonsils

FRIDAY — FEB. 08

Sun Rises 07:09
Sun Sets 17:39
Moon Rises 21:35
Moon Sets 09:15

MOON ENTERS LIBRA 06:10

moon trine jupiter-06:55. moon square neptune-10:45. moon oppos mars-13:47. moon oppos venus-15:47.

Samuel Butler 1612	Jules Verne 1828
Martin Buber 1878	Dame Edith Evans 1888
King Vidor 1894	Neal Cassady 1926
James Dean 1931	Tom Rush 1941
Nick Nolte 1941	Gary Coleman 1968

1933: Mrs. Lucinda Mills, age 67, is strangled to death by her family during religious ceremony (Tomahawk, Ky.). **1982:** Guilty plea entered by Hitachi for theft of information from IBM.

A corporation is just like any natural person, except that it has no pants to kick or soul to damn, and, by god, it ought to have both.
Ernest & Lindley

SUNDAY

Sun Rises 07:08
Sun Sets 17:41
Moon Rises 22:46
Moon Sets 09:44

MOON IN LIBRA

moon trine mercury-04:08. sun trine moon-17:11.

George Ade 1866	Amy Lowell 1874
Bill Veeck 1914	Brendan Behan 1923
Roger Mudd 1928	Robert Morris 1941
Carole King 1941	Mia Farrow 1945

1861: Jefferson Davis elected President of confederacy. **1870:** U.S. Weather Bureau established. **1964:** Beatles' first appearance on *Ed Sullivan Show*. **1981:** Bill Haley, rock 'n roller, dies of heart attack at age 55 in his home (Harlingen, Texas).

For some incredibly uncanny reason, a musician is more important than a politician these days.
Eric Clapton

Hamburger History

By John Lehndorff

The **hamburger** is the quintessential American food. Almost 40 billion beef patties in buns are eaten each year, making it our most popular meal by far. As the Golden Arches sprout across the globe, the **cheeseburger** with **French fries** has become a symbol of America and its cuisine. At some point though, every child asks the immortal question: Why is there no ham in hamburger? The answer, like the arches, spans the globe.

The evolution of the hot and juicy entree started with Russians who wanted to be more virile. The Tartars, from the steppes of Russia, ate raw ground horsemeat patties to gain the strength of the stallion. The dish came with them down the Elbe River in the 1300s as they fought and traded with the Germans in the city of Hamburg. The Hamburgians responded by changing the meat to beef and cooking it.

The raw beef dish we call **Steak Tartar** was concocted by an American and the French dubbed it "Bifteck A' L'Americaine." The Russians also have "Goviazhi Kohlety," which closely resembles **Italian meatballs**, which were invented in Brooklyn in the 1920s.

The Bifteck a' l'Hambourgeosie or **Hamburg Steak** came to America with German immigrants in the late 1800s. At that point, it was a hard-cooked loaf that was crumbled and mixed with eggs, breadcrumbs, and spices before frying. The name Hamburg stuck because most of the immigrants sailed over on the Hamburg-Amerika Line which served this meat dish on the lower decks. The dish became very popular, especially when served with **grilled onions**, a French invention.

Around 1900, Dr. J.H. Salisbury began a health fad by prescribing the eating of beef burger three times a day to cure colitis, pernicious anemia, asthma, bronchitis, rheumatism, and gout. The cure didn't work, but the **Salisbury steak** was named after him anyway.

Legend has it that the Hamburg Steak became the hamburger at the St. Louis Exposition, in 1904. Running out of clean plates, a concession stand employee in desperation, started placing the steaks between two slices of bread. People loved it so much they stopped serving it any other way.

The British claim that the true inventor was John Montagu, the Earl of Sandwich (1718-1792) and a diehard gambler, who wanted to eat with one hand so he could keep playing cards. His true contribution was the **roast beef sandwich**, although the Pueblo Indians enjoyed a corn bread version introduced by the Spanish Conquistadors.

Until after World War II the hamburger was an ethnic specialty food that was served with a variety of condiments. It was up to a blender salesman and visionary named Ray Kroc to make it our national food.

In 1954, Kroc discovered the McDonald brothers, Maurice and Richard, selling thin hamburgers on round buns with onions, ketchup, mustard, and a pickle — for a low price. He bought the idea and opened the first McDonald's in Des Plaines, Illinois the same year. Thus was **fast food** born.

The French were actually the last to make **French fries**, an authentic American food. Potatoes originated in South America and were cultivated by the Incas who introduced them to the Spaniards who in turn introduced them throughout Europe.

It was the Italians who so-named them because the potatoes were sliced into long julienne strips in the French manner. They finally returned to America at the turn of the century with emigrants from a variety of countries. French fries are now the most popular food in America, surpassing even hamburgers, and are ordered by 53 percent of us every month.

The bland, sweet dairy product called **American cheese**, which is usually melted over the hamburger to make the cheeseburger, was derived from Cheddar cheese. It was invented in the 1660s by farmers in the town of Cheddar in Bristol, England.

Ketchup or **catsup** originated in India and China from where it was imported to England; in its original form, it was a very sour condiment. The Pilgrims, in turn, brought it with them to the New World, but it didn't become the sweet sauce we now drench our burgers and fries with until 1869, when a Massachusetts pickle maker added sugar to the mix.

FEBRUARY

SUNDAY — FEB. 10

Sun Rises 07:07
Sun Sets 17:42
Moon Rises 23:57
Moon Sets 10:14

MOON ENTERS SCORPIO 07:49
moon square jupiter-09:22. moon conj pluto-15:48.

Bill Tilden 1893	Harold MacMillan 1894
Bertolt Brecht 1898	Leontyne Price 1927
Peter Allen 1944	Donovan 1946

1258: Mongols sack Baghdad. *1763:* Treaty of Paris ends French and Indian War. *1863:* Fire extinguisher patented. *1912:* Joseph Lister, surgeon, dies (Walmer, Kent, England). *1933:* Singing telegrams introduced. *1942:* First gold record awarded (sales over 1 million) for **Chattanooga Choo Choo** by Glenn Miller. *1962:* CIA pilot Gary Powers exchanged for Soviet master spy Rudolph Abel.

MONDAY — FEB. 11

Sun Rises 07:06
Sun Sets 17:43
Moon Rises ----
Moon Sets 10:46

MOON IN SCORPIO
moon square mercury-13:24. sun square moon-23:57.

LAST QUARTER MOON 23:57

Thomas Edison 1847	Florence Kennedy 1916
Sidney Sheldon 1917	King Farouk 1920
Virginia Johnson 1925	Tina Louise 1934
Burt Reynolds 1936	Sergio Mendes 1941

1794: First U.S. treaty with the Six Nation Confederacy of the Iroquois, signed by George Washington to last "forever" and broken with the building of the Kinzua Dam in the 1960s. *1927:* Tutankhamen's casket opened. *1933:* First of 56 children jumps over 1,000 feet to her death into crater of Mihara Volcano on island of Oshima in Japan—last jump is on May 9, after which police guards are installed to prevent any more. *1984:* U.S. Scientists announce discovery of crucial mutation occurring in gene's which causes cancer.

TUESDAY — FEB. 12

Sun Rises 07:05
Sun Sets 17:45
Moon Rises 01:08
Moon Sets 11:22

MOON ENTERS SAGITTARIUS 11:09
moon conj saturn-07:06. moon at desc node-22:40.

Abraham Lincoln 1809	Charles Darwin 1809
George Meredith 1828	Alice Roosevelt Longworth 1884
Omar Bradley 1893	Joe Garagiola 1926
Nina Simone 1933	Bill Russell 1934

1880: National Croquet League organized. *1940:* Superman begins as serial on radio. *1961:* Venus probe launched. *1976:* Sal Mineo, actor, dies at age 37 after being stabbed by unknown assailant (Hollywood).

It's dog-eat-dog, and if anyone tries to get me I'll get them first. It's the American way of survival of the fittest.

Ray Kroc

LINCOLN'S BIRTHDAY

WEDNESDAY — FEB. 13

Sun Rises 07:04
Sun Sets 17:46
Moon Rises 02:19
Moon Sets 12:03

MOON IN SAGITTARIUS
moon trine mars-01:10. moon trine venus-03:51.
moon conj uranus-17:48.

Bess Truman 1885	Grant Wood 1892
Georges Simenon 1903	William Shockley 1910
Tennessee Ernie Ford 1919	Eileen Farrell 1920
Kim Novak 1933	George Segal 1934
Oliver Reed 1938	Carol Lynley 1942

1866: James-Younger gang robs their first bank. *1889:* First Secretary of Agriculture appointed. *1933:* Blondie and Dagwood married. *1945:* American bombers attack Dresden, Germany in series of raids that continued through Feb. 15—final death toll was over 30,000. *1965:* African and Asian students attack U.S. consulate in Budapest.

One mouse can only fill its belly, but ten thousand mice can empty a lake.

Japanese Proverb

THURSDAY — FEB. 14

Sun Rises 07:02
Sun Sets 17:47
Moon Rises 03:26
Moon Sets 12:52

MOON ENTERS CAPRICORN 16:27
moon conj neptune-21:50.

Thomas Malthus 1766	Jack Benny 1894
Jimmy Hoffa 1913	Hugh Downs 1921
Vic Morrow 1932	Florence Henderson 1934
Carl Bernstein 1944	Tim Buckley 1947

269: St. Valentine beheaded in Rome during the persecution of Claudius the Goth. *1779:* Captain James Cook, explorer, dies at hands of Hawaiian natives, with whom he had disagreement—he was stabbed and drowned, his body rendered into pieces before it was returned to his crew. All they received was his scalp, bare bones, and both hands preserved in salt—remains were buried at sea. *1876:* Elisa Gray files notice of invention of telephone—Alexander Graham Bell is awarded the patent (March 7).

VALENTINE'S DAY

FRIDAY — FEB. 15

Sun Rises 07:01
Sun Sets 17:48
Moon Rises 04:27
Moon Sets 13:48

MOON IN CAPRICORN
moon square mars-10:13. moon square venus-13:04.

Galileo 1564	Cyrus McCormick 1809
Susan B. Anthony 1820	Cesar Romero 1907
Leonard Woodcock 1911	John Anderson 1922
James Schlesinger 1929	Susan Brownmiller 1935
Melissa Manchester 1951	Jane Seymour 1951

1879: Women admitted to practice law before the U.S. Supreme Court. *1933:* Anton Cermak, mayor of Chicago, is assassinated. *1965:* Canada's new national Maple Leaf flag is raised for first time on Parliament Hill in Ottawa. *1981:* Michael Bloomfield, blues guitarist, dies in his car (San Francisco)—a heroin overdose is suspected.

Life is a hard job.

Faye Dunaway

3-DAY WEEKEND

Presidents' Day

by Ed Quillen

On the third Monday of every February, millions of Americans stay home from work and school in honor of an event variously called "Presidents' Day," "Washington-Lincoln Day," "Washington's Birthday," or "three-day weekend."

This year that date is February 18. It comes on a Monday, of course, to allow Americans to contemplate the wisdom of the father of their nation while skiing in the Rockies or sunning on the Gulf. More respectful citizens sometimes recall that Washington's birthday is actually February 22.

But the archives of that era do not show that George Washington was born to Augustine and Mary Washington on February 22, 1732, the date given in history texts. The old records show that George Washington arrived at Pope's Creek, Westmoreland County, Virginia, on February 11, 1731. That's a difference of one year and eleven days.

The explanation goes back to another leader of another nation. In 46 b.c., Julius Caesar, on advice from the Greek astronomer Sisogenes, established a new calendar. Sisogenes set the year at 365 1/4 days long. That's close, but it wasn't close enough for long-term date keeping.

The year — the time it takes for the earth to return to the same position in relation to the sun — is actually 365 days, 5 hours, 48 minutes, and 46 seconds, not the convenient 365 days and 6 hours decreed by Sisogenes and Caesar.

This tiny difference — amounting to about a day every 128 years — began to accumulate, until the calendar was seriously out of whack with the seasons. The first recorded notice of the problem came in 730 a.d. from the Venerable Bede, an Anglo-Saxon scholar and monk. But it took another eight centuries before anyone got around to doing anything about it.

What finally occasioned the change was a curious and enduring preoccupation of the Vatican astronomers. They couldn't have cared less that through the newly invented telescope, Jupiter was discovered to have moons and Saturn to have rings. They were greatly concerned, however, that it was getting harder and harder to perform their principal task — computing the annual date for Easter. Easter Sunday is a moveable feast which was, and still is, determined by the date of the Jewish Passover celebration. Passover, in turn is established by a relationship between the New Moon and the Vernal Equinox, the beginning of spring.

The Vernal Equinox is supposed to occur about March 22. But centuries of an inaccurate calendar had pushed the date ahead to March 11. If it were to continue, Halloween would someday become a summer feast, and Christmas would occur as the leaves were changing colors. So finally, in 1582, Pope Gregory XIII decreed that October 4 of that year would be followed by October 15.

Dropping those ten days would make the calendar conform to the seasons, but unless another change was made, the error would recur and grow anew. To prevent this, the pontiff altered the leap year cycle. Under the Julian Calendar, every year evenly divisible by 4 was a leap year, meaning it acquired an extra day on February 29. Under the new Gregorian Calendar it stayed that way, except that years ending in "00" were not leap years unless they were evenly divisible by 400. Thus 1900 was not a leap year, but 2000 will be.

Had the Vatican reformed the calendar a century or two earlier, when the Pope's word was still law in Europe, matters would have been much simpler. Unfortunately, Gregory reigned after the Reformation, when the Protestant half of the European continent reviled "popery" and, therefore, any decree issued from the Vatican, regardless of scientific merit.

Only the Roman Catholic countries — France, Italy, Portugal, and Spain — immediately adopted the Gregorian Calendar in 1582. Before the 16th century was over, Belgium, the Netherlands, and Catholic

FEBRUARY

SATURDAY   FEB. 16

Sun Rises 07:00
Sun Sets 17:49
Moon Rises 05:21
Moon Sets 14:49

MOON ENTERS AQUARIUS 23:36

sun square saturn-05:16.

Mario Pei 1901	Hugh Beaumont 1909
Levar Burton 1957	John McEnroe 1959

1868: Elk's Club organized. 1918: Anti-loafing Law passed in N.J., requiring all able-bodied males to be gainfully employed. 1937: Nylon patented. 1959: Fidel Castro sworn in as Cuban Premier. 1965: FBI foils extremist plot to blow up Statue of Liberty, Liberty Bell, and Washington Monument.

You know, you win by default in this world. If you can just keep up the marathon footrace people think it's all done by expertise, but really it's just old age.

George Hamilton

SUNDAY   FEB. 17

Sun Rises 06:59
Sun Sets 17:50
Moon Rises 06:06
Moon Sets 15:53

MOON IN AQUARIUS

oon conj jupiter-04:12. moon square pluto-08:26.
mercury square saturn-11:21.

Chaim Potok 1929	Alan Bates 1930
Jim Brown 1936	Gene Pitney 1941

1876: First sardine canned (Eastport, Maine). 1908: Geronimo dies. 1934: Albert I, King of Belgium, dies from fall while mountain climbing.

PRESIDENTS' DAY continued

German states had joined them. Protestant Germans, as well as the Danes, came aboard in 1699.

Britain, however, did not relent until 1752, when George Washington, then a British subject in a colonial empire, was 20 years old. By that time, the error had grown to 11 days again. Finally, parliament and King George II accepted the Gregorian standard and decreed that September 2, 1752 would be followed immediately by September 14.

Washington subsequently adjusted his birth date to the seasons, or the date it would have been had the Gregorian Calendar been in effect at the time and place of his birth. Thus, February 22 instead of February 11.

But what about the year? Why was he born in 1732 instead of the 1731 originally recorded 1731?

Well, while dropping the 11 days, His Majesty's Government also changed the date of New Year's Day. Scrapping the ancient Roman custom of beginning the new year on March 25, the British Crown adopted the European New Year reckoned from January 1.

So when Washington adjusted his birthday party to the new calendar, he had to change the year as well. February 22, 1731 (Julian) occurred *before* March 25 (Julian New Year, 1732) but *after* January 1 (Gregorian New Year, 1732). According to the Gregorian Calendar then, George Washington was born in 1732, as history maintains.

Incidentally, the British Empire was not the last realm to adopt the Gregorian Calendar. Japan waited until 1873 and Turkey until 1916. In the Soviet Union, February 13, 1918, was the day after February 1, 1918. Greece didn't change until 1923.

Washington's Birthday, then, is more than a holiday. It reveals to us something about all our days and the ways we count and divide them.

Picking A President

"To tell who will be elected U.S. president, take two roosters, the evening before election, and name each for the respective candidates of the leading parties; place them together under a tub, and early the following morning uncover them and notice which crows first; the one crowing will indicate the election of the candidate for which he was named."

Encyclopedia of Superstitions, 1903

Electing A Corpse

A dead man was elected mayor of a small town in Colorado in 1983. The voters of Ward, population 125, elected as the mayor of this old mining town, a resident who died a week before the election. Some of the voters were undoubtedly paying tribute to the man and the community, for as one resident quipped, "Ward's a ghost town, and we decided to elect a dead man to represent the silent majority." But not everyone shared this sentiment; another voter was heard to say, "When he won, I just about died."

> "The Vice-President simply presides over the Senate and sits around hoping for a funeral. It is a very high office which consists entirely of honor and I don't have any ambition to hold an office like that."
> — *Harry Truman*

Infamous Veeps

Being a collection of short anecdotes concerning the office and office-holders of Vice-President of the United States

by Armand Legg

Richard Nixon, while serving as the thirty-sixth Vice-President (under Eisenhower), achieved the distinction of becoming the first Vice-President to be depicted on a postage stamp. The stamp was issued on May 15, 1958, by Ecuador. It was worth two *sucres*, about twelve U.S. cents.

Charles Curtis (31st Vice-President, 1929-1933, under Herbert Hoover) is the only Native American to hold that office. Although only ⅛ Indian, from Kaw Tribe in Kansas, Curtis was known to have constantly boasted of his ancestry. He was not known for a distinguished career, and was described in his own lifetime as a "mediocrity who is as faithful to his party as he is dull and dumb."

Aaron Burr (3rd Vice-President, 1801-1805, under Thomas Jefferson) was arrested just after ending his term in office, thereby becoming the first Vice-President to be so marked. The crime was treason. Burr had been trying to organize an invasion of Mexico, and was indicted on June 24, 1807. After a trial that lasted more than a month, he was acquitted on September 1.

William Rufus De Vane King (13th Vice-President, 1853, under Franklin Pierce) never campaigned for the office, nor served. He died only six weeks after being sworn-in, and is the only executive officer of the United States ever to have been inaugurated in a foreign country. Nominated in 1852, King left the U.S. for Cuba in order to recover from an illness, and was too weak to return to Washington, D.C., after the election was over. An act of Congress allowed him to receive the oath of office in Havana. A U.S. Navy steamer took him back to his home state of Alabama a few weeks later, where he died on April 18, 1853.

George Clinton (4th Vice-President, 1805-1809, under Thomas Jefferson) may have been the most vilified person to hold the office. John Quincy Adams wrote at the time, "Mr. Clinton is totally ignorant of all the most common forms of proceeding in the Senate.... His judgement is neither quick nor strong ... a worse choice than Mr. Clinton could scarcely have been made." A senator from New Hampshire wrote, "He is old, feeble & altogether uncapable of the duty of presiding in the Senate.... He has no mind — no intellect — no memory — He forgets the question — mistakes it — & not infrequently declares a vote before it's taken — & often forgets to do it after it is taken...."

Adlai Ewing Stevenson (23rd Vice-President, 1893-1897, under Grover Cleveland) achieved no great distinction that honors him in history books, but he was the only candidate for office that was ever nominated by three different parties during the same election. During the election of 1900, several years after his first term expired, he was nominated to run again by the Democrats, the Silver Republicans, and the Populists. He was not rewarded for this triple support, since he lost the election.

James Schoolcraft Sherman (27th Vice-President, 1909-1912, under William Howard Taft) is the only candidate for executive office in the U.S. to have run for office after dying. Sherman was extremely ill with a kidney problem when he was convinced by the Republican party that his candidacy was necessary for the re-election of President Taft. He did not campaign because he was sick, and he died on October 30, 1912, only a few days before the election. By then it was too late to pick an alternate candidate; Republicans asserted that it was not necessary anyway, since the votes would only elect Electoral College members. Thus, Sherman's eulogy was 3,484,980 votes, too few for victory at the polls; Taft and his dead running mate were defeated.

Thomas Riley Marshall (28th Vice-President, 1913-1921) is little noted in history except for saying, "What this country needs is a really good five-cent cigar." He also said, "Since the days of John Adams, there has been a dread and fear that some vice-president of the United States would break loose and raise hell and Maria with the administration. Everything that can be done, therefore, is done to furnish him with some innocuous occupation. They seek to put him where he can do no harm."

Alben W. Barkley (35th Vice-President, 1949-1953, under Harry S. Truman) had a grandson, who, at the age of ten years old, coined and was the first to use the term **Veep** as a nickname for the position his grandfather held.

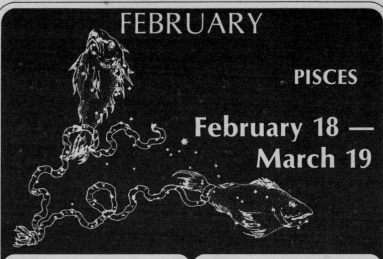

FEBRUARY

PISCES

February 18 — March 19

MONDAY
FEB. 18

Sun Rises 06:58
Sun Sets 17:51
Moon Rises 06:44
Moon Sets 16:56

MOON IN AQUARIUS

MERCURY ENTERS PISCES 15:42.
sun conj mercury-23:49.

Sun Enters Pisces 09:08

Alessandro Volta 1745
Wallace Stegner 1909
Helen Gurley Brown 1922
Yoko Ono 1933
Nikos Kazantzakis 1883
Jack Palance 1919
Milos Forman 1932
Cybill Shepherd 1950

1564: Michelangelo dies. *1678: Pilgrim's Progress Part I* published. *1688:* First vote against slavery recorded in the U.S. (Germantown, Penn.). *1930:* Ollie becomes first cow to fly in airplane and be milked in flight. *1933:* James "Gentleman Jim" Corbett, boxer, dies.

That's the truth—age is the worst thing of all. Time is what's chasing you. *Audie Murphy*

PRESIDENT'S DAY

TUESDAY
FEB. 19

Sun Rises 06:56
Sun Sets 17:52
Moon Rises 07:16
Moon Sets 17:58

MOON ENTERS PISCES 08:38

moon square saturn-04:35. sun conj moon-10:43.
moon conj mercury-11:33. moon trine pluto-17:44.

NEW MOON 10:43

Copernicus 1473
Kay Boyle 1903
Carson McCullers 1917
Andre Breton 1896
Merle Oberon 1911
Lee Marvin 1924

1725: An innkeeper's wife is consumed by flames in front of witnesses in an apparent case of spontaneous human combustion (Rheims, France) *1942:* Frank "The Dasher" Abbandando, dies in electric chair—he received his nickname for allegedly dashing away from an intended victim so fast that he caught up to him from behind. His lawyer once defended him against a murder charge by claiming, "Ballplayers don't kill people."

MARDI GRAS

WEDNESDAY
FEB. 20

Sun Rises 06:55
Sun Sets 17:54
Moon Rises 07:43
Moon Sets 18:58

MOON IN PISCES

moon square uranus-19:02.

Ansel Adams 1902
Gloria Vanderbilt 1924
Roy Cohn 1927
Buffy Sainte-Marie 1941
Jennifer O'Neill 1948
John Daly 1914
Robert Altman 1925
Bobby Unser 1934
J. Geils 1946
Patricia Hearst 1954

1937: First combination car-plane built, the Arrowbile, powered by Studebaker engine. *1962:* John Glenn circles earth three times in space capsule. *1965: Ranger 8* spacecraft, launched Feb. 17, transmits 7,000 pictures of moon before crash landing on lunar surface.

ASH WEDNESDAY
CHINESE NEW YEAR

THURSDAY
FEB. 21

Sun Rises 06:54
Sun Sets 17:55
Moon Rises 08:08
Moon Sets 19:57

MOON ENTERS ARIES 19:42

mercury trine pluto-04:49. moon trine saturn-15:39.

Antonio Santa Anna 1795
Constantin Brancusi 1876
W.H. Auden 1907
Sam Peckinpah 1925
Barbara Jordan 1936
August Von Wassermann 1866
Anais Nin 1903
Charles Scribner 1921
Erma Bombeck 1927
Christopher Atkins 1961

1795: France grants freedom of worship. *1918:* Incas, last striking green and yellow Carolina parakeet, dies in a zoo (Cincinnati, Ohio). *1962:* J. Edgar Hoover wins George Washington Award for the "most outstanding individual contribution to American freedom during 1961," *1965:* Malcolm X, leader of Black Nationalist movement, dies at age 39, the victim of an assassination (New York City).

You get to a point in your life when there aren't any obvious dragons.

Billy Joel

GROWING

BY LIZ CAILE

NOW'S THE TIME—Northeast: Plant fruit trees; finish fruit tree pruning. Set out horseradish, rhubarb, onion sets for early scallions. **Midwest:** Subtle signs of spring can be found; blackbirds whistle from pond and ditchside. **Mountain States:** Start cool weather plants indoors — broccoli, lettuce, cabbage, brussel sprouts. **Northwest:** Don't work wet ground too soon. Beware of cold, damp soil around transplant roots and of "damping off" of seedlings, where fungus weakens seedling at soil line. **Southeast:** Plant all annual flowers and vegetables. Begin staggered plantings of gladiola bulbs for large displays of flowers. **South:** Frost danger past; start cantaloupe, watermelons, pumpkins outdoors. **Southwest:** Don't delay bare-root planting any longer as spring warmth will end dormancy of nursery stock grapes, roses, fruit and ornamental trees. Till in cover crops and layers of compost or manure spread last fall.

Growing Soil

Very few of us will ever see the great productivity of fertile virgin soil just opened up to farming. No computer has yet analyzed the complex biology and chemistry of soil that nature has created over millenia into a perfect growing medium. Nor have modern farmers found a way to equal its productivity through new strains of crops and artificial fertilizers.

Gardening is a matter of growing soil to duplicate that perfection as closely as possible. Our growing efforts aren't going to reach fruition in a year or even two. We can spend many years improving our garden soil with mulches, mineral additives and compost.

Even container gardeners can "grow" their own soil by collecting and mixing free or low cost materials into local dirt to improve it. Some experts maintain the sterile, artificially created and enriched potting soils are the best to use and trouble free. They may work for you, but there's no putting down the real thing.

Don't be shy. Take a large garbage bag or feed bag into the country and collect dried cowpies. Light, easy and inoffensive to handle, they break up easily to add organic matter to your soil.

To grow soil is to nurture a host of soil microorganisms that release nutrients in turn absorbed by the fine root hairs of plants. Provide an organically-rich, aerated, mineral rich setting for these tiny life-givers.

Recognize the geological basis of your local soils; learn the native plants that prosper in these soils. Past history of your garden plot can indicate mineral deficiencies that can be remedied by the addition of rock powders. Your county extension agent can help you learn more about your garden soil.

Root Of The Matter

The root is the tip of the first growth shoot, called the *radicle*, of every germinating seed. There is tremendous power in the root and

eventually some roots can break up hard soil and pry rocks apart, having gained a hold in a narrow crack. But most vegetable plant roots depend on natural openings between soil granules to grow and extend their crucial network.

Roots conduct necessary materials to the photosynthesizing area of the plant. They also support it and anchor it against the wind and sheeting water of summer storms.

Taproots act as storage areas for photosynthesized food. These storage roots — carrots, turnips, beets, parsnips, rutabagas, etc. — are rich food sources from the vegetable garden. Grasses have spread-out systems of fibrous roots which anchor soil.

A single mature rye plant has a total root system of 300 to 500 miles. Roots of standard varieties of tomatoes, cabbage and carrots reach to depths of ten, eight and five feet respectively.

Alfalfa (a legume and not a grass) has a deep taproot that reaches to a depth of 20 feet to bring up moisture and nutrients. No wonder alfalfa is called the queen of green manures and is a rich source of nutrients for man and beast.

The roots of many plants have provided natural dyes for fabrics in many cultures, through many centuries. The roots of mountain mahogany are pounded by the Navajo weaver to collect the outer bark to dye wool a warm reddish brown.

A traditional red dye comes from the roots of the madder plant, and the coral-red of Scotch plaids was once obtained from the roots of ladies bedstraw. This color was so valued that dyers dug up too many plants, and the edges of their sandy island meadows began to unravel and erode.

So it became a crime punishable by death to dig the bedstraw. Our society could go further than it has in recognizing the importance of plant roots to holding the earth together.

FEBRUARY

FRIDAY   FEB. 22
Sun Rises 06:53
Sun Sets 17:56
Moon Rises 08:31
Moon Sets 20:54

MOON IN ARIES
moon square neptune-02:01.

George Washington 1732
Julius Erving 1950
Charlie Finley 1918
Edward Gorey 1925
Sparky Anderson 1934

Frederic Chopin 1810
Edna St. Vincent Millay 1892
Sybil Leek 1922
Edward Kennedy 1932
Ishmael Reed 1938
Amy Alcott 1956

SATURDAY   FEB. 23
Sun Rises 06:51
Sun Sets 17:56
Moon Rises 08:53
Moon Sets 21:51

MOON IN ARIES
sun trine pluto-00:13. moon conj mars-02:57.
moon conj venus-04:53. moon trine uranus-07:20.
moon at apogee-20:00.

Samuel Pepys 1633
W.E.B. Dubois 1868
Regine Crespin 1927
Louis Abolafia 1943

George Fredrick Handel 1685
Casmir Funk 1884
Peter Fonda 1939
Johnny Winter 1944

1505: *Columbus granted a license to ride a mule in Spain.* **1848:** *John Quincy Adams, 6th Pres. of U.S., dies in Speaker's Room of House of Representatives after suffering heart attack—he was 80 years and 227 days old. His last words were, "This is the last of earth. I am content."* **1885:** *John Lee survives three attempts at hanging in England.* **1905:** *Rotary Club founded.* **1965:** *Comedian Stan Laurel dies at age 74.* **1971:** *Lt. William Calley confesses he ordered the massacre of 22 My Lai civilians.*

SUNDAY   FEB. 24
Sun Rises 06:50
Sun Sets 17:57
Moon Rises 09:17
Moon Sets 22:48

MOON ENTERS TAURUS 08:27
moon trine neptune-14:58. moon square jupiter-16:50.
moon oppos pluto-17:55.

Winslow Homer 1836
Michel Legrand 1931

Michael Harrington 1928
James Farentino 1938

1530: *Last imperial coronation of a Holy Roman Emperor.* **1653:** *New York's first City Hall opens in a saloon.* **1815:** *Robert Fulton, inventor of the steamboat, dies.* **1922:** *Bluebeard executed for burning 10 of his fiancees.*

We do a great deal of expressing ourselves, in terms of slang, and it seems to please our imagination most when we can devise some odd-sounding word or phrase that applies to the ancient art of sham.

Rube Goldberg

MONDAY   FEB. 25
Sun Rises 06:49
Sun Sets 17:58
Moon Rises 09:42
Moon Sets 23:47

MOON IN TAURUS
venus trine uranus-10:48.

Pierre Renoir 1841
Enrico Caruso 1873
Zeppo Marx 1901
Tom Courtenay 1937

Benedetto Croce 1866
Meher Baba 1894
Anthony Burgess 1917
George Harrison 1943

1745: *Colonies pass legislation offering rewards for Indian scalps.* **1836:** *First greenbacks issued.* **1956:** *Hen lays 16 oz. egg.* **1970:** *Mark Rothko, modernist painter, dies (New York City).* **1983:** *Tennessee Williams chokes to death on plastic bottle cap.*

TUESDAY   FEB. 26
Sun Rises 06:47
Sun Sets 17:59
Moon Rises 10:11
Moon Sets ----

MOON ENTERS GEMINI 21:11
mars trine uranus-03:04. moon oppos saturn-17:19.

Victor Hugo 1802
Jackie Gleason 1916
Betty Hutton 1921
Robert Novak 1931

Buffalo Bill Cody 1846
Tony Randall 1920
Margaret Leighton 1922
Johnny Cash 1932

1531: *An earthquake in Lisbon, Spain kills 20,000 people.* **1815:** *Napolean escapes from Elba.* **1832:** *Chopin gives his first concert at age 21 (Paris).* **1919:** *Grand Canyon National Park established by Act of Congress.*

Literally everybody owns public lands. You can't go up and claim your square yard, but if something goes wrong with the public land and resources, everybody suffers.

Ansel Adams

WEDNESDAY   FEB. 27
Sun Rises 6:45
Sun Sets 18:00
Moon Rises 10:44
Moon Sets 00:48

MOON IN GEMINI
jupiter square pluto-01:51. moon at asc node-03:03.
moon trine jupiter-06:27. venus conj mars-12:56.
sun square moon-15:41.

FIRST QUARTER MOON 15:41

Henry Wadsworth Longfellow 1807
John Steinbeck 1902
Lawrence Durrell 1912

Hugo Black 1886
James T. Farrell 1904
Scott Momaday 1934

1814: *Beethoven's 8th Symphony premieres in Vienna.* **1915:** *First American soldier dies in WWI.* **1936:** *Ivan Pavlov, psychologist, dies (Leningrad).* **1939:** *Sit-down strikes are outlawed by Supreme Court.*

I'm often grateful that life has made it possible for me to mind my own business.

Doctor Doolittle

CELESTIAL EVENTS

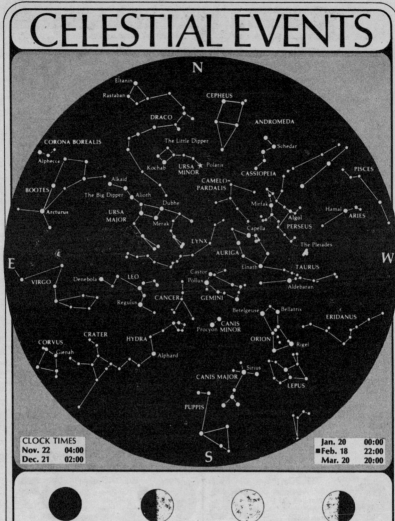

N

Eltanin
Rastaban
DRACO
CEPHEUS
ANDROMEDA
CORONA BOREALIS
The Little Dipper
Schedar
Alphecca
Kochab
URSA MINOR ★ Polaris
CASSIOPEIA
PISCES
BOOTES
Alkaid
The Big Dipper Alioth
CAMELO-PARDALIS
Mirfak
Hamal
ARIES
Arcturus
URSA MAJOR
Dubhe
Algol
PERSEUS
The Pleiades
Merak
Capella
LYNX
AURIGA
W
E
Elnath
TAURUS
VIRGO
Denebola
LEO
Castor
Pollux
GEMINI
Aldebaran
Regulus
CANCER
Betelgeuse
Bellatrix
ERIDANUS
Procyon CANIS MINOR
CORVUS
CRATER
HYDRA
ORION
Rigel
Gienah
Alphard
Sirius
CANIS MAJOR
LEPUS
PUPPIS
S

CLOCK TIMES		
Nov. 22	04:00	
Dec. 21	02:00	

Jan. 20	00:00
■Feb. 18	22:00
Mar. 20	20:00

NEW MOON
Feb. 19; 10:43

FIRST QUARTER
Feb. 27; 15:41

FULL MOON
March 6; 18:13

LAST QUARTER
March 13; 09:34

MERCURY comes to superior conjunction Feb. 19, and is visible after March 1 appearing low in the western sky at sunset, then setting about 1 hour later. **VENUS** is visible all month appearing low in the western sky at sunset, then setting 1-2 hours later. **MARS** is visible all month appearing in the western sky at sunset, then setting 2-3 hours later. **JUPITER** is visible all month rising in the east 2-3 hours before sunrise. **SATURN** is visible all month rising in the east about midnight and fading near midsky with morning twilight. **Feb. 22:** Venus 8° N. of waxing crescent Moon (evening sky); Mars 3° N. of waxing crescent Moon (evening sky). **Feb. 26:** Venus at greatest brilliancy (evening sky). **Mar. 11:** Saturn 3° N. of waning gibbous Moon (night sky). **Mar. 16:** Jupiter 5° N. of waning crescent Moon (morning sky); Mercury at gr. elong. E.(18°).

FEBRUARY—MARCH

THURSDAY
FEB. 28

Sun Rises 06:44
Sun Sets 18:01
Moon Rises 11:25
Moon Sets 01:49

MOON IN GEMINI

mercury square uranus-03:02. moon oppos uranus-08:06. moon square mercury-09:00.

Montaigne 1533	Linus Pauling 1901
Stephen Spender 1909	Vincente Minnelli 1910
Gavin MacLeod 1931	Tommy Tune 1939
Mario Andretti 1940	Bernadette Peters 1948

1940: First basketball game televised. *1966:* Elliot See and Charles Bassett, astronauts, die in plane crash on roof of Gemini Capsule building at McDonnell Aircraft Company (St. Louis, Mo.). *1968:* Frankie Lymon, 25, lead singer with the Teenagers, dies from heroin overdose in his grandmother's bathroom (New York City). *1976:* Ford calls Fidel Castro an international outlaw.

People do not deserve to have good writing, they are so pleased with bad.

Ralph Waldo Emerson

FRIDAY
MARCH 01

Sun Rises 6:42
Sun Sets 18:03
Moon Rises 12:14
Moon Sets 02:49

MOON ENTERS CANCER 07:23

moon oppos neptune-13:33.

William Dean Howells 1837	Ralph Ellison 1914
Robert Lowell 1917	Dinah Shore 1921
Roger Daltrey 1945	Ron Howard 1954

1780: First U.S. bank established. *1883:* Women's Temperance Society organized. *1910:* Train wreck in Wellington, Washington kills 96 people. *1932:* Lindbergh baby kidnapped. *1954:* Five Congressmen shot in House by Puerto Rican Nationalists; they went to the Senate first, but no one was there. *1961:* Peace Corps established by Executive Order of John Kennedy. *1965:* Brace Beemer, radio voice of "Lone Ranger" from 1941 to 1954, dies at age 62.

Ballroom conversation is the closest thing in the world to nothing.

Rube Goldberg

SATURDAY
MARCH 02

Sun Rises 06:40
Sun Sets 18:04
Moon Rises 13:11
Moon Sets 03:47

MOON IN CANCER

sun trine moon-05:23. moon square venus-20:15. moon square mars-22:09.

Sam Houston 1793	Desi Arnaz 1917
Tom Wolfe 1931	Lou Reed 1943
Karen Carpenter 1950	Laraine Newman 1952

1799: National legislation enacted for the standardization of weights and measures. *1818:* Sedon pyramid of Gizah opened. *1889:* Several dogs, four calves, and a horse electrocuted to test equipment before use on convicted criminals. *1899:* Mt. Rainier National Park established. *1901:* Forest Service formed. *1965:* Russian troops rout crowd of 2,000 in Moscow protesting U.S. conduct in Vietnam.

SUNDAY
MARCH 03

Sun Rises 06:39
Sun Sets 18:05
Moon Rises 14:17
Moon Sets 04:40

MOON ENTERS LEO 13:28

moon trine mercury-01:52. moon trine saturn-10:11. moon square pluto-21:18. moon oppos jupiter-23:11.

George Pullman 1831	Alexander Graham Bell 1847
Jean Harlow 1911	Lee Radziwill 1933

1863: America's first conscription law passed. It contained clause providing exemption in exchange for $300. *1893:* RFD mail instituted. *1923:* Joseph Gurney Cannon first person to have picture on cover of *Time* magazine. *1960:* Leonard Warren, operatic baritone, dies on stage at Metropolitan Opera in New York City during ovation from audience. He had just finished aria from Verdi's opera *La Forza del Destino.*

MONDAY
MARCH 04

Sun Rises 06:37
Sun Sets 18:06
Moon Rises 15:29
Moon Sets 05:26

MOON IN LEO

moon trine uranus-19:43.

Knute Rockne 1888	John Garfield 1913
Miriam Makeba 1932	Jimmy Clark 1936
Barbara McNair 1939	Paula Prentiss 1939

1519: Cortez lands in Mexico. *1789:* U.S. Constitution officially in effect. *1963:* William Carlos Williams, writer, dies (Rutherford, N.J.). *1969:* 150,000 barrels of oil spilled into Cook Inlet, Alaska.

I feel smog abandons me from time to time, and I feel very upset about that.

Dudley Moore

TUESDAY
MARCH 05

Sun Rises 06:36
Sun Sets 18:07
Moon Rises 16:44
Moon Sets 06:06

MOON ENTERS VIRGO 15:42

moon trine venus-00:52. moon trine mars-04:06. moon square saturn-12:39. mercury trine saturn-15:16. moon trine neptune-21:11.

Mercator 1512	James Ives 1824
Frank Norris 1870	Samantha Eggar 1929
Judd Hirsch 1935	Eugene Fodor 1950

1770: Crispus Attucks, a black, is killed in Boston Massacre—first martyr of American Revolution. *1894:* Seattle opens first municipal employment office. *1937:* New York City Mayor La Guardia calls Hitler a "brown-shirted fanatic." The U.S. officially apologizes.

If I didn't have my demons, I wouldn't have my angels.

Tennessee Williams

FORECAST

BY NAN DE GROVE

PISCES

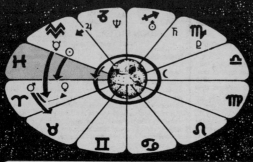

LONGITUDE OF THE PLANETS

09:08 PST; 02/18/85

Sun *00°00′* **Pisces**
Moon *17°44′* **Aquarius**
Mercury *29°29′* **Aquarius**
Venus *13°21′* **Aries**
Mars *11°58′* **Aries**
Jupiter *02°43′* **Aquarius**
Saturn *27°53′* **Scorpio**
Uranus *17°31′* **Sagittarius**
Neptune *03°03′* **Capricorn**
Pluto *04°42′* **Scorpio R**

The humanitarian urges of Aquarius lead to empathy, compassion, and forgiveness in Pisces, the last of the twelve signs. The old feeds the new as we return to the watery womb, awaiting rebirth. Boundaries dissolve in the sign of the Fishes as we experience the vulnerability of our humanity and the inherent dualities of spirit incarnate in matter.

With Venus and Mars conjunct in Aries through March 14th, spirits are high and romantic adventures offer a tempting solution to winter blues. Our passions could propel us into emotional entanglements that are somewhat premature and insubstantial. Alliances formed during this period will best succeed if they are based on common vision and mutual ideals.

Fire and water signs predominate now. This combination tends toward intensity, impulsiveness, and emotional extremes. There is tension between the self-expressive urges of fire and the self-protective tendencies of water. The Full Moon on March 6th emphasizes the need for balance and discrimination in handling these extremes.

WATER SIGNS can express the imaginative and compassionate sides of themselves now, but should avoid escapism, oversensitivity, and emotional manipulation.

Cancer: you may be grasping the meaning of a complex situation and feeling connected with universal themes. Professional life is in ferment and a romantic involvement could be complicating matters in this area.

Scorpio: seek creative outlets for explosive feelings. Work on reaffirming faith in self and faith itself.

Pisces: you are ready for a new cycle now, with more clearly defined goals. Opportunities are present to connect with others who will help you give form to your visions.

FIRE SIGNS may be baffled by complex emotional situations that do not respond to direct solutions. Unconscious factors are potent now, and demand respect.

Aries: you may be pursuing something that could be a real treasure or a flash in the pan. Learn the difference between quest and conquest; be discriminating and discreet.

Leo: finalize matters and settle accounts, before moving into a new phase. Use this time to organize, refine, and reflect.

Sagittarius: you'll probably be dealing with the past in some way, resolving old emotional issues that are in conflict with new growth. Home, family, and personal foundations demand attention.

EARTH SIGNS are dealing with intangible, subconscious factors that influence outer circumstances.

Taurus: are you sensing the larger themes and purposes that tie in with individual goals? Some things are not to be taken too literally or seriously.

Virgo: time for a new cycle of interaction with others. Full Moon brings tensions to the surface as you see the need for major changes in your work and home life. Don't underestimate your abilities.

Capricorn: open up to the unknown and linking with the universal mind. Whether you fear these new trends or welcome them, your life is changing irrevocably.

AIR SIGNS are restless and eager to try out new ideas, discovering that emotional fuel is vital to implementing plans.

Gemini: your life is in flux, making it difficult to define goals and make commitments. Watch nerves and avoid scattering your energy.

Libra: your preoccupation with relationship issues and may sweep you into extremely volatile interactions with others. Avoid being overly influenced by strong personalities, heed intuition, and watch your health.

Aquarius: you can make considerable progress now, using a combination of common sense, intellect, and intuition. Use diplomacy and tact, rather than arrogance, to overcome obstacles.

WEDNESDAY — MARCH 06
Sun Rises 06:35
Sun Sets 18:08
Moon Rises 17:59
Moon Sets 06:40

MOON IN VIRGO
MERCURY ENTERS ARIES-16:07.
sun oppos moon-18:13. moon square uranus-20:29.

FULL MOON 18:13

Michelangelo 1475 — Cyrano De Bergerac 1619
Elizabeth Browning 1806 — Ring Lardner 1885
Furry Lewis 1893 — Bob Wills 1905
Ed McMahon 1923 — Alan Greenspan 1926
Gabriel Garcia Marquez 1928 — Valentina Tereshkova 1937

1836: *"Remember the Alamo."* 1857: *Dred Scott decision handed down by Supreme Court. Blacks declared non-citizens.* 1886: *First A.C. power plant begins operation.* 1931: ***The March of Time*** *first heard on radio.* 1932: *John Philip Sousa, the "March King," dies of heart attack in hotel room (Reading, Penn.).*

THURSDAY — MARCH 07
Sun Rises 06:33
Sun Sets 18:09
Moon Rises 19:13
Moon Sets 07:12

MOON ENTERS LIBRA 15:47
saturn retrogrades-04:41. mercury at asc node-16:00.
moon oppos mercury-18:56. moon square neptune-21:12.

Luther Burbank 1849 — Maurice Ravel 1875
Anna Magnani 1908 — Janet Guthrie 1938

1799: *Pennsylvania tax revolt.* 1870: *First male-female Grand Jury impaneled.* 1906: *U.S. troops wipe out an entire Philippine Moro tribe and are congratulated by Pres. Teddy Roosevelt.* 1965: *First U.S. combat troops land in South Vietnam, at Da Nang.* 1965: *Using gas, clubs, and whips, Selma, Ala. police prevent civil rights march to Montgomery.*

FRIDAY — MARCH 08
Sun Rises 06:32
Sun Sets 18:10
Moon Rises 20:27
Moon Sets 07:42

MOON IN LIBRA
moon at perigee-00:00. moon trine jupiter-02:08.
sun square uranus-04:41. mercury square neptune-14:54.

Sophocles 496bc — Sam Jaffe 1893
Claire Trevor 1908 — Cyd Charisse 1921
Lynn Redgrave 1943 — Little Peggy March 1948

1874: *Millard Fillmore, 13th Pres. of U.S., dies at age 74 years and 60 days, suffering from paralysis and debility (Buffalo, N.Y.)—his last words were, "The nourishment is palatable."* 1894: *New York becomes first state to license dogs.* 1917: *Russian revolution begins with riots and strikes in St. Petersburg.* 1930: *William H. Taft, 27th Pres. of U.S., dies of "debility" at age 72 years and 174 days (Washington, D.C.).*

In every lie, there's a little truth.
Thomas Magnum

SATURDAY — MARCH 09
Sun Rises 06:31
Sun Sets 18:11
Moon Rises 21:41
Moon Sets 08:12

MOON ENTERS SCORPIO 15:47
moon oppos venus-02:46. moon oppos mars-09:19.
mars at asc node-16:00. moon conj pluto-23:01.

Adolf Eichmann 1906 — Samuel Barber 1910
Mickey Spillane 1918 — James Buvkley 1923
Herbert Gold 1924 — Trish Van Devere 1943

1274: *Thomas Aquinas, saint, dies on way to Council of Lyons after being struck on head and knocked off his donkey by a low-hanging tree limb—according to tradition, the donkey also died, from sorrow.* 1796: *Napolean marries Josephine.* 1822: *Artificial teeth patented.* 1916: *Pancho Villa and 1,500 Mexican guerillas attack Columbus, New Mexico, killing 17 American citizens.* 1945: *Most destructive air raid in history—U.S. Army Air Corps destroy over 16 sq. miles of Tokyo in nighttime incendiary bomb attack, using 2,000 tons of bombs dropped from 334 B-29 bombers to shatter and burn 250,000 buildings. Official death count on ground was 83,793, with unofficial estimate of over 100,000.*

SUNDAY — MARCH 10
Sun Rises 06:29
Sun Sets 18:132
Moon Rises 22:56
Moon Sets 08:44

MOON IN SCORPIO
moon square jupiter-03:03.

Immanuel Velikovsky 1895 — Frederick Lowe 1904
Heywood Hale Broun 1918 — Katharine Houghton 1945

1892: *Capitol of New York moved from New York City to Albany.* 1913: *Harriet Tubman, ex-slave and abolitionist, dies (Auburn, N. Y.) at Harriet Tubman Home for Aged Negroes, which she founded.* 1974: *Japanese soldier discovered in the Philippines—nobody had told him that WWII was over.* 1980: *First time a woman is jailed for non-payment of child support.* 1980: *Scarsdale Diet doctor, Dr. Herman Tarnower, slain.*

You got to have a dream/ If you don't have a dream/ How you gonna have a dream come true?
Bloody Mary

MONDAY — MARCH 11
Sun Rises 06:27
Sun Sets 18:14
Moon Rises ----
Moon Sets 09:20

MOON ENTERS SAGITTARIUS 17:29
sun trine moon-01:56. moon conj saturn-14:16.

Dorothy Gish 1898 — Ralph Abernathy 1926
Rupert Murdoch 1931 — Sam Donaldson 1934

1302: *Romeo marries Juliet.* 1779: *Army Corps of Engineers established.* 1816: *Shenandoah, Chief of the Oneidas, dies.* 1824: *Bureau of Indian Affairs created as part of the War Department.* 1948: *Zelda Sayre Fitzgerald, wife of F. Scott Fitzgerald, dies in fire that burned through mental hospital where she was a patient (Asheville, N.C.).* 1965: *White Boston minister, James. J. Reeb, dies from beating administered by 3 white men during March 8 civil rights march.* 1965: *14 young civil rights workers stage White House sit-in demanding federal intervention in Selma, Ala.* 1970: *Erle Stanley Gardner, age 80, dies (Temecula, Calif.).*

GOOD-BYE

Badminton

by Bob Conrow

In case you haven't noticed, badminton — not tennis or racquetball — happens to be the most popular racquet sport in the world. If this little tidbit surprises you, that's simply because you (like most Americans) equate the sport with summertime frolics rather than serious play.

More than 70 countries around the world, however, honor badminton with a "national status" and defend it with a passion. Britons, for example, would rather "be badmintoning" than playing soccer. And Indonesians, who may muster 1,000 fans just to watch a practice session, have profiled their badminton "hero," Rudy Hartono, on a postage stamp.

Contrary to its pity-pat image, professional badminton is at once a highly aggressive and curiously catlike game — a graceful mixture of freedom and flow, smooth deception, and instant action. The object of badminton is not so much to catch the bird, as it is to pursue the feathered object with stealth, cunning, and a certain degree of style.

And when it comes to birds, professional badminton players can be as fussy as a pedigreed Siamese. As Tom Carmichael of the United States Badminton Association puts it, "if the bird doesn't come from a real goose it's going to be either too fast, too slow, or else it will spin out on the turns." While many companies have tried, so far, none has succeeded in manufacturing a synthetic counterpart that in any way flies like the "real thing."

The real thing in this case weighs in at less than an ounce and is made from the choicest goose feathers. Geese from the Far East are preferred and, even then, just four select feathers are plucked from each goose. This tidy missile is then topped off with an immaculately-tailored, kidskin-covered cork.

The name of the game in badminton is precision movement, and a bird of any other feather will simply not do. Just the slightest flick of the wrist, often delayed until the last possible instant, can determine whether the bird will zip like a bullet — at close to 200 mph — or else plop gingerly over the net like an overly-ripe plum. High speed photographers report that a bird in flight may dart back and forth between players in a mere half second. And typically in competitive play, a bird will rebound between racquets in just under a second. Compare this with tennis where racquet-to-racquet timings average around one and a half seconds.

For a competitive player to keep up with such a swiftly moving object is no mean feat. During a singles match, a player may have to run as much as a mile, change direction (90 degrees or more) 150 times, and hit the bird (on the "head") nearly 200 times. If all this leaves you somewhat breathless just thinking about it, no wonder! Be advised that the professional badminton player in a 45 minute match must not only run farther than either a running back or an end, but he or she will also exert more arm action than a baseball pitcher in a typical nine-inning game.

All this, of course, bears not the slightest resemblance to the game commonly played amidst the scent of charcoal-flavored hamburgers and potato chips on American patios. Nor, for that matter, does it have much to do with the game's origins.

While images of racquets and birds (or shuttlecocks) can be found in paintings dating back almost 2,000 years, the game's present version was first "officially observed" by British officers stationed in India in the 1870s. The soldiers returned to native soil, taking the game but not the name with them.

In India, it was called Poona, after the city where it was played. In England, with rather unfortunate consequences, the sport became better known as the "game at Badminton."

At Badminton, an upper-class British estate, sports enthusiasts were more inclined to fashion than to game finesse. High-button shoes and Prince Albert coats were definitely "in" and shirtsleeves were "out." In fact, "out" is exactly what happened to one club player for daring to remove his Prince Albert during a game. Moreover, because the doors of Victorian salons opened inwards, the court was forced into a most unreasonable "hourglass" shape. Not until 1901, did the court resume its more practical, rectangular form.

Although badminton made its way to American shores by late 19th century, it soon fell victim to style and circumstance. Neglected by the rich and regarded casually by the middle classes, badminton proved ill fit to compete in the rough-and-tumble arena of American sports.

For a few brief moments in the thirties, the U.S. led the world in both champions and participants. Then basketball moved swiftly onto the courts, and the badminton players discovered almost overnight that they had hardly a bench left to sit on.

Today, while the Chinese, Indonesians, and Japanese cart home most of the international badminton trophies, America's estimated 50,000 serious players remain optimistic. Patiently, they wait for the basketball players to clear the floor and dream of the day when their own Rudy Hartono will step boldly into the limelight.

MARCH

TUESDAY   MARCH **12**
Sun Rises 06:26
Sun Sets 18:15
Moon Rises 00:09
Moon Sets 10:01

MOON IN SAGITTARIUS
moon at desc node-01:43. moon trine mercury-09:36.

Henry The Navigator 1394   Jack Kerouac 1922
Edward Albee 1928   Andrew Young 1932
Liza Minnelli 1946   James Taylor 1948

1888: *The Blizzard of '88 kills 400 in northeastern states.* **1912:** *Girl Scouts organized.* **1926:** *Edward Scripps, newspaperman, dies on board a ship off coast of Liberia.* **1930:** *Gandhi begins 200-mile salt march to protest salt tax.* **1933:** *FDR delivers first Fireside Chat.* **1951:** ***Dennis the Menace** appears.*

Mercury is visible above the Western Horizon just after evening twilight. Most people have never seen it. You can get out and see it!

WEDNESDAY   MARCH **13**
Sun Rises 06:25
Sun Sets 18:16
Moon Rises 01:19
Moon Sets 10:48

MOON ENTERS CAPRICORN 21:54
moon conj uranus-00:29. moon trine venus-08:10.
sun square moon-09:34. venus retrogrades-10:17.
moon trine mars-20:34.

LAST QUARTER MOON 09:34

Joseph Priestly 1733   Percival Lowell 1855
William Bolger 1923   Deborah Raffin 1953
    1781: *Planet Uranus*

discovered. **1877:** *Earmuffs patented.* **1884:** *Standard Time established in U.S.* **1901:** *Benjamin Harrison, 23rd Pres. of U.S., dies from pneumonia at age 67 years and 205 days (Indianapolis, Ind.)—his last words were, "Are the doctors here?"* **1964:** *Kitty Genovese stabbed to death in three separate attacks over half an hour on a New York street as 37 witnesses stand idly by.* **1968:** *More than 6,400 sheep reported killed by nerve gas escaping from Army test at Dugway Proving Grounds (Utah).*

THURSDAY   MARCH **14**
Sun Rises 06:23
Sun Sets 18:17
Moon Rises 02:23
Moon Sets 11:42

MOON IN CAPRICORN
moon conj neptune-04:12. moon square mercury-20:57.
MARS ENTERS TAURUS-21:07.

Maxim Gorky 1868
Hank Ketcham 1920
Quincy Jones 1933
Albert Einstein 1879
Diane Arbus 1923
Michael Caine 1933

1883: *Karl Marx dies— he once said, "Last words are for fools who haven't said enough."*

FRIDAY   MARCH **15**
Sun Rises 06:21
Sun Sets 18:18
Moon Rises 03:20
Moon Sets 12:42

MOON IN CAPRICORN
moon square venus-14:33.

Lightnin' Hopkins 1912   Harry James 1916
Phil Lesh 1940   Mike Love 1941
Sly Stone 1944   Ry Cooder 1947

44bc: *Julius Caesar assassinated.* **1493:** *Columbus returns to Spain after getting lost on his way to China.* **1882:** *Longfellow writes his last poem "The Bells of San Blas."* **1913:** *First Presidential press conference.*

Question: My wife says cigars stink.
Answer: She's right.

Question: Why do many people dislike cigar smokers?
Answer: Who cares?

The Cigar Almanac

SATURDAY   MARCH **16**
Sun Rises 06:20
Sun Sets 18:18
Moon Rises 04:07
Moon Sets 13:45

MOON ENTERS AQUARIUS 05:11
moon square mars-07:07. moon square pluto-13:22.
moon conj jupiter-20:50.

Pat Nixon 1912   Jerry Lewis 1926
Daniel Moynihan 1927   Bernado Bertolucci 1940
Jerry Jeff Walker 1942   Erik Estrada 1949

1915: *Federal Trade Commission organized.* **1926:** *Robert Goddard launched first liquid-fueled rocket.* **1940:** *1st civilian death from air raid in World War II—Germans attack Orkney Islands in Great Britain, killing one person.* **1968:** *My Lai Massacre—109 Vietnamese men, women, and children are killed during raid on their village by U.S Army's Charlie Company, 1st Battalion, 20th Infantry, led by 1st Lieutenant William L. Calley.*

A well-written life is almost as rare as a well-spent one.

Thomas Carlyle

SUNDAY   MARCH **17**
Sun Rises 06:18
Sun Sets 18:19
Moon Rises 04:46
Moon Sets 14:48

MOON IN AQUARIUS

Mercedes McCambridge 1918   Nat King Cole 1919
James Irwin 1930   John Sebastian 1944
Kurt Russell 1951   Lesley-Anne Down 1954

180: *Marcus Aurelius dies.* **1845:** *Stephen Perry invents rubber bands.* **1938:** *Franco bombs Barcelona.* **1959:** *Dalai Lama flees from Tibet to India.* **1965:** *Soviet cosmonaut performs first spacewalk.*

ST. PATRICK'S DAY

The Mystery Of
The Uvula
by Robert B. McFarland M.D.

The uvula is that curious, pink, worm-like appendage that hangs from the soft palate in the back of the mouth. Behind the uvula is the throat or pharynx, and above the soft palate is the nasopharynx.

Usually the uvula looks like FIGURE 1 below, but occasionally anatomic variations occur and it looks like FIGURE 2. Long uvulas sometimes touch the tongue, but most are short and resemble letter "U" or "V," which may explain how the name arose.

world and the people who request it don't often tell strangers their reasons. Usually this simple but useless operation is performed by a traditional or barber surgeon as a ritual in early childhood.

In November, 1981, the *Journal of Laryngology and Otology* described "Uvulectomy in Nigeria," and in 1982 the *Israel Journal of Medical Sciences* described "Mutilation of the Uvula Among Bedoins of the South Sinai." Both articles exhibit a trace

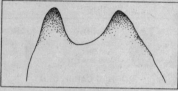

FIGURE 1

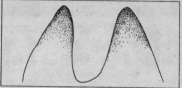

FIGURE 2

Some uvulas tilt to one side or the other, but most hang straight down. In rare circumstances, the uvula is greatly enlarged, and appears bulbous and pendulous; in such cases, this causes no apparent disfunction or discomfort to the individual. Like most body organs that form in the midline, however, there is a possibility of incomplete fusion of the uvula in embryonic life.

Just what the uvula does, is another question altogether — a question that not only remains unanswered, but one that, apparently, is rarely asked. In fact, there is an extraordinary, and therefore disturbing scarcity of both information and curiosity concerning the nature and function of this bizarre appendage, in both technical and popular sources.

The uvula may play a role in enhancing certain vibrato sounds or "tra-la-la" sounds. Just saying the word uvula rapidly and repeatedly is a good way to exercise this mysterious organ.

But to the question, "What is the uvula for?", the only answer of any certainty appears to be: "No one knows, and no one cares!"

Doctors have been trimming the uvula with impunity, if not glee, for a long time. One doctor in my childhood hometown always removed the uvula when he took out the tonsils, and no one had the nerve to ask him why. To remove the uvula is customary in many underdeveloped countries of the

of condescension on the part of the scientifically trained observers over the ritual customs of tribal people.

The uvula will often be swollen when a person has a sore throat, and the surrounding tissue of the palate, the pharynx, and the tonsils can be even more swollen. This occurs mainly with throat infections, but a swollen uvula can sometimes occur when no other signs of infection are present.

The uvula is not removed nearly as often as the nearby tonsils, but there is undoubtedly a similar reason for both operations. Ever since anesthesia became practical more than 100 years ago, removing tonsils has been the most common surgical procedure done in hospitals. (This does not include male circumcision which is not called a surgical procedure because anesthesia is withheld.)

No one is even sure why tonsils are removed, but I think the reasons are similar to the reasons for trimming uvulas or climbing mountains; that is, because they are there. The tonsils are made up of lymphatic tissue which helps resist infection; so in theory, they should be left intact.

Most infections of humans are caused by bacteria or viruses and are spread from person to person by coughing or sneezing. As a sore throat begins, the tonsils enlarge, become sore, and often have yellow pus or exudate on their surface.

It seems reasonable to believe that cutting out these red, swollen tonsils might be

MONDAY   MARCH 18

Sun Rises 06:16
Sun Sets 18:20
Moon Rises 05:19
Moon Sets 15:50

MOON ENTERS PISCES 14:50

sun trine saturn-08:28. moon square saturn-10:58.
moon trine pluto-23:13.

Amerigo Vespucci 1454	Grover Cleveland 1837
Edgar Cayce 1877	Richard Condon 1915
Andy Granatelli 1923	George Plimpton 1927
John Updike 1932	Wilson Pickett 1941

1584: *Ivan the Terrible, Czar of Russia, dies while playing chess—cause of death was suspected to be related to unknown ailment that caused him "grievously to swell in the cods."* **1937:** *Natural gas explosion kills 294 people (New London, Tex.).* **1961:** *Pillsbury Dough Boy born.* **1965:** *Farouk I, exiled King of Egypt, dies in Italy 2 hours after eating dozen oysters, leg of lamb, fried potatoes, beans, 2 oranges, 2 bottles of Coca-Cola, bottle of ginger soda, glass of mineral water, and smoking Havana cigar.*

TUESDAY   MARCH 19

Sun Rises 06:14
Sun Sets 18:21
Moon Rises 05:47
Moon Sets 16:50

MOON IN PISCES

mars trine neptune-18:31.

Wyatt Earp 1848	William Jennings Bryan 1860
Earl Warren 1891	John Sirica 1904
Eugene McCarthy 1916	Irving Wallace 1916
Pauline Kael 1919	Philip Roth 1933
Phyllis Newman 1935	Ursula Andress 1936

721bc: *Babylonians observe lunar eclipse—first recorded in history.* **1950:** *Edgar Rice Burroughs, writer, dies.*

The immortality of a writer is to be taken literally. Whenever anyone reads his words, the writer is there. He lives in his readers.
William Burroughs

UVULA continued

justified, at least on a primitive level: "If it offend thee, cast it out." Unfortunately, almost all studies show that children get just as many sore throats after having their tonsils removed as do children the same age who keep their tonsils.

As children grow up, the tonsils gradually shrink in size and finally disappear. Rarely can one tell whether a twenty-five-year-old has had their tonsils removed or not, unless they remember. And most people remember, because anesthesia and surgery are easily confused with death threats in the minds of children.

So I suspect the uvulectomy is done for

similar reasons. The uvula can sometimes be seen to swell with sore throats and it does not have any crucial function. This type of surgical ritual persists in many parts of the underdeveloped world and is probably related to ritualistic sexual mutilations, such as male and female circumcision.

And to remind us that ritual mutilation is always in vogue, even in the overdeveloped world, there is a new proposed reason for removing the uvula and the adjacent tissue of the palate and pharynx. This procedure is now being tried on people with sleep apnea, a rare condition that occurs in very fat people, usually those who weigh more than 300 lbs.

Such individuals often have difficulty breathing, which results in poor sleep at night and, in turn, frequent falling asleep in the daytime. Just because they are unhappy enough to become obese and thus can not breath well is a poor reason to attack their uvulas, unless sadistic and ritualized mutilations have a deeper and more profound purpose than we now understand.

With the aid of a flashlight and a spoon handle to depress the tongue, one may observe the state of the uvula in any friend who will humor your curiosity. After observing several uvulas, get ready for the coming controversy over the mysterious uvula. Scientific doctors will be attempting to restrain untrained practitioners from performing uvulectomies in Nigeria, while devising new excuses to perform them in the United States.

THE PHENOMENON OF KULKULCAN

by Jim Walton

The major events of our calendar rarely fall upon days of astronomical significance. However, the calendars of our cultural ancestors, the Egyptians, the Greeks, and the Persians, were timed to coincide with the important passages of the sun into the seasons.

We still have a vestige of this custom in the system of astrology which begins the zodiacal cycle on March 21, the first day of Aries and also the day when the sun passes through the Spring (or Vernal) Equinox. Although our new year is celebrated on January 1, the day of the equinox is still celebrated as the beginning of the year in other traditions, for example, as the Persian New Year.

A remarkable reaffirmation of the timing of astronomical phenomena with the calendar has recently been popularized in Mexico. Every spring thousands of tourists, and not a few dedicated cultists, converge on the ancient ceremonial city of Chichen Itza in the Yucatan, to witness a unique phenomenon that only occurs at the time of the vernal and autumnal equinox.

This event, fast becoming a national holiday, is the appearance of a serpent of light on the pyramid of Kukulcan — the Mayan Quetzalcoatl. As the sun gradually descends to the horizon, a set of seven brilliantly lit diamonds appear on the northeast balustrade of the pyramid, formed by the zigzag shadows cast by its stepped platforms. At the bottom of the stairway, the sculptured head of a feathered rattlesnake, now joined briefly to its luminous body, seems to guard some arcane mystery.

Today, archaeologists are still trying to unlock the secrets of the ancient Mexican temples. The pyramid at Chichen Itza, also affectionately known as the Castillo (castle), is a textbook in stone of pre-Hispanic numerology. Its four sides represent the four cardinal directions and their elements. Its four stairways each contain 91 steps which,

with the platform at the top, make 365 stairs representing the days of the solar year.

The 52 shallow niches on each side may represent the 52 years of the calendar round (a conjunction of the 365 day solar year with the 260 day sacred almanac). Its nine platforms symbolize the nine lords of the night, or the nine mansions of the Mayan underworld called the Bolon-na.

None of this rather dry numerical symbolism expresses the pageantry and religious meaning that must have accompanied the original ceremonies. It might have been a potent experience, for in the words of the modern discoverer of the phenomenon, J. Rivard: "To the ancient people who worshipped at this site, a manifestation such as this must have seemed a most awe-inspiring hierophany, since the serpent was one of the meaningful aspects of their religious experience."

It is possible that the serpent's sinuous grace was a metaphor for the oscillation of the sun between its northern and southern extremes on the horizon (at the solstices). An equinoctal festival is recorded for the Aztec Temple Major where celebrants carrying a huge paper serpent danced on the steps of the temple.

Symbolically, the passage of the sun through the equinoxes is also associated with agricultural rhythms. As the Maya were an agricultural people, their rituals largely expressed the growing cycle of their staff of life, corn or, more properly speaking, maize. The biannual appearance of the fiery feathered serpent represented the arrival and departure of the major growing season. Just after the vernal equinox, the rainy season begins.

Whether or not numerology and symbolism are represented in additional aspects of Mayan architecture the phenomenon of Kukulcan is an impressive wedding of astronomy, art, and life.

MARCH

ARIES

March 20 – April 18

WEDNESDAY
MARCH 20

Sun Rises 06:13
Sun Sets 18:21
Moon Rises 06:12
Moon Sets 17:49

MOON IN PISCES

moon square uranus-02:19. mars oppos pluto-17:34. moon trine saturn-22:15.

Sun Enters Aries 08:14
VERNAL EQUINOX

Ovid 43bc
Henrik Ibsen 1828
B.F. Skinner 1904
Alfonso Garcia Robles 1911
John Ehrlichman 1925

Ned Buntline 1823
Max Brand 1892
Ozzie Nelson 1907
Carl Reiner 1922
Mr. Rogers 1928

1727: Isaac Newton dies in England. 1751: Act of Parliament changes calendar—new year to begin on January 1 for the first time. 1852: Uncle Tom's Cabin, by Harriet Beecher Stowe, published (Boston). 1896: U.S. Marines land in Nicaragua to protect U.S. property.

THURSDAY
MARCH 21

Sun Rises 06:12
Sun Sets 18:22
Moon Rises 06:35
Moon Sets 18:46

MOON ENTERS ARIES 02:20

sun conj moon-03:59. mercury trine uranus-06:11. moon square neptune-09:30.

NEW MOON 03:59

Johann Sebastian Bach 1685
James Coco 1929

Phyllis McGinley 1905
Karen Kain 1951

1617: Pocahontas, Powhatan Indian, dies in London, England, as she was preparing to return to America. 1821: First treaty between Wampanoags and the Plymouth colony. 1859: First zoo in U.S. incorporated (Philadelphia). 1907: U.S. Marines land in Honduras to protect American-owned banana plantations from revolutionaries. 1958: Michael Todd, film producer, dies at age 49 in plane crash about 35 miles southwest of Grants, New Mexico. 1965: Martin Luther King leads thousands from Selma, Ala. on first day of 54-mile march to Montgomery under protection of 4,000 federal troops.

FRIDAY
MARCH 22

Sun Rises 06:10
Sun Sets 18:23
Moon Rises 06:57
Moon Sets 19:43

MOON IN ARIES

uranus retrogrades-14:09. moon trine uranus-14:40. moon conj mercury-15:36. moon conj venus-19:45.

Van Dyck 1599
Chico Marx 1891
Werner Klemperer 1920
William Shatner 1931

Robert Millikan 1868
Karl Malden 1913
Marcel Marceau 1923
May Britt 1933

1794: U.S. Congress prohibits foreign slave trading. 1820: Stephen Decatur, war hero, is shot and killed in duel. 1895: First demonstration of cinematography (by Lumiere). 1965: U.S. discloses use of tear gas against Vietnamese insurgents denying any violation of international law. 1972: ERA Amendment passed in the U.S. Senate. 1978: Aerialist Karl Wallenda, 73, falls from a wire suspended 123 feet in air between 2 hotels (San Juan, Puerto Rico), and dies instantly.

Immature artists imitate. Mature artists steal.
Lionel Trilling

SATURDAY
MARCH 23

Sun Rises 06:09
Sun Sets 18:24
Moon Rises 07:20
Moon Sets 20:41

MOON ENTERS TAURUS 15:06

moon at apogee-07:00. moon trine neptune-22:24. sun square neptune-22:48. moon oppos pluto-23:36.

Juan Gris 1887
Erich Fromm 1900
Roger Bannister 1929
Chaka Khan 1953

Dane Rudhyar 1895
Akira Kurosawa 1910
Maynard Jackson 1938
Moses Malone 1954

1752: First newspaper printed in Canada— The Halifax Gazette. 1775: Patrick Henry delivers speech—"Give me liberty or give me death." 1794: Rivet patented. 1901: Melba toast recipe disclosed by Dame Nellie Melba. 1928: First private execution in Quebec—George McDonald hanged for murder of taxi driver. 1942: Japanese-Americans interned in California. 1966: Pope meets the Archbishop of Canterbury—first meeting of these leaders in 400 years. 1983: Barney Clark dies after living for 112 days with an artificial heart.

GROWING
BY LIZ CAILE

NOW'S THE TIME—The last killing frost may register sometime this month for Northwest, Southwest and upper Southeast regions. Check locally before setting out frost sensitive plants. **Southeast, South:** Feed bulbs, roses, shrubs with compost and fertilizers such as bonemeal dug into top inch of soil. Frost-free sections, full speed ahead with sweet potatoes, cucurbits, tomatoes and eggplants. **Southwest:** Mulch to conserve moisture. Clear plastic mulch increases soil heat around warmth lovers. Let vegetation keep growing after blooms fade to store nutrients in bulbs for next year's blooms. Cooler regions, sow cukes, and squashes in individual pots indoors so they can be transplanted without root trauma. **Northeast:** Set out hardy flowers like pansies and iceland poppies. Set lily of the valley pips in shaded parts of the yard for longest blooming season. Sprout wheat grass for long silky green Easter basket lining. **Midwest:** Avoid compacting wet soils. But add rock phosphate, bonemeal to soil where needed. **Northwest:** Get early potatoes, peas, beets and lettuce into the ground early in the month. Harden off young broccoli and cabbage plants before this month's planting.

Starting Seedlings

Seed packets always specify "time until germination," or when plants will emerge from the soil. For this and other information, it's a good idea to hold onto empty seed packets through the growing season.

Seeds sprout quicker if germinated in moist layers of paper, either to test their viability or to speed up outdoor growing. Germinated seeds can be planted in containers or in outdoor beds and gently covered with a light layer of soil for a quick, even start.

Vegetable and flower seeds have a wide range of preferences when it comes to ideal temperatures for germination.

Quick sprouters in cool soil (at or below 68° F.) include: lettuce, radish, turnip, pea and onions. Parsley seed, though slow to germinate, likes cool soils.

Some seeds will not germinate in cool soil and like temperatures of 70° F. and above: lima bean, snap bean, cucumber, okra, pepper, eggplant and watermelon.

Lettuce will grow to maturity when sown in the garden in almost any climate. But if you live in a northern region and are in a hurry for fresh, homegrown salad, sow seeds in flats many weeks before you could plant lettuce outdoors. The seedlings can be transplanted from the flats to individual pots or an outdoor coldframe when they are about three inches tall, after the first true leaves have appeared. **Be sure flats are well watered before transplanting.**

The key to good flavor in lettuce started indoors is to maintain a consistent supply of warmth, water and nutrients. Harvest lettuce at its prime, rather than in bland youth or bitter old age.

Fast germinating flower seeds include ageratum, alyssum, balsam, candytuft, cockscomb, cornflowers, cosmos, English daisy, marigold, strawflowers, and zinnias. Soak nasturtium seed 24 to 48 hours before planting to speed germination; nick seeds of morning glory and lupine to weaken outer coat before planting.

Coriander & Silantro

Coriander, also known as cilantro, is the parsley of oriental and Spanish cuisines. Known in ancient times around the Mediteranean, the herb has a long history of medicinal and flavoring uses. The seeds are used in cooking, worldwide, and the green leaves are added sparingly to sauted vegetables, soups and salads.

Coriander should be sown directly in the garden in a sunny, well-drained spot, and can be interspersed with other garden vegetables. Or, start from seed in indoor pots. Its featherly leaves and pungent, dried seeds are characteristic of the parsley family, as are its umbels of delicate pink flowers.

Don't count on growing seeds from indoor plants, but enjoy the greens. On the other hand, outdoors in a dry, sunny spot, coriander may bolt into seed too early for the greens to be enjoyed.

When the seeds have formed and are beginning to ripen, pick the stalks with the seed heads and dry them in an airy location in paper bags. Rub seeds from fruits when dry and use them in vegetable and fish dishes, beef or lentil soups, or on puddings, applesauce or in coffeecake.

In The Kitchen

According to Kathy Hoshijo, author of *Kathy Cooks Naturally*, you can increase nutritional values by germinating nuts and seeds. She suggests "germinating" almonds, hazelnuts, peanuts, hulled sunflower seeds, corn, pumpkins, squash and sesame seeds rather than "sprouting" them. The distinction lies in using them before the emergent sprout grows any longer than half an inch.

Nutritional values of nuts and seeds double when soaked overnight before eating, because of increased digestibility, and double again when they sprouted for two days or more.

SUNDAY — MARCH 24

Sun Rises 06:08
Sun Sets 18:25
Moon Rises 07:45
Moon Sets 21:39

MOON IN TAURUS

moon conj mars-04:51. moon square jupiter-10:49.
mercury retrogrades-11:02.

William Morris 1834	Fatty Arbuckle 1887
Wilhelm Reich 1897	Malcolm Muggeridge 1903
Clyde Barrow 1909	Lawrence Ferlinghetti 1919
Norman Fell 1925	Steve McQueen 1930

1882: First public demonstration of pancake making (New York City). **1882:** Henry Wadsworth Longfellow, poet, dies (Cambridge, Mass.). **1905:** Jules Verne, writer, dies (Amiens, France). **1935:** *Major Bowes' Original Amateur Hour* debuts coast-to-coast on radio. **1976:** Isabel Peron overthrown by military in Argentina.

Dressing a pool player in a tuxedo is like putting whipped cream on a hot dog.
Minnesota Fats

MONDAY — MARCH 25

Sun Rises 06:06
Sun Sets 18:26
Moon Rises 08:12
Moon Sets 22:39

MOON IN TAURUS

moon oppos saturn-23:40.

Ed Begley 1901	Howard Cosell 1920
Simone Signoret 1921	Flannery O'Conner 1925
Gloria Steinem 1936	Hoyt Axton 1938
Aretha Franklin 1942	Bonnie Bedelia 1946
Elton John 1947	Nick Lowe 1949

1892: Walt Whitman, poet, dies. **1900:** Socialist Party organized in U.S. **1953:** Polio vaccine announced by Dr. Salk. **1954:** RCA begins color TV production. **1965:** Selma march concludes with 25,000 demonstrating in Montgomery for voting rights—civil rights worker Mrs. Viola Liuzzo, Detroit housewife, is murdered by Ku Klux Klansmen. **1975:** King Faisal of Saudi Arabia assassinated.

The softer you sing, the louder you're heard.
Donovan

TUESDAY — MARCH 26

Sun Rises 06:05
Sun Sets 18:27
Moon Rises 08:43
Moon Sets 23:39

MOON ENTERS GEMINI 04:02

moon at asc node-05:30.

A.E. Housman 1859	Conde Nast 1874
Robert Frost 1874	Joseph Campbell 1904
Tennessee Williams 1911	Sterling Hayden 1916
Bob Elliott 1923	Gregory Corso 1930

JIVE

WEDNESDAY — MARCH 27

Sun Rises 06:03
Sun Sets 18:28
Moon Rises 09:20
Moon Sets ----

MOON IN GEMINI

moon trine jupiter-00:20. moon oppos uranus-15:50.
mercury trine uranus-19:09.

Gloria Swanson 1898	Pee Wee Russell 1906
Cyrus Vance 1917	Sarah Vaughan 1924
Arthur Mitchell 1934	Cale Yarborough 1939
Michael York 1942	Maria Schneider 1952

1945: Last German V-2 rocket hits England, landing in Orpington, Kent at 4:54 p.m. and killing one person. **1964:** Alaska earthquake kills 117. **1968:** Yuri Gargarin, first man to travel in space, dies in jet crash.

THURSDAY — MARCH 28

Sun Rises 06:02
Sun Sets 18:29
Moon Rises 10:04
Moon Sets 00:39

MOON ENTERS CANCER 15:13

venus trine uranus-04:02.moon oppos neptune-22:07.
moon trine pluto-22:58.

Raphael 1483	August Anheuser Busch 1899
Rudolf Serkin 1903	Nelson Algren 1909
Edmund Muskie 1914	Zbigniew Brzezinski 1928
Mario Vargas Llosa 1936	Rick Barry 1944

1941: Virginia Woolf commits suicide. **1969:** Dwight D. Eisenhower, 34th Pres. of U.S., dies from heart disease, at age 78 years and 165 days (Washington, D.C.)—his last words were, "I've always loved my wife. I've always loved my children. I've always loved my grandchildren. And I have always loved my country." **1979:** Emmett Kelly dies. **1979:** Three Mile Island nuclear power plant overheats. **1980:** Mt. St. Helens volcano in Washington erupts for the first time in more than a century.

FRIDAY — MARCH 29

Sun Rises 06:00
Sun Sets 18:30
Moon Rises 10:57
Moon Sets 01:37

MOON IN CANCER

sun square moon-08:11. mars square jupiter-12:50.
moon square mercury-23:03. moon square venus-23:09.

FIRST QUARTER MOON 08:11

Cy Young 1867	Man O'War 1917
Walt Frazier 1945	Earl Campbell 1955

1923: War Resisters League founded. **1945:** Last German V-1 flying bomb is launched against England, and is destroyed in air over Sittingbourne, Kent—a total of 9,200 V-1s were launched toward England, with over half malfunctioning or destroyed before hitting. Total deaths from bombs was 6,139, giving a final score of 1.5 deaths per bomb. **1971:** Charles Manson sentenced to life imprisonment. **1971:** Lt. William Calley convicted of the murder of 22 Vietnamese civilians (the My Lai massacre)— Calley sentenced to 3 years in his apartment.

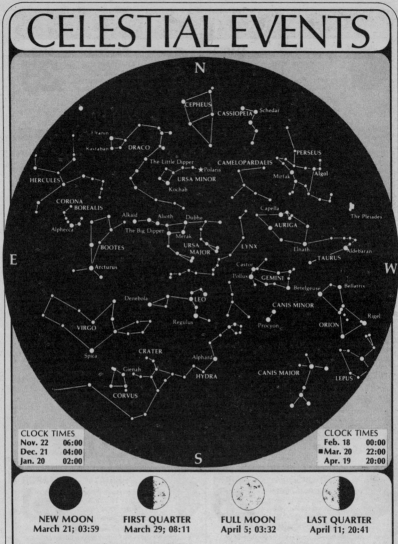

N

CLOCK TIMES	
Nov. 22	06:00
Dec. 21	04:00
Jan. 20	02:00

CLOCK TIMES	
Feb. 18	00:00
■Mar. 20	22:00
Apr. 19	20:00

S

NEW MOON	FIRST QUARTER	FULL MOON	LAST QUARTER
March 21; 03:59	March 29; 08:11	April 5; 03:32	April 11; 20:41

MERCURY comes to inferior conjunction April 3, becoming visible thereafter, rising in the east 1-1½ hours before sunrise. **VENUS** follows exactly the same pattern, coming to inferior conjunction April 3, becoming visible thereafter, rising in the east 1-1½ hours before sunrise. **MARS** is visible all month appearing in the western sky at sunset, then setting about 2 hours later. **JUPITER** is visible all month rising in the east 3-5 hours before sunrise, then fading near midsky with morning twilight. **SATURN** is visible all month rising in the east 2-4 hours after sunset, then fading in the western sky with morning twilight. **Mar. 20:** VERNAL EQUINOX, first day of Spring. **Mar. 22:** Mercury 6° N. of waxing crescent Moon (evening sky); Venus 12° N. of waxing crescent Moon (evening sky); Mercury 5° S. of Venus (evening sky). **Mar. 24:** Mars 1.4° N. of waxing crescent Moon (evening sky). **Apr. 07:** Saturn 3° N. of waning gibbous Moon (morning sky). **Apr. 13:** Jupiter 5° N. of waning crescent Moon (morning sky). **Apr. 17:** Venus 10° N. of waning crescent Moon (morning sky); Mercury 3° N. of waning crescent Moon (morning sky).

SATURDAY — MARCH 30

Sun Rises 05:59
Sun Sets 18:31
Moon Rises 11:58
Moon Sets 02:30

MOON ENTERS LEO 22:51
moon trine saturn-18:41.

Maimonides 1135
Paul Verlaine 1844
Sean O'Casey 1880
Peter Marshall 1930
Jerry Lucas 1940

Goya 1746
Vincent van Gogh 1853
McGeorge Bundy 1919
Warren Beatty 1937
Eric Clapton 1945

1867: Alaska purchased. **1950:** Invention of transistor announced. **1965:** House UnAmerican Activities Committee (HUAC) votes to investigate Ku Klux Klan. **1965:** Bomb explosion at U.S. Embassy in Saigon kills 13 and wounds 180.

Eccentricity, n. A method of distinction so cheap that fools employ it to accentuate their incapacity.

The Devil's Dictionary

SUNDAY — MARCH 31

Sun Rises 15:57
Sun Sets 18:32
Moon Rises 13:05
Moon Sets 03:18

MOON IN LEO
moon square pluto-05:57. moon oppos jupiter-18:08.
sun trine moon-18:47. moon square mars-20:20.

Rene Descartes 1596
Nikolai Gogol 1809
Jack Johnson 1878
John Fowles 1926
Shirley Jones 1933

Franz Josef Haydn 1732
Sergei Diaghilev 1872
Octavio Paz 1914
Cesar Chavez 1927
Gabe Kaplan 1945

1889: Eiffel Tower opens. **1913:** John Pierpont Morgan, banker, dies (Rome, Italy). **1959:** Dalai Lama granted political asylum in India. **1976:** Court rules that Karen Quinlan may die.

The daily news tells us again and again that, with all his knowledge and with all his refined ways, modern man remains the wildest animal. *Isaac Bashevis Singer*

PALM SUNDAY

MONDAY — APRIL 01

Sun Rises 05:55
Sun Sets 18:33
Moon Rises 14:17
Moon Sets 03:59

MOON IN LEO
moon trine mercury-01:54. moon trine venus-02:14.
moon trine uranus-06:09. moon square saturn-22:23.

Sergei Rachmaninoff 1873
Toshiro Mifune 1920
Debbie Reynolds 1932

Wallace Beery 1881
William Manchester 1922
Ali MacGraw 1938

1841: Brook Farm founded. **1866:** U.S. Congress passes Civil Rights Bill, giving equal rights to all persons born in the U.S. except Indians. **1960:** U.S. launches first weather satellite.

ALL FOOL'S DAY

TUESDAY — APRIL 02

Sun Rises 05:53
Sun Sets 18:34
Moon Rises 15:30
Moon Sets 04:35

MOON ENTERS VIRGO 02:25
moon trine neptune-08:23.

Casanova 1725
Emile Zola 1840
Kurt Adler 1905
Alec Guinness 1914
Leon Russell 1941

Hans Christian Andersen 1805
Max Ernst 1891
Buddy Ebsen 1908
Marvin Gaye 1939
Emmylou Harris 1949

1792: Congress authorizes first U.S. Mint and passes legislation for "E. Pluribus Unum" to be on all coins. **1877:** First human shot from a cannon. **1963:** Mass demonstrations begin in Birmingham, Ala., demanding civil rights and an end to segregation. **1979:** First black woman appointed to U.S. Court of Appeals.

Let every eye negotiate for itself, and trust no agent. *William Shakespeare*

WEDNESDAY — APRIL 03

Sun Rises 05:52
Sun Sets 18:35
Moon Rises 16:45
Moon Sets 05:07

MOON IN VIRGO
moon trine mars-00:59. sun conj mercury-06:05.
moon square uranus-07:38. sun conj venus-14:01.

Washington Irving 1783
Henry Luce 1898
Marlon Brando 1924
Marsha Mason 1942

George Jessel 1898
Herb Caen 1916
Helmut Kohl 1930
Eddie Murphy 1961

1860: Pony Express inaugurated. **1882:** Jesse James, outlaw, age 34, shot to death while standing on chair to straighten a picture in his house (St. Joseph, Missouri).

THURSDAY — APRIL 04

Sun Rises 05:50
Sun Sets 18:36
Moon Rises 18:00
Moon Sets 05:38

MOON ENTERS LIBRA 02:53
moon square neptune-08:37. neptune retrogrades-17:44.
moon trine jupiter-21:16. moon oppos mercury-22:28.
moon oppos venus-23:43.

Dorothea Dix 1802
Robert E. Sherwood 1896
A. Bartlett Giamatti 1938

Arthur Murray 1895
Anthony Perkins 1932
Hugh Masekela 1939

431bc: Peloponesian War begins. **1870:** Golden Gate Park established by California legislature. **1887:** Susanna Sater elected first woman mayor in U.S. (Argonia, Kansas). **1968:** Rev. Martin Luther King, Jr. assassinated in Memphis, Tenn.— riots and violence in 26 cities. **1969:** *Star Trek* cancelled.

SIGN OUT

FORECAST

BY NAN DE GROVE

ARIES

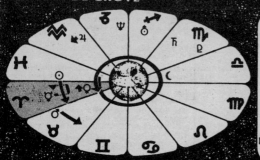

LONGITUDE OF THE PLANETS
08:14 PST; 03/20/85

Sun 00°00′ Aries
Moon 20°56′ Pisces
Mercury 17°32′ Aries
Venus 21°18′ Aries R
Mars 03°57′ Taurus
Jupiter 08°55′ Aquarius
Saturn 27°58′ Scorpio R
Uranus 17°59′ Sagittarius
Neptune 03°33′ Capricorn
Pluto 04°15′ Scorpio R

The spring quarter begins at a rather slow, uncertain pace. The ardor and passion of the Ram are subdued and the Arien spirit of initiative and self-determinism is underground—still active, but mixed in with unconscious drives and urges.

Use of personal will is a critical issue. Individual ego drives, combined with unconscious complexes and archetypal themes, are setting the stage for compulsive, irrational behavior which could be difficult to undo. Power drives and aggressiveness need to be tempered, especially around the 20th, when the Mars-Pluto opposition could trigger a violent eruption of repressed emotions and hostilities.

People from the past may reappear in our lives now, in flesh or in spirit. In some cases, old contacts will resurface and have an unexpected impact on our present lives. This is a reevaluation period; we may have to backtrack before we can move ahead. Major decisions and commitments should be postponed if at all possible. The Ram likes to act now and think later, but we must all consider the long-range implications of our actions now.

FIRE SIGNS may be struggling with the contradiction between conscious ideals and goals, and unconscious factors.

Aries: is getting in touch with a new-self image and has a potential for long-range success if efforts can be sustained. Getting resources and support from others may be a key issue; be patient and diplomatic.

Leo: is feeling a return of vitality and enthusiasm after last month's confusion. Obstacles that appear now will reveal areas where unconscious factors are blocking new beginnings.

Sagittarius: has creative fire, but doesn't quite know what to do with it. A blocked feeling could be the result of suppressed emotions or a neglected material plane.

EARTH SIGNS are experiencing the slow breakdown of old values and the emergence of new directions in their lives. An uncertain, shaky feeling may be part of this transition.

Taurus: is concerned in some way with deep, unconscious forces which shape the outer world. Look carefully at motives and inner urges; excessive control could trigger a volcanic eruption around the 20th.

Virgo: is also dealing with the unconscious and is particularly concerned with negative beliefs that deny success. Work on inner levels now will bring tangible improvements next month.

Capricorn: begins a new cycle in personal and domestic life now, and may be sorting through conflicting goals and desires. Avoid self-sacrifice.

AIR SIGNS should avoid making hasty judgments or alliances. Reversals and complications are likely to occur after March 25th.

Gemini: may be organizing a group or collaborating on a project. Review and revise after the 25th.

Libra: will see unconscious issues or unresolved past problems surface in relationships, especially around the Full Moon on April 5th.

Aquarius: may also be haunted by the past while trying to launch new projects. Be clear about motives; deal openly with opposition.

WATER SIGNS are striving to get a more secure footing in the world before moving into new territory.

Cancer: may have conflicts between professional life and personal relationships. Avoid projecting a "savior" role onto others, as they will find it burdensome.

Scorpio: needs to examine a resistance to positive changes and avoid defensiveness and manipulation of others.

Pisces: is concerned with resources, finances, and other mundane matters. The union of spirit and matter could be a revelation in your life now.

APRIL

FRIDAY APRIL 05

Sun Rises 05:49
Sun Sets 18:37
Moon Rises 19:15
Moon Sets 06:08

MOON IN LIBRA

sun oppos moon-03:32. moon at perigee-10:00.

FULL MOON 03:32

Algernon Swinburne 1837	Booker T. Washington 1856
Spencer Tracy 1900	Melvyn Douglas 1901
Bette Davis 1908	Gregory Peck 1916
Arthur Hailey 1920	Frank Gorshin 1934
Michael Moriarty 1941	Jane Asher 1946

2348bc: Noah's ark grounded at Mt. Ararat (traditional date). **1614:** Pocahontas, daughter of Indian Chief Powhatan, marries John Rolfe in Virginia. **1977:** 300 disabled demonstrators picket and begin "sit-in" at HEW in Washington to demand equal rights for the handicapped.

GOOD FRIDAY

SATURDAY APRIL 06

Sun Rises 05:47
Sun Sets 18:38
Moon Rises 20:32
Moon Sets 06:39

MOON ENTERS SCORPIO 02:10

moon oppos pluto-08:14. moon square jupiter-21:09.

Lincoln Steffens 1866	Harry Houdini 1874
Baba Ram Dass 1931	Merle Haggard 1937
Michelle Phillips 1944	Bob Marley 1945

1832: Black Hawk War begins. **1917:** U.S. declares war on Germany. **1957:** Last electric trolley run in New York City. **1965:** U.S. launches Earlybird, world's first communications satellite. **1971:** Igor Stravinsky, composer, dies (New York City). **1972:** U.S. begins regular sustained bombing of North Vietnam.

FIRST DAY OF PASSOVER

SUNDAY APRIL 07

Sun Rises 05:46
Sun Sets 18:39
Moon Rises 21:49
Moon Sets 07:14

MOON IN SCORPIO

moon oppos mars-04:49. sun trine uranus-10:27. moon conj saturn-21:54.

Francis Xavier 1506	St. Teresa of Avila 1515
Percy Faith 1908	Billie Holiday 1915
Ravi Shankar 1920	James Garner 1928
Daniel Ellsberg 1931	Jerry Brown 1938

30: Crucifixion of Christ. **1652:** Capetown, South Africa established. **1739:** Richard Turpin, "The Highwayman," executed. **1832:** An English farmer sells his wife for 20 shillings and a Newfoundland dog. **1864:** Camel race in Sacramento, California. **1869:** Sherman becomes commanding General of the U.S. Army; Sherman's motto—"The only good Indian I ever saw was dead." **1909:** Matthew Henson, black explorer, first human to set foot on the North Pole, 45 minutes before Admiral Peary.

EASTER SUNDAY

MONDAY APRIL 08

Sun Rises 05:45
Sun Sets 18:39
Moon Rises 23:04
Moon Sets 07:53

MOON ENTERS SAGITTARIUS 02:17

moon at desc node-07:30. moon trine mercury-18:04. moon trine venus-20:17.

Ian Smith 1919	Jacques Brel 1929

1513: Ponce de Leon discovers Florida. **1887:** The Charity Hospital of Louisiana (New Orleans) records death of a 45-year-old patient from masturbation.

TUESDAY APRIL 09

Sun Rises 05:43
Sun Sets 18:40
Moon Rises ----
Moon Sets 08:40

MOON IN SAGITTARIUS

moon conj uranus-08:03. sun trine moon-11:30.

Baudelaire 1821	Paul Robeson 1898
Howard Rusk 1901	J. William Fulbright 1905
Hugh Hefner 1926	Paul Krassner 1932

1865: Lee surrenders to Grant (Appomattox, Va.). **1963:** Winston Churchill made an honorary citizen of U.S. **1976:** Phil Ochs, folksinger, commits suicide at age 36 by hanging himself in closet at his sister's house.

The reward for conformity is everybody likes you but yourself.

Rita Mae Brown

Death doesn't like crowds. It comes to you when you're alone.

Tennessee Williams

WEDNESDAY APRIL 10

Sun Rises 05:42
Sun Sets 18:41
Moon Rises 00:13
Moon Sets 09:33

MOON ENTERS CAPRICORN 04:57

moon conj neptune-11:16. moon square mercury-19:36. moon square venus-22:07.

Joseph Pulitzer 1847	Clare Boothe Luce 1903
Roy Hofheinz 1912	Harry Morgan 1915
Chuck Connors 1921	Jane Kean 1928
Max Von Sydow 1929	Omar Sharif 1932
David Halberstam 1934	Don Meredith 1938

1864: Maximilian becomes emperor of Mexico. **1872:** First Arbor Day. **1979:** Idi Amin flees Kampala, Uganda.

If you have been fortunate enough to latch on to some of the better things in life, as we were, try throwing a few of them away. You don't know how superior it makes you feel.

Rube Goldberg

1985 Produce Calendar

by Liz Caile

This calendar is designed to help you get the best value from supermarket produce by shopping for foods that are in season and local to your area. In spite of the great range of fruits and vegetables that is available to us through the wonders of modern transportation and storage techniques, our choices are really limited by what can be produced in the most mechanized way, and stored and transported without spoiling.

Seasonal specialties offer a wonderful range of flavor and texture that may have been deleted from the run of the mill selection at the produce counter.

To get the best from the market, shop early in the day and avoid shopping on weekends. Then you will have more choices and the produce you purchase will be fresher and will have been handled less.

Many fruits and vegetables store better at home in brown bags than plastic bags, because the paper bags breath. You may want to purchase some produce, such as apples and onions, in sufficient quantities to store at home — not because you can improve on the storage time of commercial techniques but because you will have more choices in varieties, and you can avoid some of the treatments applied to prolong storage life, such as anti-sprouting compounds and waxes.

Often a low price-per-pound indicates a good fresh supply of fruits or vegetables — for instance, most avocadoes, greens, summer squash and oranges are best when they are cheapest.

Fruits and vegetables listed below under certain months may vary in availability and quality depending on weather and planting conditions affecting crops for this year.

JANUARY

Best Values .... □ carrots □ coconuts □ grapefruit □ California navel oranges

Other Values .... □ apples □ broccoli □ Brussel sprouts □ cabbage □ mushrooms □ greens □ turnips □ rutabagas (skins may be waxed to improve appearance) □ parsnips (storage sweetens these roots!) □ celery (coming from Florida and California in winter and early spring) □ endive (from Florida during winter and early spring, from New Jersey and Ohio during summer and fall)

FEBRUARY

Best Values .... □ California citrus □ Washington apples

Other Values .... □ first new potatoes are in from Southern fields □ scallions □ cauliflower □ winter squash □ peas □ spinach □ granny smith apples (may be coming from New Zealand, Chili, Australian, South Africa, or California) □ bananas □ pineapples

MARCH

Best Values .... □ new potatoes □ beets □ mushrooms □ broccoli □ smooth-skinned avocados (Fuerte avocados from California mature from November to May) □ pineapples

Other Values .... □ first asparagus □ strawberries from California

APRIL

Best Values .... □ Sweet onions, such as bermudas, fresh from Southern U.S. □ radishes □ asparagus □ garlic (from California and Mexico) □ strawberries (coming in now until July 1)

Other Values .... from Chile and Mexico, look for: □ peppers □ zucchini □ yellow squash □ eggplants □ lettuce

MAY

Best Values .... □ strawberries □ rhubarb □ peas (from local growers) □ sweet onions

Other Values .... from California, look for: □ cantaloupe □ grapes □ peaches □ nectarines □ cherries (May to June) □ kiwi fruits (from New Zealand, May to November) □ mangos (harvested in Florida and Hawaii from mid-May to October) □ pineapples □ wild mushrooms (Morels)

THURSDAY   APRIL 11

Sun Rises 05:40
Sun Sets 18:42
Moon Rises 01:15
Moon Sets 10:33

MOON IN CAPRICORN
moon trine mars-16:30. sun square moon-20:41.

LAST QUARTER MOON 20:41

Paul Douglas 1907   Oleg Cassini 1913
Ethel Kennedy 1928   Joel Grey 1932

1831: First loan from a Building and Loan Association. 1926: Luther Burbank, horticulturalist, dies at age 76 (Santa Rosa, Calif.). 1928: King of Afghanistan has his tonsils removed in Berlin. 1945: Buchenwald liberated by Allied Forces. 1965: Rash of tornadoes rages through Midwest killing 253, causing $250 million in property damage.

An author ought to write for the youth of his own generation, the critics of the next, and the schoolmasters of ever afterwards.

F. Scott Fitzgerald

FRIDAY   APRIL 12

Sun Rises 05:39
Sun Sets 18:43
Moon Rises 02:06
Moon Sets 11:37

MOON ENTERS AQUARIUS 11:04
moon square pluto-17:54.

Henry Clay 1777   Ann Miller 1919
Tiny Tim 1932   David Cassidy 1950

1858: First national billiard championship (Detroit, Mich.). 1861: Confederates fire on Fort Sumter—Civil War begins. 1945: Pres. Franklin Delano Roosevelt dies from cerebral hemorrhage at age 63 years and 72 days (Warm Springs, Ga.)—earlier that day, he had torn up his draft card, remarking that he wouldn't be needing it any more. His last words were, "I have a terrific headache." 1961: Cosmonaut Yuri Gagarin becomes the first person to orbit the earth. 1981: Joe Louis, the "Brown Bomber," dies. 1983: Harold Washington elected first black mayor of Chicago.

The opposite of talking isn't listening. The opposite of talking is waiting.

Fran Lebowitz

SATURDAY   APRIL 13

Sun Rises 05:37
Sun Sets 18:44
Moon Rises 02:48
Moon Sets 12:41

MOON IN AQUARIUS
moon conj jupiter-11:30.

Thomas Jefferson 1743   F. W. Woolworth 1852
Samuel Beckett 1906   Harold Stassen 1907
Eudora Welty 1909   Al Green 1946

1788: First riot in America begins (New York City). 1796: First elephant arrives in U.S. 1854: First agricultural school chartered. 1917: "Diamond Jim" Brady, financier, dies after several years of ill health, supposedly caused by his tremendous appetite (Atlantic City, N.J.).

Religion is a topic which should never be introduced in society. It is the one subject on which persons are most likely to differ, and least able to preserve temper.

Collier's Cyclopedia, 1882

SUNDAY   APRIL 14

Sun Rises 05:36
Sun Sets 18:45
Moon Rises 03:23
Moon Sets 13:44

MOON ENTERS PISCES 20:30
moon square mars-04:18.moon square saturn-14:33. mercury at desc node-23:30.

Arnold Toynbee 1889   Papa Doc Duvalier 1907
Rod Steiger 1925   Loretta Lynn 1932
Erich Von Daniken 1934   Frank Serpico 1936
Julie Christie 1941   Pete Rose 1941

1775: First Abolition Society established—Ben Franklin is first president. 1788: Doctor's Riot, Columbia University—New York students and neighbors oppose doctors because medical cadavers were stolen from local graveyards. 1806: First Webster's Dictionary published. 1865: Lincoln assassinated by John Wilkes Booth. 1930: Ripley's Believe It or Not debuts on radio.

Man is but an animal with ideas, but an animal is not a man without them.

Old Bore's Almanac

MONDAY   APRIL 15

Sun Rises 05:34
Sun Sets 18:46
Moon Rises 03:52
Moon Sets 14:44

MOON IN PISCES
moon trine pluto-03:34.

Leonardo Da Vinci 1452   Henry James 1843
Asa Randolph 1889   Bessie Smith 1894
Roy Clark 1933   Elizabeth Montgomery 1933
Claudia Cardinale 1939   Dave Edmunds 1944

1865: Abraham Lincoln, 16th Pres. of the U.S., dies after being shot by John Wilkes Booth at Ford Theater (Washington, D.C.)—he was 56 years and 62 days old. 1912: Titanic sinks—1517 lost. 1934: Blondie gives birth to Alexander—Dagwood is the proud father.

TUESDAY   APRIL 16

Sun Rises 05:33
Sun Sets 18:47
Moon Rises 04:17
Moon Sets 15:43

MOON IN PISCES
moon square uranus-07:38. mercury directs-21:21.

Wilbur Wright 1867   John Millington Synge 1871
Charlie Chaplin 1889   Peter Ustinov 1921
Kingsley Amis 1922   Ike Pappas 1933
Dusty Springfield 1939   Kareem Abdul-Jabbar 1947

69: Marcus Salvius Otho, Emperor of Rome, commits suicide. 1862: Congress abolishes slavery in District of Columbia. 1879: Saint Bernadette, religious hallucinator, dies. 1935: Fibber McGee and Molly premieres on radio. 1947: Fertilizer ship explosion kills 500 (Texas City, Texas).

INCOME TAX DEADLINE

JUNE

Best Values . . . . □ **apricots** □ **cherries** (mid-June to July from Washington, Oregon, Michigan, New York) □ **green beans** (from Florida, California, North Carolina, Georgia, New Jersey and New York)

Other Values . . . . □ **lemons** □ **limes** □ **mangos** □ **peas** (from local growers)

JULY

Best Values . . . . □ **sweet corn** □ **bell peppers** (from Florida, California, New Jersey, Texas, North Carolina and Michigan) □ **blueberries** (New Jersey and Michigan are top producers, also North Carolina, Maine, Washington and Oregon) □ **beets** □ **tomatoes** □ **cucumbers** □ **green onions**

Other Values . . . . □ **blackberries** □ **cantaloupe** □ **watermelon** □ **okra** (available occasionally in northern markets) □ **wild mushrooms** (Chanterelles)

AUGUST

Best Values . . . . □ **muskmelons** (from California, Texas, Arizona, Indiana, Georgia, Michigan, Colorado, South Carolina. Varieties include Persian, honeydew, Casaba, Crenshaw, cantaloupe) □ **peaches**   □ **nectarines** □ **plums** □ **summer squash** □ **bell peppers** □ **tomatoes**

Other Values . . . . □ **raspberries** (from Washington, Oregon, Canada) □ **avocados** (Hass from California, Florida. Florida avacado harvest from August to January) □ **pears** (summer Bartlett pears from California)

SEPTEMBER

Best Values . . . . □ **grapes** □ **eggplant** □ **tomatoes** □ **bell peppers** □ **chili peppers** □ **hot peppers** □ **cucumbers** □ **plums** □ **beets** □ **dill**

Others Values . . . . □ **pears** □ **summer squash** □ **cauliflower** □ **romaine lettuce** □ **potatoes** (85 percent of harvest in fall) □ **grapefruit** (Florida harvest from September to July)

OCTOBER

Best Values . . . . □ **pumpkin** □ **cauliflower** □ **pomegranates** (from California) □ **California artichokes** □ **apples** □ **tomatoes**

Other Values . . . . □ **parsnips** (from Pennsylvania, Illinois, New York) □ **grapefruit** (October to April is Texas harvest) □ **pears** (winter varieties include Bosc, Anjou, Comice)

NOVEMBER

Best Values . . . . □ **sweet potatoes** □ **brussel sprouts** □ **pears** □ **parsley** □ **persimmons** □ **winter squash** □ **cranberries** (from Massachusetts, Wisconsin, New Jersey, Washington, Oregon)

Other Values . . . . □ **walnuts** □ **pecans** □ **sweet onions** (buy yellow and white pungent varieties from northeast and northcentral states for home storage to avoid anti-sprouting treatment) □ **leeks** □ **celery** (late fall and early winter from New York and Michigan) □ **grapefruit** (Arizona harvest from November to August) □ **kiwi fruits** (from California)

DECEMBER

Best Values . . . . □ **bananas** □ **parsley** □ **celery** □ **tangerines** □ **oranges** □ **winter squash** □ **cabbage**

Other Values . . . . □ **onions** □ **cucumbers** □ **grapefruit** (California harvest from December to October) □ **turnips** □ **rutabagas** □ **celeriac**

WEDNESDAY   **APRIL 17**

Sun Rises 05:32
Sun Sets 18:48
Moon Rises 04:40
Moon Sets 16:40

MOON ENTERS ARIES 08:18

moon trine saturn-01:52. moon square neptune-15:31. moon conj mercury-21:59. moon conj venus-22:17.

Nikita Khrushchev 1894	Thornton Wilder 1897
Gregor Piatigorsky 1903	Rebekah Harkness 1915
William Holden 1918	Harry Reasoner 1923

1521: Martin Luther excommunicated by Diet of Worms. **1790:** Benjamin Franklin dies. **1861:** First oil well fire. **1864:** Bread riot in Savannah, Georgia. **1942:** Doolittle raids Tokyo. **1945:** American war correspondent Ernie Pyle, 44, is killed by a Japanese sniper on Ie Island. **1961:** Bay of Pigs Invasion. **1965:** 15,000 protestors picket White House, staging first national demonstration against Vietnam War—LBJ rejects appeals to suspend bombing. **1969:** Sirhan Sirhan convicted of assassinating Robert Kennedy.

THURSDAY   **APRIL 18**

Sun Rises 05:31
Sun Sets 18:49
Moon Rises 05:03
Moon Sets 17:37

MOON IN ARIES

mercury conj venus-07:42. moon trine uranus-20:07.

Clarence Darrow 1857	Leopold Stokowski 1882
Hayley Mills 1946	Nate Archibald 1948

1775: Paul Revere's ride. **1853:** William King, former Vice Pres., dies—labelled "a hero of many a well-fought bottle," he is only executive of U.S. government to have been sworn into office in a foreign country, Cuba. **1906:** San Francisco earthquake. **1946:** League of Nations votes itself out of existence. **1955:** Albert Einstein, physicist, dies at age 75 (Princeton, N.J.). **1956:** First umpire wears glasses at a baseball game.

> My impression of people is that their attention span is about two minutes.
>
> Ralph Nader

Weaning Traditions

In recent years, historians have developed many theories relating to the psychology of the past or "psychohistory." One of the most outspoken supporters of this research is Lloyd DeMause. In his book, Foundations of Psychohistory, DeMause focuses attention on patterns of child rearing. This is particularly relevant to current public interest in understanding child abuse.

This table, which is excerpted from his book, lists the average age of children from different countries and historical periods at the time of weaning. In comparison with current practices, these figures prompt questions which might be useful in trying to understand the influences and effects of environment and enforced behavior on children.

APPROXIMATE DATE	NATIONALITY	AGE WHEN WEANED
367 B.C.	Greek	24
100 A.D.	Roman	12-24
400	Roman	35
1314	Italian	24
1497	German	10-24
1538	English	18
1540	English	9
1540	German	12
1540	English	34
1550	English	8-14
1552	Italian	15-30
1579	English	7-36
1603	French	25
1620	English	14
1643-79	English	12-19
1697	English	10-12
1753	English	3-4
1762	English	12-48
1770	English	4
1797	English	6
1807	English	15
1810	English	12
1839	English	10-12
1859	American	15
1878-82	German	1-6

Table reprinted with permission from: Foundations of Psychohistory, by Lloyd DeMause. The Institute for Psychohistory, 2315 Broadway, New York, New York 10024.

ABANDON SHIP!

by William Casey

Before a sinking ship slowly gurgles beneath the waves, the captain usually has the courtesy to alert everyone on board to abandon ship. Company bosses aren't always so thoughtful. When the minions of the corporation have been told "not to worry," how can they be prepared to jump ship before it goes belly up?

Here are some tell-tale signs of a floundering corporate vessel. These signs hold true **only if they represent a recent, fairly sudden change** in the company's *modus operandi*. If your company has always operated this way .....well, we're all entitled to a little masochism.

PANIC Managers develop symptoms of panic when doom threatens their workplace; the more panicked the managers, the fuzzier their thinking becomes. Some will take refuge in fantasies that no drastic action is needed — things will get better if they just stay the course. Others develop short fuses or deep depressions. But, in their panic, all of them perform complex decision making in a clearly inept manner. They'll eschew complexities in favor of simpler realities, for example — spending hours fussing with the format of a report rather than the content.

BUDGET PROBLEMS Managers preoccupy themselves with pennies when the big picture indicates fiscal collapse. A wide-eyed spending paranoia stalks the management elite, but the fears seem focused on trivia. As an example, a salesman is verbally attacked for printing too many business cards. Here, the style indicates more than the content. Expect violent, over-reactive responses from management in these situations.

STRESS Look for signs of stress and sleepless nights among the top managers. Baggy eyes, stuporous fatigue, and short tempers all give away a management that's under siege. Hours away from work may be spent hitting the bottle, and even the wives.

AVOIDANCE Managers will become unavailable to staff. Not only will they be hard to find, but once cornered, will have no straight answers for the big questions. In part, they are avoiding the discomfort of facing the troops, while pretending that everything is okay. Otherwise, they have less time for their staffs since preoccupation with the impending shipwreck takes more of their time.

SILENCE Expect more hush-hush communications between owners and managers. Conversations will stop abruptly as you enter the room. Check to see if others are experiencing this. If not, the only ship about to sink may be your own.

MEETINGS You may also see managers abruptly converging for frequent closed-door meetings. These meetings are usually held on short notice and may occur several times in a single day. The white-lipped managers will emerge saying little, and head for their desks to await the next group panic attack. Because of their difficulty in thinking clearly, many managers will seek increased numbers of meetings. Meetings are substituted for action.

RATS You'll be the last to hear the swan song. The major creditors and principals will be way ahead of you. But you'll know that they know because some of them will practically move in. If you are the switchboard operator — or know the switchboard operator — you'll smell a rat earlier than most, since the major creditors and principals will be on the phone constantly. If the president asks you to tell them he's out, it's a clue to start looking for gainful employment. If the company lawyers are around so often their mail is being forwarded (you can bet **they've** got positive cash flow), its a good sign that trouble is terminal. In this scenario, lawyers get paid twice, once for delivering the last rites and again for embalming the body.

ADVANCE WARNING Here are a couple of not-so-smart moves that will warn you well in advance when your ship is headed for a reef.

Whoever coined the phrase "If you're so smart, why aren't you rich?," should be shot. Because now people who are rich are convinced that they're smart — your firm decides that it can succeed at enterprises outside of its expertise. Even though it took years to get good at their trade, corporate honchos think they can enter another field and do just as well overnight. A widget factory will decide to make computers; an ice cream parlor will decide to sell vitamins. Some succeed. Those are the smart ones.

Giddy with success, managers may perform another classic corporate blunder: overexpansion. They leverage themselves onto thin ice, opening branches and buying competitors as fast as they can wheedle credit from their bankers. If demand dips, or suppliers can't come through, make sure you're watching the action from the deck of another ship.

There is no such thing as job security. If you sense from these simple guidelines that your job is about to sink under you, it might be prudent to abandon it before it abandons you.

APRIL

TAURUS

April 19 — May 19

FRIDAY   APRIL **19**

Sun Rises 05:30
Sun Sets 18:50
Moon Rises 05:25
Moon Sets 18:34

MOON ENTERS TAURUS 21:12

moon at apogee-09:00. sun conj moon-21:22.

Sun Enters Taurus 19:26

NEW MOON 21:22

Anthony Bliss 1913   Hugh O'Brian 1925
Kenneth 1927   Don Adams 1927
Jayne Mansfield 1932   Dudley Moore 1935

1892: First gasoline automobile operated in U.S. 1910:
Halley's Comet reappears. 1910: Successful treatment for
syphilis announced. 1918: Congress rewrites Espionage Act
to include women spies. 1961: Cuban rebels overwhelmed
by Castro's troops.

**How to sow Beans: One for the mouse, one
for the crow, one to rot, one to grow.**

Farmers' Proverb

SATURDAY   APRIL **20**

Sun Rises 05:28
Sun Sets 18:51
Moon Rises 05:49
Moon Sets 19:32

MOON IN TAURUS

moon oppos pluto-04:14. moon trine neptune-04:26.

Adolf Hitler 1889   Joan Miro 1893
Stanley Marcus 1905   Paul Stevens 1920
Nina Foch 1924   Ryan O'Neal 1941

1657: Jews win equal rights of citizenship in the colonies.
1769: Chief Pontiac assassinated. 1848: Walter Reuther
seriously wounded by an assassin's bullet. 1969: People's
Park planted (Berkeley, Calif.).

**My ever-present realization of the material
virtues of kidney stew and Gorgonzola
cheese has permanently destroyed whatever
of the ethereal that may have been born
within me.**

Rube Goldberg

SUNDAY   APRIL **21**

Sun Rises 05:26
Sun Sets 18:52
Moon Rises 06:15
Moon Sets 20:32

MOON ENTERS GEMINI 10:00

moon square jupiter-01:38. mars oppos saturn-02:51.

Charlotte Bronte 1816   John Muir 1838
Max Weber 1864   Charles Grodin 1935

1910: Mark Twain, writer, dies at age 75 (Redding, Conn.).
1918: Red Baron shot down. 1966: First artificial heart
implant.

**In the past, I didn't say what I am saying now
about humanity because I had read in books
that the 20th century was blessed. Being a
young man, I didn't dare to say that the
whole thing was a lie. But now that I'm an old
man, why shouldn't I say how I feel?**

Isaac Bashevis Singer

MONDAY   APRIL **22**

Sun Rises 05:25
Sun Sets 18:53
Moon Rises 06:44
Moon Sets 21:33

MOON IN GEMINI

moon oppos saturn-02:57. moon conj mars-04:34.
moon at asc node-12:05.

Henry Fielding 1707   Immanuel Kant 1724
Nikolai Lenin 1870   Ellen Glasgow 1874
O.E. Rolvaag 1876   J. Robert Oppenheimer 1904
Yehudi Menuhin 1916   Jack Nicholson 1937
Glen Campbell 1938   Peter Frampton 1950

1370: Construction of French Bastille begins. 1889:
Homestead land rush (Okla.). 1915: First use of poison gas
(Germans at Ypres, Belgium). 1932: Lightning bolt is
witnessed striking a flock of geese, killing 52, which are
distributed as dinner fare (Manitoba, Canada). 1970: First
Earth Day. 1983: Hitler Diaries announced by W. German
magazine—they are later proven to be forged.

FLIM FLAM

GROWING
BY LIZ CAILE

NOW'S THE TIME—Northeast, Midwest, Mountain States: If you haven't broken ground yet, take another look at your yard to find a sunny, well-drained garden spot. Last chance to purchase and set out bare-rooted shrubs and trees. Plant hardy crops outside this month. Grape hyacinths and plum blossoms will be found in May baskets. **Northwest:** Plant bulbs for summer blooms: gladiolas, dahlias and ornamental alliums. Add compost to berry patches. Apply mulch where dry summer period is just around the corner, but not before soil is warmed for summer crops. **South:** Plant heat-loving seeds of squash, watermelon, cukes, cantaloupes, and okra, in the ground. **Southwest:** Coming dry season is the biggest factor. Take a tip from the Hopi, and plant small salad gardens of lettuce, tomato and pepper plants near the water tap for efficient watering. Plant pumpkins in zones where there will be a frost to sweeten them, in the middle of beds with lettuce and snap beans. Pumpkins will grow into borders where beans and lettuce have been harvested.

Transplants

Barerooted transplants most often fail because the roots of the plant dry out too much. Barerooted shrubs and trees need to be transplanted when the plant is dormant. The roots, with soil shaken or washed from them, are often packed in spaghnum moss or some other protective material.

Soak the roots of these trees and shrubs after purchase, and plant as soon as possible. Prepare the hole large enough to accommodate the spread-out roots; make soil porous, and moist to invite new root growth. The upper part of the transplant can be pruned back substantially.

Container grown plants, whether individual marigolds, single tomato plants, rosebushes or evergreen trees, have root systems adapted to the container. Even when transplanted into a limitless growth medium, the roots may stay tightly wound within the growth confines of the original container, throughout the growing season.

If the roots of container grown plants are in a tight ball, make vertical shallow cuts in several places to tease old roots into new growth. Remove severely twisted or deformed roots.

The **ideal soil** for a transplant is: 45 percent soil particles, 5 percent organic matter, 30 percent air and 20 percent water. The proportion of air to water will fluctuate with periodic watering (statistics from R.L. Snodsmith, *Brooklyn Botanic Gardens Handbook #97*).

Choose young **bedding plants** and nursery stock vegetables such as tomatoes — avoid the temptation to purchase plants in full bloom or with fruits already set.

Tomatoes will grow new roots along the stem if it is buried in the ground, but most plants must be transplanted at the same depth that they were in the container or ground. Some fruit tree varieties, developed from grafts, will alter if their graft is set below soil level.

New transplants need more water until they are established. In the case of shrubs and trees transplanted in the Fall, give them special attention when the growing season commences the following spring.

Hardening-Off

Harden-off seedlings of lettuce, tomatoes, cabbage, and peppers by setting them out in the sun and breeze for progressively longer periods of time — a process that can take up to two weeks. Hardening-off creates physiological changes in young plants. Sunflowers and beans are two plants that cannot be hardened in this way.

Okra

Also known as gumbo, gobo or ladies fingers, okra seeds will not germinate in cold soil. Like eggplant, it is a tender garden vegetable, but it can be grown in some northern gardens, where it begins producing its edible seed pods in 60 to 70 warm growing days. Soak seeds for 24 hours before planting.

The pods must be harvested young and continuously to further production, and they should be used soon after picking. Use them in soups, as a steamed vegetable or in fritters — sliced, dipped in cornmeal or batter, and fried in oil. Don't cook okra in aluminum or iron pans — metal reaction will blacken pods.

Okra is relatively high in thiamine and riboflavin, vitamins B-1 and B-2, respectively. These B vitamins are necessary for using food energy, and like all the water soluable B vitamins, must be replaced daily as they cannot be stored in the body. Folklore says okra is good for healing stomach ulcers, sore throats and constipation.

Related to the hibiscus plant, okra has characteristic mallow flowers and would be interesting to try as a container plant.

The young pods of the edible broadleaf milkweed can be used in soups and stews like okra, but caution: the narrowleaved milkweed plant is considered poisonous.

APRIL

TUESDAY — APRIL 23

Sun Rises 05:23
Sun Sets 18:54
Moon Rises 07:19
Moon Sets 22:33

MOON IN GEMINI

sun oppos pluto-06:13. sun trine neptune-10:10.
moon trine jupiter-14:36. moon oppos uranus-21:02.

Shakespeare 1564	Vladimir Nabokov 1899
J.P. Donleavy 1926	Shirley Temple 1928
Halston 1932	Roy Orbison 1936
David Birney 1939	Lee Majors 1939
Sandra Dee 1942	Herve Villechaize 1943
Joyce Dewitt 1949	Valerie Bertinelli 1960

1928: Gene Tunney, heavyweight boxing champion of world, lectures at Yale U. about Shakespeare. *1965:* Rev. Martin Luther King and 18,000 demonstrators bring civil rights movement north to Boston, protesting school segregation.

Egotist, n. A person of low taste, more interested in himself than in me.
The Devil's Dictionary

WEDNESDAY — APRIL 24

Sun Rises 05:22
Sun Sets 18:55
Moon Rises 08:01
Moon Sets 23:31

MOON ENTERS CANCER 21:26

venus directs-16:07.

Willem de Kooning 1904	Robert Penn Warren 1905
Shirley MacLaine 1934	Barbra Streisand 1942

1704: First American newspaper, **Boston News Letter**, published. *1833:* Soda fountain patented. *1880:* Library of Congress created. *1967:* Vladimir Komarov, Soviet cosmonaut, dies during re-entry of space capsule when parachute becomes tangled with capsule and falls 4.3 miles to earth—he is first person known to have died during execution of a space mission.

ARBOR DAY

THURSDAY — APRIL 25

Sun Rises 05:21
Sun Sets 18:56
Moon Rises 08:50
Moon Sets ----

MOON IN CANCER

moon trine pluto-03:51. moon oppos neptune-04:14.
moon square venus-09:03. moon square mercury-16:18.

St. Louis 1214	Oliver Cromwell 1599
Guglielmo Marconi 1874	William Brennan, Jr. 1906
Edward R. Murrow 1908	Ella Fitzgerald 1918
Albert King 1925	Meadowlark Lemon 1932
Al Pacino 1939	Talia Shire 1946

1859: Digging on the Suez Canal begins. *1959:* St. Lawrence Seaway opens. *1964:* Statue of the "Little Mermaid" in Copenhagen loses head to thieves. *1965:* Dominican Republic military coup ousts U.S.-supported government.

FRIDAY — APRIL 26

Sun Rises 05:19
Sun Sets 18:57
Moon Rises 09:47
Moon Sets 00:25

MOON IN CANCER

MARS ENTERS GEMINI-01:13.
moon trine saturn-23:07.

David Hume 1711	James Audubon 1785
Ma Rainey 1886	Ludwig Wittgenstein 1889
Lowell Thomas 1892	Anita Loos 1893
Bernard Malamud 1914	I.M. Pei 1917
Bruce Jay Friedman 1930	Carol Burnett 1933

1819: First Odd Fellows Lodge organized. *1865:* John Wilkes Booth shot. *1901:* "Black Jack" Ketchum, train robber, dies on gallows (Santa Fe, New Mex.)—due to incorrect way noose was placed around his neck and weights tied to his body, he was decapitated by the hanging. *1952:* First broadcast of **Gunsmoke** on radio. *1970:* Gypsy Rose Lee dies at age 56 (Los Angeles, Calif.).

SATURDAY — APRIL 27

Sun Rises 05:18
Sun Sets 18:58
Moon Rises 10:51
Moon Sets 01:14

MOON ENTERS LEO 06:10

moon square pluto-12:06. moon trine venus-17:26.
sun square moon-20:25.

FIRST QUARTER MOON 20:25

Jack Klugman 1922	Coretta King 1927
Sandy Dennis 1937	Sheena Easton 1959

1521: Magellan dies. *1865:* Worst marine disaster in U.S. history—steamer **Sultana** explodes on Mississippi River, killing 1,700 passengers, most of them Union soldiers returning from Confederate prison camps. *1870:* Floor of Supreme Court building in Richmond, Vermont, collapses, killing 61 people. *1882:* Ralph Waldo Emerson dies. *1932:* Hart Crane gets drunk and jumps into the sea from a ship. *1937:* German Air Force, at invitation of Francisco Franco, experiments with aerial saturation bombing on Guernica, Spain, destroying it. *1965:* Soviet communications satellite, launched April 23, is first to relay TV signals from space.

SUNDAY — APRIL 28

Sun Rises 06:16
Sun Sets 19:59
Moon Rises 12:59
Moon Sets 02:56

MOON IN LEO

moon trine mercury-04:11. moon oppos jupiter-09:58.
moon trine uranus-14:31.

James Monroe 1758	Sidney Toler 1874
Lionel Barrymore 1878	Robert Anderson 1917
Harper Lee 1926	Ann Margret 1941

1686: Isaac Newton delivers his first volume of Principia to British Royal Society. *1789:* Mutiny on the **Bounty**. *1945:* Benito Mussolini, dictator of Italy during most of WWII, is shot by anti-Fascist partisans after brief trial—he had been caught trying to escape to Switzerland on April 26.

DAYLIGHT SAVINGS TIME BEGINS
SET CLOCKS AHEAD 1 HOUR

CELESTIAL EVENTS

N

Schedar

CASSIOPEIA

PERSEUS

Algol

Deneb

CEPHEUS

Mirfak

CYGNUS

CAMELOPARDALIS

LYRA

DRACO

Polaris

Capella

AURIGA

Eltanin

The Little Dipper

Vega

URSA MINOR

Rastaban

Kochab

LYNX

ORION

Dubhe

HERCULES

Alkaid

Alioth

Merak

URSA

Castor

GEMINI

Betelgeuse

CORONA

BOREALIS

The Big Dipper

MAJOR

Pollux

E

Rasalhague

W

Alphecca

BOOTES

CANCER

CANIS MINOR

OPHIUCHUS

Arcturus

LEO

Proxyon

Denebola

Regulus

VIRGO

CRATER

Alphard

SCORPIO

LIBRA

Spica

Gienah

HYDRA

CORVUS

S

CLOCK TIMES	
Dec. 21	06:00
Jan. 20	04:00
Feb. 18	02:00

CLOCK TIMES	
Mar. 20	00:00
■Apr. 19	22:00
May 20	21:00

NEW MOON
April 19; 21:22
May 19; 14:41

FIRST QUARTER
April 27; 20:25

FULL MOON
May 4; 12:53

LAST QUARTER
May 11; 10:34

MERCURY is visible all month rising in the east 1½ hours before sunrise. **VENUS** is visible all month rising in the east 2-3 hours before sunrise. **MARS** is visible all month appearing low in the western sky at sunset, then setting 1-2 hours later. **JUPITER** is visible all month rising in the east about midnight, then fading near midsky with morning twilight. **SATURN** is visible throughout the night all month rising in the east at sunset, then setting in the west at sunrise; it comes to opposition May 15. **Apr. 22:** Mars 0.4° S. of waxing crescent Moon-OCCULTATION-(evening sky). **May 01:** Mercury at gr. elong. W.(27°). **May 04:** TOTAL ECLIPSE OF THE MOON (Not visible from N. America). **May 05:** Saturn 3° N. of waning gibbous Moon (night sky). **May 09:** Venus at greatest brilliancy. **May 10:** Jupiter 5° N. of waning gibbous (night sky). **May 11:** Mars 6° N. of *Aldebaran*. **May 15:** Venus 3° N. of waning crescent Moon (morning sky). **May 17:** Mercury 1.5° S. of waning crescent Moon (morning sky). **May 19:** PARTIAL ECLIPSE OF THE SUN (Visible from northern Canada and northern Asia).

APRIL—MAY

MONDAY — APRIL 29

Sun Rises 06:15
Sun Sets 20:00
Moon Rises 14:09
Moon Sets 03:32

MOON ENTERS VIRGO 12:24

moon square saturn-05:32. moon square mars-16:41. moon trine neptune-18:18.

William Randolph Hearst 1863
Rod McKuen 1933
Peter Jennings 1938
Jeremy Thorps 1929
Zubin Mehta 1936
Jim Ryan 1947

TUESDAY — APRIL 30

Sun Rises 06:14
Sun Sets 20:01
Moon Rises 15:20
Moon Sets 04:05

MOON IN VIRGO

sun trine moon-05:33. moon square uranus-17:39.

Alice B. Toklas 1877
Eve Arden 1912
Willie Nelson 1933
John Crowe Ransom 1888
Cloris Leachman 1926
Jill Clayburgh 1944

1871: Mob massacres 100 Apaches under U.S. protection at Camp Grant, Ariz. **1888:** 246 people are killed by hailstones as large as cricket balls (New Delhi, India). **1900:** Casey Jones killed in the wreck of the *Cannonball Express.* **1928:** Harvard wins first intercollegiate competition in English Literature over Yale. **1945:** Hitler commits suicide in Berlin bunker. **1965:** Anti-American demonstrations over U.S. intervention in Dominican Republic erupt in Chile, Panama, and New York City. **1975:** Vietnam War formally ends.

I believe in the presumptive reluctance to abandon tradition.

William F. Buckley, Jr.

WEDNESDAY — MAY 01

Sun Rises 06:13
Sun Sets 20:02
Moon Rises 16:33
Moon Sets 04:35

MOON ENTERS LIBRA 14:22

moon square neptune-19:55. moon trine mars-20:31.

Dante 1265
Glenn Ford 1916
Scott Carpenter 1925
Judy Collins 1939
Kate Smith 1909
Joseph Heller 1923
Terry Southern 1928
Rita Coolidge 1944

1707: Great Britain formed with the uniting of England and Scotland. **1883:** Buffalo Bill's first "Wild West Show." **1898:** Battle of Manila Bay during Spanish-American War— American ships virtually destroy Spanish fleet, killing 381 Spanish sailors with no American loss of life. **1928:** 6 children are killed by hail the size of hens' eggs (Rumania). **1960:** Francis Gary Powers shot down in U-2 spy plane over Russia. **1965:** Spike Jones dies. **1975:** Smokey the Bear retires.

I yam what I yam. *Popeye*

MAY DAY

THURSDAY — MAY 02

Sun Rises 06:12
Sun Sets 20:03
Moon Rises 17:47
Moon Sets 05:04

MOON IN LIBRA

moon oppos venus-01:41. moon trine jupiter-14:56. moon oppos mercury-15:41.

Phillipe Halsman 1902
Bing Crosby 1904
Benjamin Spock 1903
Larry Gatlin 1948

1519: Leonardo da Vinci dies. **1957:** Joseph McCarthy dies. **1960:** Caryl Chessman, convicted "Redlight Bandit," dies in gas chamber at San Quentin Prison (Calif.)—he had successfully delayed his own execution for 12 years with legal appeals. **1965:** *Earlybird* satellite relays TV signal—first U.S. broadcast from space. **1972:** J. Edgar Hoover, director of FBI, dies at age 77 in his sleep at home (Washington, D.C)— he was suffering from high blood pressure at the time.

I know wimmins, and wimmins is difficult.
Ernest Hemingway

FRIDAY — MAY 03

Sun Rises 06:11
Sun Sets 20:04
Moon Rises 19:02
Moon Sets 05:34

MOON ENTERS SCORPIO 14:17

moon conj pluto-19:08. moon at perigee-22:00.

Niccolo Machiavelli 1469
Roberto Rossellini 1906
William Inge 1913
Sugar Ray Robinson 1920
Frankie Valli 1937
Walter Slezak 1902
Earl Wilson 1907
Pete Seeger 1919
James Brown 1928
Doug Henning 1947

1375bc: Earliest recorded eclipse of the sun (Ugarit, Syria). **1965:** Cambodia severs relations with U.S. **1965:** El Salvador earthquake kills 150. **1972:** 7 office workers die at their desks on 36th floor of skyscraper in New York City when steam pipe explodes.

I do not believe that the Great Society is the ordered, changeless and sterile battalion of the ants.

Lyndon Johnson

SATURDAY — MAY 04

Sun Rises 06:10
Sun Sets 20:05
Moon Rises 20:20
Moon Sets 06:06

MOON IN SCORPIO

mercury trine uranus-01:10. sun oppos moon-12:53. moon square jupiter-14:47.

FULL MOON 12:53

St. Vincent de Paul 1576
Thomas Huxley 1825
Audrey Hepburn 1929
Horace Mann 1796
Maynard Ferguson 1928
Roberta Peters 1930

1886: Haymarket Riot in Chicago. **1970:** U.S. National Guard murders four students at Kent State. **1976:** Australia makes "Waltzing Matilda" national anthem.

FORECAST

BY NAN DE GROVE

TAURUS

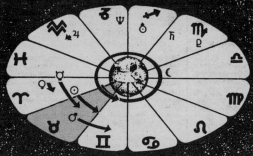

LONGITUDE OF THE PLANETS
19:26 PST; 04/19/85

Sun 00°00′ **Taurus**
Moon 29°07′ **Aries**
Mercury 07°05′ **Aries**
Venus 06°28′ **Aries R**
Mars 25°39′ **Taurus**
Jupiter 13°49′ **Aquarius**
Saturn 26°38′ **Scorpio R**
Ura 17°39′ **Sagittarius R**
Nept 03°34′ **Capricorn R**
Pluto 03°28′ **Scorpio R**

The **New Moon of April 19th sets off a pattern of oppositions** between the Sun, the Moon, and Mars in Taurus and Pluto and Saturn in Scorpio. The Bull is stubborn, ornery, and inclined to see red now. Obstacles, confrontations, and aggression are typical of this configuration.

Since Pluto and Saturn, the "heavies" in the line-up, are in Scorpio, we must deal with conflicting forces within ourselves and acknowledge unconscious motives and attitudes that are blocking creativity and productivity.

The **Mars-Saturn opposition, exact on April 21st, is conducive to violent displays of ego** and clashes of will. It is all too easy to project problems onto others, especially authority figures or a nebulous "them." We can avoid behavior we might later regret if we can recognize the origins of these projections before we start blaming and scapegoating.

With **Saturn and Pluto retrograde,** the source of frustration lies in the past. Problems arise in relation to issues that have been nagging at us for quite some time. Some of these are the result of events that began taking shape around mid-February, 1984 when Mars and Saturn were last conjunct.

Financial and business deals tend to be blocked in the early part of Taurus. With Venus still retrograde, partnership and agreements of all kinds are being reevaluated.

EARTH SIGNS make progress now through perseverance and nonattachment to results.

Taurus: you most personally affected by the month's general trends and needs to cultivate flexibility and tolerance.

Virgo: an unexpected financial opportunity is likely, but should use discrimination and intuition to avoid being misled.

Capricorn: use opportunities to actualize dreams through the right combination of traditional methods and innovative ideas.

Self-confidence is an important for positive results.

AIR SIGNS may need to make practical adjustments before things can get off the ground.

Gemini: you may be making significant contacts, or be giving something or someone a second chance. A big boost in energy and confidence comes after the 26th.

Libra: Successful settlements, agreements, and business negotiations are favored. Be straightforward, discreet, and ask for what you want.

Aquarius: you may need to slow down and consider the practical and emotional ramifications of plans. Things take a turn for the better around May 18th.

FIRE SIGNS need to work with things as they are rather than over-idealizing and over-theorizing.

Aries: be charming and persuasive, but circumspect in business dealings and partnerships; look below the surface.

Leo: you have some important endings and new beginnings to sort through. In deciding whether an attractive opportunity is worth the sacrifice, take a chance.

Sagittarius: consolidate projects and conserve energy to avoid an overload. Partners are challenging and demanding around April 26th.

WATER SIGNS may be better able than other signs to use the potential of this month's planets, due to their instinctive understanding of dualities and sensitivity to subconscious currents.

Cancer: exercise caution around the May 4th eclipse and stay tuned to emotional frequencies at home.

Scorpio: you may find yourself on the defensive; be careful not to alienate others through paranoid behavior.

Pisces: you may find your philosophical and spiritual foundations shifting. Adjust and adapt concepts from experience rather than the other way around.

SUNDAY — MAY 05

Sun Rises 06:09
Sun Sets 20:05
Moon Rises 21:38
Moon Sets 06:43

MOON ENTERS SAGITTARIUS 13:56

moon conj saturn-06:52. moon at desc node-18:01.
sun square jupiter-21:31.

Mohammed 570
Karl Marx 1818
Tyrone Power 1913
Tammy Wynette 1942

Soren Kierkegaard 1813
Alice Faye 1912
Ann B. Davis 1926
Bob Woodward 1943

1847: A.M.A. organized. 1945: Only deaths in U.S. from enemy action during WWII—hydrogen balloon launched in Japan and carrying explosives landed in a wooded area of Oregon, where it was discovered and accidentally set off by a local minister's child, killing the child, his 4 other children, and his wife. The balloon was one of about 1,000 thought to have reached U.S.

CINCO DE MAYO

MONDAY — MAY 06

Sun Rises 06:08
Sun Sets 20:06
Moon Rises 22:53
Moon Sets 07:27

MOON IN SAGITTARIUS

moon oppos mars-01:02. moon trine venus-03:25.
moon conj uranus-17:49. moon trine mercury-23:38.

Robespierre 1758
Toots Shor 1905
Stewart Granger 1913
T.H. White 1915

Sigmund Freud 1856
Weeb Ewbank 1907
Orson Welles 1915
Bob Seger 1945

1642: Montreal founded by Paul de Chomedey. 1811: James Fenimore Cooper resigns commission in Navy. 1851: Yale patents lock. 1862: Henry David Thoreau dies after battling tuberculosis for several years (Concord, Mass.)—his last words were, "Moose, Indian." 1877: Crazy Horse surrenders. 1937: German dirigible Hindenberg explodes as it docks at Lakehurst, N.J., killing 36 people on board.

TUESDAY — MAY 07

Sun Rises 06:07
Sun Sets 20:07
Moon Rises ----
Moon Sets 08:19

MOON ENTERS CAPRICORN 15:11

moon conj neptune-20:50.

Robert Browning 1812
Tchaikovsky 1840
Archibald MacLeish 1892
Edwin Land 1909
Totie Fields 1930

Johannes Brahms 1833
Gabby Hayes 1885
Gary Cooper 1901
Eva Peron 1919
Teresa Brewer 1931

1912: Pulitzer Prize established. 1915: Lusitania sinks off coast of Ireland after being torpedoed by a German U-boat—about 2,000 people died. 1928: Judge exonerates blind dog after it bit a deaf man. 1954: Viet Minh defeat French at Dien Bien Phu.

Listen, when you feel you are morally right, you just have to act and let people catch up later. That's the way it is in war.

Audie Murphy

WEDNESDAY — MAY 08

Sun Rises 06:06
Sun Sets 20:08
Moon Rises 00:01
Moon Sets 09:18

MOON IN CAPRICORN

moon square venus-06:59. sun trine moon-23:12.

Bakunin 1814
Theodore Sorenson 1928
Thomas Pynchon 1937
Peter Benchley 1940
Keith Jarrett 1945

Don Rickles 1926
Gary Snyder 1930
Rick Nelson 1940
Toni Tennille 1943
Melissa Gilbert 1964

1794: Lavoisier guillotined. 1876: Truganini, last Aborigine from Tasmania, dies. 1886: First Coca-Cola sold (Jacob's Pharmacy, Atlanta, Ga.). 1911: England and China sign treaty to trade opium. 1945: Germany surrenders. 1979: Violence grips San Salvador as civil war begins.

You can no more win a war, than you can win an earthquake.

Jeanette Rankin

THURSDAY — MAY 09

Sun Rises 06:05
Sun Sets 20:09
Moon Rises 00:59
Moon Sets 10:23

MOON ENTERS AQUARIUS 19:38

moon square mercury-08:20.

John Brown 1800
Jose Ortega y Gasset 1883
Glenda Jackson 1936
Candice Bergen 1946

Henry John Kaiser 1882
Mike Wallace 1918
Albert Finney 1936
Billy Joel 1949

1502: Columbus begins his last voyage. 1933: Hitler burns 25,000 books in Berlin. 1944: Eye bank opens (New York City).

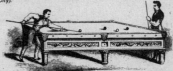

FRIDAY — MAY 10

Sun Rises 06:04
Sun Sets 20:10
Moon Rises 01:46
Moon Sets 11:29

MOON IN AQUARIUS

moon square pluto-00:54. moon trine mars-13:59.

John Wilkes Booth 1838
Fred Astaire 1899
Mother Maybelle Carter 1909
Stephen Bechtel Jr. 1928
Judith Jamison 1944

Ariel Durant 1898
David O. Selznick 1902
Nancy Walker 1921
Pat Summerall 1930
Dave Mason 1946

1775: Ethan Allen and his Green Mountain Boys storm British positions at Ticonderoga, New York. 1818: Paul Revere, silversmith and patriot, dies (Boston, Mass.). 1869: Transcontinental railroad completed—Leland Stanford drives golden spike. 1910: Glacier National Park created by Act of Congress. 1948: Rex Morgan, M.D., debuts as comic strip. 1960: Triton returns to New London—first submarine to circumnavigate the earth under the water. 1971: Armed marshals and U.S. Coast Guard force Indians from Alcatraz Island after 19 months of occupation.

"Something rather subtle seems to be at work." — Sir Frederick Sanger

The Antidote To Entropy

by Jane Waterman & George Nash

The world is going to hell in a handbasket. And so, it would seem, is the universe — at least according to the Second Law of Thermodynamics. Simply put, this law states that the energy of any given system will always tend to flow down a gradient from order and complexity toward disorder and chaos until it reaches a state of uniform randomness or equilibrium.

From this, it would seem to follow that the probability of any system being arranged in an orderly fashion will be very small and that the probability of randomness will continue to increase with the passage of time. The "arrow of time," Sir Arthur Eddington's metaphor for this irreversible one-way flow, is called entropy, a concept at once both a scientific law and a poetic insight of compelling power.

Consider the paradox: all around us is complexity — bacteria, flora, forests, ecosystems of extreme subtlety, civilizations and all their artifacts. All are highly-ordered and growing more so with time. Why, in the face of the odds against it, is there so much structure and so little randomness? It is not that the Second Law is false, but that there seems to be a tendency which counteracts it. Long before the principle of action and equal reaction was codified into Newton's Third Law of Motion, it was intuitively grasped. The history of this knowledge is the history of human thought and philosophy.

From this, it would seem to follow that the probability of any system being arranged in an orderly fashion will be very small and that the probability of randomness will continue to increase with the passage of time. The "arrow of time," Sir Arthur Eddington's metaphor for this irreversible one-way flow, is called entropy, a concept at once both a scientific law and a poetic insight of compelling power.

St. Augustine and Goethe's Faust both spoke of the devil as the lord of chaos, the "spirit which always negates" and opposes the work of the Creator's love. Philosophy grapples with the questions of how one can know and the limits of the knowing. In both these endeavors, the role of human consciousness is pivotal. The various disciplines of science also struggle to reconcile their observations with coherent theories on how the universe hangs together. The history of science is littered with half-buried monuments to the fascination of this fateful dichotomy.

Jeremy Campbell, writing in *Grammatical Man*, draws upon the seminal work of information theorist Claude Shannon, linguist Noam Chomsky, biophysicist Lila Gatlin, and the Nobel-prize-winning "poet of thermodynamics," Ilya Prigogine, to advance the idea that the "arrow of history" and the thermodynamic arrow are "complimentary, and not in conflict."

Campbell suggests, like Prigogine, that order is something which arises naturally out of disorder. In an open system that is thermodynamically consistent when viewed as a whole, such as the universe, it is possible under certain conditions for local "fluctuations" to occur, and even more important, to persist.

Think of the universe not as a uniform mix, but rather as a sort of lumpy pudding. Some of these local "lumps" can reach and maintain a steady state that is far from the equilibrium of maximum entropy. Thus, non-equilibrium can be a source of order, an anti-entropy generator. The key to this "equifinal" state is complexity.

Campbell says that complexity is "not just a matter of a system having a lot of parts which are related to one another in non-simple ways. Instead, it turns out to be a special property in its own right, and it makes complex systems different in kind from simple ones, enabling them to do things and be things one might not have expected."

In other words, there is a local loophole in the Second Law. There seems to be something about the very structure of matter which generates order: things are arranged in only some ways and not others, although any of an infinity of arrangements are theoretically possible. It is almost as if complexity is a threshold. And once crossed, it allows a previously ordinary system to burgeon into increasing order.

If entropy is seen as a function of information, the growth of order from disorder becomes understandable. The amount of entropy in a system is related to the information about that system possessed by its observer. Disorder is, at least on some level, a highly subjective concept. For example, a newborn baby has no knowledge

MAY

SATURDAY — MAY 11

Sun Rises 06:03
Sun Sets 20:11
Moon Rises 02:24
Moon Sets 12:34

MOON IN AQUARIUS

moon conj jupiter-01:14. sun square moon-10:34.
moon square saturn-18:30.

LAST QUARTER MOON 10:34

Irving Berlin 1888
Clifton Wharton 1899
Phil Silvers 1912
Eric Burdon 1941

Ellsworth Bunker 1894
Salvador Dali 1904
Mort Sahl 1927
Robert Jarvik 1946

1872: First woman nominated for President—Victoria Clafin Woodhull. 1981: Bob Marley dies of cancer in Miami.

Euphemisms are words that prettify; euphemists are people who mistake words for things and think by renaming unpleasant things they can render them pleasant.
William Safire

SUNDAY — MAY 12

Sun Rises 06:02
Sun Sets 20:12
Moon Rises 02:55
Moon Sets 13:36

MOON ENTERS PISCES 03:56

moon trine pluto-09:26. venus at desc node-16:00.

Socrates 467bc
Florence Nightingale 1820
Philip Wylie 1902
Tom Snyder 1936
Ron Ziegler 1939

Dolley Madison 1768
Theodor Reik 1888
Howard K. Smith 1914
George Carlin 1938
Steve Winwood 1948

1896: New York City prohibits spitting in public. 1933: Emergency Relief Administration created. 1975: S.S. Mayaguez captured by Cambodia.

MOTHER'S DAY

MONDAY — MAY 13

Sun Rises 06:01
Sun Sets 20:13
Moon Rises 03:22
Moon Sets 14:36

MOON IN PISCES

moon square mars-02:55. moon square uranus-13:13.
MERCURY ENTERS TAURUS-19:10.

Daphne Du Maurier 1907
Mary Wells 1943

Roger Zelazny 1937
Stevie Wonder 1950

1896: Ford makes his first car. 1904: 382,000 acres of Sioux Indian land opened for settlement in South Dakota. 1916: First Indian Day held by Society of American Indians. 1918: First airmail stamp issued. 1981: Would-be assassin shoots and wounds Pope John Paul II (Rome).

Men are not necessities, they're luxuries. You don't need them, but they're really wonderful.
Cher

TUESDAY — MAY 14

Sun Rises 06:00
Sun Sets 20:14
Moon Rises 03:46
Moon Sets 15:34

MOON ENTERS ARIES 15:25

moon trine saturn-05:12. moon square neptune-21:54.

Gabriel Fahrenheit 1686
George Lucas 1944

Patrice Munsel 1925
David Byrne 1952

1607: Jamestown settled. 1804: Lewis and Clark leave St. Louis for Pacific coast. 1884: Anti-Monopoly Party formed. 1904: First Olympics in U.S. (St. Louis). 1948: Israel granted statehood. 1965: Red China explodes its 2nd nuclear device. 1970: 2 students die at Jackson State College (Miss.) during confrontation with police.

OKAY

I have never had criticism from anybody I really respect.
James Watt

WEDNESDAY — MAY 15

Sun Rises 05:59
Sun Sets 20:15
Moon Rises 04:08
Moon Sets 16:31

MOON IN ARIES

sun oppos saturn-10:56. mercury oppos pluto-14:28.
moon conj venus-18:24. mercury trine neptune-21:07.

Frank Baum 1856
Katherine Anne Porter 1890
James Mason 1909
Anna Maria Alberghetti 1936
Lainie Kazan 1942

Pierre Curie 1859
Joseph Cotten 1905
Wavy Gravy 1936
Trini Lopez 1937
George Brett 1953

1886: Emily Dickinson, poet, dies at age 56 (Amherst, Mass.). 1905: Las Vegas founded. 1918: Humphrey Bogart, age 18, expelled from Phillips Academy (Andover, Mass.). 1965: Organization of American States Commission negotiates cease-fire in Dominican Republic.

THURSDAY — MAY 16

Sun Rises 05:58
Sun Sets 20:15
Moon Rises 04:30
Moon Sets 17:28

MOON IN ARIES

moon trine uranus-01:36. moon at apogee-17:00.

Studs Terkel 1912
Frank Mankiewicz 1924
Billy Martin 1928

Liberace 1919
Robert Pierpoint 1925
Olga Korbut 1956

1763: Samuel Johnson meets his biographer, James Boswell. 1965: Series of accidental explosions kills 27 Americans in South Vietnam. 1966: Stokely Carmichael elected chairman of SNCC, beginning a shift from civil rights to black power in the black movement. 1969: Russian space vehicle lands on Venus. 1980: Elvis Presley's physician indicted for illegally prescribing dangerous drugs to Presley and others.

Freedom is not free. *Rev. Jesse Jackson*

or information about its surroundings. Its birth, to the attendants, is a rather routine affair, the order obvious. To the parents, it is a new experience, although they have some idea of what to expect. To the baby, it is total chaos. The amount of entropy in this system would vary with the viewpoints of each participant.

What could seem more random than the continual erosion of landforms by the action of wind and water and the deposition of sediments upon the sea bottom? Yet this debris is exquisitely graded in the act of deposition and will eventually give rise to the fantastic and unique features of some future landscape. Most people look at a swamp and see only a hodge-podge of weeds and shrubs mired in sloppy black mud, but an ecologist marvels at the intricate harmony of a fragile and delicately balanced system. Likewise, early studies of the atom postulated a "raisin pudding" model consisting of negatively charged particles swimming in a positively charged soup — quite a contrast to the atom of modern quantum physics. The phenomena themselves did not change, but as our understanding of them increased, the inherent order became more apparent.

Modern information theory, as generalized by Shannon, applies to all exchanges — chemical, verbal, social, and thermo- or biodynamical. It traces its origins to the nineteenth-century physicist Ludwig Boltzman, who was among the first to have an inkling of the link between information and entropy, which he called "missing information." A system high in entropy is one about which little useful information can be known. Because all the contrasts between the parts of the system have been averaged out, it contains very little of value or interest to the observer.

In Shannon's view, such a system is like the static in the background of a radio transmission. Introducing order into a system is akin to sending a message over the same radio. The problem is how to ensure that the transmission be received with an acceptable freedom from error and not be swallowed up by the entropic noise. That is, how are a limited number of possibilities manifested by an infinite probability?

Shannon's Theorem also says that there can be no information without uncertainty. To be sure, a message repeated ad infinitum possesses a high degree of order. But although its entropy is very low, it cannot carry very much information. In order for complex systems to develop, complicated messages must be transmitted. There needs to be a balance between variety and reliability.

For example, if the generation of a list of letters is determined only by statistical probability, it is virtually impossible that anything resembling intelligible language will emerge. If, however, the selection is determined by a few simple rules which take into account the context of each letter, the random generation soon begins to resemble the patterns of real language and syntax.

The most striking example of the affinity between living and non-living matter which is suggested by information theory is the DNA molecule found in all living systems. Here is a superlative balance indeed: the four basic "letters" of the genetic alphabet provide just enough redundancy to insure accurate transmission of the genetic message while allowing for enough variation so that the messenger, RNA, transmits the algorithms which allow the infinitely complex and utterly unique possibilities of life to unfold in an orderly, controlled, yet open-ended process.

Evolution then is essentially an information process, one that maximizes freedom of expression and freedom from error. The history of evolution is the gradual refinement of the transmission and reception of the DNA message and the counterbalancing of entropy by information. Information is not only gathered by individual members of a species to be lost when death of the organism degrades it. That would be entropic indeed.

Instead, it is coded and transmitted from generation to generation, both within the genetic and (for very complex species such as humans) cultural archives. Species evolve and become better adapted as information is compiled. Complexity breeds flexibility. Those species which are capable of creative response to change are those which are best adapted for survival.

One might argue that this is all a poetic conceit; that although life increases in complexity, it is ultimately dependent on energy, specifically solar energy, and therefore doomed to extinction when that energy is finally degraded, as it must be. This assumes that our solar system and the universe is an isolated or closed system — an idea open to dispute.

We exist in a universe that we do not fully comprehend. What of black holes that suck up matter, time, and energy like vacuum cleaners of unfathomable magnitude? Could these holes be a transition point in a timeless cycle beyond our present sphere of knowledge? Are we like astronomers before Galileo, insisting that the world is flat because we cannot see past the horizon?

Homo Sapiens is the product of some 500 million years of dispersed energy and accumulated information. How much longer we have left is a matter of conjecture. Assuming that life will continue as it has, we may in time gather enough information and understanding to prove Einstein right when he said that "God does not play dice with the universe." It's more likely that God plays video games, using a coin whose faces are information and entropy.

FRIDAY — MAY 17

Sun Rises 05:57
Sun Sets 20:16
Moon Rises 04:53
Moon Sets 18:25

MOON ENTERS TAURUS 04:23

moon oppos pluto-09:54. moon trine neptune-10:49. moon conj mercury-16:48.

Ayatollah Khomeini 1900   Maureen O'Sullivan 1911
Stewart Alsop 1914   Dennis Hopper 1936

1291: The city of Acre in Israel captured by Moslems—60,000 Christians killed or enslaved. 1875: First Kentucky Derby. 1927: Graumann's Chinese Theater opens. 1979: Heirs of Karen Silkwood awarded $10.5 million in damages from Kerr-McGee Corp.

A man who hits the peak at twenty-seven has a tough job ahead. People will be expecting me to pull rabbits out of the hat for the rest of my life.

Martin Luther King, Jr.

SATURDAY — MAY 18

Sun Rises 05:56
Sun Sets 20:17
Moon Rises 05:18
Moon Sets 19:25

MOON IN TAURUS

moon square jupiter-13:53.

Bertrand Russell 1872   Meredith Willson 1902
John Paul II 1918   Pernell Roberts 1930
Dwayne Hickman 1934   Reggie Jackson 1946

1852: 1st compulsory school attendance law enacted in U.S. (Mass.). 1899: Permanent Court of International Arbitration established at The Hague. 1919: Nabokov learns to foxtrot. 1974: India's first nuclear blast. 1980: Mt. St. Helens volcano explosion devastates three states with ash, killing 14—more than 40 missing.

PEACE DAY

SUNDAY — MAY 19

Sun Rises 05:55
Sun Sets 20:18
Moon Rises 05:47
Moon Sets 20:25

MOON ENTERS GEMINI 17:01

moon oppos saturn-06:05. sun conj moon-14:41. moon at asc node-16:21.

NEW MOON 14:41

John Hopkins 1795   Ho Chi Minh 1890
Malcolm X 1925   Harvey Cox 1929
David Hartman 1935   Peter Townshend 1945

1911: First conviction using fingerprints as evidence. 1964: American Embassy in Moscow found to be bugged. 1965: Cyclone devastates Pakistan, killing 12,000. 1979: First National Conference on Women in Crisis (New York City).

On calm days, I know that it is not possible to remake the world. You can fix parts, but you can't remake the world.

Edward Koch

The Pond by Linda Hogan

The pond is one of the world's hearts.
From time to time
some scaly fish of the past
beats up from the slime
like an old ache or love, then sinks again.

Crickets are pulsing in the wrist of night.
Sleep lays a hand on them and me
but forgets to count.

By morning, sit up! The pond is in
the clouds. Night in a robe of stars
did some alchemy, changed water
to nothing
and the old creatures are exposed
in hard air. What kind
of motel is this anyway?

Maybe it's Oklahoma
with rains of fish
and the frogs, evicted for weeping,
falling out of Room 103,
their toes spread like stars.

SATELLITES

by Larry C. Sessions

Since the Russians launched their tiny beeping *Sputnik* in 1957, thousands of satellites have rocketed into Earth orbit to gather weather and other scientific data, revolutionize the communication industry, and even spy on military installations. Approximately 5,000 satellites and other orbiting objects are tracked regularly by NORAD in Colorado Springs, Colorado, and the number grows each year. Most of these satellites are no longer operating; they are either out of control and simply following the unyielding law of gravity, or they are not really satellites at all, but rather orbital debris such as spent booster rockets.

The vast majority of those 5,000-plus orbiting objects are far too faint to be seen without a telescope, but there are still dozens bright enough to be observed by anyone with normal vision who takes the time to look.

You have probably observed a satellite cross the evening sky, even if you didn't recognize what you were watching. Satellites normally appear as faint stars coursing slowly through the constellations. They travel in just about any direction, but you are not likely to see one moving from east to west because the orbital dynamics make such orbits more difficult.

A satellite may appear as a high-flying airplane with no running lights. Many people mistakenly report satellites as UFOs. Further, satellites should not be confused with meteors or "shooting stars." Meteors streak across the sky and are gone in a matter of seconds; a satellite in orbit moves much more slowly. Often, it may be observed for several minutes.

At the height of 180 miles, which is in the range at which the space shuttles operate, an orbit around the globe takes about 91 minutes. At a thousand miles, it takes about two hours. The higher the satellite, the longer it takes to orbit.

A satellite orbiting over the equator in the same direction as the Earth and at a height of about 23,000 miles above the Earth's center will orbit once in 24 hours. Consequently, the satellite will seem to hover over one location, day and night. These are usually communications and weather satellites. Unfortunately, they are far too faint to be seen without powerful telescopes.

Well, what about those you can see? What can you tell about them? Generally speaking, it's a good guess that any satellite you see orbits the Earth in 90 minutes to two hours and is anywhere from about 120 miles to 1,000 miles up. Satellites in higher orbits are usually faint and difficult to see with the unaided eye.

If a satellite is fluctuating in brightness, you can say with some confidence that it is tumbling through space. Bright sunlight reflects from the shiny portions of the satellite, causing the brightness to vary as it rotates. This may be intentional for gyroscopic stabilization, or the satellite may simply be out of control.

Unfortunately, without certain pieces of difficult-to-obtain data or a knowledgeable mentor, it will be next to impossible to identify most satellites. You can't tell what kind of satellite it is — whether it is American or Soviet (of course, we should mention that the Canadians, British, Indians, French, Japanese, Indonesians, and Chinese also have a limited number of satellites in orbit) — or when you can see it again.

You can guess when and where to look for the satellite on subsequent orbits, but about all you can say is that it is likely to pass on its next orbit in 90 to 120 minutes, and that it will appear, if at all, to the west of its original track. It will appear to the west because of the Earth's east-west rotation.

You can increase your chances of seeing a satellite by looking when the conditions are favorable. It is best to look in the western half of the sky for a couple of hours after sunset. Then the sunlight can still illuminate a satellite several hundred miles up, just as the sun will shine at the top of a tall building or mountain longer than it does at ground level. By the same reasoning, it is also good to look in the eastern sky for a few hours before dawn.

You may not be able to identify the particular satellites you observe, but that preserves some of the mystery and intrigue of your sightings. After all, you might be watching Soviet spy satellites or, perhaps, just an empty booster rocket. At any rate, dozens of them are there for you to observe, hurtling above the Earth at thousands of miles per hour, symbols of our first faltering steps to the stars.

MAY

GEMINI

May 20 — June 20

MONDAY
MAY
20

Sun Rises 05:55
Sun Sets 20:18
Moon Rises 06:20
Moon Sets 21:26

MOON IN GEMINI

mars trine jupiter-05:34. mars oppos uranus-08:42.
venus trine uranus-18:49.

Sun Enters Gemini 19:43

Honore de Balzac 1799	James Stewart 1908
Edward Whitehead 1908	Mary and Margaret Gibb 1912
George Gobel 1919	Charles Reich 1928
Joe Cocker 1944	Cher 1946

526: Antioch earthquake—250,000 people killed. **1899:** First driver arrested in U.S. for speeding—Jacob German, driving a taxi at 12 mph (New York City). **1902:** Cuban Independence Day. **1921:** Mme. Curie is presented with $100,000 of radium by Pres. Harding—representing gift from American women. **1946:** Army C-45 airplane crashes into side of the Manhattan Building in New York City, 58 floors above street—5 people are killed.

VICTORIA DAY

TUESDAY
MAY
21

Sun Rises 05:54
Sun Sets 20:19
Moon Rises 07:00
Moon Sets 22:26

MOON IN GEMINI

moon trine jupiter-02:00. moon oppcs uranus-02:02.
moon conj mars-03:07.

Plato 427bc	Albrecht Durer 1471
Alexander Pope 1688	Gaspard de Coriolis 1792
Henri Rousseau 1844	Raymond Burr 1917
Dennis Day 1917	Rennie Davis 1940

1819: First bicycle is ridden on streets of New York City. **1863:** Seventh Day Adventists form church. **1881:** Clara Barton organizes American Red Cross. **1928:** Frank Johns, Socialist Labor Party candidate for Pres. of U.S., drowns while attempting rescue of boy from river (Ore.). **1952:** John Garfield, actor, dies of heart attack at age 39 (New York City). **1975:** Col. Paul Shaffer, U.S. rep. in Iran, is assassinated.

FIRST DAY OF RAMADEN

WEDNESDAY
MAY
22

Sun Rises 05:54
Sun Sets 20:19
Moon Rises 07:47
Moon Sets 23:22

MOON ENTERS CANCER 04:04

moon trine pluto-09:04. moon oppos neptune-09:58.

Arthur Conan Doyle 1859	Vance Packard 1914
Judith Crist 1922	Peter Nero 1934
Richard Benjamin 1938	Paul Winfield 1941

1919: Explosion of starch dust kills 44 (Cedar Rapids, la.). **1949:** James Forrestal, who had resigned as Sec. of Defense only a few days before, dies after leaping from 16th floor window of Nat'l Naval Medical Center (Bethesda, Md.)—he was 57 years old at time, the victim of sudden mental and physical collapse. A note was found in room that quoted Sophocles on subject of death. **1954:** Bob Dylan celebrates his Bar Mitzvah. **1965:** Columbian government announces state-of-seige following student protests over U.S. intervention in Dominican Republic.

LIFTOFF

THURSDAY
MAY
23

Sun Rises 05:53
Sun Sets 20:20
Moon Rises 08:42
Moon Sets ----

MOON IN CANCER

moon square venus-15:56. mercury square jupiter-19:07.

Scatman Crothers 1910	Helen O'Connell 1920
Rosemary Clooney 1928	Barbara Barrie 1931
Joan Collins 1933	Anatoly Karpov 1951

1498: Savonarola burned as a heretic. **1785:** Benjamin Franklin invents bifocals. **1878:** UN special session on world disarmament opens. **1934:** Bonnie and Clyde die in police ambush in which they receive 23 and 25 bullet wounds, respectively—she was 23 years old and he was 25. **1977:** Univ. of Calif. researchers disclose a gene-splitting technique to attack human diseases.

Even the posterior of a great man is of interest.

John L. Lewis

GROWING
BY LIZ CAILE

NOW'S THE TIME — Around the country there's no end of things to do in the garden — sowing, thinning, weeding and mulching. If young plants are stunted, or yellowish and you suspect soil deficiencies, try feeding with manure tea. (Steep the manure in a bucket or drum of water for several days. Dilute before using, and avoid using on root crops.) **Northeast:** Plant seeds and transplants of tender garden annuals outside. **Southeast:** check leaves of beans, squash, other garden plants, top and underside, for egg clusters of pests and for aphids. Take these measures — pick off, crush, spray with a blast of water. Add companion plants or dose with manure tea to strengthen plantings. **Mountain States:** Potato sets should already be in the ground and poking up their flannel leaves; many seeds and transplants go into the ground now; set out geraniums and other plants wintered indoors. **Northwest:** Thin young fruits from apple and peach trees where set is thick. **Southwest:** Keep shrubs and trees well-watered; water them deeply. Build up a circular wall a few inches high to direct water to roots of trees. Mulch after watering.

Do Plants Feel?

Our tendency in talking about animals is to **anthropomorphize** — that is, to interpret them as human forms, with human motives and thoughts. In talking and writing about plants we **anthropopathize** — we give plants human passions and feelings: they "like" us, they "don't like" us. They "like" sweet or sour soil, sun or shade, sand or clay. Some plants "hate" to "get their feet wet" — a case of anthropopathizing and -morphizing at the same time.

More accurately, plants respond well or poorly to given environmental conditions. The range of responses in the plant world is astonishing. In the garden or in the wild, in the apartment or greenhouse, we begin to think of plants as individuals because of this diverse range of responses.

In every garden, some plant or crop will unexpectedly flourish, and another flounder, regardless of the good intentions of the grower. Sometimes a change in watering habits or transplanting to a new location will revive the ailing plant or species.

With environmental catastrophes at hand — insect plagues, long rainy spells or drought, exceptionally cold or warm weather, some garden plants will show superior hardiness and stay healthy while others fail.

Tomatoes Are Tops

In just about every part of the country, tomatoes respond well to good soil, clear days, warm temperatures and regular watering. They've always been a popular fruit, since discovered in Spain's New World and introduced to Europe as a decorative plant. For awhile, Europeans had a prejudice against eating this red fruit. But it wasn't long before the tomato became a staple flavoring, starting with Italian and Spanish cuisines.

Besides the incomparable flavor of homegrown tomatoes, they contribute significant amounts of vitamin A to our diets. Not water soluble, vitamin A is stored in body cells, and is a building block of healthy tissue surfaces inside and outside the body. Some consider it a major component of the dietary prevention of cancer and to contribute to healing tissues.

Tomatoes are the most popular garden plant in the U.S., and thrive in containers indoors or out. Some miniature varieties will fit in a four inch flower pot, while a standard variety has plenty of room in a four or five gallon tub. Three plants will fit in half a wine cask or a section of 55 gallon drum cut as a container.

For container grown plants, remember that the tomato is normally wind pollinated — so be sure to twitch the flower clusters, or give them a gentle shake, if you want them to set fruit. Pollen is produced most abundantly during the brightest hours of the day. If tomatoes are growing madly but not blossoming, slow watering and let the soil dry out a bit.

Bone meal dug into the container or outdoor bed is a good preparation; it provides minerals for flowering and fruiting. Too much available nitrogen will make for very leafy but unfruitful plants.

When transplanting, you can pinch off the lower leaves of the young plant and bury the stem as far as possible in the soil for greater root development, but tip the rootball horizontally so it stays in the warmer layer of soil. The stem will straighten out of its slightly horizontal position by itself.

Some fine touches include companion planting — spearmint and garlic, for instance, to repel aphids; or marigolds to discourage white flies; onions, asparagus, parsley, to stimulate growth; basil, beebalm, borage, for good measure. Avoid planting tomatoes with or near potatoes, dill or cabbage.

In warm climates, a mulch applied after the ground has warmed helps to keep even moisture around the roots and the result is a longer lasting plant and longer fruiting period. But unmulched plants may come into fruit a week or two earlier.

FRIDAY — MAY 24

Sun Rises 05:53
Sun Sets 20:21
Moon Rises 09:43
Moon Sets 00:12

MOON ENTERS LEO 12:54

moon trine saturn-02:05. moon square pluto-17:35.

Jean Paul Marat 1744	Queen Victoria 1819
Elsa Maxwell 1883	Suzanne Lenglen 1899
Sam Giancana 1908	Bob Dylan 1941
Gary Burghoff 1943	Rosanne Cash 1955

1543: Copernicus dies. **1856:** John Brown band murders and mutilates 5 people in Kansas. **1883:** During official opening of Brooklyn Bridge, a crowd of pedestrians panics, causing deaths of 12 people. **1965:** Civil war erupts in Bolivia.

SATURDAY — MAY 25

Sun Rises 05:52
Sun Sets 20:22
Moon Rises 10:49
Moon Sets 00:56

MOON IN LEO

moon trine uranus-18:59. moon oppos jupiter-19:36.

Ralph Waldo Emerson 1803	Bennett Cerf 1898
Lindsey Nelson 1919	Beverly Sills 1929
John Gregory Dunne 1932	Ron Nessen 1934
Leslie Uggams 1943	Karen Valentine 1947

1888: International Council of Women meets (Washington, D.C.). **1895:** U.S. troops battle Geronimo (Blue River, Ariz.). **1960:** First air express from New York to Washington, D.C. **1983:** Navy Lt. Cmdr. Albert Schaufelberger is assassinated in El Salvador.

3-DAY WEEKEND

SUNDAY — MAY 26

Sun Rises 05:52
Sun Sets 20:23
Moon Rises 11:57
Moon Sets 01:33

MOON ENTERS VIRGO 19:06

moon trine venus-02:31. moon square mercury-03:28.
moon square saturn-08:31.

Norma Talmadge 1897	John Wayne 1907
Peter Cushing 1913	Jay Silverheels 1919
James Arness 1923	Brent Musburger 1939
Stevie Nicks 1948	Hank Williams, Jr. 1949

1868: Last public execution in England with hanging of Michael Barrett, convicted of complicity in deaths of 13 on a reservation. **1877:** Crazy Horse, last of Sioux Chiefs, is confined to a reservation. **1972:** First Watergate break-in attempt.

Killing someone is easy, and instantly you're famous. I want to be infamous. I want to be controversial. It's much more colorful.
Brian de Palma

MONDAY — MAY 27

Sun Rises 05:51
Sun Sets 20:24
Moon Rises 13:06
Moon Sets 02:06

MOON IN VIRGO

moon trine neptune-00:17. sun square moon-05:56.
mercury oppos saturn-13:04. moon square uranus-23:34.

FIRST QUARTER MOON 05:56

Cornelius Vanderbilt 1794	Julia Ward Howe 1819
Wild Bill Hickok 1837	Isadora Duncan 1878
Dashiell Hammett 1894	Rachel Carson 1907
John Cheever 1912	Herman Wouk 1915
John Barth 1930	Lou Gossett 1936

1679: Habeas Corpus becomes part of British statute law. **1964:** Jawaharlal Nehru, Prime Minister of India, dies at age 74—cause of death was heart attack. **1965:** Israeli forces raid Jordan in reprisal for recent attacks. **1965:** Federal government funds "Head Start Program" with $18 million.

MEMORIAL DAY

TUESDAY — MAY 28

Sun Rises 05:51
Sun Sets 20:25
Moon Rises 14:15
Moon Sets 02:36

MOON ENTERS LIBRA 22:40

moon square mars-09:21. moon trine mercury-16:17.

Thomas Moore 1779	Ian Fleming 1908
T-Bone Walker 1910	Walker Percy 1916
Beth Howland 1941	Sondra Locke 1948

1962: "Blue Monday" at the New York Stock Market—biggest drop since Oct. 1929. **1972:** Duke of Windsor, ex-King of England, dies of cancer at age 77 in his home (Paris).

My reflexes aren't conditioned to accept non-violence. My immediate instinct under the threat of physical attack...is instant defense and total retaliation.
Jackie Robinson

WEDNESDAY — MAY 29

Sun Rises 05:50
Sun Sets 20:26
Moon Rises 15:26
Moon Sets 03:04

MOON IN LIBRA

moon square neptune-03:32. sun trine moon-12:38.

Patrick Henry 1736	Beatrice Lillie 1898
T.E. White 1906	John Kennedy 1917
Paul Ehrlich 1932	Al Unser 1939

1911: W.S. Gilbert, playwright, dies of heart attack while trying to rescue young female guest who was swimming with him in private lake—he was 74. **1933:** Gold standard authorized. **1942:** John Barrymore, actor, dies at Presbyterian Hospital at age 59 (Hollywood, Calif.)—causes of death were listed as myocarditis, chronic nephritis, cirrhosis of liver, and gastric ulcers. **1965:** 99 whites and blacks arrested in Selma for violating boycott laws.

The idea of being in a rock-and-roll band is not having to go to work.
Chrissie Hynde

CELESTIAL EVENTS

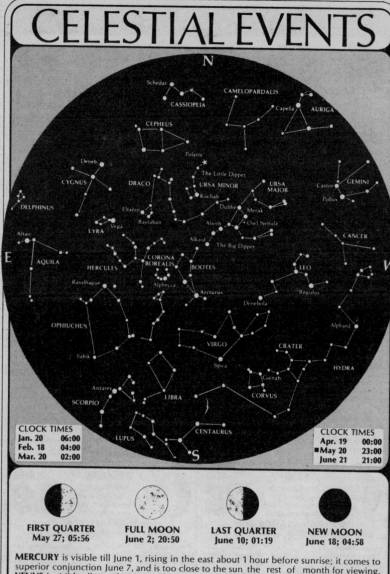

N

Schedar · CASSIOPEIA · CAMELOPARDALIS · Capella · AURIGA

CEPHEUS

Polaris ★

Deneb · The Little Dipper

CYGNUS · DRACO · URSA MINOR · URSA MAJOR · Castor · GEMINI

Kochab · Pollux

DELPHINUS · Eltanin · Dubhe · Merak

Rastaban · Alioth · Owl Nebula · CANCER

Vega · LYRA · Alkaid · The Big Dipper

Altair

AQUILA · CORONA BOREALIS · BOOTES · LEO

E · HERCULES · BOOTES · Regulus · W

Rasslhague · Alphecca · Arcturus

Denebola

OPHIUCHUS · Alphard

Sabik · VIRGO · CRATER

Spica · HYDRA

Antares · Gienah

SCORPIO · LIBRA · CORVUS

LUPUS · CENTAURUS

S

FIRST QUARTER
May 27; 05:56

FULL MOON
June 2; 20:50

LAST QUARTER
June 10; 01:19

NEW MOON
June 18; 04:58

MERCURY is visible till June 1, rising in the east about 1 hour before sunrise; it comes to superior conjunction June 7, and is too close to the sun the rest of month for viewing. **VENUS** is visible all month rising in the east 3 hours before sunrise. **MARS** is visible till the end of May appearing low in the western sky at sunset, then setting about 1 hour later. **JUPITER** is visible all month rising in the east shortly after sunset, then fading in the western sky with morning twilight. **SATURN** is visible all month appearing in the eastern sky at sunset, then setting in the west shortly before dawn. **May 21:** Mars 1.9° S. of waxing crescent Moon (evening sky). **June 01:** Saturn 3° N. of waning gibbous Moon (night sky). **June 07:** Jupiter 5° N. of waning gibbous Moon (night sky). **June 12:** Venus at gr. elong. W.(46°). **June 14:** Venus 1.9° S. of waning crescent Moon (morning sky).

MAY—JUNE

THURSDAY
MAY 30
Sun Rises 05:50
Sun Sets 20:26
Moon Rises 16:38
Moon Sets 03:32

MOON IN LIBRA
moon trine jupiter-02:45.
MERCURY ENTERS GEMINI-12:44.
moon trine mars-13:40. moon oppos venus-14:55.

Stepin Fetchit 1892
Irving Thalberg 1899
Howard Hawks 1896
Frank Blair 1915

1431: Joan of Arc burned at the stake. 1896: First automobile accident—car hits bicyclist. 1945: U.S. Marines take Okinawa. 1965: Vivian Malone becomes first black graduate of Univ. of Ala. 1972: Lod Airport Massacre—using machine guns and hand grenades, 3 terrorists from Japan kill 28 people as they get off plane from Paris at the Tel Aviv airport.

FRIDAY
MAY 31
Sun Rises 05:49
Sun Sets 20:27
Moon Rises 17:53
Moon Sets 04:02

MOON ENTERS SCORPIO 00:07
moon conj pluto-04:00.

Walt Whitman 1819
Norman Vincent Peale 1898
Prince Rainier 1923
Brooke Shields 1965
Fred Allen 1894
Edward Bennett Williams 1920
Johnny Paycheck 1941

1779: George Washington orders destruction of the Iroquois. 1913: Popular vote for U.S. Senators becomes law.

SATURDAY
JUNE 01
Sun Rises 05:49
Sun Sets 20:28
Moon Rises 19:10
Moon Sets 04:36

MOON IN SCORPIO
moon square jupiter-03:30. moon at perigee-06:00.
moon conj saturn-14:12.

Jacques Marquette 1637
Nelson Riddle 1921
Marilyn Monroe 1926
Reverend Ike 1935
Brigham Young 1801
Andy Griffith 1926
Christopher Lisch 1932
Ron Wood 1947

1868: James Buchanan, 15th Pres. of U.S., dies of rheumatic gout at age 77 years and 39 days (Lanchester, Penn.)—his last words were, "O Lord God Almighty, as Thou wilt." 1965: U.S. communities begin passing laws against latest and "dangerous" fad, the skateboard. 1968: Helen Keller, age 87, dies from stroke (Westport, Conn.)—Mark Twain considered her and Napolean to be the 2 most interesting people of 19th century.

SUNDAY
JUNE 02
Sun Rises 05:48
Sun Sets 20:29
Moon Rises 20:26
Moon Sets 05:15

MOON ENTERS SAGITTARIUS 00:33
moon at desc node-04:26. moon oppos mercury-10:29.
mercury at asc node-16:00. sun oppos moon-20:50.

FULL MOON 20:50

Marquis de Sade 1740
Hedda Hopper 1890
Marvin Hamlisch 1944
Thomas Hardy 1840
Stacy Keach 1941
Jerry Mathers 1948

1967: Beatles' "Sergeant Pepper's Lonely Hearts Club Band" released.

I can think of nothing more boring for the American people than to have to sit in their living rooms for a whole half an hour looking at my face on their television screens.
Dwight Eisenhower

MONDAY
JUNE 03
Sun Rises 05:48
Sun Sets 20:30
Moon Rises 21:39
Moon Sets 06:03

MOON IN SAGITTARIUS
moon conj uranus-02:43. moon oppos mars-19:39.
moon trine venus-22:22.

Jefferson Davis 1808
Milton Cato 1915
Allen Ginsberg 1926
Gordon Sinclair 1900
Paulette Goddard 1915
Hale Irwin 1945

1916: ROTC authorized. 1953: Billy Joe McAllister jumps off the Tallahatchee Bridge. 1980: Defense computer goofs—signals Soviet attack.

I have not lived as a woman. I have lived as a man. I've just done what I damn well wanted to and I've made enough money to support myself and I ain't afraid of being alone.
Katharine Hepburn

TUESDAY
JUNE 04
Sun Rises 05:47
Sun Sets 20:30
Moon Rises 22:43
Moon Sets 07:00

MOON ENTERS CAPRICORN 01:34
moon conj neptune-06:09. jupiter retrogrades-15:21.

Mitch Miller 1911
Howard Metzenbaum 1917
Bruce Dern 1936
Charles Collingwood 1917
Robert Merrill 1919
Freddy Fender 1937

1784: First flight by a woman—hot-air balloon (France). 1798: Casanova, legendary lover, dies (Bohemia). 1844: Last great auk dies. 1928: Lawsuit against U.S. Radium Corp. settled out of court with 5 women who were dying of radium poisoning. 1940: Allied evacuation from Dunkirk completed. 1963: Jimmy Hoffa indicted.

In trying to keep unnecessary expenditures down I believe the President ought to be as unsatisfied as a little boy's appetite.
Lyndon Johnson

FORECAST

BY NAN DE GROVE

GEMINI

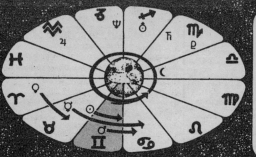

LONGITUDE OF THE PLANETS
19:43 PDT; 05/20/85

Sun *00°00′* Gemini
Moon *13°26′* Gemini
Mercury *11°23′* Taurus
Venus *16°42′* Aries
Mars *16°59′* Gemini
Jupiter *16°37′* Aquarius
Saturn *24°25′* Scorpio R
Ura *16°40′* Sagittarius R
Nept *03°05′* Capricorn R
Pluto *02°38′* Scorpio R

Jupiter's beneficient and visionary influence is a central motif as Gemini begins. A lively and felicitous grouping of Venus, Mars, Jupiter, and Uranus provides an exciting change of pace from last month's pattern of inertia. Old gripes and grudges can be dropped now since we are feeling generally magnanimous and eager to forget the past.

This is a time to be attentive and cautious when traveling (whether across the continent or across the street) and when handling explosives, electricity, or fire. Critical periods are May 20th-28th and June 2nd-8th, with emphasis on the Full Moon of June 2nd.

Some could become fanatical with these influences, taking it upon themselves to proclaim "truth" for everyone else. Self-will could masquerade as divine inspiration. This applies not only to the lunatic fringe (which will be quite visible this month), but to everyone—we could all be tempted to resort to mental coercion.

As Jupiter retrogrades on June 4th, the pace will slacken and we may find we have further inner work to do before we can realize the potentials we've glimpsed. On June 9th, Mars leaves Gemini and enters Cancer; if we were over-inflamed and zealous earlier, we're sure to feel burned-out now.

AIR SIGNS are vitalized, inspired, and communicative.

Gemini: Initiate a new cycle with high hopes and determination. An urge to break away from any restraint or commitment could result in loneliness later; give it enough thought.

Libra: you have benefits coming from many directions and an active social life. Avoid over-idealizing and suppressing feelings. A turning point comes around June 6th.

Aquarius: at the hub of interesting and innovative activities, you may welcome a slower pace around the 4th of June. Avoid scattering your energies.

EARTH SIGNS may be providing stability for their flightier friends and feeling somewhat flustered by the shifting winds of change.

Taurus: capitalize on new opportunities related to finances and prepare for a turning point the first week of June.

Virgo: you may have a crisis brewing involving work, homelife, and personal needs. Watch nerves and don't overcommit.

Capricorn: be prepared for a revelation of some kind around June 9th that could necessitate revising a relationship. Strong emotional undercurrents are operating; avoid defensiveness.

FIRE SIGNS are inflamed and may be igniting the passions of others. Try moderating energy to avoid burnout.

Aries: lucky in love, you may make important connections now. Communication skills and diplomacy are vital to maintaining popularity.

Leo: take advantage of creative and literary opportunities; you may connect socially with others who aid success.

Sagittarius: turning points arising in relationships will require some important decisions. Take it easy around Full Moon when nervous tension could erupt in anger. Avoid defensiveness and hasty judgments.

WATER SIGNS can easily get feelings hurt now by taking things too personally.

Cancer: you may feel especially sensitive and intuitive. Hidden feelings and motives will surface when energy changes dramatically around the 9th of June.

Scorpio: an opportunity to invest or merge with another is likely to increase mutual resources. A turning point in relationships comes around June 6th.

Pisces: avoid the tendency to become scattered and over-stressed; no need to over-react to challenges. An important decision regarding career or home life may be necessary now.

JUNE

WEDNESDAY   JUNE
05
Sun Rises 05:47
Sun Sets 20:31
Moon Rises 23:37
Moon Sets 08:04

MOON IN CAPRICORN

Federico Garcia-Lorca 1898	Alfred Kazin 1915
Bill Moyers 1934	Joe Clark 1939

1876: *Visitors to the Centennial Exposition at Philadelphia are delighted with the first bananas they have ever tasted—before this time bananas were rarely available in the U.S.* **1900:** *Stephen Crane, writer, dies of tuberculosis at age 28 (Badenweiler, Germany).* **1965:** *U.S. acknowledges for first time that American ground troops are engaging in combat in South Vietnam.* **1967:** *Ries Tijerina band takes over Tierra Amarilla County Court House (New Mexico).*

Politics is about how we ought to live. Television is politics. Literature is politics. You can't hermetically seal these things; that's the whole point. Life is a seamless web.
George Will

THURSDAY   JUNE
06
Sun Rises 05:47
Sun Sets 20:31
Moon Rises ----
Moon Sets 09:11

MOON ENTERS AQUARIUS 04:52
VENUS ENTERS TAURUS-01:52.
moon square venus-05:05. moon square pluto-08:53.
sun oppos uranus-11:50. mercury oppos uranus-22:34.

Beau Brummell 1778	Alexander Pushkin 1799
George Gurdjieff 1872	Thomas Mann 1875
David Scott 1932	Dalai Lama 1935

1932: *Federal tax on gasoline begins.* **1933:** *First "drive-in" (Camden, N.J.).* **1944:** *D-Day—Allied forces invade Europe.* **1965:** *Gemini 4 Astronaut Edward White makes America's first spacewalk.* **1966:** *James Meredith shot and wounded in Mississippi.* **1968:** *Robert Kennedy, U.S. Senator from New York, dies after hours of surgery at Good Samaritan Hospital, the victim of an assassination attack the day before in Hotel Ambassador (Los Angeles).*

COME BACK

FRIDAY   JUNE
07
Sun Rises 05:47
Sun Sets 20:32
Moon Rises 00:20
Moon Sets 10:19

MOON IN AQUARIUS
sun conj mercury-07:10. mercury trine jupiter-09:15.
sun trine moon-11:22. moon conj jupiter-11:24.
moon trine mercury-11:50. sun trine jupiter-11:57.
moon square saturn-22:53.

Paul Gauguin 1848	Jessica Tandy 1909
Gwendolyn Brooks 1917	Rocky Graziano 1922
Tom Jones 1940	Thurman Munson 1947

632: *Muhammad dies.* **1816:** *20 feet of snow fall on Dannville, Vt.* **1905:** *Norway and Sweden separated.* **1937:** *Jean Harlow dies from cholecystitis, (inflammation of gall bladder) at age 26 (Los Angeles)—her mother, a Christian Scientist, would not allow medical treatment, and infection that was out of control could not be treated by the time she was admitted to a hospital.* **1955:** *The $64,000 Question premieres on TV.* **1965:** *U.S. Supreme Court establishes birth control as constitutional right to privacy.* **1980:** *Henry Miller dies.*

SATURDAY   JUNE
08
Sun Rises 05:47
Sun Sets 20:32
Moon Rises 00:55
Moon Sets 11:24

MOON ENTERS PISCES 11:46
moon trine mars-10:53. venus oppos pluto-12:20.
moon trine pluto-16:01. venus trine neptune-22:38.

Giovanni Cassini 1625	Grant Lewi 1902
Robert Preston 1913	Byron White 1917
Nancy Sinatra 1940	Boz Scaggs 1944

1872: *One-cent postage authorized.* **1874:** *Cochise dies on Chirachahua Reservation.* **1947:** *Lassie first heard on radio.* **1967:** *USS Liberty, U.S. Navy ship, is attacked by Israeli torpedo boats and fighter planes in international waters north of Sinai Peninsula—34 U.S. sailors die. Israel apologized for attack, claiming it was accidental.* **1977:** *Gerald Ford shoots hole-in-one during a golf game.*

If I were a slicer, I'd be dead. So it's good to be a hooker.
Jan Stephenson

SUNDAY   JUNE
09
Sun Rises 05:46
Sun Sets 20:33
Moon Rises 01:24
Moon Sets 12:26

MOON IN PISCES
MARS ENTERS CANCER-03:41.
moon square uranus-18:21.

Marvin Kalb 1930	Jackie Wilson 1934

CHILDREN'S DAY

MONDAY   JUNE
10
Sun Rises 05:46
Sun Sets 20:34
Moon Rises 01:49
Moon Sets 13:25

MOON ENTERS ARIES 22:24
sun square moon-01:19. moon trine saturn-08:27.
moon square mercury-09:34.

LAST QUARTER MOON 01:19

Frederick Loewe 1904	Prince Philip 1921
Judy Garland 1922	Maurice Sendak 1928
James McDivitt 1929	F. Lee Bailey 1933

1791: *Canada Act—British divide Canada at Ottawa River.* **1893:** *Miss Fitzsimmons, kangaroo boxer, dies in Australia.* **1935:** *Former alcoholics form Alcoholics Anonymous (New York City).*

Most of the people who do well in golf do so because they're not emotional. They're boring people.
Jan Stephenson

Cat Signs

by Dr. Carrot

During the Great Depression, tramps and hobos developed a secret code for sharing information. This code — in the form of chalk marks on fences, gates, and doors — informed their transient colleagues of what to expect from households they frequented in search of charity.

These hobo signs were used to indicate the best place for free food, warn of an unpleasant reception, or signify the possibility of part-time work. This shorthand of the road was a useful tool and helped many a homeless soul find solace and sustenance.

Unfortunately, as is often the case with useful things, this coding system has developed a new and sinister use with the passage of time...a use that has dangerous implications for every home in America.

The problem? Millions of cats living in this country have developed their own code, based on the original hobo signs. Passed from ear to ear in midnight alley rendezvous, this new cat code is now known in every major city from coast to coast. Cats everywhere in the U.S. are using it to infiltrate homes without cats. Their goal: the felinization of every household in America.

If you, like many other concerned citizens, fear for the safety and freedom of your home, it is not too late to act. Check every outside surface of each building on your property for telltale marks. These marks are difficult to recognize, as they are only cat-height above the ground, and may appear to be random scratches on the surfaces of doors, sashes, fence posts, or bird baths. Do not confuse these deliberate cat markings with sloppy, illiterate dog scratches.

Once located, evidence of feline undercover activity can be altered to confuse other cats. Just add marks that indicate undesirable conditions; this will discourage all but the most persistent tabby. Any sharp instrument can be used for this purpose, including the tines of a fork, or a pocket knife. Good luck!

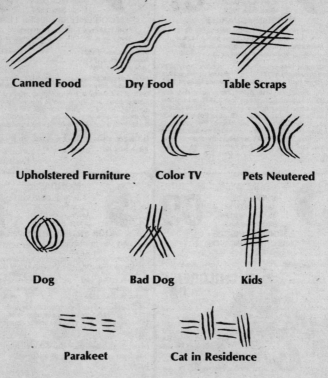

Canned Food   **Dry Food**   **Table Scraps**

Upholstered Furniture   **Color TV**   **Pets Neutered**

Dog   **Bad Dog**   **Kids**

Parakeet   **Cat in Residence**

JUNE

TUESDAY   JUNE 11
Sun Rises 05:46
Sun Sets 20:34
Moon Rises 02:12
Moon Sets 14:23

MOON IN ARIES
moon square mars-00:55. moon square neptune-03:34.

Ben Jonson 1572   Jeannette Rankin 1880
Anandamayima 1896   Lawrence Spivak 1900
Richard Loeb 1906   William Styron 1925

1825: Daniel Tompkins, former Vice Pres., dies—he had written that he suffered from "toilsome days, sleepless nights, anxious cares, domestic bereavements, impaired constitution, debilitated body, unjust abuse and censure, and accumulated pecuniary embarrassments." **1912:** First airplane to take off from a hotel roof—Multnomah Hotel (Portland, Ore). **1965:** Queen Elizabeth names Beatles to Order of the British Empire.

And in the end the love you take is equal to the love you make.

The Beatles

WEDNESDAY   JUNE 12
Sun Rises 05:46
Sun Sets 20:34
Moon Rises 02:34
Moon Sets 15:20

MOON IN ARIES
moon trine uranus-06:12. mars trine pluto-09:46.
mars oppos neptune-22:40.

David Rockefeller 1915   Ivan Tors 1916
George Bush 1924   Vic Damone 1928
Jim Nabors 1932   Chick Corea 1941

1849: Gas mask patented. **1939:** Baseball Hall of Fame dedicated (Cooperstown, N.Y.). **1965:** 300 civil rights marchers arrested in Chicago. **1975:** Indira Ghandhi found guilty of corruption in 1971 elections (India). **1979:** First man-powered flight across English Channel—the **Gossamer Condor. 1982:** Biggest disarmament rally in U.S. history (Central Park, New York City).

It's living in America that does it. Manly, at all times. Can't read poetry or play in a string quartet.

Randy Newman

THURSDAY   JUNE 13
Sun Rises 05:46
Sun Sets 20:34
Moon Rises 02:57
Moon Sets 16:17

MOON ENTERS TAURUS 11:11
moon at apogee-07:00.
MERCURY ENTERS CANCER-09:11.
moon oppos pluto--15:34. moon trine neptune-16:17.

William Butler Yeats 1865   Red Grange 1903
Ralph Edwards 1913   Paul Lynde 1926

1948: Babe Ruth gives farewell speech (Yankee Stadium). **1965:** Jewish philosopher Martin Buber, 87, dies in Jerusalem. **1971:** New York Times begins publishing "The Pentagon Papers." **1980:** Rep. John Jenrette indicted by Federal Grand Jury for bribery and conspiracy.

The whole idea of manhood in America is pitiful, a little like having to wear an ill-fitting coat for one's entire life.

Paul Theroux

FRIDAY   JUNE 14
Sun Rises 05:46
Sun Sets 20:34
Moon Rises 03:21
Moon Sets 17:16

MOON IN TAURUS
moon conj venus-02:30. mercury trine pluto-09:29.
mercury oppos neptune-13:26. moon square jupiter-21:16.

Harriet Beecher Stowe 1811   Burl Ives 1909
Lash La Rue 1917   Dorothy McGuire 1918
Pierre Salinger 1925   Che Guevara 1928
Jerzy Kosinski 1933   Eric Heiden 1958

1801: Benedict Arnold, traitor, dies (London, England). **1846:** Republic of California flag first raised (Sonoma).

In the march up the heights of fame there comes a spot close to the summit in which man reads nothing but detective stories.

Heywood Hale Broun

SATURDAY   JUNE 15
Sun Rises 05:46
Sun Sets 20:34
Moon Rises 03:49
Moon Sets 18:16

MOON ENTERS GEMINI 23:45
mercury conj mars-08:18. moon oppos saturn-09:09.
moon at asc node-23:16.

Herbert Simon 1916   Erroll Garner 1921
Morris Udall 1922   Mario Cuomo 1932
Waylon Jennings 1937   Harry Nilsson 1941

1215: Magna Carta signed. **1752:** Ben Franklin flies his kite in a thunderstorm. **1844:** Charles Goodyear patents vulcanized rubber. **1849:** James Knox Polk, 11th Pres. of U.S., dies at age 53 years and 225 days (Nashville, Tenn.)—diarrhea was cause of death. **1867:** First gallstone removed by surgery. **1877:** First black to graduate from West Point. **1965:** Folk singer Bob Dylan records "Like A Rolling Stone," his first "electric" recording.

I'm only human, and to be human is to be violent.

Archie Bunker

SUNDAY   JUNE 16
Sun Rises 05:46
Sun Sets 20:35
Moon Rises 04:20
Moon Sets 19:17

MOON IN GEMINI

Nelson Doubleday 1889   Jack Albertson 1910
Erich Segal 1937   Joyce Carol Oates 1938
Joan Van Ark 1943   Ron Leflore 1952

FATHER'S DAY

Bird Brains by Bob Conrow

If you have seen the kingfisher, perched like a lone sentinel beside a stream or pond, you may appreciate a tale passed down from olden times in England. The kingfisher, so the story goes, was once a most ordinary bird, dressed in drabbest gray from wingtip to wingtip. Noah understandably sympathized with the kingfisher's plight, and gave it an equal berth with the other creatures upon the ark.

One day, when the weather was particularly clear, Noah brought this pitiful creature topside for a breath of fresh air. In a wink — and without so much as a "thank you" — the kingfisher circled high up into the heavens until its wings became tinged with the delicate hues of clouds and sky. And then, soaring even higher, it touched the sun, which scorched the bird's breast to a bright, rusty, orange.

When the kingfisher plummeted back to earth, Noah no longer took pity on it. Forbidden to return aboard ship, the kingfisher was forced forevermore to perch outside and seek its own food from the waters.

According to some theories, birds' brains might be bigger today were it not for the flyaway nature of birds like the kingfisher. Unique among all the animals, birds were given the freedom of flight. Had they not had it so easy, had they not flown away from disagreeable situations, they might very well have developed an entirely different mental apparatus.

As Harold E. Burtt puts it in The Psychology of Birds, "If winged vertebrates can fly away from the problem instead of facing it and still survive, evolution has less of a chance. Perhaps" adds Burtt, "we should be grateful that our ancestors did not have wings."

What Burtt is alluding to is the fact that humans more than doubled their brain capacities when they emerged from sheltering forests to do battle with saber-toothed tigers, lions, and other temperamental beasts. Birds, by contrast, have kept to a relatively simple life requiring little mental clout. While the brain of a small perching bird may be ten times larger than that of similarly sized lizard, it is significantly smaller than that of a comparably sized carnivore or primate.

Despite their obvious limitations on a pound-for-pound brain basis, birds have nonetheless managed to fly circles around man since the time of Noah. What birds have in their compact craniums that we do not have, is a kind of intricate "trip-tik," complete with travel advice on how to navigate by using sun and stars, barometric pressure, and even the low-frequency sounds given off by the earth.

The tiny blackpoll warbler, for example, flies 2,000 nonstop miles from the coniferous forests of North America to the tropics of Latin America. What's more, it knows precisely which days to schedule for departures.

During the six years that New England biologists Timothy and Janet Williams have been watching warblers and other songbirds take off on their southbound flights, only two departures (out of a total of ninety-three) have headed into severe storm fronts. Even when the storms are far out to sea, the birds instinctively know when it's best to lay over.

Their success rate as well as their remarkable recall is attested to in a story told by J.M. Harvey of Jamaica. By offering a tempting morning-after breakfast of scrambled egg, Mr. Harvey was able to play host to the same banded warbler for seven consecutive winters.

While some might fault these birds for allowing their appetites to dictate their memories, such excesses may be excusable considering the circumstances. By flying without food or rest for three-and-a-half days (or longer), the endurance of these lighter-than-an-ounce creatures can be compared to that of a man running the four minute mile — for eighty hours straight!

Besides, birds (like people) are individuals, and it's a gross underestimation to figure that every bird's brain is in its belly. Alex, the talking parrot at Purdue University, provides a celebrated case in point. For the past six years, Alex has been learning complex communication skills — including identification of more than fifty objects — and in the process qualifying himself as fair competition with the best of chimps and dolphins.

What's most remarkable about Alex, however, is not what he has learned, but how he has learned it. Most trained animals learn their responses by being fed. Alex has learned mainly by watching others and imitating their behavior.

Despite Alex's unusual accomplishments,

JUNE

MONDAY   JUNE 17

Sun Rises 05:47
Sun Sets 20:35
Moon Rises 04:58
Moon Sets 20:18

MOON IN GEMINI

moon oppos uranus-06:26. moon trine jupiter-08:41.

John Wesley 1703   **Ralph Bellamy 1904**
Red Foley 1910   **Dean Martin 1917**

1950: First kidney transplant. **1965:** For first time, U.S. engages B-52 bombers in Vietnam War.

TUESDAY   JUNE 18

Sun Rises 05:47
Sun Sets 20:35
Moon Rises 05:43
Moon Sets 21:16

MOON ENTERS CANCER 10:22

sun conj moon-04:58. moon trine pluto-13:20.
moon oppos neptune-14:54. moon conj mars-22:45.

NEW MOON 04:58

Igor Stravinsky 1882   **Jeanette MacDonald 1901**
E.G. Marshall 1910   **Sylvia Porter 1913**
Richard Boone 1916   **Paul McCartney 1942**

1777: Stars and Stripes becomes official U.S. flag. **1898:** Steel Pier opens (Atlantic City, N.J.). **1965:** Nguyen Cao Ky becomes president of South Vietnam. **1975:** Prince Museid beheaded for assassination of King Faisal (Saudia Arabia). **1983:** Sally Ride becomes first woman U.S. astronaut.

Immobility is corruption, the lack of courage to move on.

Sting

WEDNESDAY   JUNE 19

Sun Rises 05:47
Sun Sets 20:36
Moon Rises 06:36
Moon Sets 22:09

MOON IN CANCER

moon conj mercury-09:36.

Duchess Of Windsor 1896   **Guy Lombardo 1902**
Lou Gehrig 1903   **Louis Jourdan 1921**
Nancy Marchand 1928   **Pier Angeli 1932**
Gena Rowlands 1936   **Malcolm McDowell 1943**

1924: Filibuster in the Rhode Island Senate is broken by explosion of gas bomb. **1934:** FCC established. **1964:** U.S. Civil Rights Bill passes after longest debate in history of U.S. Senate. **1965:** Algerian coup ousts president Ben Bella. **1972:** Hurricane Agnes comes ashore in Florida, beginning 10-day excursion along Atlantic coast, killing 118 people.

Respect the children of the poor—from them come most poets.

Mendele Mocher Sforim

THURSDAY   JUNE 20

Sun Rises 05:47
Sun Sets 20:36
Moon Rises 07:36
Moon Sets 22:55

MOON ENTERS LEO 18:32

moon trine saturn-04:35. moon square pluto-22:17.

Lillian Hellman 1905   **Errol Flynn 1909**
Audie Murphy 1924   **Mariette Hartley 1940**
Anne Murray 1946   **Cynthia Berenson 1947**

1834: Bureau of Indian Affairs established. **1910:** Krazy Kat debuts in comics. **1947:** "Bugsy" Siegel, gangster, dies from 3 rifle shots to head while sitting in living room of mansion (Beverly Hills, Calif.). **1948:** First Ed Sullivan Show broadcast on TV. **1963:** U.S. and U.S.S.R. agree on plans for hot line.

CHA CHA

You don't have to suffer to be a poet. Adolescence is enough suffering for anyone.

John Ciardi

BIRD BRAINS continued

we may discover in the long run that we've been using the wrong word to describe his behavior. What we recognize and test as "intelligence" in animals, is often limited to the ways these creatures respond on our terms. Some researchers are now coming to believe that a better criterion might be "adaptability." In other words, if an animal survives, it is intelligent. And here, man will prove no exception.

In terms of the adaptability model, birds just may be the most successful animals ever to have landed upon the surface of the earth. Many creatures have come and gone, the victims of volcanoes, earthquakes, and perhaps even Biblical floods.

Birds, on the other hand, have prevailed. Bird fossils predate human fossils by over 100 million years. That kingfisher who left the ark was no dumb bird.

THE BICYCLE

A Tale Of Two Wheels

Bob Conrow

Exactly one hundred years ago, in 1885, a daring young man on a rather flimsy contraption pedaled his way into the annals of bicycle history. Thomas Stevens, the "bicycle explorer," bravely wheeled his way through distant lands, meeting with bone-chilling cold, desert heat, and wild animals.

By the time Stevens arrived by ship in San Francisco, on January 4, 1887, he would be hailed as the "first ever" to circle the globe on a bicycle. All told, Stevens logged 13,500 miles of wheeled travel, including visits that took him first across the United States to New York, then by ship to Europe, and finally on to Persia, China, and Japan. He completed the last lap of his journey, from Yokohama to San Francisco, on the *City of Peking*.

During Stevens' absence from America, bicycle design changed drastically. By the time of his return, Stevens' **Ordinary-style** (the manufacturer's name) bicycle would not seem either very ordinary or, for that matter, very practical.

To begin with, the **Ordinary**, with its immense front wheel and its miniaturized rear wheel, was a frustrating slow poke; the large driving wheel turned only once for each evolution of the pedals. Moreover, it was admittedly hazardous, even for such stalwarts as Stevens. Mounting was nearly impossible, but that was just the first half of it. Once one was successfully launched — seated precariously atop the highest wheel — there was always the problem of getting down!

By 1885, **Dwarf Ordinaries** competed with **Xtraordinaries** and something called the **Facile** contended with the **Kangaroo**. All of them claimed to be superior to the "ordinary" **Ordinary**. However, one particular design stood out. "Many novelties are again introduced," commented a visitor to the Stanley Bicycle Show in February 1885, "but the most observable specialty is the **safety** bicycle." Included among the **safety** features in 1885, were wheels of comparatively equal size, a chain for added pumping power, and a new triangular frame that indicated the potential for deleting the top bar altogether.

By 1888, a veterinary surgeon by the name of John Boyd Dunlop, patented the first pneumatic tire and started the wheels rolling for what might be termed the **modern day** bicycle.

By this time, however, it was not just the gents who were bicycling. In September 1893, an event occurred in England that shook the very girders of genteel society. A 16-year-old girl by the name of Miss Tessie Reynolds, dared to pedal forth on a most unthinkable adventure.

Wearing a "rational" dress (patterned after bloomers), Miss Reynolds not only rode, she *raced* a man's bicycle from Brighton to London and back again. In just eight and a half hours, she had travelled almost 120 miles and, in the process, managed to become a cause celebre not only for rational dress, but for women's emancipation as well.

Women had begun to push for voting privileges and minor dress reforms prior to the Nineties — they had even ridden bicycles — but most respectable citizens of both sexes uniformly opposed rational dress and women's racing. A correspondent who signed her letter G. Lacy Hillier, however, spoke up on Miss Reynolds' behalf: "Why should the weaker sex be handicapped with the skirt? If practical female dress reform originates with cyclists, I for one shall be delighted."

In the long run, the correspondent would have just cause for elation. By the turn of the century, bicycles had moved to the side of the road to make way for automobiles, but the **safety** bicycle (and the implied mobility that went with it) had aptly served as a liberating force more powerful than any invention before or since.

The lowly bicycle has made its way briefly and bravely across the frontiers of human imagination. During the peak of the "Great American Bicycle Craze," between 1890 and 1896, Americans spent more than $100 million on the two-wheeled machines and, in the process, gained an undreamed-of freedom.

Although a full century has now passed since the time when Stevens was merrily rolling his way around the world, there is ample indication that the humble bicycle never did lose either its momentum or its mettle.

During the past decade, transportation analysts were astounded to discover that bicycles outsold automobiles by more than a million units. All of which goes to show that in times of uncertainty, the ever-efficient bicycle stands ready and able to give people a fair ride for their money.

JUNE

CANCER

June 21 — July 21

FRIDAY   JUNE 21

Sun Rises 05:47
Sun Sets 20:36
Moon Rises 08:41
Moon Sets 23:34

MOON IN LEO

moon square venus-22:17. moon trine uranus-22:26.

Sun Enters Cancer 03:44
SUMMER SOLSTICE

Ben Johnson 1572
Al Hirschfeld 1903
Judy Holliday 1921
Francoise Sagan 1935
Meredith Baxter Birney 1947
Rockwell Kent 1882
Jean-Paul Sarte 1905
Maureen Stapleton 1925
Ray Davies 1944
Prince William 1982

1960: *Chinese-Russian ideological split.* **1965:** *The Charlatans, very first "San Francisco rock band" play their first gig (Red Dog Saloon, Virginia City, Nev.).* **1982:** *Would-be Presidential assassin, John Hinckley Jr., found innocent by reason of insanity.*

SATURDAY   JUNE 22

Sun Rises 05:48
Sun Sets 20:36
Moon Rises 09:49
Moon Sets ----

MOON IN LEO

moon oppos jupiter-00:27. moon square saturn-10:54.

Rider Haggard 1856
Billy Wilder 1906
Dianne Feinstein 1933
Pete Maravich 1948
Lindsey Wagner 1949
Julian Huxley 1887
Joseph Papp 1921
Ed Bradley 1941
Meryl Streep 1949
Freddie Prinze 1954

1611: *Crew of Henry Hudson's ship mutiny, set Henry and son adrift.* **1797:** *First New York City bank opens.* **1940:** *France surrenders to Germany.* **1964:** *Supreme Court rules **Tropic of Cancer** not obscene.* **1965:** *Demonstrators clash with police in Tokyo and Seoul—protests are result of signing by 2 governments of their first treaty since 1910... 593 arrested.* **1969:** *Judy Garland, actress, dies at age 47 (London).*

He who does not enjoy his own company is usually right.

Coco Chanel

SUNDAY   JUNE 23

Sun Rises 05:48
Sun Sets 20:36
Moon Rises 10:58
Moon Sets 00:09

MOON ENTERS VIRGO 00:32

venus square jupiter-01:26. moon trine neptune-04:31.
sun trine pluto-06:43. moon oppos neptune-12:08.

Jakob Boehme 1575
Duke Of Windsor 1894
Irene Worth 1916
Empress Josephine 1763
Jean Anouilh 1910
Richard Bach 1936

1868: *Typewriter patented.* **1938:** *Marineland opens in Florida.* **1944:** *FDR delivers last Fireside Chat.* **1973:** *Last person drafted by Armed Forces under Selective Service Act.*

You think a concern for correct spelling is for sissies? You think haranguing pundits and fearsome lawyers overlook the niceties of orthography?...Tough guys care about spelling.

William Safire

MONDAY   JUNE 24

Sun Rises 05:49
Sun Sets 20:37
Moon Rises 12:06
Moon Sets 00:39

MOON IN VIRGO

moon square uranus-03:21. moon trine venus-07:34.
mercury trine saturn-19:17.

Henry Ward Beecher 1813
Norman Cousins 1912
Billy Casper 1931
Michele Lee 1942
Chief Dan George 1899
John Ciardi 1916
Pete Hamill 1935
Mick Fleetwood 1947

1497: *Cabot discovers Canada.* **1647:** *Margaret Brent seeks vote and voice in Maryland Assembly.* **1948:** *Berlin blockade begins.* **1964:** *FTC rules that "Cigarette smoking can be injurious to health" must be printed on cigarette packages.* **1965:** *Saigon government breaks diplomatic relations with France.*

We are all in some measure the creatures of organization and its constraints.

John Kenneth Galbraith

GROWING
BY LIZ CAILE

NOW'S THE TIME — If there's a crux in the gardening year, this is it. Garden plants need a lot of protection against heat and drought; chewing and sucking insects, attuned to the plants' budding maturity, begin to proliferate. Thinning and harvesting are important to keep fruits and vegetables bearing and healthy through the season. **Midwest, Southeast, South, Southwest:** Tomatoes should be mulched heavily, nurtured through hot spells — they will not set fruit if night temperatures stay at 75° F., but will return to production in cooler periods. Cayenne pepper, hot sauces, diluted and sprayed help protect against insects. Search and destroy tomato hornworms, which look as though they many have come from a Lewis Carroll book. **Northeast:** Begin snap bean harvest when pods are ripe; don't pick when plants are wet to avoid spreading rust fungus from plant to plant. **Northwest:** Plant green manures, clovers and grasses, where early veggies have been harvested. Begin planting leeks, kale, parsnips for autumn feasts; plant onion seeds for next year's sets. Kale will flourish and be sweetened by fall's frosts. **Mountain States:** In milder parts of this region, cherries and apricots will be ready for picking. Apricots on outside and top of tree ripen first. Fruit is ripe when: flesh separates from seed, and skin is golden; flesh is light yellow-green.

Water

An average of 30 inches of rain per year falls on the United States, but half the country is, climatically speaking, arid or semi-arid. Of the total U.S. rainfall, two-thirds occurs in the eastern third of the country.

All growing plants use a large amount of water in the **transpiration** process. One ploy of water engineers is to poison willows and other creekside plants in hopes of making more water available for human use. The process of transpiration, of course, puts oxygen into the air and moisture that will eventually create precipitation somewhere else. The result of decimating the great moisture-breathing rainforests in Africa and South America is droughts in adjacent areas. **For every pound of lettuce, about 400 pounds of water have been used in its growth. A corn plant transpires about ten c r 15 gallons of water per day. Mature crops of corn or tomatoes require from 12 to 24 inches of total rainfall and/or irrigation during the growing season. In warm summer weather, a vegetable garden uses about one-fourth inch, or more, of soil water per day. Much more soil water is lost through transpiration than soil evaporation.**

Conserving Water

Well prepared soil is the first defense against drought. If organic material is incorporated and the soil is well aerated to deep levels, top levels of the soil may dry out while the lower levels still provide nutrients in solution.

Thick mulches add a moderating factor to soil moisture. Mulches can be used in container gardening effectively, where water is lost through evaporation more readily than from the insulated ground. Potatoes, cantaloupe and tomatoes want an even moisture condition rather than lots of watering, and are particularly benefitted by mulches.

Plants exposed to direct sunlight lose water through transpiration much more rapidly, so transpiration and water use can be slowed by providing sun shades. These can be small, individual shades, such as a board or cardboard placed to shade plants, or continuous screens of lathe protecting beds or rows. Snow fence could be supported horizontally or vertically to create a sunscreen.

If drought is expected, why not make crop and landscaping choices with this in mind. Plants native to arid climates have natural defenses against heat and low rainfall.

Deep rooted tepary beans or Hopi watermelon, prickly pear cactus and carob trees can be planted. Jerusalem artichokes and sunflowers are derived from arid regions.

Watering Techniques

●Water deeply and not too frequently. Except for transplants and germinating seed beds, allow top soil (four to eight inches) to dry out before applying more water. Encourage deep root systems.

●If possible, use a furrow system of watering or a canvas soaker or perforated hose to direct water into soil. Overhead sprinkling can contribute to disease: downy mildew on mustard family greens; anthracnose (fungal spots) on melon and squash leaves; white mold on bean pods; fungal blight or bacterial blight on bean leaves.

●Water containers and elsewhere, when possible, with lukewarm water, so as not to cool soil drastically.

●Try dilute manure or compost tea when watering small plots or individual plants; make nutrients available in solvent.

●You can use grey water — soapy household waste water — in some cases, but not on acid loving plants, as it is alkaline. Don't dose blackberries, blueberries, potatoes, eggplant, melons, parsnips, or winter squash with suds. Provide good drainage to soils when you are using grey water.

TUESDAY — JUNE 25

Sun Rises 05:49
Sun Sets 20:37
Moon Rises 13:14
Moon Sets 01:07

MOON ENTERS LIBRA 04:47

moon square neptune-08:32. sun square moon-11:53.
moon square mars-23:51.

FIRST QUARTER MOON 11:53

George Orwell 1903
Willis Reed 1942
June Lockhart 1925
Phyllis George 1949

1868: 8-hr. day authorized for government workers. **1876:** Battle of Little Bighorn—Gen. George Armstrong Custer and 211 U.S. soldiers are killed by Indians from various tribes led by Sitting Bull. **1950:** Korean War begins. **1962:** Supreme Court rules prayer in public school unconstitutional. **1965:** Vietcong bomb Saigon cafe killing 29 and wounding 100. **1965:** Vietcong execute American serviceman Sgt. Harold Bennet. **1965:** U.S. military transport plane crashes in Calif., killing all 84 servicemen aboard.

WEDNESDAY — JUNE 26

Sun Rises 05:49
Sun Sets 20:37
Moon Rises 14:24
Moon Sets 01:34

MOON IN LIBRA

moon trine jupiter-08:26.

Abner Doubleday 1819
Colonel Tom Parker 1910
John Tunney 1934
Pearl Buck 1892
Colin Wilson 1931
Anna Moffo 1935

THURSDAY — JUNE 27

Sun Rises 05:50
Sun Sets 20:37
Moon Rises 15:35
Moon Sets 02:32

MOON ENTERS SCORPIO 07:37

moon square mercury-00:55. moon conj pluto-10:57.
sun trine moon-18:08.

Helen Keller 1880
Captain Kangaroo 1927

1787: Edward Gibbon finishes writing **The Decline and Fall of the Roman Empire. 1844:** Joseph Smith and Hyrum Smith, Mormon leaders, shot to death by mob which broke into jail in Carthage, Ill., where the Smiths were being held on charges of arson, treason, and polygamy. **1950:** 35 U.S. military advisors go to South Vietnam. **1963:** Him and Her, LBJ's beagles, born.

My idea of shows with animals is that they must always be done with the consent of the animals themselves.

Doctor Doolittle

FRIDAY — JUNE 28

Sun Rises 05:50
Sun Sets 20:37
Moon Rises 16:49
Moon Sets 02:33

MOON IN SCORPIO

moon trine mars-04:40. moon square jupiter-10:25. venus oppos saturn-12:20. moon conj saturn-20:18. moon oppos venus-20:56.

Richard Rogers 1902
Eric Ambler 1909
Dave Kopay 1942
Ashley Montagu 1905
Mel Brooks 1926
Gilda Radner 1946

1836: James Madison, 4th Pres. of U.S., dies at age 85 years and 104 days from debility—his last words were, "I always talk better lying down." **1905:** Battleship **Potemkin** taken over by crew in mutiny. **1965:** 437 Univ. of Calif. Berkeley students from Free Speech Movement sit-in of Dec. 1964, convicted of tresspassing and resisting arrest—Mario Savio is sentenced to 4 months in jail. **1968:** A man is killed after falling out the door of DC-3 airplane as it flies at 8,000 feet over southwest Missouri—he did not have a parachute.

SATURDAY — JUNE 29

Sun Rises 05:50
Sun Sets 20:37
Moon Rises 18:04
Moon Sets 03:09

MOON ENTERS SAGITTARIUS 09:30

moon at perigee-02:00. moon trine mercury-09:08.
moon at desc node-12:19.
MERCURY ENTERS LEO 12:34.

William Mayo 1861
Nelson Eddy 1901
Harmon Killebrew 1936
Antoine de Saint-Exupery 1900
Odessa Komer 1925
Stokely Carmichael 1941

1904: Prohibition Party holds national convention, nominates Silas Swallow for president. **1965:** For first time, American troops abandon defensive posture and enter jungles of South Vietnam in pursuit of Vietcong.

It is time to discard the fiction that in a country of 200 million people, everyone is qualified to quarterback the government.

Spiro Agnew

SUNDAY — JUNE 30

Sun Rises 05:50
Sun Sets 20:37
Moon Rises 19:17
Moon Sets 03:52

MOON IN SAGITTARIUS

moon conj uranus-10:26. mercury square pluto-19:15.

Lena Horne 1917
Dave Van Ronk 1936
Susan Hayward 1919
Nancy Dussault 1936

1864: Govt. levies tax on cigarettes. **1892:** "Shower of frogs" recorded in England. **1899:** "Mile-a-minute" Murphy reaches 60 mph on bicycle. **1933:** Fatty Arbuckle, actor and director, dies of heart attack in hotel bed (New York City). **1980:** Synthetic Fuel Bill signed by President Carter.

A lot of people are so concerned about endangered species. They seem to forget there are a lot of neurotic cats and dogs around.

Koo Stark

CELESTIAL EVENTS

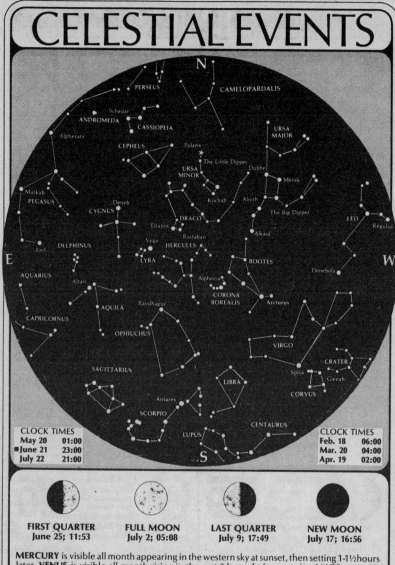

N

PERSEUS   CAMELOPARDALIS

Schedar
ANDROMEDA   CASSIOPEIA

Alpheratz   CEPHEUS   Polaris   URSA MAJOR

The Little Dipper   Dubhe

URSA MINOR   Merak

Markab   Kochab   Alioth   The Big Dipper
PEGASUS   Deneb

CYGNUS   DRACO   LEO
Eltanin   Regulus

Enif   Vega   Rastaban   Alkaid
DELPHINUS   HERCULES

E   LYRA   BOOTES   W

AQUARIUS   Alphecca   Denebola
Altair

AQUILA   Rasslhague   CORONA BOREALIS   Arcturus

CAPRICORNUS   OPHIUCHUS

VIRGO
CRATER

SAGITTARIUS   Spica   Gienah

LIBRA   CORVUS

Antares
SCORPIO   CENTAURUS

LUPUS

S

CLOCK TIMES	
May 20	01:00
■June 21	23:00
July 22	21:00

CLOCK TIMES	
Feb. 18	06:00
Mar. 20	04:00
Apr. 19	02:00

FIRST QUARTER
June 25; 11:53

FULL MOON
July 2; 05:08

LAST QUARTER
July 9; 17:49

NEW MOON
July 17; 16:56

MERCURY is visible all month appearing in the western sky at sunset, then setting 1-1½hours later. **VENUS** is visible all month rising in the east 3 hours before sunrise. **MARS** comes to conjunction July 17 and is too close to the sun all month for viewing. **JUPITER** is visible all month rising in the east just after sunset then fading in the western sky with morning twilight. **SATURN** is visible all month appearing in the eastern sky at sunset, then setting in the west 2-3 hours before sunrise. **June 21:** SUMMER SOLSTICE, first day of Summer. **June 25:** Mercury 5° S. of *Pollux* (evening sky). **June 28:** Saturn 3° N. of waxing gibbous Moon (night sky). **July 04:** Jupiter 5° N. of waning gibbous Moon (night sky). **July 05:** EARTH AT APHELION. **July 13:** Mercury at gr. elong. E.(27°). **July 14:** Venus 5° S. of waning crescent Moon (morning sky). **July 15:** Venus 3° N. of *Aldebaran* (morning sky). **July 19:** Mercury 7° S. of waxing crescent Moon (evening sky).

JULY

MONDAY   JULY 01

Sun Rises 05:50
Sun Sets 20:37
Moon Rises 20:25
Moon Sets 04:43

MOON ENTERS CAPRICORN 11:22
moon conj neptune-14:46.

George Sand 1804   Charles Laughton 1899
Olivia De Havilland 1916   Jean Stafford 1918
Leslie Caron 1931   Jamie Farr 1934
Jean Marsh 1934   Karen Black 1942
Deborah Harry 1946   Dan Aykroyd 1952

1546: Martin Luther, religious reformer, dies (Germany).
1867: Canadian confederation formed. **1896:** Harriet
Beecher Stowe, writer, dies (Hartford, Conn.). **1962:** Algeria
votes for independence from France. **1968:** Nuclear non-
proliferation treaty signed (Washington, D.C.). **1980:** C.P.
Snow dies.

God gave us kittens to teach us how to pity.
Jack Kerouac

DOMINION DAY

TUESDAY   JULY 02

Sun Rises 05:51
Sun Sets 20:37
Moon Rises 21:24,
Moon Sets 05:44

MOON IN CAPRICORN
sun oppos moon-05:08. moon oppos mars-13:32.

FULL MOON 05:08

Hermann Hesse 1877   Rene Lacoste 1905
Thurgood Marshall 1908   Cheryl Ladd 1951

1566: Nostradamus dies. **1961:** Ernest Hemingway, writer,
dies at his home (Ketchum, Idaho), the victim of a self-
inflicted bullet wound. **1964:** Civil Rights Act passes. **1967:**
Thurgood Marshall becomes first black U.S. Supreme Court
Justice. **1976:** North and South Vietnam officially reunited
with Hanoi as the capitol. **1977:** Vladimir Nabokov dies.

**A touch of art may nourish the soul, but a
good laugh always aids the digestion.**
Rube Goldberg

WEDNESDAY   JULY 03

Sun Rises 05:51
Sun Sets 20:37
Moon Rises 22:12
Moon Sets 06:51

MOON ENTERS AQUARIUS 14:46
moon trine venus-09:41. moon square pluto-18:00.

Franz Kafka 1883   Dorothy Kilgallen 1913
Tom Stoppard 1937   Geraldo Rivera 1943
Walt Garrison 1944   Jean Claude Duvalier 1951

1964: Lester Maddox chases 3 blacks from his restaurant
with ax handle. **1969:** Brian Jones, a founder of the Rolling
Stones, dies at age 25 in Cheltenham, England—he drowned
while swimming alone and under influence of drugs and
alcohol. **1971:** Jim Morrison, singer and composer with the
Doors, dies at age 28, in bathtub of room in Paris—death
attributed to heart failure, with popular speculation that an
overdose of heroin was involved.

**I never desire to converse with a man who
has written more than he has read.**
Samuel Johnson

THURSDAY   JULY 04

Sun Rises 05:52
Sun Sets 20:37
Moon Rises 22:51
Moon Sets 07:59

MOON IN AQUARIUS
moon oppos mercury-02:27. moon conj jupiter-18:13.

Nathaniel Hawthorne 1804   Gertrude Lawrence 1898
Louis Armstrong 1900   Lionel Trilling 1905
Tokyo Rose 1916   Eva Marie Saint 1924
Neil Simon 1927   Gina Lollobrigida 1927

1826: John Adams, 2nd Pres. of U.S., dies at age 90 years and
247 days of debility—his last words were "Independence
forever."**1826:** Thomas Jefferson, 3rd Pres. of U.S. dies at age
83 years and 82 days, of diarrhea—his last words were, "I
resign my spirit to God, my daughter to my country." **1831:**
James Monroe, 5th Pres. of U.S., dies of debility at age 73
years and 67 days (New York City). **1845:** Henry David
Thoreau moves to Walden Pond.

INDEPENDENCE DAY

FRIDAY   JULY 05

Sun Rises 05:52
Sun Sets 20:37
Moon Rises 23:23
Moon Sets 09:07

MOON ENTERS PISCES 20:40
moon square saturn-05:32. moon square venus-20:16.

Henry Cabot Lodge, Jr. 1902   Warren Oates 1928
Grant Devine 1944   Robbie Robertson 1944

SATURDAY   JULY 06

Sun Rises 05:52
Sun Sets 20:37
Moon Rises 23:50
Moon Sets 10:12

MOON IN PISCES
moon trine pluto-00:17.
VENUS ENTERS GEMINI-01:01.

Maximilian 1832   Laverne Andrews 1915
Nancy Reagan 1921   Merv Griffin 1925
Janet Leigh 1927   Della Reese 1932
Ned Beatty 1937   Sylvester Stallone 1946

1893: Guy de Maupassant, writer, dies at age 42 from
advanced case of syphillis—he had searched unsuccessfully
for years for relief from pain, and a year before his death
wrote, "I am in my death agony. I have a softening of the brain
brought on by bathing my nostril with salt water. The salt has
fermented in my brain, and every night my brains are dripping
away through my nose and mouth in a sticky paste." **1944:**
Fire during a performance at Ringling Brothers and Barnum
and Bailey Circus in Hartford, Conn., causes panic and
stampede inside tent, resulting in deaths of 168 people.

FORECAST

BY NAN DE GROVE

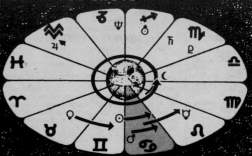

CANCER

LONGITUDE OF THE PLANETS
03:44 PDT; 06/21/85

Sun *00°00′* Cancer
Moon *18°20′* Leo
Mercury *17°27′* Cancer
Venus *15°30′* Taurus
Mars *08°38′* Cancer
Jupiter *16°28′* Aquarius R
Saturn *22°19′* Scorpio R
Uranus *15°21′* Sagittarius R
Nept *02°16′* Capricorn R
Pluto *02°02′* Scorpio R

A more conservative mood prevails this month. Emphasis on water and earth signs draws our attention to tangible reality and immediate personal concerns rather than abstract ideals or future plans.

Roots, foundations, security, and emotional bonds with others are vital issues. Like the Crab who scurries back into its hole when threatened, we may feel a need to retreat now and make adjustments wherever our ground is shaky or we've skipped over basic needs in our eagerness to expand.

The Sun aspects both Neptune and Pluto in the first few days of Cancer and trines Saturn on July 13th. Sweeping changes that come around these dates could be the result of long-term pressure and effort.

In many lives, the time is ripe for new beginnings and those who are intuitive enough to seize the moment and act could experience major gains. In some cases, crises will erupt and this will have a positive cathartic effect, sweeping away past attachments and making available new spiritual, emotional, and material resources.

This is a time to pay heed to hunches, intuition, and emotional atmospheres. Those who are overly rational could miss the boat. If it doesn't feel right this month, it probably isn't.

WATER SIGNS are in their element now and can flow with the tide, finding the right moment to launch new projects.

Cancer: try letting go of an illusion or unrealistic expectations in relationships. Begin a new cycle with enhanced self-awareness and sensitivity to the needs of partners.

Scorpio: you may sense a larger purpose or plan underlying your actions. A new sense of self-worth begins to emerge in mid-July.

Pisces: you may need to take risks in romantic and creative opportunities. Be more assertive in exploring new avenues of self-expression.

FIRE SIGNS are working behind the scenes, dealing with emotional issues and hidden factors that effect external reality.

Aries: keep a low profile. Focus on home base and generate energy for future accomplishments.

Leo: this is a time for letting go. The outcome of a situation has been determined already by past actions; further effort could do more harm than good.

Sagittarius: take a respite from mounting pressures over finances and responsibilities. With needs and feelings in flux, relationships intensify around July 6th.

EARTH SIGNS are feeling the benefits of increased stability and a clearer sense of goals and values.

Taurus: show magnetism and persuasiveness, but avoid being intimidated or manipulated around the end of June. Emotions and romantic feelings will be unreliable around the 19th of July.

Virgo: create the future now through dreams and imagination. This is a time to start planning for career changes that are becoming more urgent. Think of yourself as being worthy of your desires.

Capricorn: now's the time for making major decisions concerning relationships and personal needs. Intense emotions need expression.

AIR SIGNS: may feel in suspension as they are tying up loose ends and dealing with emotional and practical concerns.

Gemini: focus attention on finances, resources, and values; you may need to clear up a debt or complete a commitment before taking on new projects.

Libra: look for opportunities to further your career or express yourself publicly in a new way. Financial picture changes around July 12th.

Aquarius: work out details and organizational aspects of long-range plans. This is an opportune time to seek new employment, attend to health needs, and make practical improvements in all areas.

SUNDAY — JULY 07

Sun Rises 05:53
Sun Sets 20:37
Moon Rises ----
Moon Sets 11:13

MOON IN PISCES

moon square uranus-00:42. sun trine moon-01:22.
moon trine mars-08:01. moon trine saturn-02:05.

Gustav Mahler 1860	Marc Chagall 1887
Satchel Paige 1906	Gian Carlo Menotti 1911
Lawrence O'Brien 1917	Mary Ford 1924
Vince Edwards 1928	Ringo Starr 1940

578bc: Jerusalem destroyed. **1846:** California annexed from Mexico by U.S. **1937:** First Sino-Japanese War clash. **1959:** Billie Holiday, "Lady Day," singer, dies at age 44 in Metropolitan Hospital (New York City) while under arrest for narcotic addiction. **1965:** Civil rights campaign is resumed in Bogalusa, La. with march to city hall.

A restaurant is only as good as its worst meal. Just as a cookbook is only as good as its worst recipe.

Julia Child

MONDAY — JULY 08

Sun Rises 05:54
Sun Sets 20:36
Moon Rises 00:14
Moon Sets 12:12

MOON ENTERS ARIES 06:20

moon square neptune-10:00.

Franz Boas 1858	Nelson Rockefeller 1908
Billy Eckstine 1914	Faye Emerson 1917
Marty Feldman 1933	Steve Lawrence 1935

1796: First U.S. passport issued. **1822:** English poet Shelley drowns when boat capsizes in squall (Gulf of Spezzia, Italy)—corpse is found 10 days later by friends Byron, Leigh Hunt, and Edward Trelawny, who later snatches heart from burning corpse and arranges to have it buried in the English cemetery in Rome. **1932:** Stock Market hits all time low in wake of Black Tuesday crash of Oct. 29, 1929, with Dow closing at 41.22. Over this period, $9 out of every $10 invested in market was obliterated. **1976:** Nixon disbarred in New York.

Remember, a big cigar becomes a little cigar after it's been smoked for a while.

The Cigar Almanac

TUESDAY — JULY 09

Sun Rises 05:54
Sun Sets 20:36
Moon Rises 00:37
Moon Sets 13:10

MOON IN ARIES

moon trine mercury-09:14. moon trine uranus-11:47.
sun square moon-17:49. moon square mars-23:04.

LAST QUARTER MOON 17:49

Nikola Tesla 1856	Ed Ames 1927
Richard Roundtree 1942	O.J. Simpson 1947

1850: Zachary Taylor, 12th Pres. of U.S., dies in office, at age 65 years and 227 days, of bilious fever, typhoid fever, and cholera—his last words were, "I regret nothing, but am sorry that I am about to leave my friends." **1893:** First successful open heart surgery. **1918:** Worst train wreck in U.S. history—101 die (Nashville, Tenn). **1955:** Nine scientists, led by Bertrand Russell, call for abolition of war.

This is a funny world. And we humans, I often think, are the funniest animals in it.

Doctor Doolittle

WEDNESDAY — JULY 10

Sun Rises 05:55
Sun Sets 20:36
Moon Rises 01:00
Moon Sets 14:07

MOON ENTERS TAURUS 18:44

mercury trine uranus-11:17. mercury oppos jupiter-17:22.
moon trine neptune-22:21. moon oppos pluto-22:39.

John Calvin 1509	Camille Pissarro 1830
Marcel Proust 1871	Mary McLeod Bethune 1875
Saul Bellow 1915	Jake Lamotta 1921
Jean Kerr 1923	Richard Hatcher 1933
Arthur Ashe 1943	Virginia Wade 1945

1917: Emma Goldman sentenced to 2 years in prison for obstructing selective service process. **1926:** Bolt of lightning hits army arsenal (N.J.)—explosion kills 16, blows debris 22 miles away. **1972:** In India, it is reported that elephants on rampage had attacked 5 villages and killed at least 24 people.

THURSDAY — JULY 11

Sun Rises 05:55
Sun Sets 20:35
Moon Rises 01:23
Moon Sets 15:05

MOON IN TAURUS

moon at apogee-01:00. mars trine saturn-23:01.
mercury at desc node-23:32.

E.B. White 1899	Leon Spinks 1953

FRIDAY — JULY 12

Sun Rises 05:56
Sun Sets 20:34
Moon Rises 01:49
Moon Sets 16:05

MOON IN TAURUS

moon square jupiter-00:54. pluto directs-01:46.
moon square mercury-04:18. moon oppos saturn-14:32.

Henry David Thoreau 1817	Jean Hersholt 1886
Buckminster Fuller 1895	Pablo Neruda 1904
Andrew Wyeth 1917	Mark Hatfield 1922
Bill Cosby 1937	Christine McVie 1943

1942: Max Geller, owner of Green Parrot Bar (New York City) dies from gunshot during robbery—none of customers in the bar admitted seeing the shooting, but detective who studied the case for several years finally identified the culprit with the help of bar's resident parrot, who kept repeating the name of the murderer. **1967:** "Disorder" kills 26 and injures 1500 in Newark, N.J.

WHAT'S UP

Beacons Past And Present

LIGHTHOUSE LORE

by Kevin McCarthy

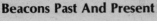

*My father was the keeper of the Eddystone Light
And he slept with a mermaid one fine night
From this union there came three
A porpoise and a porgy, and the other was me.
Yo, ho, ho, the wind blows free,
Oh, for a life on the rolling sea.*

The most common early navigational aids were simply hilltop bonfires, buckets of burning coal, or lanterns hung in trees. And then came the lighthouse; the monoliths stretching skyward at land's edge represented the finest examples of manmade, graceful utility in nature's sublime aggregation.

The oldest documented lighthouse was also the largest ever constructed, and one of the Seven Wonders of the World. The **Pharos of Alexandria** was completed on an island at the harbor entrance to the Egyptian city in about 280 b.c. The massive structure was composed of huge marble blocks cemented with molten lead, and rose over 400 feet high. The great monument required 20 years to construct and lasted over 1500 years, until a severe earthquake finally reduced it to rubble.

Some have suggested that another of the Seven Wonders, the **Colossus of Rhodes**, was also a lighthouse. In this view, the gargantuan statue of Apollo, straddling a Greek harbor, had blazing eyes of fire. Although unsubstantiated, this idea offers a practical explanation for the construction of the divine replica.

The Romans built at least thirty lighthouses. One of the most famous was the **Tower of Hercules**, at Corunna, Spain. The 130-foot tower was supposedly built by the god himself, who kept the flame burning continuously for 300 years. The Spanish later restored the pillar to make it the oldest functioning lighthouse known.

Many lighthouses were constructed in Europe over the next several centuries, the most notable being the ornate towers of the French. In the ninth century, traders who came to Bordeaux to buy wine threatened to take business elsewhere unless something was done to illuminate the dangerous, periodically submerged islet of Cordovan, near the port. Various beacons shone from small towers beginning about 880.

Finally, in 1584, a French architect took 27 years to build a combination palace, cathedral, fort, and land lighthouse that was a Renaissance masterpiece. Although no monarch apparently ever used the royal suite provided, the beautiful building set new standards of architectural engineering and design.

Encouraged by this example, the British began looking toward placing a beacon at **Eddystone Rocks**, a world-famous ship graveyard in the English Channel. The ingenious Henry Winstanley, having lost two newly acquired ships to the reed, proposed to undertake the impossible task, and began in the spring of 1696.

The first light beamed from the lonely reef in the fall of 1698, but the tower had to be repaired and made taller the next summer. By 1703, the structure badly needed repairs.

The flamboyant Winstanley boasted that his greatest wish was to be in his beloved lighthouse during the biggest storm ever. So, on November 26, 1703, the cavalier fellow and his workmen made their way out to the Eddystone Light, just in time for a storm of historic proportions. That evening, hundreds in English cities were killed by falling trees and chimneys, and the gale on the sea was worse. The following morning, tower, creator, and crew were gone. Winstanley's wish had been ruthlessly granted.

A new tower was built on the rocks in 1708. This structure lasted fifty years until the wooden sheathing on the stone building caught fire. Strangely, a glob of molten lead fell down the gullet of one of the keepers as he stood below watching the blaze. The man showed no ill effects, and his physician discounted the story. Several days later the man died suddenly. An autopsy revealed a seven-ounce piece of lead in his stomach.

JULY

SATURDAY
JULY 13
Sun Rises 05:57
Sun Sets 20:34
Moon Rises 02:19
Moon Sets 17:06

MOON ENTERS GEMINI 07:23

moon at asc node-03:40. sun trine saturn-18:53.

SUNDAY
JULY 14
Sun Rises 05:58
Sun Sets 20:33
Moon Rises 02:54
Moon Sets 18:07

MOON IN GEMINI

moon conj venus-00:33. moon oppos uranus-12:11.
moon trine jupiter-12:12.

James Whistler 1834	Irving Stone 1903
Isaac Bashevis Singer 1904	Woody Guthrie 1912
Gerald Ford 1913	Douglas Edwards 1917
John Chancellor 1927	Polly Bergen 1930

1789: *Bastille Day (France).* **1899:** *James Cagney born—date later changed to July 14, 1904 by Warner Bros.* **1953:** *Hail from large storm in Alberta, Canada kills 36,000 ducks.* **1965:** *Ecuador declares martial law after student demonstrations.* **1966:** *8 student nurses die in their apartment in Chicago, victims of an attack by Richard Speck—5 are strangled and 3 are stabbed to death.*

The profession of book-writing makes horse racing seem like a solid, stable business.

John Steinbeck

MONDAY
JULY 15
Sun Rises 05:59
Sun Sets 20:33
Moon Rises 03:36
Moon Sets 19:07

MOON ENTERS CANCER 17:54

moon oppos neptune-21:03. moon trine pluto-21:34.

Rembrandt 1606	Alex Karras 1935
Linda Ronstadt 1946	Nan Hayes 1948

1876: *First no-hitter pitched, by Washington Bradley.* **1922:** *First duckbill platypus exhibited in U.S.* **1940:** *Robert Wadlow, tallest man in world, dies at age 22, the victim of a severe infection caused by braces he wore to help him stand up—he was 8 feet 11 inches tall and weighed 491 pounds.* **1978:** *Hailstones the size of baseballs kill over 200 sheep (Montana).*

Writing is a dog's life, but the only life worth living.

Gustave Flaubert

TUESDAY
JULY 16
Sun Rises 05:59
Sun Sets 20:32
Moon Rises 04:27
Moon Sets 20:02

MOON IN CANCER

Mary Baker Eddy 1821	Barbara Stanwyck 1907
Bess Myerson 1924	Stewart Copeland 1952

1945: *First explosion of an atomic bomb—Trinity Site, near Alamagordo, New Mex.* **1956:** *Last Barnum & Bailey Circus performed under canvas.* **1965:** *Adlai Stevenson, U.S. statesman, dies from heart attack at age 65 while walking near U.S. Embassy in London.*

There's a curious paradox about television. Anyone who appears on it for half an hour five nights a week has influence, but the moment you use it you lose it.

Ted Koppel

WEDNESDAY
JULY 17
Sun Rises 06:00
Sun Sets 20:31
Moon Rises 05:25
Moon Sets 20:51

MOON IN CANCER

moon trine saturn-10:01. sun conj moon-16:56.
moon conj mars-17:00. sun conj mars-19:41.
mercury square saturn-19:52.

NEW MOON 16:56

John Jacob Astor 1763	Erle Stanley Gardner 1889
James Cagney 1899	Art Linkletter 1912
Lucie Arnaz 1951	Phoebe Snow 1952

1850: *First photograph of a star—Vega.* **1974:** *Lightning kills circus elephant that is chained to tree (Oquawka, Ill.).* **1975:** *Apollo-Soyuz link up.* **1979:** *Somoza resigns and leaves Nicaragua.*

The important question is how long you should go without exercise before eating.

Miss Piggy

THURSDAY
JULY 18
Sun Rises 06:01
Sun Sets 20:31
Moon Rises 06:30
Moon Sets 21:33

MOON ENTERS LEO 01:25

moon square pluto-04:55. venus trine jupiter-22:39.

William Thackeray 1811	Clifford Odets 1903
Hume Cronyn 1911	Harriet Nelson 1911
John Glenn 1921	Martha Reeves 1941

64: *Rome burns, Nero fiddles, according to legend.* **1972:** *3 Muckleshoot Indians arrested for fishing in their own stream (Wash.).* **1981:** *At the Hyatt Regency Hotel in Kansas City, a walkway collapses, killing 110 people.*

WARM
&
MOIST

97

After scores of shipwrecks in perilous Boston Harbor, the first American lighthouse was built on **Little Brewster Island** in the harbor in 1716. The keeper and his family were lost two years later when their boat capsized as they tried to reach the island before a storm.

The event inspired young Ben Franklin's first poem, "Lighthouse Tragedy." A large cannon was installed at the light, and fired frequently during fog. The pillar was often struck by lightning, but Bostonians refused to attach a lightning rod, thinking "it vanity and irreligion for the arm of flesh to presume to avert the stroke of heaven."

The lighthouse became a pawn during the Revolutionary War, and was twice destroyed by American troops during the British occupation of the port. Finally blown up by the lobster backs as they retreated, the structure wasn't rebuilt until 1783.

Bogus lighthouses proved as treacherous as the deadliest storm for early merchant men working the eastern seaboard. Outlaws called "moon-cursers" set up false, moveable lights to lure craft onto reeds and rocks. The shipwrecked crews were drowned or shot by the wreckers who became rich from the ship's booty.

Wrecking became so common that some local economies were propped up by the brisk trade in shipwrecked cargo. Ralph Waldo Emerson visited Cape Cod during this period, and found much opposition to the proposed Federal installation of lighthouses. The reason, he was told, was a fear of injuring the wrecking business.

The earliest West Coast lighthouse was built as an extension of **Baranof's Castle**, at New Archangel (Sitka) Alaska in 1837. Baranof, a successful but tyrannical lord of the Russian territory, never lived in the castle, but left his mark on the building nevertheless.

The story is told that Baranof sent a beautiful princess' lover to Siberia, telling her that he had been lost at sea. Forced to marry another, she mysteriously vanished from the wedding party and was found dead in her chamber. Twice a year thereafter, the castle was filled with the scent of wild briar roses as her spirit, searching for the lost lover, roamed the corridors, swishing her wedding gown and extinguishing fires.

Probably no vocation has been so romanticized as that of lighthouse keeper. The image of the unfailing sender of hope in a lonely, beautiful wilderness symbolizes the best that we may hope to be. But the rugged life of a "wickie" on a remote outpost included great peril, hard work, and enormous responsibilities. Often the duty was a family affair, with the lion's share of the toil falling to the wife, who served as assistant keeper as well as chef, mother, seamstress, and gardener.

Interestingly, the roster of the old U.S. Lighthouse Service lists a surprising number of women keepers. Kate Waller minded the light at **Robbins Reef** near Staten Island for over thirty years. She estimated that she rescued fifty shipwrecked fishermen before she retired in 1919. Julia Williams tended the **Santa Barbara Lighthouse** for forty years. And Ida Lewis Wilson, a keeper at **Lime Rock**, Rhode Island served thirty-two years and was awarded a gold medal for bravery.

One of the most famous remote duty stations was **Tillamook Rock**, Oregon. Many thought it would be impossible to build a lighthouse on the storm-swept islet and they were almost right. The structure was finally complete in 1881 — at a cost of $125,000 and one life. Since no boat could approach the sheer cliffs of the basalt pinnacle in the prevailing weather and swells, a derrick with a long boom was installed for transfer of personnel and supplies.

Although the light was nearly 150 feet above the sea, walls of water sometimes crested the pillar and damaged the beacon. Several times the keepers toiled in salt water literally up to their necks in order to repair the lantern. The roof was holed so frequently by boulders that a two-foot thick reinforced concrete roof was installed in 1898. A further problem was the alarming erosion of the volcanic rock perch itself.

Tillamook is very remote — so much so that supposedly, first keeper was led away in a straight jacket. Even mundane tasks became an adventure at "Tilly." The privy lay at the end of a steep, exposed staircase, and was prone to geyser visitors four feet high during a storm.

During a gale in 1934, the derrick was devoured by the boiling maelstrom, the lens was shattered, the outer railings were ripped away, and the entire lighthouse was filled with water. Although suffering from exposure, the keepers feverishly attended to their duties. One man installed the standby light despite a serious gash in his arm from flying glass. Another ingeniously built a shortwave transmitter from spare parts, and was able to alert those ashore to the conditions of the light.

Many keepers were killed while manning a dangerous post or pulling others from the sea. The debris of the **Scotch Cap Lighthouse** remains a memorial to the five Coast Guardsmen killed there by the tidal wave after the 1946 Alaskan Earthquake.

All of the famous exposed American Lighthouses such as **Minots Ledge** near Boston and Lake Superior's **Stannard Light** have been replaced by automated navigational aids. But we keepers of the flame reside with the mystic sentinels in spirit.

FRIDAY   JULY **19**
Sun Rises 06:02
Sun Sets 20:30
Moon Rises 07:39
Moon Sets 22:10
MOON IN LEO

moon oppos jupiter-02:31. moon trine uranus-03:13. venus oppos uranus-06:32. moon square saturn-15:38. moon conj mercury-17:54.

Lizzie Borden 1816   Herbert Marcuse 1898
George McGovern 1922   Pat Hingle 1924
Vikki Carr 1942   Ilie Nastase 1946

1881: Sitting Bull and followers surrender. 1969: Mary Jo Kopechne dies of undetermined causes after car in which she was riding plunges off bridge on Chappaquiddick Island (Mass.).

I do not see why people should dress like garage mechanics on space trips, particularly when they are going to be on worldwide television.

Miss Piggy

SATURDAY   JULY **20**
Sun Rises 06:02
Sun Sets 20:30
Moon Rises 08:49
Moon Sets 22:41
MOON ENTERS VIRGO 06:29

moon trine neptune-09:11.

Theda Bara 1890   Hart Crane 1899
Diana Rigg 1938   Carlos Santana 1947

1714: The Bridge of San Luis Rey falls—5 die. 1801: First cheese factory in U.S. produces its first cheese and presents it to Thomas Jefferson. 1890: Kiowa Indians forbidden to perform Sundance. 1965: Supreme Court justice Arthur Goldberg is named to succeed Adlai Stevenson as U.N. Ambassador. 1973: Bruce Lee, actor, dies at age 33 in Hong Kong from health problems relating to a convulsive disorder. 1976: Viking I lands on Mars.

GORILLA
DANGEROUS
Please not to approach too close to the bars

SUNDAY   JULY **21**
Sun Rises 06:03
Sun Sets 20:29
Moon Rises 09:58
Moon Sets 23:10
MOON IN VIRGO

moon square uranus-07:23. moon square venus-11:43.

Ernest Hemingway 1899   Marshall McLuhan 1911
Don Knotts 1924   John Gardner 1933
Edward Herrmann 1943   Robin Williams 1952

1798: Battle of Pyramids—Napoleon takes Cairo. 1979: Coca-Cola for sale again in Cairo, Egypt.

All my major works have been written in prison.... I would recommend prison not only to aspiring writers but to aspiring politicians, too.

Jawaharlal Nehru

Eclipses

May 4 — Total Eclipse of the Moon. Visible from Australasia, Asia, Europe and Africa.
May 19 — Partial Eclipse of the Sun. Visible from N.E. Asia, Japan, North of N. America, Greenland, Iceland, extreme N.W. Europe and Arctic regions.
October 28 — Total Eclipse of the Moon. Visible from Australasia, Asia, Europe and Africa.
November 12 — Total Eclipse of the Sun. Visible from Antarctica and South of S. America.

Balloon Briefs

A 30-foot-high balloon landed in an orchard in Israel in 1983, and was immediately surrounded by police and military personnel who suspected a terrorist bomb. "We hear strange things, we respond, we act. You see a strange balloon, you don't think twice," a local police official was quoted as saying. However, instead of a bomb, the investigators found packages of underwear and pamphlets written in Chinese. According to the final explanation, the balloon had been launched from Taiwan on a propaganda mission toward mainland China, but had been blown 6,000 miles off course.

Free Attractions

by Mary Van Meer and Michael Anthony Pasquarelli

It's no surprise to most people that a vacation can be costly. Even sticking close to home, the expense of transportation and food — let alone admission costs for entertainment — can exhaust an average vacation budget. Here are some amusements any family can afford and they're all *free!*

COON DOG MEMORIAL PARK A cemetery for hounds, with interesting and sentimental tombstones dating from 1937, when "Old Troop" was buried by his owner. Cherokee, Alabama, 12 miles south of State Highway 72 on Colbert County Road 21. Open year-round, 24 hours a day.

BOXING HALL OF FAME Historical exhibits, plaster casts of the greatest fists in boxing, plus Joe Lewis' gloves. 120 West 31st Street, 6th Floor, New York, New York. Open year-round, Monday to Friday, 10:00 to 3:30.

THE ORIGINAL McDONALD'S A plaque and the original golden arch mark the spot where Ray Kroc opened the first McDonald's "Speedee Service" restaurant on April 15, 1955. A modern version of the franchise operates in close proximity to provide refreshments for those taking the pilgrimage (normal charges in effect for food). 400 Lee Street, Des Plaines, Illinois. Open year-round, regular business hours.

DRY FALLS The geological remains of a huge waterfall, over three and a half miles wide, with a drop of over 400 feet. Coulee City, Washington, 4 miles SW of town, off State Highway 17, in Sun Lakes State Park. Open year-round.

EEL INSTITUTE A hatchery for eels under a geodesic dome. Milford Hall on the University of Bridgeport campus, Bridgeport, Connecticut. Open year-round, 24 hours a day.

CLOCK MUSEUM Exhibits of over 18,000 locks and related items. 114 Main Street, Terryville, Connecticut. Open May through October, Tuesday-Sunday, 1:30 to 4:00, or by appointment during the rest of the year.

CROAKER COLLEGE Tours by appointment of a school for frogs. 430 Park Fair Drive, Sacramento, California. Open year-round.

FIDDLING HALL OF FAME Exhibits of fiddles, including one made of matchsticks, plus Fiddlers' Hall of Fame. 44 West Commercial Street, Weiser, Idaho. Open year-round, daily, 10:00 to 5:00.

MAYTAG HISTORICAL CENTER Exhibits of Maytag appliances, including, from 1907, the first washer. Authentic period settings and slide show. 300 West Fourth Street North, Newton, Iowa. Open year-round, daily, 8:00 to 8:00.

WORLD'S LARGEST GLOBE A huge globe, 28 feet in diameter, which rotates on a 24 hour cycle. Nearby, in the Coleman Map Building, is a large, detailed relief map of the U.S. which spans 65 feet. Great Plain Avenue on the Babson College campus, Babson Park, Massachusetts. Open year-round, sunrise to sunset. (Relief map is open April-October, daily, 10:00 to 5:00, and 2:00 to 5:00 the rest of the year.)

ELEPHANT HOUSE A six-story house built in 1881, in the shape of an elephant. 9200 Atlantic Avenue, Margate, New Jersey. Open June to September, daily, 10:00 to 5:00.

POPEYE STATUE A monument to the world's most famous spinach eater, in the heart of spinach-growing country. City Square, Crystal City, Texas. Open year-round, daily, sunrise to sunset.

CHATTANOOGA CHOO CHOO The original train from the 19th Century. 1400 Market Street, Chattanooga, Tennessee. Open year-round, daily.

WORLD'S LARGEST ORCHID NURSERY A one-hour tour through acres of orchids, roses, gardenias, and other flowers. 1450 El Camino Real, San Francisco, California. Open year-round except major holidays, tours at 10:30 and 1:30.

TUPPERWARE MUSEUM A collection of food containers from 4,000 b.c. to the present. Kissimmee, Florida, 2 miles north of town on U.S. 441. Open year-round, Monday-Friday, 9:00 to 4:00.

This information is excerpted with permission from *FREE ATTRACTIONS, U.S.A.*, by Mary VanMeer and Michael Anthony Pasquarelli, published by John Muir Publications.

JULY

LEO

July 22 — August 21

MONDAY   **JULY**
Sun Rises 06:04
Sun Sets 20:28
Moon Rises 11:07
Moon Sets 23:37

22

MOON ENTERS LIBRA 10:10

moon square neptune-12:44.

Sun Enters Leo 14:36

Edward Hopper 1882   Karl Menninger 1893
Stephen Vincent Benet 1898   Amy Vanderbilt 1908
Robert Dole 1923   Orson Bean 1928

1298: *First use of the English Longbow.* **1869:** *John Roebling, chief engineer for construction of Brooklyn Bridge, dies from tetanus infection received when the toes on one of his feet were amputated after an accident on bridge site.* **1918:** *Lightning kills 504 sheep in single strike (Wasatch National Forest, Utah).*

Leisure as a concept implies that the work you do is unpleasant.

Ansel Adams

TUESDAY   **JULY**
Sun Rises 06:05
Sun Sets 20:27
Moon Rises 12:16
Moon Sets ----

23

MOON IN LIBRA

moon trine jupiter-09:17. moon trine venus-19:25.

Raymond Chandler 1888   Pee Wee Reese 1918
Gloria De Haven 1924   Bert Convy 1934

1885: *Ulysses S. Grant, 18th Pres. of U.S., dies from carcinoma of the tongue and tonsils at age 63 years and 87 days (Mt. McGregor, N.Y.)—his last word was, "Water."* **1979:** *Ayatollah Khomeini bans non-religious music in Iran.*

WEDNESDAY   **JULY**
Sun Rises 06:06
Sun Sets 20:26
Moon Rises 13:26
Moon Sets 00:05

24

MOON ENTERS SCORPIO 13:16

moon square mars-12:53. sun square pluto-16:13.
moon conj pluto-16:37. sun square moon-16:39.
MARS ENTERS LEO-21:04.

FIRST QUARTER MOON 16:39

Alexandre Dumas 1802   Ambrose Bierce 1842
Amelia Earhart 1898   Zelda Fitzgerald 1900
John MacDonald 1916   Ruth Buzzi 1936

1872: *Ralph Waldo Emerson's house burns.* **1910:** *First Paul Bunyan stories published.* **1974:** *Cass Elliot, singer, dies at age 33 in London—official autopsy report stated that death was due to heart attack brought on by overweight condition, although popular reports had her choking to death on ham sandwich.*

OH OH

THURSDAY   **JULY**
Sun Rises 06:07
Sun Sets 20:26
Moon Rises 14:37
Moon Sets 00:34

25

MOON IN SCORPIO

moon at perigee-11:00. moon square jupiter-11:49.
saturn directs-12:36.

Maxfield Parrish 1870   Jack Gilford 1907
Dotson Raider 1942   Steve Goodman 1948
Walter Payton 1954   Steve Podborski 1957

1967: *Detroit blacks in open revolt against police.* **1973:** *Vietnam War ruled illegal by Federal Judge.*

Moi is told that some brisk exercise is also excellent for nerves, but I find that just the idea of exercise makes me so nervous that it doesn't help.

Miss Piggy

GROWING
BY LIZ CAILE

NOW'S THE TIME —Northern gardeners, harvest to keep plants producing into fall, while southern gardeners, begin planning late fall and winter gardens. **Mountain States:** For best flavor, cut lettuce heads and leaf lettuce plants right at the crown. **Northeast, Midwest:** Harvest carrots by digging from one end of the row and completing the harvest in regular increments. Pulling carrots one at a time, may leave a convenient egg-laying hole for carrot rust flies. **Northwest:** Cut chard to just above the crown, and new leaves will come in. Greens have the greatest vitamin C content just after picking and after a full day of sunlight. **South, Southeast:** Depending on frost-free period, many vegetables can be started now, as well as winter flowering pansies, lupine, and sweet pea. Keep seedbeds moist. If insects are severe, consider new varieties of vegetables and insect-resistant hybrids, noting word of caution below (Plant Toxins).

Natural Cotton?

Just one of the many inconsistencies that plagues our complex lives is the fact that cotton, exalted as an all-natural fiber, is the most pesticide intensive crop grown in the United States.

According to Walter Ebeling in *The Fruited Plain*, only a small portion of our total crop acreage is treated with insecticides. But close to half of the insecticides used in this country are used on cotton, which is host to a long list of insects throughout its growing cycle.

Environmentally destructive pesticides take enough of a toll on the ecosystem of the cottonfield that growers have found it an economic necessity to approach insect control from the angle of **integrated pest management.**

The integrated system uses **sanitation, biological controls** such as confusing mating insects with synthesized sex attractants; and **fast maturing varieties** that are harvested before the insects reach population peaks.

Plant Toxins

All plants, including garden vegetables, have or produce toxic substances that protect them from diseases, insect infestations and other natural threats. In making use of these natural toxins to develop disease- and insect-resistant crop varieties, plant breeders are increasing percentages of these chemicals, some of which are now being identified as carcinogenic or mutagenic.

Plants respond to damage by increasing their production of protective toxins or by producing new ones. It goes to show what complex metabolisms apparently simple garden vegetables have.

Not all hybrids depend on the toxicity principal to strengthen disease resistance, and not all hybrids are necessarily more resistant to disease or insects. Some simply produce more, even in the face of attack. Other hybrids lack an ingredient of attrac-

tion or a nutrient necessary for a particular insect species' well being.

And in her complexity, nature provides antidotes in food for the toxins that are also present. For example, beets contain high percentages of carcinogenic nitrate; beet greens are also high in beta-carotene, an anticarcinogenic substance.

Home Bug Remedies

Rhubarb leaves, poisonous but usually plentiful, reportedly make a good spray for aphids. Boil a generous number of leaves in enough water for treating aphid-hosting plants. Strain the oxalic-acidic brew, add liquid soap to make it stick, and apply with a garden sprayer.

To attract beneficial predator insects to your garden and to hold onto those you purchase from a nursery supply store or mail order company, the old variety principal triumphs again. Cultivate a variety of flowering plants as well as a variety of vegetables in varying stages of maturity throughout the growing season, and keep the garden world moist.

Keeping the garden free of decomposing plant material, fruit and debris where insects breed is essential. For an easy to use and constructive approach to sick gardens try *Rx For Your Vegetable Garden*, by Duane Newcomb.

Kitchen Root Tip

Start root vegetables cooking in cold water. Immerse above-ground parts of vegetables in steam or boiling water. Vegetables retain the most vitamins and minerals when cooked quickly in as little water as possible.

Water from root vegetables should be saved for soup stock, or just add to canned soup or powdered soup mixes. The water from boiled potatoes adds flavor and tenderness when used as all or part of the liquid in both yeast breads and quick breads.

FRIDAY — JULY 26
Sun Rises 06:07
Sun Sets 20:25
Moon Rises 15:50
Moon Sets 01:08

MOON ENTERS SAGITTARIUS 16:12

moon conj saturn-01:43. moon square mercury-08:07.
moon at desc node-14:26. moon trine mars-18:16.
sun trine moon-23:17.

George Catlin 1796
Carl Jung 1875
Robert Graves 1895
Salvador Allende 1908
Blake Edwards 1922
Mary Jo Kopechne 1940
Estes Kefauver 1903
Vivian Vance 1913
Jean Shepherd 1923

George Bernard Shaw 1856
Aldous Huxley 1894

SATURDAY — JULY 27
Sun Rises 06:08
Sun Sets 20:24
Moon Rises 17:03
Moon Sets 01:47

MOON IN SAGITTARIUS

moon conj uranus-16:25. mercury retrogrades-17:50.
mars square pluto-23:26.

Confucius 551bc
Peggy Fleming 1948

Norman Lear 1922
Maureen McGovern 1949

SUNDAY — JULY 28
Sun Rises 06:09
Sun Sets 20:24
Moon Rises 18:11
Moon Sets 02:34

MOON ENTERS CAPRICORN 19:21

moon oppos venus-10:17. moon trine mercury-11:17.
moon conj neptune-21:41.

Corot 1794
Harry Bridges 1901
Jacques D'Amboise 1934
Mike Bloomfield 1943

Joe E. Brown 1892
Rudy Vallee 1901
Peter Duchin 1937
Vida Blue 1949

1814: Shelley elopes to France. **1859:** First oil well drilled. **1914:** Austria-Hungary declares war on Serbia—WWI begins. **1928:** An egg is fried on the steps of the Capitol building (Washington, D.C.). **1945:** Army B-25 bomber crashes into side of Empire State Building, 915 ft above the ground—3 people in plane and 10 people in building were killed. **1965:** Abe Fortas named to replace Arthur Goldberg as U.S. Supreme Court justice. **1965:** LBJ announces doubling draft quota in order to increase immediately number of U.S. troops in Vietnam from 75,000 to 125,000.

MONDAY — JULY 29
Sun Rises 06:09
Sun Sets 20:23
Moon Rises 19:12
Moon Sets 03:30

MOON IN CAPRICORN

Booth Tarkington 1869
William Powell 1892
Thelma Todd 1905

William Beebe 1877
Clara Bow 1904
Melvin Belli 1907

1492: First almanac published. **1754:** First international boxing match. **1870:** First road paved with asphalt. **1958:** NASA authorized. **1965:** Police officials in Bogalusa, La. are convicted of civil contempt for not protecting civil rights demonstrators. **1967:** Fire on U.S. aircraft carrier Forrestal in Gulf of Tonkin off the coast of North Vietnam kills 134 sailors—worst catastrophe in Navy since WWII.

If you've got clown paintings, you've got serious problems. I don't understand clowns, anyway.

Joe Piscopo

TUESDAY — JULY 30
Sun Rises 06:10
Sun Sets 20:22
Moon Rises 20:04
Moon Sets 04:33

MOON ENTERS AQUARIUS 23:25

Emily Bronte 1818
Casey Stengel 1891
Peter Bogdanovich 1939
Pat Schroeder 1940

Henry Ford 1863
Henry Moore 1898
Eleanor Smeal 1939
Arnold Schwarzenegger 1947

1784: Diderot, writer, dies after eating apricot his wife had warned him not to eat—his last words were, "How in the devil can it hurt me?" **1866:** White Democrats attack meeting of black and white Republicans (New Orleans)—massacre 40. **1933:** Man in Cumberland Gap, Tenn. shouts loud enough to be heard for 8 1/2 miles by listeners in Tenn., Kent., and Virg. **1965:** LBJ signs Medicare Social Security bill—first U.S. public health care bill. **1965:** Honduran government declares state-of-seige after demonstrators clash with police outside presidential palace.

SNICKERS

WEDNESDAY — JULY 31
Sun Rises 06:11
Sun Sets 20:21
Moon Rises 20:46
Moon Sets 05:41

MOON IN AQUARIUS

moon square pluto-03:01. moon oppos mars-06:44.
sun oppos moon-14:41. moon conj jupiter-21:35.

FULL MOON 14:41

Madam Blavatsky 1831
Susan Flannery 1943

Milton Friedman 1912
Evonne Goolagong 1951

1790: First U.S. patent issued. **1845:** Saxophone invented by Adolphe Sax. **1912:** First federal motion picture censorship law enacted. **1949:** Lightning hits infield at baseball game, kills shortstop, 1st baseman, 2nd baseman, ducks ditch 20 feet long, and injures 30 fans. **1958:** Last 3-cent first class letter delivered in U.S. **1981:** Major League baseball strike ends after 50 days.

Freedom of the press is limited to those who own one.

A.J. Liebling

CELESTIAL EVENTS

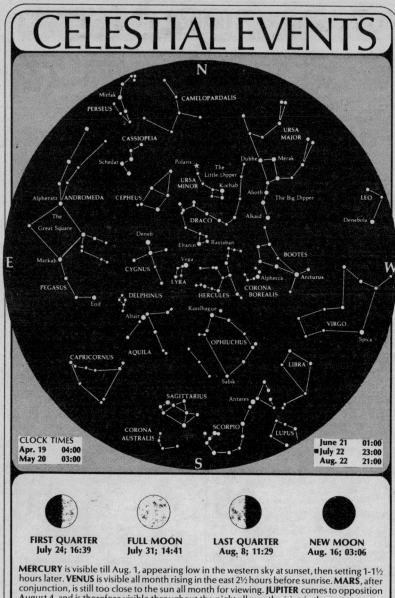

CLOCK TIMES
Apr. 19   04:00
May 20   03:00

June 21   01:00
■ July 22   23:00
Aug. 22   21:00

FIRST QUARTER
July 24; 16:39

FULL MOON
July 31; 14:41

LAST QUARTER
Aug. 8; 11:29

NEW MOON
Aug. 16; 03:06

MERCURY is visible till Aug. 1, appearing low in the western sky at sunset, then setting 1-1½ hours later. **VENUS** is visible all month rising in the east 2½ hours before sunrise. **MARS**, after conjunction, is still too close to the sun all month for viewing. **JUPITER** comes to opposition August 4, and is therefore visible throughout the night all month, rising in the east at sunset, then setting in the west at sunrise. **SATURN** is visible all month appearing near midsky at sunset, then setting in the west shortly after midnight. **July 26:** Saturn 3° N. of waxing gibbous Moon (night sky). **July 31:** Jupiter 4° N. of full Moon (night sky). **Aug. 13:** Venus 5° S. of waning crescent Moon (morning sky).

104

THURSDAY AUG. 01

Sun Rises 06:12
Sun Sets 20:20
Moon Rises 21:21
Moon Sets 06:49

MOON IN AQUARIUS

moon square saturn-13:57. moon oppos mercury-18:56.

Jean Baptiste Lenmarck 1744   Richard Henry Dana 1815
Helman Melville 1819   Paul Horgan 1903
Jack Kramer 1921   Ramblin' Jack Elliott 1931
Dom Deluise 1933   Jerry Garcia 1942

1918: Joyce Kilmer, poet, killed in battle in France. 1946: U.S. Atomic Energy Commission established. 1966: Charles Whitman, ex-Marine, age 24, shot by Austin, Texas policeman at top of tower on University of Texas campus, after killing 20 people, including his wife and his mother. 1974: Greek Constitution reinstated after military dictatorship is deposed. 1977: First oil from Alaskan pipeline transferred to tanker.

Unlocking the atom can help save the race or destroy it.

Ansel Adams

FRIDAY AUG. 02

Sun Rises 06:13
Sun Sets 20:18
Moon Rises 21:50
Moon Sets 07:56

MOON ENTERS PISCES 05:33

VENUS ENTERS CANCER 02:10.
moon trine venus-05:53. moon trine pluto-09:22.

Paul Laxalt 1922
James Baldwin 1924
Peter O'Toole 1932
Myrna Loy 1905

SATURDAY AUG. 03

Sun Rises 06:14
Sun Sets 20:17
Moon Rises 22:15
Moon Sets 08:59

MOON IN PISCES

venus oppos neptune-04:31. moon square uranus-08:03.
venus trine pluto-21:48. moon trine saturn-22:16.

John Thomas Scopes 1900   Dolores Del Rio 1904
Neal Miller 1909   Leon Uris 1924
Tony Bennett 1926   Richard Lamm 1935

1610: Henry Hudson enters Hudson Bay. 1829: Rossini's *William Tell* premieres (Paris). 1832: Sauk Indian massacre. 1903: Martha "Calamity Jane" Cannary, age 50, dies in hotel bed in Terry, South Dakota—her last words were, "Bury me next to Bill." (apparently referring to Wild Bill Hickok). 1958: USS *Nautilus* makes first undersea crossing of North Pole. 1958: J.S. Sordelet becomes first sailor to reenlist while under the North Pole. 1966: Lenny Bruce, comedian, dies at age 41 of "acute morphine poisoning" (Hollywood).

LAUGH

SUNDAY AUG. 04

Sun Rises 06:15
Sun Sets 20:16
Moon Rises 22:39
Moon Sets 10:00

MOON ENTERS ARIES 14:43

sun oppos jupiter-04:41. moon square neptune-17:07.
moon square venus-20:57.

Percy Bysshe Shelley 1792   Maurice Richard 1921
Richard Lugar 1932   Mary Decker Tabb 1958

1735: Precedent for freedom of press established in English North American colonies when John Peter Zenger wins acquittal of libel charges. 1790: U.S. Gov't bonds authorized. 1874: Chautauqua forms. 1917: U.S. acquires the Virgin Islands. 1956: Motorcycle first exceeds 200 mph. 1977: Dept. of Energy added to Cabinet.

Great people talk about ideas, average people talk about things, and small people talk about wine.

Fran Lebowitz

MONDAY AUG. 05

Sun Rises 06:16
Sun Sets 20:15
Moon Rises 23:01
Moon Sets 10:58

MOON IN ARIES

moon trine mars-05:06. sun trine moon-17:25.
moon trine uranus-18:36.

Guy de Maupassant 1850   Robert Taylor 1911
Richard Kleindienst 1923   Roman Gabriel 1940

1858: Undersea cable completed across Atlantic Ocean—it quit working after 27 days. 1861: Congress abolishes flogging in the Army. 1870: Knights of Pythias incorporated. 1924: *Little Orphan Annie* debuts in comics. 1962: Actress Marilyn Monroe, 36, dies of an apparent accidental overdose of barbiturates in her home in Hollywood. 1963: Nuclear Test Ban Treaty signed.

Do you turn on your friends when they do something wrong? Do you renounce them? I think that's the time to be a friend.

Diane Sawyer

TUESDAY AUG. 06

Sun Rises 06:17
Sun Sets 20:14
Moon Rises 23:25
Moon Sets 11:56

MOON IN ARIES

mercury square saturn-07:35. sun trine uranus-07:54.
moon trine mercury-09:32.

Alfred Lord Tennyson 1809   Alexander Fleming 1881
Louella Parsons 1881   Scott Nearing 1883
Hoot Gibson 1892   Dutch Schultz 1902
Lucille Ball 1911   Robert Mitchum 1917

1890: William Kemmler, ax murderer, is first person to be executed in electric chair (Auburn Prison, N.Y.). 1945: Hiroshima, Japan is hit by atomic bomb, killing about 78,000 people, including at least 10 captured American flyers. 1965: LBJ signs Voting Rights Act.

FORECAST

BY NAN DE GROVE

LEO

LONGITUDE OF THE PLANETS
14:36 PDT; 07/22/85

Sun 00°00′ Leo
Moon 02°35′ Libra
Mercury 24°14′ Leo
Venus 18°09′ Gemini
Mars 28°32′ Cancer
Jupiter 13°37′ Aquarius R
Saturn 21°28′ Scorpio R
Ura 14°21′ Sagittarius R
Nept 01°30′ Capricorn R
Pluto 01°58′ Scorpio

Crises, challenges, confrontations, and power struggles create a tense and generally stressful atmosphere in the early part of Leo. Tense aspects between the Sun, Mercury, and Mars in Leo and Pluto and Saturn in Scorpio will trigger the release of unconscious urges and motives that may be contrary to conscious intentions.

The self-confidence and exuberance of Leo is tempered and subdued by the watery, emotionally-charged nature of Scorpio. This is a time when hidden problems and repressed emotional issues are sure to surface. The dramatic tendencies of Leo could become wildly exaggerated, causing over-reaction and defensiveness.

Important turning points and resolutions come in the first ten days of this month. For some, this will be a result of successfully meeting challenges and mobilizing energy toward goals that have some kind of essential personal value; for others, a radical change of perspective is necessary to move out of an impasse. Some changes due now are a result of failure to take action last month.

FIRE SIGNS can benefit by moderating their ego-centered urges and impulses. Goals that have a mutual purpose will prosper.

Aries: you'll feel a surge of energy around the end of July, but may meet with opposition at the same time. Avoid defensiveness and overreacting to challenge.

Leo: your abundance of energy will endure despite setbacks and feelings of self-doubt. Work on areas where foundations are weak and lack of trust is stifling growth. Look for benefits to come through others.

Sagittarius: confront hidden emotional attitudes that may be inhibiting growth and sabotaging plans. Ideas and theories need to be reconciled with experience.

EARTH SIGNS are feeling unsettled, irritated perhaps by the rapidly changing forces around them.

Taurus: you may be at an impasse, procrastinating over necessary changes in home life, relationships, career, or all of the above. Tensions ease in the first few days of August.

Virgo: you could benefit from a period of retreat to sort things out and recover energy. Critical elements of a situation are hidden now, so avoid major decisions until after August 20th.

Capricorn: look for returns on investments or the conclusion of long-term efforts. Working with others for mutual benefit is a key issue.

AIR SIGNS are making important connections and communications now.

Gemini: can benefit through relationships, creative work, and pursuing new areas of learning. Avoid taking on too much or planning too far ahead; review and revise until August 20th.

Libra: events that transpire this month may necessitate reviewing your goals and reevaluating your social life. Avoid overcommitting and being too dependent on others.

Aquarius: you are reaching a turning point or a plateau; you have important choices to make involving career, relationships, and personal freedom.

WATER SIGNS are caught between the security of an old familiar routine and the uncertainty of new possibilities.

Cancer: problems with money could result from your changing values and overuse of resources. Popularity and prosperity increase after August 2nd, but avoid financial decisions until after August 20th.

Scorpio: review career and life goals; you may have a new vocation. Consider ways to mobilize untapped resources.

Pisces: look for more meaningful work opportunities and outlets for your creative energies. Take care of health and focus on improving self-image.

WEDNESDAY   AUG. 07

Sun Rises 06:18
Sun Sets 20:13
Moon Rises 23:49
Moon Sets 12:54

MOON ENTERS TAURUS 02:41

moon trine neptune-05:05. moon oppos pluto-07:00. moon at apogee-19:00. moon square mars-21:00.

Rahsaan Roland Kirk 1936
Lana Cantrell 1944
B. J. Thomas 1942
Rodney Crowell 1950

1789: War Dept. organized. **1888:** Jack the Ripper murders for the first time. **1904:** Train wreck kills 96 (Eden, Colorado). **1933:** Alley Oop debuts in comics. **1956:** 7 dynamite trucks explode in Cali, Columbia—1200 die. **1959:** Satellite sends first pictures of surface of the Earth. **1963:** Patrick Bouvier Kennedy, premature son born to Pres. Kennedy and his wife, dies at age 2 days.

Never change your act. I know people who did, and they always lost out. Never change your act.

Eubie Blake

THURSDAY   AUG. 08

Sun Rises 06:19
Sun Sets 20:12
Moon Rises ----
Moon Sets 13:53

MOON IN TAURUS

sun square moon-11:29. moon square mercury-18:42. moon oppos saturn-22:38.

LAST QUARTER MOON 11:29

Marjorie Rawlings 1896
Jesse Stuart 1907
Sylvia Sidney 1910
Rory Calhoun 1922
Mel Tillis 1932
Ernest Lawrence 1901
Arthur Goldberg 1908
Dino De Laurentiis 1919
Esther Williams 1923
Keith Carradine 1949

1588: Spanish Armada destroyed by the British—Francis Drake is hero. **1846:** Smithsonian Institution founded. **1876:** Mimeograph patented. **1945:** U.S. ratifies UN Charter. **1955:** First International Conference on Peaceful Use of Atomic Energy. **1963:** The Great Train Robbery—$7 million taken from British train. **1981:** Pres. Reagan endorses production of neutron bomb.

FRIDAY   AUG. 09

Sun Rises 06:20
Sun Sets 20:10
Moon Rises 00:17
Moon Sets 14:53

MOON ENTERS GEMINI 15:31

moon at asc node-05:57.

Izaak Walton 1593
Robert Shaw 1925
Rod Laver 1938
Jean Piaget 1896
Bob Cousy 1928
Ken Norton 1945

1639: Jonas Bronck settles the Bronx (New York). **1902:** King Edward VII crowned (England). **1945:** Nagasaki, Japan is hit by atomic bomb, killing over 30,000 people, including as many as 1,000 Allied P.O.W.s. **1969:** Sharon Tate, actress, and 4 friends are murdered at her home in Beverly Hills, Calif., by members of Charles Manson's "Family."

PERSEID METEOR SHOWER. For the next 2 or 3 nights stars will be falling. These meteors best can be seen between 10 pm and moonrise, about midnight. Get out and see 'em!

SATURDAY   AUG. 10

Sun Rises 06:21
Sun Sets 20:09
Moon Rises 00:50
Moon Sets 15:54

MOON IN GEMINI

moon trine jupiter-13:53. sun conj mercury-15:08. moon oppos uranus-19:27.

Norma Shearer 1900
Karl Hess 1923
Rhonda Fleming 1923
Eddie Fisher 1928

SUNDAY   AUG. 11

Sun Rises 06:22
Sun Sets 20:07
Moon Rises 01:29
Moon Sets 16:54

MOON IN GEMINI

mars oppos jupiter-04:04.

Mike Douglas 1925
Virna Lisi 1937

1894: Kelly's Hobo Army leaves Washington, D.C., escorted by federal troops. **1965:** Race riot, worst since 1943, erupts in Watts area of Los Angeles. **1983:** Newspaper story first reports of young computer hackers breaking into sophisticated systems, including military installations.

PAY UP

They give you driver's license tests and fishing license tests, but they never give you any license for a child.

George Hamilton

MONDAY   AUG. 12

Sun Rises 06:23
Sun Sets 20:06
Moon Rises 02:15
Moon Sets 17:51

MOON ENTERS CANCER 02:28

moon oppos neptune-04:34. moon trine pluto-06:40.

Diamond Jim Brady 1856
Jane Wyatt 1912
Porter Wagoner 1927
Christy Mathewson 1878
John Derek 1926
Buck Owens 1929

1827: William Blake, artist and writer, dies after singing song about heaven—a witness to the death said, "I have been at the death, not of a man, but of a blessed angel." **1865:** Joseph Lister demonstrates antiseptic surgery. **1934:** Li'l Abner appears in comics. **1965:** Syrian and Israeli troops clash at Jordan River. **1965:** Race riot erupts in Chicago, leaving 1 dead and 67 injured. **1977:** Space shuttle makes its maiden free flight.

To leave positions of great responsibility and authority is to die a little.

Dean Acheson

DEFECTIVE DOGS

by Ken Freed

Consider the Boston bulldog. The dog has a big head with powerful undershot jaws and a small body. Originally bred for baiting bulls, these dogs could bite into the flank of a rampaging bull and not be thrown off. Breeders encouraged a wrinkled face so that a bull's blood would flow away from the dog's eyes. Although virtually no one uses bulldogs for bull baiting any more, the breeding standards remain.

Beyond being downright ugly, all bulldogs inherit a mass of genetic defects. Listen to one of these dogs breathe sometime. Their short face and neck make bulldogs belch bits of food into their lungs, and forces them to breathe too fast and shallow. Their underbite often causes bulldogs to be born with soft or too-long palates. With their narrow flanks, few bulldogs can free-whelp, so great is the risk that bulldog pups will become lodged in the birth canal. Yet those who love bulldogs say they wouldn't have their breed any other way.

Those who love collies are just as adamant about their breeding standards. Their favored traits are expressed by the American Kennel Club breeding standards: "... a large, round, full eye seriously detracts from the desired sweet expression."

Hence, most collies suffer from an ailment the experts call **collie eye anomaly**, a weak spot on the eyeball that collapses as the dogs age. Eventually, the retina becomes detached, leaving the dogs blind. The dogs now called collies once had big round eyes set in square heads. By selecting for narrower heads and smaller eyes, purebred collie fanciers chose the traits that cause blindness in most collies.

In the late 1930s and early 1940s, breeders decided German shepherds should have high shoulders and sloping rumps. Many veterinary orthopedic surgeons assert that this choice leads to **hip dysplasia**, a structural genetic defect where the upper leg bone does not mesh with the hip socket. While dog lovers tend to think shepherds and dysplasia are synonymous, practically all large dogs have this problem.

A separate disease plaguing many large breeds is **gastric torsion** or **bloat**. In this hereditary illness, the stomach suddenly becomes inflated, twists painfully, and presses on the heart and lungs. Bloat tends to appear without warning and usually kills the dog in fifteen minutes.

Where did all of these genetic defects come from? Ten thousand years ago, in the region known as Mesopotamia, our ancestors domesticated wild wolves and other canines, selectively breeding them for traits most beneficial to man. This continuing process eventually created the dog breeds we know today. Such human meddling has replaced healthy traits with flaws.

Purebred dog breeders, most veterinary health authorities agree, are primarily responsible for today's epidemic of genetic defects. The majority of today's inherited ailments come from the selection and awarding of championships to dogs with certain prized, but genetically defective, characteristics.

Show breeders strive for conformity to certain standards — a dog's style is too often more important than its health. In many cases, the two are mutually exclusive. Such standards have allowed genetic defects to proliferate.

Most **glaucoma** in cocker spaniels, for example, can be traced to a three-time winner of the big Madison Square Garden show back in the 1940s. That spaniel, *My Own Brucie*, was bred to hundreds of females. His eye disease spread throughout the breed, and now almost every cocker tends to have glaucoma.

A purebred dog with a good pedigree can mean big dollars in sire or dam fees from commercial breeders and private **fancy**

TUESDAY   AUG. **13**
Sun Rises 06:24
Sun Sets 20:05
Moon Rises 03:10
Moon Sets 18:43
MOON IN CANCER
moon conj venus-02:21. moon trine saturn-19:05.

Felix Adler 1851	Ben Hogan 1912
Rex Humbard 1919	Pat Harrington, Jr. 1929
Don Ho 1930	Dan Fogelberg 1951

1844: First university on West Coast opens (Willamette Univ., Oreg.). **1930:** National Beet Grower's Assoc. incorporates. **1935:** Roller Derby begins in Chicago—50 skaters try to skate distance equal to that from New York to California. **1965:** Birth of the Jefferson Airplane. **1965:** Governor orders Calif. National Guard into Watts to control rioting—more than 14,000 troops are required before violence ends.

Original thought is like original sin: both happened before you were born to people you could not possibly have met.
Fran Lebowitz

WEDNESDAY   AUG. **14**
Sun Rises 06:25
Sun Sets 20:04
Moon Rises 04:13
Moon Sets 19:28
MOON ENTERS LEO 09:57
sun square saturn-08:45. moon square pluto-13:58.

Ernest Dichter 1907	Russell Baker 1925
Buddy Greco 1926	David Crosby 1941
Robyn Smith 1944	Susan Saint James 1946

1912: U.S. Marines sent to Nicaragua. **1935:** Social Security Act passes Congress. **1945:** Japan surrenders—unofficial end of WWII.

Music is a thing that has optimism built into it. Optimism is another way of saying "space." Music has infinite space. You can go as far into music as you can fill millions of lifetimes. Music is an infinite cylinder, it's open-ended, it's space.
Jerry Garcia

THURSDAY   AUG. **15**
Sun Rises 06:26
Sun Sets 20:03
Moon Rises 05:22
Moon Sets 20:07
MOON IN LEO
moon oppos jupiter-04:46. moon conj mars-10:26. moon trine uranus-10:39. moon conj mercury-11:59. mars trine uranus-15:00.

Napoleon Bonaparte 1769	Sir Walter Scott 1771
Thomas de Quincy 1785	Edna Ferber 1887
T.E. Lawrence 1888	Thomas Hart Benton 1889
Wendy Hiller 1912	Oscar Peterson 1925
Stanley Milgram 1933	Barbara Bouchet 1943

1848: Dentist's chair patented. **1876:** U.S. Congress passes law allowing the Powder River and Black Hills country to be taken from the Lakota Nation. **1914:** Panama Canal formally opens. **1935:** Will Rogers, humorist and actor, and Wiley Post, aviator, die in plane crash near Point Barrow, Alaska—Rogers was 56 and Post 36. **1967:** Rosebud Sioux delegation marches to protest Vietnam War. **1969:** Woodstock Festival opens.

FRIDAY   AUG. **16**
Sun Rises 06:26
Sun Sets 20:02
Moon Rises 063:33
Moon Sets 20:41
MOON ENTERS VIRGO 14:15
moon square saturn-00:16. sun conj moon-03:06. mercury conj mars-05:21. moon trine neptune-16:01.

NEW MOON 03:06

George Meany 1894	J.I. Rodale 1898
Eydie Gorme 1931	Julie Newmar 1935
Suzanne Farrell 1945	Lesley Ann Warren 1946

1949: Margaret Mitchell, author of **Gone With The Wind**, dies in Atlanta, Ga. hospital of injuries received after being hit by taxi while on way to see a movie—cab driver was later convicted of involuntary manslaughter. **1977:** Elvis Presley, singer and actor, dies at age 42 on bathroom floor of Graceland home (Tenn.), apparently the victim of misuse of drugs although autopsy report indicated death from natural causes.

SATURDAY   AUG. **17**
Sun Rises 06:27
Sun Sets 20:01
Moon Rises 07:44
Moon Sets 21:11
MOON IN VIRGO
mercury trine uranus-01:58. moon square uranus-13::53.

Davy Crockett 1786	Llewellan George 1876
Mae West 1893	John Hay Whitney 1904
John Hawkes 1925	Robert De Niro 1942
Guillermo Vilas 1952	Belinda Carlisle 1958

1896: Gold deposits discovered in Bonanza Creek (Klondike, Alaska). **1915:** Automobile electric starter patented. **1915:** Leo Frank, factory manager, lynched in Marietta, Georgia, after his death sentence was commuted to life imprisonment—lynching was believed by many to be related to his being Jewish.

This is a time when things must be done before their time.
Robert Redford

SUNDAY   AUG. **18**
Sun Rises 06:28
Sun Sets 20:00
Moon Rises 08:55
Moon Sets 21:41
MOON ENTERS LIBRA 16:44
moon square neptune-16:24.

Marshall Field 1834	Max Factor 1904
Casper Weinberger 1917	Walter J. Hickel 1919
Shelly Winters 1922	Brian Aldiss 1925
Rosalynn Carter 1927	Roman Polanski 1933
Rafer Johnson 1935	Robert Redford 1937

1938: **Wizard of Oz** premieres on the silver screen. **1965:** Curfew is lifted as Watts riot ends, leaving 35 dead, 900 injured, 4,000 arrests, and $200 million in property damage. **1965:** Mass. governor John Volpe signs first statute in U.S. outlawing racial imbalance in public schools. **1976:** 2 U.S. soldiers are killed by North Korean soldiers while pruning a tree in demilitarized zone. **1978:** Rosalynn Carter pilots Goodyear blimp over Virginia.

Einstein would have been a computer pirate.
Steve Wozniak

breeders — who together handle most of the AKC registered dogs being bred — to the many **backyard breeders** who earn tidy sums by arranging mates for their AKC certified dogs.

The primary source of uncertified pure-bred dogs is the **puppy mills**, large operations mass-producing dogs for pet stores. The less reputable of these breeders either do not check their breeding pairs for defects, or ignore any obvious genetic problems, or both. They also ship defective dogs without spaying or neutering, which allows defects to spread.

Pet stores compound the problem; few inspect their *merchandise* for genetic defects. Though veterinarians are called in for crises and cursory check-ups, dealers say costs for regular genetic screenings are prohibitive.

Shop owners also set prices according to each breed's popularity, frequently without regard for an individual animal's condition. And when consumers favor a particular breed, efforts to supply the increased demand furthur encourage unrestrained production of defective dogs.

Pet owners who fail to neuter their dogs, yet allow them to roam the neighborhood must also share the blame. If their pet has a defect, the faulty trait is perpetuated through any future breeding. Similarly, when pet owners choose to home-breed their dogs — whether as a genetic experiment or for economic opportunity — it's the pups who must live with tinkered genetics.

High veterinary fees encourage more defects too, because many masters can only afford vet visits for emergencies or rabies shots. So most genetic defects are neither diagnosed nor treated. Pet owners who avoid regular pre-natal visits for pregnant canines also risk creating new genetic disorders among the unborn litter.

Veterinarians share the responsibility directly as well. Despite a code of ethics that requires vets to discourage the breeding of defective animals, they often perform artificial insemination on dogs incapable of coitus.

Finally, the humane movement could do more to curb genetic defects in dogs. While animal shelters play an important role as pet adoption agencies, few shelters require sterilization of obviously defective dogs before releasing the animals to new owners. There are at least 35 million dogs alive in America today; just how many suffer congenital defects is uncertain. But eliminating these hereditary ailments among our canine kin will require enormous effort and cooperation. If something isn't done to save the dogs soon, we're likely to breed them into extinction.

EVERYDAY WONDERS

The Birth of the Mail
by Micki Magyar

When you have finished writing a letter, you put it into an envelope, put a stamp on it, and post it in a mail box. But these three common items have not always been around. Envelopes were first used in 1609. Before the introduction of uniform postage, envelopes, or enclosing sheets were seldom used, as they were charged as an extra sheet. In 1830, a stationer at Brighton, the fashionable resort in England, manufactured some envelopes which were popular at the resort, but the use of this separate "enclosing folder" did not become common until some time later.

Postage stamps came into popular use at about the same time. Various private postal services had operated on the continent and in England in the 1600s, and some of them used stamps to indicate that payment for delivery had been made.

In 1838 in Sydney, Australia, the Post Office issued a prepaid envelope with an embossed stamp on it. A letter enclosed in one of these envelopes would be delivered anywhere in the Sydney district. Eventually, with the invention of the adhesive stamp in 1834, the stamps and the envelopes became separate items.

Letter boxes were first used in France by one of the private postal services. The first known letter box in England was a cast-iron box in the side of the postal building in Wakefield, dated 1809. This device was copied in the United States — first by the many private postal companies that provided service in the colonies, and later by the governmental service.

MONDAY — AUG. 19

Sun Rises 06:29
Sun Sets 19:58
Moon Rises 10:06
Moon Sets 22:07

MOON IN LIBRA

moon trine jupiter-09:35. moon at perigee-21:00.

Coco Chanel 1883	Alfred Lunt 1892
P.D. Ouspensky 1897	Ogden Nash 1902
James Cozzens 1903	Malcolm Forbes 1919
Willie Shoemaker 1931	Diana Muldaur 1938

1929: *Amos an' Andy* debuts on radio. **1965:** *U.S. troops destroy Vietcong stronghold in first major battle as independent force.* **1974:** *Rodger Davies, U.S. ambassador to Cyprus, is assassinated.*

The time of our grandfathers is past. But were those proud old men here today, they would probably have already registered Republican.

Spiro Agnew

TUESDAY — AUG. 20

Sun Rises 06:30
Sun Sets 19:56
Moon Rises 11:17
Moon Sets 22:37

MOON ENTERS SCORPIO 18:51

moon square venus-03:38. mercury directs-15:47.
moon conj pluto-22:50.

Oliver Hazard Perry 1785	H.P. Lovecraft 1890
Jacqueline Susann 1921	Don King 1931
Isaac Hayes 1942	Graig Nettles 1944

1968: *Last Imperial Pheasant dies in U.S. zoo.*

WEDNESDAY — AUG. 21

Sun Rises 06:31
Sun Sets 19:54
Moon Rises 12:29
Moon Sets 23:09

MOON IN SCORPIO

venus trine saturn-02:35. moon square jupiter-11:26.
moon square mercury-17:13.

Chris Schenkel 1923	Princess Margaret 1930
Wilt Chamberlain 1936	Kenny Rogers 1938
Peter Weir 1944	Jackie Deshannon 1944

1831: *Nat Turner and followers rebel—murder 55 whites over next 2 days.* **1901:** *Iron Man McGinnity thrown out of National Baseball League for stepping on Umpire's toes and spitting in his face.* **1971:** *George Jackson, Black Panther and one of the Soledad Brothers, is shot and killed while attempting to escape from San Quentin Prison (Calif.).* **1979:** *Nicaragua issues Bill of Rights.* **1983:** *Benigno Aquino, Jr., leader of political opposition in Philippines, is assassinated upon his return from exile.*

RETREAT

EVERYDAY WONDERS

The Birth of Gum
by Micki Magyar

Anyone who has found a wad of used chewing gum on a theater seat may wonder why it should have been invented in the first place. But Americans consume tons of the sticky stuff every year, in an ever-growing variety of flavors and types.

The first gum sold for chewing was a spruce gum, made in 1848 by John Curtis, in Bangor, Maine. People had been chewing on the sticky sweet gum of pine and spruce trees since they got the habit from the Indians, but this was the beginning of chewing gum as we know it today.

The various types of spruce gum were quite popular. So much so that when Thomas Adams came up with the idea of using chicle, with flavoring added, he was told it would never sell. He tried it anyway, starting up a small factory in 1872.

As we know, the new gum did sell, and he made a small fortune. And in 1888, the first vending machine gum, *Tutti-Frutti*, appeared in the stations of the elevated trains in New York. Production has only increased since then, and with new varieties appearing each year, it seems as though the supply for theater seats won't run out soon.

WEATHER

To interpret the forecasts presented here, one must first understand the importance of the ten regions depicted on this map. These geographical areas are distinguished, one from another, by the differences in their weather patterns. Regional topography is a primary factor influencing these distinct regional weather patterns. For example, when westerly winds stretch from the west coast to the great plains, remarkably different weather occurs from place to place. Where the winds create an upslope condition on the windward side of mountains, precipitation is likely. At the same time, a downslope condition on the leeward side would produce the opposite effect.

Even within the boundaries of one region, vast weather differences may occur. One mountain, for instance, can create local weather variances within close proximity. Furthermore, a relatively cool body of water greater than three miles in diameter may have a quieting effect on convective precipitation such as thunderstorms. These same water surfaces may create local temperature differences (fronts). Because thunderstorms affect an area in a "hit or miss" fashion, a general forecast cannot account for all the vagaries within a region.

The following are general forecasts for each of the ten regions depicted on the map. It is possible, therefore, that your particular location may have considerably different weather. In addition, the dates indicated for precipitation and periods of warm or cold weather are approximate. Temperature averages are projected for lower elevations only.

Thank you. If you have any questions or comments, please write to us.

— **Ed Pearl, Meteorologist**

December 1984

1 Wet early and late in the month; cold early, then seasonal to mild temperatures. Temperatures should average from 40° to 45°. Steady rain most of the first week. Relatively dry weather is expected December 8-21, then showery periods will increase through month's end. Showers are expected December 21-23, 25-27, and 29-31. Coldest weather with heavy mountain snows December 1-7.

2 Average precipitation; cool late in the first week through mid-month, otherwise near normal temperatures. Temperatures will average 48° coastal areas, 39° inland north to 50° in the deserts. Showers in California about December 3-6, then general showers possible all areas December 14-18 with snow in the mountains. Possible snow in the northern Arizona mountains December 24-27. Cold weather is expected December 9-16. More cloudiness than normal.

3 Mild early in the month and briefly at mid-month, otherwise colder and wetter than normal. Temperatures at lower elevations should average from 26° to 32°. Showers at lower elevations the start of first week accompanied by mountain snows, snow increasing toward end of week. Repeated periods of mostly snow at 3-5 day intervals after first week increasing again December 25-31. Coldest weather is anticipated December 8-14 and again December 26-31.

4 Mild first ten days, then considerably colder remainder of month; precipitation near or slightly below normal falling mainly as snow. Temperatures should average from 16° north to 28° south. Coldest readings should occur about December 6-8, 12-14, 18-20, 25-26, and 30-31. Very strong winds will accompany and precede cold air outbreaks.

5 Mild early in month, then below normal temperatures; precipitation will be near normal east and much above normal west. Temperatures should average from 32° north to 45° south. Warmest readings should occur December 5-8 and coldest weather December 12-16 and 25-31. Light showers or rain are possible December 1-2 and 9-10, then heavier precipitation will occur later. In the west most likely dates are December 14-18 and 25-29 for significant precipitation, the east

FORECAST

will have a greater chance for rain and snow December 11-14, 21-23, and 24-27.

6 **Colder than normal with near normal precipitation.** Average temperatures will likely range from 17° north to 28° south. Frequent light snows should start about December 10 and occur at about 3-4 day intervals. Rainshowers are possible south early in the period. Temperatures near normal December 1-7 except below normal north. Below normal temperatures should dominate from December 8-31 with only brief reading near normal.

7 **A gradual cooling trend through the month, precipitation near or slightly above normal.** Temperatures should average from 35° north to 49° south. Precipitation

should be most likely about December 1-2, 5-7, -12, 17-20, and 25-28. Snow may occur into the deep south December 26-27. Temperatures slightly above normal. Coldest period December 27-31.

8 **Cold at mid-month, otherwise a cool month; precipitation above normal.** Temperatures most likely will average from 24° west and north to 34° near the coast. Snow inland and coastal rain is most likely December 2-5, 8-10, 14-15, 19-20, 24-27, and 30-31. Snow should be moderate or light through December 20 and heavier thereafter. Coldest weather will probably occur from December 16-20 and December 31.

9 **Cooler than normal, near or slightly above normal precipitation.** Tem-

peratures should average from 32° west and north to 39° south coastal areas. Light to moderate precipitation should occur frequently, most likely dates are December 2-4, 7, 9-10, 15-16, 19-20, 24-26, and 29-31. Snow is quite likely in the mountains with rain along the coast and rain and snow elsewhere. Coldest weather December 26-31.

10 **Temperature mild most of month, cool at month's end; precipitation above normal.** Temperatures should average from 57° north to 63° south. Periods of showers and thundershowers, some heavy, are most likely December 3-5, 17-20, and 28-30. Possible freeze north and central about December 31. Although mild, it will likely be cloudier than normal except extreme south.

January

1 **Near normal temperatures and average rainfall.** Temperatures should average from 36° to 40°. Precipitation is likely at frequent intervals lasting 2-3 days. Heaviest precipitation will probably occur at mid-month about January 12-15 and 17-20. Very little fluctuation in temperatures except for that associated with the precipitation.

2 **Near normal temperatures and slightly below normal precipitation.** Temperatures should average from 48° along the coast, 40° across the inland north to about 51° in the deserts. More temperature variation east and north than the west. Coldest weather in the east January 2-6 and 24-28. Greatest likelihood of showers and mountain snows January 2-3, 15-17, and 24-26.

3 **Cold early and late, mild mid-month; precipitation near normal.** Temperatures should average from 23° to 28° at lower elevations. Snow mainly east January 2-5, 23-25, and 28-30. General precipitation January 14-15 and 18-20. Coldest temperatures January 5-6 and 23-31. Warmest readings January 12-20. Windy mid-month.

4 **Very cold at start and end of month, mild mid-month; normal precipitation.** Average temperatures should range from 8° north to 25° south. A series of light snows are expected January 1-3, 6-8, 10, 22-24, and 29-30. Some snow, north only, January 13-14 and 18-19. Coldest weather is anticipated January 1-9 and again January 23-31. Windy periods.

5 **Cold early in the month and cold** late in the north, otherwise mild; precipitation near normal. Temperatures should range from 29° north to 44° south. Rain south and snow north January 1-3 and 7-8, lighter isolated showers possible January 14-15 and 19-20. Heavier rain, some snow north, is expected January 23-25 and 30-31. Cold January 1-9 and mainly north January 25-31. Very warm extreme south January 25-27.

6 **Gradual moderation in temperature, precipitation near normal.** Temperatures should average from 11° north to 27° south. Coldest weather most likely will occur January 1-11, then gradually warming. Possibly much colder January 30-31. Warmest January 25-29. Light snows possible every other day January 1-8 and north only January 13-15 and 19-20. General rain south and snow north January 29-31.

7 **Cold early, then cool east and mild west mid-month and warm at end of month; wet early, then relatively dry.** Temperatures should range from an average of 35° north to 52° south. Rain south and snow north January 9-10, 15-17, 22-23, and possible heavy thunderstorms January 30-31.

8 **Normal temperatures and near normal precipitation.** Temperatures should range from an average of 22° north and west to 31° near the coast. Snow inland and rain along the coast is especially likely January 1-4, then lighter precipitation is expected at 3-4 day intervals for much of the month. Better than average skiing expected. The chance for major cold outbreaks or warm periods is low.

9 **Cool mid-month, otherwise near normal temperatures; precipitation slightly above normal.** Temperature averages should range from 31° west to 39° east. No significant above or below normal temperatures expected, except cooler than normal January 15-19. Precipitation as mainly snow west and mainly rain along the coast January 2-5, 8-9, 14-15, 21-22, and 28-29.

10 **Warmer than normal most of month; near normal precipitation.** Temperatures should range from an average of 57° north to 63° south. A period of moderate to heavy thunderstorms January 2-5, then lighter precipitation on or about January 9, 14-15, 22, and 31. Cool weather north January 15-19. Probably more sunshine than normal for southern Florida.

February

1 **Temperatures slightly below normal, above normal precipitation.** Temperatures should average from 39° to 43°. Windy especially along the coast and higher terrain. Frequent precipitation at 1-3 day intervals producing some local flooding. A brief pause in the precipitation between February 10 and 14. Coldest weather should occur the first eleven days. More cloud cover than the usual.

2 **Cold mid-month, otherwise generally mild; precipitation above normal north to near normal south.** Temperatures should average from 51° along the coast, 40° across the inland north to 54° in the deserts. Showers on the coast and snow mainly inland north February 1-3 and 6-7, snow and rain mostly inland February 12-15, then scattered rain and snow mostly north February 19-28 at 3-4 day intervals. Windier than normal northern mountains and coast.

3 **Above normal temperatures start of month, below mid-month and near normal at end; precipitation should be well above normal.** Temperature averages should range from 27° to 33° at lower elevations. Heavy snows at high elevations and rain and snow at low elevations are expected February 2-4, 7-8, 12-15, 19-21, and 24-28. Coldest weather February 13-17, warmest conditions February 1-2. Windy especially in the mountains.

4 **Wet and cold mid-month, otherwise most of area will be dry, windy, and mild.** Average temperatures should range from 17° north to 32° south. Precipitation, as mainly snow, is expected February 7-9 and 14-18. Snowshowers west and north at 2-3 day intervals between those dates and at month's end. Warm weather is expected February 4-7 and 24-28, a cold period February 15-19. Windy especially west and north.

5 **Above normal temperatures and near to below normal precipitation.** Temperatures should average from 36° north to near 50° south. Precipitation dates are difficult to forecast, however rain and possibly some snow should occur from February 14-18. A period or two of light rain or showers are possible at other undetermined dates. Coldest weather is likely February 14-19, warmest weather is likely February 11-13 and almost all month extreme south.

6 **Below normal temperatures warming last week; below normal precipitation.** Temperatures should

February

average from 10° north to 25° south. Precipitation will probably occur as light snow periods February 1-3, 7-8, 11-12, 17-18, and mainly north February 21-22 and 26-27. Coldest weather through February 17 then milder, especially south. Warmest south February 24-26.

7 **Cool early in month then gradual warming, precipitation near normal except dry last week.** Temperatures should average from 39° north to 54° south. Coldest weather probably February 1-7, warmest likely February 24-28. Precipitation, mainly as rain February 2-4 (snow north),

7-8, 12-13, and 17-18. Dry period February 22-28.

8 **Cool most of month becoming mild last week, above normal precipitation.** Temperatures should average from 21° west and north to 31° near the coast. Precipitation as frequent snow and possible coastal showers is expected on or about February 2-3, 5-6, 8-9, 12-13, and 17-18. Rain and snow is expected February 22-23 and 27-28. Coldest February 3-10 and warmest February 24-28.

9 **Cold early in the month followed by gradual warming to above normal readings; precipitation near normal.** Temperatures should range

from 34° inland and north to 41° near the coast. Precipitation should fall February 2-3, 8-9, 12-13, and 18-19 as snow inland and rain along the coast. Mild to warm and dry February 21-28.

10 **A variable cold/warm period through mid-month, then mild and dry; precipitation near normal.** Temperatures should average from 58° north to 62° south. Precipitation is most likely as showers and thunderstorms February 1-2, 6-7, 12-14, and 18-20. February 21-28 should be mainly dry with possible isolated showers and thunderstorms. Coldest weather February 2-4.

March

1 **Slightly above normal precipitation and below normal temperatures.** Temperature averages should range from 41° to 46°. Heavy coastal rain and higher elevation snow March 1-3, then additional rain heaviest about March 6-7, 10-11, 15-16, 19-20, 25-26, and 30-31. Coldest weather March 2-4, then brief mild spells before each precipitation event. Local flooding possible from precipitation combined with melting high country snows March 4-11.

2 **Above normal precipitation and below normal temperatures.** Temperatures should average from 51° along the coast, 44° inland north to 57° in the deserts. Rain with snow in the mountains March 1-5, showers and mountain snow March 11-12, 16-17, and 20-21. General rain with mountain snows moving slowly from west to east March 26-31. Coldest weather will be associated with each precipitation period.

3 **Above normal precipitation and slightly below normal temperatures.** Temperatures should average from 34° to 39° at lower elevations. Some rain at lowest elevations otherwise heavy snows especially in the mountains March 2-4, 7-8, 11-13, 20-23, and 30-31. Coldest weather should be coincidental with the precipitation. Mild weather just preceding each precipitation event.

4 **Above normal precipitation and slightly below normal tempera-**

tures. Temperature averages should range from 27° north to 39° south. Heavy snows in areas prone to upslope conditions, snow and rain elsewhere. Most likely dates for precipitation are March 3-5, 8-9, 12-14, 21-24, and 30-31. Coldest weather will be directly associated with the precipitation. Mild to warm conditions should just precede each storm system.

5 **Slightly above normal precipitation and near normal temperatures.** Although sharp changes are expected, temperatures should average from 44° north to 56° south. Significant precipitation falling mainly as rain showers and thunderstorms should occur March 3-5, 9, 12-14, 22-24, and 31. Coolest weather should occur March 4-5, 13-15, and 23-24. Warm conditions are likely between each precipitation event.

6 **Temperatures near normal and precipitation near normal.** Temperature averages should range from 28° north to 37° south. Precipitation should fall mainly as snow north and west and rain elsewhere. Most likely dates for precipitation are March 4-6, 13-15, 22-25, and 31. Coldest weather March 1-6, warmest weather March 10-12 and 18-21. A cloudy month especially north.

7 **Cool first of month, then mainly above normal temperatures; precipitation near normal.** Temperatures should average from 47° north to near 60° south. Precipitation as rain

March 1-3, then mainly showers and thunderstorms March 7-8, 15-16, 24-26, and west March 31. Severe thunderstorms likely March 15-16, 24-26, and 31. Very humid at times March 20-31. Coldest weather March 2-6 and warmest March 20-31.

8 **Near normal temperatures and slightly below normal precipitation.** Temperatures should range from averages of 33° west and north to 39° near coastal areas. Precipitation should fall as snow and rain west and rain east. Most likely dates for precipitation are March 1-4, 7-8, 15-16, and 24-25. Coldest weather is expected March 3-7. A very cloudy month.

9 **Slightly above normal temperatures and below normal precipitation.** Temperatures should average from 43° north and west to 59° along south coastal areas. Showers March 2-4, 8, 16-17, 25, and 30-31. Coldest weather March 4-6 and again March 31, mild or warm weather much of the month.

10 **Warm early, then cool late in the month; slightly below normal precipitation.** Temperatures should average from 63° north to 69° south. Precipitation should occur as isolated thunderstorms at almost anytime, more organized heavier thunderstorms can be expected March 2-3, 16, 25-26, and 31. Coolest weather March 28-31. Severe weather in north central areas is likely on precipitation dates.

April

1 **Frequent periods of showers and slightly below normal temperatures.** Temperatures should average from 48° to 52°. Showers and periods of rain should occur at 2-3 day intervals through April 20, dates are too difficult to ascertain. April 21-30 showers should be less frequent and lighter occurring April 23-24 and 27-28. Coldest weather first week of month and warmest last week. Very windy along the north coast.

2 **Below normal precipitation and**

above normal temperatures. Temperatures should average from 56° along the coast, 52° inland north and 70° in the deserts. Most likely chance for precipitation will be April 24-27 mainly in the eastern mountains. Very dry weather much of the region. Warmest weather April 1-5, coolest east April 24-30. More than the usual amount of sunshine.

3 **The month starting dry, then wetter; above normal temperatures, then cooler.** Temperatures should range from an average of 44° to 49°. Most likely precipitation should fall April 6-8, 10-11, 4-5, 7-8, 20-21, and 24-28. Precipitation

should mainly be rain at lower elevations and snow in the mountains. Warmest April 1-4 and coolest east April 25-29. Cloudier than normal east.

4 **Cool and wet at start and end of the month; mild, windy, and dry at mid-month.** Temperatures should range from an average of 44° north to 51° south. Snow west and rain east April 1-5 and 25-29, otherwise widely scattered showers, especially east at about 4 day intervals. Very windy with the storms at start and end of month, also windy at mid-month. Warmest weather at mid-month and coldest with the storms.

WEATHER FORECAST

April

5 **Wet at start and end of month, temperatures slightly below normal.** Temperatures should average from 55° north to 63° south. Heaviest precipitation falling as rain west and possible severe thunderstorms east April 2-5 and 26-30. Only isolated showers and thunderstorms between the storm dates. Coldest weather April 4-6 and 28-30, warmest April 2-20. Coldest weather will be enhanced west by cold upslope rains.

6 **Near normal temperatures and above normal precipitation.** Temperatures should range from averages of 44° north to 50° south. Most precipitation should fall as showers and thunderstorms south and snow and rain near the Canadian border. Most likely precipitation dates April 2-5, 9-10, 5-6, 20-21, and 26-30. Coldest all areas April 5-7 and 28-30 northwest. Cloudier than normal. Colder along the shores of the Great Lakes.

7 **Near normal precipitation, near normal temperatures west and above normal east.** Temperature averages should range from 59° northwest to 68° southeast. Severe

or heavy thunderstorms expected from west to east April 3-7 and 26-30, widely scattered showers and thunderstorms between those dates most frequent and heaviest near the Gulf. Warm most of month east and mainly between storms west.

8 **Cool early in month, then near or slightly above normal temperatures; near normal precipitation.** Temperature averages should range from 46° west and north to about 50° near the coast. Precipitation is most likely April 1-3, 6-8, 10-11, 6-7, 21-22, and 29-30. Coldest first few days of the month, warmest April 24-26. A very cloudy month.

9 **Slightly above normal temperatures and near normal precipitation.** Temperatures should average from 55° inland to 60° along the coast.

Heaviest organized precipitation April 1-3, then widely scattered showers or thunderstorms at 3-4 day intervals. Possible heavy or severe storms April 29-30. Coolest April 2-4 and warmest April 27-29. A very humid month.

10 **Slightly above normal precipitation and above normal temperatures.** Average temperatures should range from 71° to 78°. Most likely heavy thunderstorms April 2-4 then scattered thunderstorms at almost any time. A very humid summery type month. Coolest April 4-5, warm rest of period.

May

1 **Showery periods with near normal precipitation, slightly below normal temperatures.** Average temperatures should range from 54° to 58°. Precipitation should occur mainly as light showers at 3-4 day intervals. Mild just prior to the onset of showers and cool during precipitation. Quite cloudy with somewhat less than normal sunshine. No specific precipitation dates can be given.

2 **Normal precipitation west, wetter east; slightly below normal temperatures.** Temperatures should average from 58° along the coast, 50° inland north and 74° in the deserts. Snow in northern Arizona mountains and showers at lower elevations May 1-4 and May 11-14, widely scattered showers and thunderstorms inland and deserts May 23-25 and 29-31. Coolest weather east May 11-14, warmest May 19-22.

3 **Above normal precipitation south, near normal north; slightly below normal temperatures.** Temperature averages should range from 51° to 56° at lower elevations. Most likely general precipitation dates are May 1-4, 7-8, 11-14, and 19-20. Widely scattered thunderstorms and showers May 23-25 and 29-31. Heaviest precipitation south. Snow in higher mountains on general precipitation dates. Cloudier than normal. Coolest weather on general precipitation dates.

4 **Above normal precipitation and**

below normal temperatures. Temperature averages should range from 54° north to near 60° south. Precipitation is most likely May 2-5, 8-10, 13-14, and 20-21. Scattered thunderstorms are possible at any time May 22-31. Precipitation west part of region May 8-10 may fall as snow. Much cloudier than normal. Coolest weather should coincide with precipitation, warmest at end of month.

5 **Above normal precipitation west and near normal elsewhere; temperatures slightly below normal north to near normal south.** Temperatures should average from 64° north to 73° south. Widely scattered thunderstorms are possible at almost anytime south, organized precipitation north is expected May 2-5, 8-10, 13-14, and 20-21. Becoming very warm and humid the last week. Coolest weather May 13-15.

6 **Cool at start and warm at the end of the month, near or slightly below normal precipitation.** Temperatures should range from an average of 56° north to 60° south. Most likely precipitation May 4-6, 9-10, 13-15, and 21-24. Coldest May 1-4, warmest May 26-31. Humid, especially south, May 26-31. Cooler along the shores of the Great Lakes.

7 **Cool at mid-month, otherwise above normal temperatures; slightly below normal precipitation.** Temperatures should average from 69° north to 76° south. General showers and thunderstorms May 13-15, otherwise a threat of isolated

to scattered thunderstorms on an almost daily basis. Coolest weather May 15-16, warm rest of month. A very humid month.

8 **Cool early in month, then warmer than usual; near normal precipitation.** Temperatures should range from 59° north and west to 62° near the coast. Cool and showery May 1-2, general precipitation May 14-16 and 23-25. Otherwise only a few showers or thundershowers possible. Coldest May 2-5, warmest from May 18 through 311.

9 **Cool early in month, then above normal temperatures; near normal precipitation.** Temperatures should average from 65° west and north to 70° in south coastal areas. Other than organized showers and thunderstorms May 14-16, a few thunderstorms may be expected at almost any time. Cool May 1-5, then generally warm and humid. Slow moving thunderstorms may cause small areas of flooding north late in the month.

10 **Slightly above normal temperatures; stormy early in the month, then relatively dry.** Temperatures should average from 76° north to 82° south. Heavy thunderstorms May 3-5, then only isolated thunderstorms at times thereafter. More sunshine than normal and slightly less humid.

June

1 **Near normal precipitation and temperatures.** Temperatures should average from 60° to 64°. Precipitation should be light and infrequent as weak weather systems move on to the north coast. Very difficult to define dates for the precipitation. Coolest weather will accompany the showers. Cloudier north than south. No unusual weather activity.

2 **A changing month, warm to hot and dry, then wetter and cooler in Arizona and western New Mexico at month's end.** Temperature averages should range from 62° along the coast, the mid 70s inland north and 85° in the deserts. Clear skies most of the month, except for coastal fog and stratus. June 25-30 significantly wetter and cooler weather in eastern Arizona and western New Mexico. Locally heavy thunderstorms southeastern Arizona.

3 **Near normal temperatures and precipitation.** Average temperatures should range from 63° to 67°. Precipitation should occur as mainly isolated shower and thunderstorm activity, heaviest thunderstorms extreme southeast June 1-6 and again June 28-30. Very little in terms of significant weather anticipated. Warmest weather June 20-27.

4 **Cool early in month, then very warm; near normal precipitation.** Temperatures should average from 67° to 72°. Showers and thunderstorms should be most prevalent June 1-3, 12-16 (east-central), and southwest June 28-30. Isolated locally heavy thunderstorms are possible at almost any time, but mainly in the afternoon west and at night east. Coolest weather June 3-5, then quite warm except for brief cooling Montana and North Dakota.

5 **Very warm month; isolated areas of very heavy rainfall.** Temperatures should range from 76° to 83° for averages. Minimum organized thunderstorm activity, however isolated thunderstorms or squall lines are anticipated. Most numerous storms in Texas and eastern New Mexico. Local flash flooding is likely along with an increased threat of tornado activity.

6 **Cool early and late in month, very hot and humid at mid-month.** Temperatures should average from the mid-60°s north to near 70° south, 5 to 10 degrees cooler along the Great Lakes. Coolest weather June 3-7 and then cooling north June 26-30. Thunderstorms mainly south June 2-4, general storms June 14-18, otherwise isolated thunderstorms anticipated. A high likelihood for severe weather June 15-17.

7 **Below normal precipitation and above normal daytime temperatures.** Temperatures should average from 80° to 83°. Two notable exceptions to a general drying trend: (I) isolated very heavy thunderstorms along the Gulf and in Texas and (2) a period of heavy thunderstorms east June 16-19. Above normal sunshine, but quite hazy.

8 **Slightly below normal temperatures and near normal precipitation.** Temperatures should average from 66° to 69°. Showers and thundershowers should accompany weak cool fronts at about 4-5 day intervals. No specific dates for precipitation can be given. Greater than normal cloud cover anticipated. Warm only on the day prior to each cool front.

9 **Near normal temperatures, above normal precipitation north and below normal south.** Temperatures should average from 72° west and north to 76° near the south coast. Cool air outbreaks in section 8 should produce periods of moderate to heavy thunderstorms north, some possibly severe. Across the southern area mainly dry air should persist except for thunderstorms June 17-19.

10 **Near to below normal precipitation; near normal temperatures.** Temperatures should average form near 80° north to 83° south. About below normal precipitation except for numerous thunderstorms at times across south Florida. Daytime highs primarily above normal and nighttime lows slightly below normal. Most of region will have above normal sunshine.

July

1 **Near normal temperatures and precipitation.** Temperatures should average from 65° to 69°. Only a few showers possible the entire month, no specific dates of occurrence can be given. Night and morning fogs should be a regular event along the coast. A very sunny month.

2 **Cooling temperatures and above normal precipitation should mark the month.** Temperatures should average from 63° along the coast, 76° inland north to 89° in the deserts. Surges of thunderstorms, some very heavy, should gradually spread west and north from eastern Arizona. Much daytime cooling is expected in and near the thunderstorms. Little or no storm activity in western California. Cloudier than normal inland, also humid.

3 **Above normal precipitation and below normal temperatures.** Temperatures should average from 72° to 75° at lower elevations. Frequent afternoon and evening scattered thunderstorms should gradually spread northward. Locally heavy rains should develop south by mid-month. Since the storms will not affect all areas, there will be a few locations with relatively little rainfall. Very strong winds in and near the thunderstorms.

4 **Above normal precipitation and near normal temperatures.** Temperatures should average from 71° north to 76° south. Thunderstorms east July 1-2, then scattered thunderstorms will increase July 13-31. Locally heavy thunderstorms especially southwest and southeast portion of the area. Although temperatures will be near normal, rapid cooling will occur near thunderstorms. Coolest weather expected north July 2-4, warmest weather July 6-II.

5 **Above normal precipitation north, near or slightly below normal south; near normal temperatures.** Temperatures should average from 80° north to 86° south. A brief heat wave July 2-6 east. Scattered thunderstorms increasing north July 13-31; only isolated, locally heavy thunderstorms south. Above normal sunshine.

6 **Above normal precipitation west and below east, near or slightly above normal temperatures.** Temperatures should range from 72° north to 76° south. Scattered thunderstorms west at 2-3 day intervals through most of the month. Organized severe thunderstorms north about July 15. Only isolated thunderstorms elsewhere.

7 **Below normal precipitation and near normal temperatures.** Temperatures should average from 81° to 84° and should be slightly above normal for daytime highs and below for nighttime lows. A hazy, but sunny month. Most thunderstorm activity should occur along the Gulf. Very heavy precipitation along the Gulf July 24-29 from a possible tropical storm. Drought conditions inland.

8 **Above normal temperatures and below normal precipitation.** Temperatures should average from 74° to 79°. A rather dry month, isolated very heavy thunderstorms will locally cause above normal precipitation. No specific dates can be set for the thunderstorms. Above normal sunshine and a very warm to hot month.

9 **Below normal precipitation and near normal temperatures.** Temperatures should average from 75° to 80°. Very little precipitation. Drought conditions may be widespread. Above normal sunshine, however, there will be a significant haze and pollution build-up. Above normal daytime highs and below normal at night.

10 **Above normal precipitation and somewhat below normal temperatures.** Temperatures should average from 79° to 84°. Bands of showers and thunderstorms should cross from east to west at 4-5 day intervals, locally heavy rains especially south half. A possible tropical storm July 19-24 could cause flooding conditions. A relatively cloudy month and therefore somewhat cooler days.

WEATHER FORECAST
August

1 Very little precipitation and near or above normal temperatures. Temperatures should average from 66° to 70°. Coastal areas should remain cool. Precipitation will be minimal with only an isolated shower or thunderstorm expected inland. Significant drying is generally anticipated. A sunny month except for coastal fog and haze inland. No major cool outbreaks foreseen. Very warm at times inland with a high fire danger.

2 Above normal precipitation inland, below normal temperatures inland and near normal near the coast. Temperatures should average from 63° near the coast, 75° inland north to 86° in the deserts. Locally heavy thunderstorms inland through mid-month likely causing some flooding. Much cooling in areas with storms. Very little, if any, coastal precipitation. A very cloudy month inland. Thunderstorms should end in all areas except southeast by month's end.

3 Above normal precipitation south, near normal north; near normal temperatures. Temperatures should average from 70° to 75°. Heavy, mainly late day, thunderstorms south through August 15; general drying trend thereafter. Only isolated mountain thunderstorms north through the month. Coolest weather south with thunderstorms and cooler east August 26-31. Local flooding and hail likely south through August 15.

4 Near or slightly above normal temperatures, then much cooler at month's end; near normal precipitation. Temperatures should average near 70°. Precipitation should fall as frequent periods of scattered thunderstorms through August 20, then a widespread thunderstorm outbreak August 26-29. A warm month, except for very cool weather spreading from north to south August 27-30. Possible frost north areas about August 30.

5 Above normal precipitation and near normal temperatures. Temperatures should average from 78° north to 82° south. Scattered thunderstorms with locally heavy precipitation most of the month. Heaviest storms southwest at mid-month. Local flooding will be likely along with potentially large hail. Turning much cooler north and east August 29-31. Very humid.

6 Near normal precipitation west and relatively dry elsewhere, except for a general wet period at end of month; above normal temperatures, cooling at month's end. Temperatures should average from 70° to 75°. Widely scattered thunderstorms mainly west through August 10, drying through August 25 then thunderstorms moving from northwest to south and east August 26-31. Coldest period August 28-31, otherwise mostly warm.

7 Above normal precipitation west and below elsewhere; near normal temperatures. Temperatures should average from 78° north to 83° south. Periods of showers and thunderstorms west at about four day intervals, most intense thunderstorms will probably occur August 29-30. Potential for a tropical storm or hurricane along the Gulf Coast will be high from August 20 to month's end. No significant cool periods.

8 Near normal temperatures and precipitation. Temperatures should range from 70° north and west to 73° near the south coast. Very little significant weather to report. A few thunderstorms possible mainly in the late afternoons through August 20. A general cooling trend August 22 through 31. Probably the best weather of the summer. Very comfortable except for heat and humidity near the major south coast cities.

9 Slightly above normal temperatures and near normal precipitation. Temperatures should average from 75° to 78°. Precipitation probably will occur as widely scattered or isolated thunderstorms. A few of those storms will likely be heavy. Another hazy month, but less so. Turning cooler with heavy thunderstorms north on or about August 24.

10 Above normal precipitation south and near normal north, slightly below normal temperatures. Temperatures should average form 80° to 85°. Thunderstorms probably will move across southern Florida at about 4-5 day intervals. Isolated to widely scattered thunderstorms elsewhere at almost any time. An increasing threat for a hurricane or tropical storm the last II days of the month.

September

1 Temperatures near normal becoming above normal at month's end; precipitation near normal. Temperatures should average from 60° to 64°. Periods of showers at 4-5 day intervals through September 17 mainly north, then very dry. Cool weather with the showers. Hot weather September 20-30 and the heat may build to the coast by month's end.

2 Near normal precipitation and temperatures. Temperatures should average from 64° near the coast, 70° across the inland north to 84° in the deserts. Thunderstorms at times across south-central Arizona, otherwise typical area wide drying. Coolest weather northeast at mid-month otherwise seasonally mild to warm temperatures. Abundant sunshine, light winds except for daytime gustiness in the deserts and on the coast.

3 Near normal precipitation; below normal temperatures northeast and near or above southwest. Temperatures should average from 60° to 67° at lower elevations. A few thunderstorms in so. mountains through September 10, mountain snows and valley rains September 14-18 eastern area only, scattered mountain snows northeast September 28-30, a few showers at almost anytime north through September 13, otherwise mainly dry.

4 Below normal temperatures and slightly above normal precipitation. Temperatures should average from 56° north to 63° south. Mainly dry and warm through September 10. Much colder with possible snow west and north and showers, rain and thunderstorms elsewhere September 15-18. Briefly warm again September 20-24 then generally cool, especially north, through September 30. Additional showers are possible September 25-26 and 29-30. Frosts and freezes north and west on or about September 18-19.

5 Temperatures near normal except cool mid-month, near normal precipitation. Temperatures should average from 68° north to 75° south. Major thunderstorm outbreak about September 16-17, otherwise only isolated activity primarily south through the month. Very cool, particularly north, September 17-19. Generally a sunny and very pleasant month. Very gusty winds prior to and with thunderstorms at mid-month.

6 Rapidly changing weather, overall temperatures will be a couple of degrees below normal and precipitation slightly above normal. Temperatures should average from 57° north to 65° south. Precipitation as primarily showers north and shower and thunderstorms south September 4-5, 9-10, 16-19, 23-24, and 29-30. Warmest period September 12-15 and coolest September 19-20 and 25-30. Frosts and freezes September 20 and 28-30.

7 Temperatures slightly above normal and precipitation near normal. Temperatures should average from 70° north to 79° south. Only isolated thunderstorms, mainly within 100 miles of Gulf, September 1-15, widespread thunderstorms from west to east September 17-19, then relatively dry through Septem-

ber 30. Warmest weather September 12-16, coolest September 19-21 and north September 26-30.

8 Mild early in month, warm midmonth then cool; near normal precipitation. Temperatures should average from 62° west and north to 66° south coast areas. Showers most likely September 1, 5-6 and at almost any time September 19-30. Warmest September 15-18, coolest September 25-30. Rather cloudy September 25-30. On clear nights frosts or light freezes are likely.

9 Above normal temperatures, except below normal end of month; slightly below normal precipitation.

Temperatures should average from 70° to 72°. Only isolated showers and thunderstorms expected through the month. Potential for hurricane near the coast about mid-month could greatly increase precipitation in the area. Impossible to pinpoint this event. Cool September 26-30.

10 Normal precipitation and temperatures. Temperature averages should range from 79° north to 83° south. Isolated thunderstorms at anytime. Most noteworthy will be a threat of hurricane activity mainly along or near the Atlantic coast about mid-month. Otherwise a great, typical month of September.

October

1 The month will start hot and dry and end cold and wet. Temperatures should average from 52° to 55°. Sunny, hot and dry October 1-9. Showers at 2-3 day intervals October 10-24 then heavier precipitation October 25-27 and 30-31. An incredible contrast this month going from summer to winter.

2 Temperatures near or above normal; very little precipitation. Temperatures should average from 61° along the coast, 58° across the inland north to 74° over the deserts. A very sunny month with little or no precipitation through October 24. Possible rain and snowshowers in the Arizona and New Mexico high country October 26-27 and 31 and showers at lower elevations northeast.

3 Temperatures to average near normal; near normal precipitation. Temperatures should average from 47° to 52° at lower elevations. Showers at lower elevations and snow and rainshowers in the mountains at 3-4 day intervals October 11-24, significant rain and snow developing October 25-27 and 30-31. Warmest west October 1-9, coldest October 26-28 and 31.

4 Cooling first week, mild midmonth then colder and stormy at end of month. Temperatures should average from 49° north to 55° south. Showers mainly north October 1-3 and 8-9, general heavier precipitation of rain and snow October 26-28. Warmest October 9-16, coldest October 27-31.

5 Temperatures averaging near normal with slightly below normal precipitation. Temperatures should average from 59° north to 67° south. Only a few isolated showers and thundershowers, except for general showers and thunderstorms October 26-29. Overall a very sunny and pleasant month.

6 Temperatures averaging above normal with slightly below normal precipitation. Temperatures should average from 52° north to 57° south. A few showers at times north otherwise very little precipitation until general precipitation develops October 27-30. Showers and thunderstorms should fall south and snow and rain northwest.

7 Temperatures slightly above normal; slightly below normal precipitation. Temperatures should average from 62° north to nearly 70° south. Precipitation will be scarce

with only isolated showers and thunderstorms October 1-25 and most areas dry. General showers and thunderstorms are expected October 28-31, some could be locally heavy.

8 Cool early in month, warm late; near normal precipitation. Temperatures should average from 51° north and west to 57° near the south coast. Showery October 1 and every 3-4 days October 6-20, heavy showers and thunderstorms possible October 30-31. Coolest weather with frost and freezes October 2-4 and warmest October 25-29.

9 Slightly below normal temperatures and near normal precipitation. Temperatures should average from 57° west to 61° near the coast. Showers and thunderstorms October 1-2, isolated showers at times October 6-20, and possible heavy precipitation October 30-31 especially north. Coldest October 3-6 and warmest October 26-29.

10 Near normal precipitation and temperatures. Temperatures should average from 72° to 77°. Two threats from potential hurricanes or tropical storms, one about midmonth and another about October 25.

November

1 Temperatures slightly below normal; above normal precipitation. Temperatures should average from 43° to 47°. Periods of rain and showers heavy at times at 2-3 day intervals through most of the month.

2 Temperatures starting above normal, cooling to below normal before end of the month; near to above normal precipitation. Temperatures should average from 56° along the coast, 43° inland north to close to 60° in the deserts. Sunshine or high clouds and mild to warm through November 18.

3 Above normal precipitation and near normal temperatures. Temperatures should average from 34° to 39° at lower elevations. Frequent periods of mainly rain and snow showers at lower elevations and snow in the mountains starting north and spreading south by

November 15.

4 Near normal precipitation and above normal temperatures. Temperatures should average from 34° north to 43°. Scattered showers of mainly rain at about 5 day intervals, no specific dates can be given.

5 Temperatures above normal and precipitation below normal. Temperatures should average from 46° north to 58° south. A very sunny month and very little precipitation is expected, greatest chance for showers north at 5 day intervals.

6 Temperatures above normal and precipitation near normal. Temperatures should average from 35° north to 42° south. Precipitation falling mainly as showers south and snow showers extreme north on or about November 4-5, 9-10, 14-16, 21-22, and 27-28.

7 Temperatures slightly above normal with near normal precipitation.

Temperatures should average from 48° north to 59° south. Precipitation as showers and a few thunderstorms on or about November 5-6, 9-10, 15-16, 22-23, and 27-28.

8 Temperatures slightly below normal; near normal precipitation. Temperatures should average from 37° north and west to 41° near the south coast. Precipitation mainly as showers near the coast and snow and rain north and west on or about November 1-2, 7-8, 14-15, 18-20, 23-24, and 28-30.

9 Near normal temperatures and precipitation. Temperatures should average from 43° west and north to 50° near the coast. Showers and a few thunderstorms on or about November 5-6, 10-11, 15-17, 22-23, and 28-29.

10 Slightly above normal temperatures and near normal precipitation. Temperatures should average from 64° north to 70° south.

City Weather Forecasts

Chicago
Dec: Below normal temperatures. Near normal precipitation.
Jan: Near normal temperatures. Above normal precipitation.
Feb: Slightly below normal temperatures and precipitation.
Mar: Near normal temperatures. Slightly above normal precipitation.
Apr: Near normal temperatures. Above normal precipitation.
May: Slightly below normal temperatures, warm late. Slightly above normal precipitation.
Jun: Near or above normal temperatures. Above normal precipitation.
Jul: Above normal temperatures. Slightly below normal precipitation.
Aug: Near normal temperatures and precipitation.
Sep: Near normal temperatures. Above normal precipitation.
Oct: Above normal temperatures. Near normal precipitation.
Nov: Slightly above normal temperatures. Slightly below normal precipitation.

Phoenix
Dec: Slightly below normal temperatures. Above normal precipitation.
Jan: Mild mid-month, otherwise below normal temperatures. Near or slightly above normal precipitation.
Feb: Near normal temperatures and precipitation.
Mar: Above normal precipitation. Below normal temperatures.
Apr: Near normal precipitation. Slightly above normal temperatures. —
May: Above normal temperatures. Below normal precipitation.
Jun: Slightly above normal temperatures. Near normal precipitation.
Jul: Below normal temperatures. Much above normal precipitation.
Aug: Slightly below normal temperatures. Above normal precipitation.
Sep: Near normal temperatures and precipitation.
Oct: Above normal temperatures. Below normal precipitation.
Nov: Near normal temperatures and precipitation.

Denver
Dec: Near normal temperatures and precipitation.
Jan: Below normal temperatures. Above normal precipitation.
Feb: Above normal temperatures. Near normal precipitation.
Mar: Below normal temperatures. Above normal precipitation.
Apr: Below normal temperatures. Slightly above normal precipitation.
May: Near normal temperatures. Above normal precipitation.
Jun: Near or above normal temperatures. Near normal precipitation.
Jul: Near normal temperatures. Variable precipitation, mostly above normal.
Aug: Near normal temperatures. Above normal precipitation.
Sep: Below normal temperatures. Above normal precipitation.
Oct: Near normal temperatures. Above normal precipitation.
Nov: Above normal temperatures. Below normal precipitation.

Salt Lake City
Dec: Near normal temperatures. Above normal precipitation.
Jan: Below normal temperatures. Above normal precipitation.
Feb: Near normal temperatures and precipitation.
Mar: Rapid changes. Slightly below normal temperatures. Above normal precipitation.
Apr: Slightly above normal temperatures. Near normal precipitation.
May: Below normal temperatures. Above normal precipitation.
Jun: Above normal temperatures. Below normal precipitation.
Jul: Near normal temperatures. Above normal precipitation.
Aug: Near normal temperatures. Slightly above normal precipitation.
Sep: Near normal temperatures and precipitation.
Oct: Above normal temperatures. Near normal precipitation.
Nov: Above normal temperatures and precipitation.

San Francisco
Dec: Slightly above normal precipitation. Near normal temperatures.
Jan: Below normal precipitation. Above normal temperatures.
Feb: Above normal precipitation, except dry at mid-month. Below normal temperatures.
Mar: Above normal precipitation. Below normal temperatures, becoming milder after mid-month.
Apr: Above normal temperatures. Near normal precipitation.
May: Near normal temperatures, except cool near end of month. Above normal precipitation.
Jun: Near normal temperatures and precipitation.
Jul: Slightly above normal temperatures. Near normal precipitation.
Aug: Near normal temperatures and precipitation.
Sep: Above normal temperatures, especially at end of month. Near or below normal precipitation.
Oct: Above normal temperatures first week cooling to below normal by last week. Above normal precipitation, most falling at end of month.
Nov: Below normal temperatures. Above normal precipitation.

Los Angeles
Dec: Slightly above normal precipitation. Temperatures slightly below normal.
Jan: Above normal temperatures. Below normal precipitation.
Feb: Above normal precipitation especially at start and end of month. Below normal temperatures.
Mar: Above normal precipitation, particularly first half of month. Below normal temperatures.
Apr: Near normal precipitation. Slightly above normal temperatures.
May: Near normal temperatures and precipitation.

City Weather Forecasts

Jun: Above normal temperatures, near normal precipitation.
Jul: Near normal temperatures and precipitation.
Aug: Slightly above normal temperatures. Near normal precipitation.
Sep: Above normal temperatures. Below normal precipitation.
Oct: Near normal precipitation. Slightly above normal temperatures.
Nov: Above normal precipitation. Near normal temperatures, except cool at end of month.

Seattle

Dec: Temperatures below normal first week, then returning to near normal. Above normal precipitation, showers and rain at times except for break in precipitation about mid-month.
Jan: Temperatures mostly near or slightly above normal, slightly below normal precipitation.
Feb: Dry February 10-14 otherwise frequent showers with above normal precipitation Slightly below normal temperatures.
Mar: Much above normal precipitation in a series of heavy storms. Below normal temperatures.
Apr: Showery, above normal precipitation. Slightly below normal temperatures.
May: Slightly above normal precipitation, showery. Temperature just under normal.
Jun: Temperatures and precipitation near normal.
Jul: Near normal temperatures and precipitation.
Aug: Above normal temperatures. Little or no precipitation, below normal.
Sep: Near normal precipitation. Above normal temperatures last week of month, otherwise near normal.
Oct: Above normal temperatures and below normal precipitation first week changing to below normal temperatures and above normal precipitation by mid-month.
Nov: Above normal precipitation. Slightly below normal temperatures.

Toronto

Dec: Below normal temperatures. Near normal precipitation.
Jan: Near normal temperatures and precipitation.
Feb: Below normal temperatures. Slightly above normal precipitation.
Mar: Near normal precipitation. Slightly above normal temperatures.
Apr: Above normal precipitation. Near normal temperatures.
May: Below normal temperatures, becoming above normal. Near normal precipitation.
Jun: Slightly below normal temperatures. Above normal precipitation.
Jul: Near normal temperatures. Above normal precipitation.
Aug: Near normal temperatures and precipitation.
Sep: Near normal temperatures. Above normal precipitation.
Oct: Cool early, then near or above normal temperatures. Near normal precipitation.
Nov: Near normal temperatures and precipitation.

Miami

Dec: Near normal temperatures. Slightly above normal precipitation.
Jan: Above normal temperatures. Near normal precipitation.
Feb: Near normal temperatures and precipitation.
Mar: Near normal temperatures. Below normal precipitation.
Apr: Above normal temperatures. Near normal precipitation.
May: Slightly above normal temperatures. Near normal precipitation.
Jun: Near normal temperatures. Above normal precipitation.
Jul: Below normal temperatures. Above normal precipitation.
Aug: Below normal temperatures. Above normal precipitation.
Sep: Near normal temperatures and precipitation.
Oct: Near normal temperatures and precipitation.
Nov: Slightly above normal temperatures. Near normal precipitation.

New York

Dec: Below normal temperatures. Near normal precipitation.
Jan: Near normal temperatures and precipitation.
Feb: Near normal temperatures. Above normal precipitation.
Mar: Above normal temperatures. Near normal precipitation.
Apr: Near normal temperatures. Much above normal precipitation.
May: Near normal temperatures and precipitation.
Jun: Near normal temperatures. Slightly above normal precipitation.
Jul: Above normal temperatures. Below normal precipitation.
Aug: Slightly above normal temperatures. Slightly below normal precipitation.
Sep: Near normal temperatures and precipitation.
Oct: Slightly below normal temperatures. Slightly above normal precipitation.
Nov: Slightly below normal temperatures. Near normal precipitation.

Dallas

Dec: Above normal precipitation. Slightly below normal temperatures.
Jan: Above normal precipitation. Near normal temperatures.
Feb: Above normal temperatures. Below normal precipitation.
Mar: Near normal temperatures. Slightly above normal precipitation.
Apr: Above normal temperatures. Near normal precipitation.
May: Above normal temperatures. Near or below normal precipitation.
Jun: Above normal temperatures. Below normal precipitation.
Jul: Near normal precipitation and temperatures.
Aug: Slightly above normal precipitation. Near normal temperatures.
Sep: Near normal temperatures and precipitation.
Oct: Above normal temperatures. Below normal precipitation.
Nov: Above normal temperatures. Below normal precipitation.

Volcano Eruption Forecast by Bob Conrow

Predicting volcanic eruptions is like playing Russian roulette: it's not really a question of *if*, it's a matter of *when*. Unlike many other natural phemena, volcanoes erupt with whimsical unpredictably.

Just how unpredictable are they? The "when" of volcanic activity can vary from a few brief seconds to millennia.With the possible exception of a few Indian medicine men, no one really knows when to expect a volcano to blow. The rest of us must rely on intuition or the admittedly fallible "experts."

Volcanoes, like stray dogs, come in various shapes, sizes, and dispositions. In most cases, their bark is worse than their bite. Some, however, such as Mount St. Helens, have a manner of huffing and puffing that tantalizes volcanologists. Since that spring day in 1980, when Mount St. Helens blew her stack, scientists successfully predicted, weeks in advance, more than thirteen subsequent eruptions. Scientists have yet to score as well in predicting the likes of such a volcano as Mexico's Paricutin.

Until 1943, Paricutin was nothing more than a twinkle in the Creator's eye. On the morning of Februrary 20th of that year, a farmer by the name of Dionisio Pulido rolled out of bed to discover that during the night, an 80-foot-long fissure had opened in the middle of his cornfield. As the Pulido family looked on in awe, the fissure began to spew a mixture of gas and ash.

Within a day, the molten mound reached a height of 33 feet; by the end of the first week, a 550-foot-tall mountain was made out of a molehill. By February, 1944, Paricutin grew to the incredible height of more than 1,000 feet. Paricutin developed slowly for nine more years, until, in 1952, at the majestic stature of 1,353 feet, the celebrated mountain gave its last steamy gasp, and retired from action.

Despite the Pulido family's loss of home and farm, and the destruction of two villages, Paricutin struck a relatively modest bargain with the local residents. Because Dionisio and his neighbors had the time and good sense to evacuate, no deaths occurred. Moreover, because volcanic ash contains valuable agricultural nutrients, in time it created some of the earth's most fertile soil.

The volcanologists responsible for making volcanic eruption predictions increasingly find themselves faced with a dilemma. "This is a terrible problem for many of us in earth sciences," notes University of California professor Tanya Atwater. "If we had been better able to predict (the first) Mount St. Helen's eruption, we would have saved some lives. Now, that has been completely turned around. By predicting the possibility of a volcanic eruption in Mammoth (California) we are ruining the economy — so it is claimed by the people in Mammoth."

As many scientists willingly admit, far too little is understood about volcanoes to predict imminent disasters with accuracy. If calculations are in error, local residents suffer unnecessarily. In issuing its recent Volcano Hazards report, the United States Geologic Survey knew that it was treading on sensitive toes,

Considering the fact that more than 100,000 lives have been lost to volcanic activity during the past two centuries, the agency decided to proceed with its volcanic "hit list." Based on historic patterns of recurring eruptions, the report pinpoints 33 potential hot spots in Hawaii, Alaska, and the western contiguous United States. This list begins with the most dangerous spots, and ends with the least dangerous, divided according to the time of most recent eruption.

ERUPTIONS IN THE PAST 200 TO 300 YEARS

1. *Aleutian volcanoes*, Alaska (1983)
2. *Augustine Volcano*, Alaska (1976)
3. *Iliamna Volcano*, Alaska (1978)
4. *Katmai Volcano*, Alaska (1931)
5. *Mount Spurr*, Alaska (1954)
6. *Redoubt Volcano*, Alaska (1968)
7. *Lassen Peak*, California (1917)
8. *Mono-Inyo craters*, California (c.1750)
9. *Mount Shasta*, California (1786)
10. *Haleakala*, Hawaii (1790)
11. *Hualalai*, Hawaii (1801)
12. *Kilauea*, Hawaii (1983)
13. *Mauna Loa*, Hawaii (1975)
14. *Mount Hood*, Oregon (1906)
15. *Mount Baker*, Washington (1859)
16. *Mount Ranier*, Washington (1882)
17. *Mount St. Helens*, Washington (1983)

ERUPTIONS MORE THAN 1,000 YEARS AGO

18. *Mount Edgecumbe*, Alaska
19. *Mount Wrangell*, Alaska
20. *Medicne Lake Volcano*, California
21. *Glacier Peak*, Washington
22. *Mount Adams*, Washington
23. *Crater Lake*, Oregon
24. *Mount Jefferson*, Oregon
25. *Mount McLoughlin*, Oregon
26. *Newberry Volcano*, Oregon
27. *Three Sisters*, Oregon

ERUPTIONS MORE THAN 10,000 YEARS AGO, BUT STILL DANGEROUS

28. *San Francisco Peak*, Arizona
29. *Clear Lake volcanoes*, California
30. *Coso volcanoes*, California
31. *Long Valley caldera*, California
32. *Socorro*, New Mexico
33. *Yellowstone caldera*, Wyoming

VIRGO

August 22 — September 21

THURSDAY AUG. **22**

Sun Rises 06:31
Sun Sets 19:53
Moon Rises 13:42
Moon Sets 23:46

MOON ENTERS SAGITTARIUS 21:36

moon square mars-01:21. moon conj saturn-08:07.
moon trine venus-10:42. moon at desc node-15:04.
uranus directs-17:21.sun square moon-21:36.

Sun Enters Virgo 21:36

FIRST QUARTER MOON 21:36

Dave Dellinger 1915
Ray Bradbury 1920
Ray Marshall 1928
Carl Yastrzemski 1939

John Lee Hooker 1917
Denton Cooley 1920
Diana Sands 1934
Valerie Harper 1940

1906: Victor patents phonograph. **1922:** Michael Collins, one of founders of I.R.A., is assassinated in Ireland. **1972:** 30,000 Yippies, Zippies, Viet Vets, and SDS'ers converge on Republican Convention (Miami).

FRIDAY AUG. **23**

Sun Rises 06:33
Sun Sets 19:53
Moon Rises 14:54
Moon Sets ----

MOON IN SAGITTARIUS

sun trine neptune-21:11. moon trine mercury-21:26.
moon conj uranus-21:34.

Edgar Lee Masters 1869
Gene Kelly 1912
Charles Lee Brown 1921
Patricia McBride 1942

Ernie Bushmiller 1905
Tex Williams 1917
Vera Miles 1929
Rick Springfield 1949

1838: First graduates get degrees from first women's college in U.S. **1927:** Nicola Sacco and Bartolomeo Vanzetti, factory worker and fish peddler, are executed in Mass. for armed robbery and murder—they are later cleared by proclamation. **1947:** Roy Chadwick, airplane designer, and 3 others die in England immediately following takeoff of new plane he had designed—an investigation revealed that the aileron controls had been installed in reverse.

SATURDAY AUG. **24**

Sun Rises 06:33
Sun Sets 19:52
Moon Rises 16:03
Moon Sets 00:30

MOON IN SAGITTARIUS

mercury trine uranus-01:42. moon trine mars-07:11.

Max Beerbohm 1872
Jorge Luis Borges 1899

Malcolm Cowley 1898
Rene Levesque 1922

79: Pliny the Elder, Roman writer, dies in eruption of Mt. Vesuvius—he had deliberately approached the erupting volcano in order to study it, and apparently died from inhaling poisonous fumes. **1944:** French troops liberate Paris. **1965:** 58 U.S. servicemen returning to Vietnam are killed when their transport plane crashes into Hong Kong Harbor. **1970:** First UFW lettuce boycott begins.

Rich is strong, poor is weak, and the government works for whoever pays its salaries.

Hunter Thompson

SUNDAY AUG. **25**

Sun Rises 06:34
Sun Sets 19:51
Moon Rises 17:06
Moon Sets 01:22

MOON ENTERS CAPRICORN 01:24.

moon conj neptune-03:02. sun trine moon-05:19.

Bret Harte 1836
Walt Kelly 1913
Mel Ferrer 1917
Althea Gibson 1927
Carter Burden 1941

Ruby Keeler 1909
Eugene Rostow 1913
Monty Hall 1923
Cecil Andrus 1931
Anne Archer 1947

1879: Ann Rutledge, age 22, dies in New Salem, Ill.—she was said to be Abraham Lincoln's true love. **1921:** Treaty with Germany. **1940:** First parachute wedding. **1967:** George Lincoln Rockwell, 49, leader of American Nazi Party, dies in parked car outside laundromat (Arlington, Va.)—he was shot by another member of the group which he headed.

There's no painkiller equal to the adrenalin of stagefright.

Carol Channing

GROWING
BY LIZ CAILE

NOW'S THE TIME — Midwest, Mountain States, Northeast: Dig, divide and replant crowded perennials such as horseradish, sorrel, lavender, chives, mint, yarrow and tansy. Cut tender shoots of herbs for rooting indoors and potting for the winter windowsill herb garden. Plant hardy bulbs this month and next, as appropriate to your area. **Mountain States:** Apple harvest begins; dark seeds indicate ripe apples. **Southwest:** Plant spring bulbs, locating bulbs on a northern exposure if you want to delay the blooming somewhat. **South:** Water fall blooming perennials for the most and biggest flowers. Divide and transplant dormant bulbs. **Far south:** Start sweet potatoes for early spring meals. **Northwest:** Some green manure crops to sow in the fall in mild regions include — bur clover, buckwheat, barley, clover, Scotch kale, winter oats, field pea, winter wheat, vetch. Where winters are colder, try white sweet clover. Replant spinach and radishes. Many spring flowering bulbs can be planted where there is good drainage, this month and next. Send for bulb catalogues for greatest variety of plants to choose from.

Bulbs

Fall flower bulbs are really potent growing packages, ready to bloom and thrust up stout green leaves with only a minimum of preparation by the gardener. They're easy, do-it-yourself florist kits, as simple to purchase as a bag of onions.

Daffodils, hyacinths, tulips, crocuses, and narcissus are some of the most familiar bulbs now available and ready to be set in the ground. Paperwhite narcissus and yellow-blossomed Soleil d'or narcissus may be available later in the season as they are the easiest for "forcing," or growing indoors for mid-winter bloom. The other bulbs are soon gone from the bins at the nursery.

Anemones — or wind flowers and ranunculous — of the buttercup family are tender or semi-hardy flowering bulbs that can be coaxed gently along in a mild winter situation or indoors.

Bulbs Outdoors

Where winters are moderate to severe, hardy bulbs are your best bet. Daffodils are in this group, along with tulips and bearded irises (really grown from rhizomes). Daffodils have an added advantage of not appealing to the tastes of ubiquitous rodents.

Choose bulbs for firmness, bright skins and good weight. In the case of true bulbs, examine the plate where the new roots will be growing for a healthy appearance.

All bulbs need good drainage, with a possible exception of the beautiful siberian iris that grows in damp and shaded soils and is available for spring planting.

Plant bulbs so they will develop a healthy root system as a first priority. Bulbs use a slow acting fertilizer best; they have already stored their growth rations and needn't take it all at once from the soil. Bonemeal is the recommended fertilizer. Well-rotted manure or compost can underline the hole for bulbs, covered with a layer of soil before the bulb is planted.

Bulb groups need ample water in the fall and spring. After fall planting protect bulbs from raucous frost heave (alternate freezing and thawing) by mulch, which will be removed for spring watering and spring growth.

Plenty of sun will insure blooms and healthy foliage, which will in turn feed bulbs for next season. Not only will well-placed bulbs produce flowers unstintingly, they will multiply underground and increase your supply from year to year.

Bulbs Indoors

Most of the fall bulbs can be planted in pots for indoor winter bloom. The principles of indoor growing include: pot so roots can reach water but the bulb won't be submerged and rot. Provide plenty of room for root growth below, but bulbs can be almost touching each other and can protrude slightly above the soil line. Tulip bulbs should be planted with the flat side toward the edge of the pot, because this is where the first leaf will appear.

The next step is to provide a cool, dark storage period, when the roots will grow strong and numerous. Lilies of the valley may already have been cooled and are ready to grow in the light.

Temperatures for this storage period should be around 40°F. You can bury pots of tulips, hyacinths, daffodils, and crocus, outside in a trench under loose soil or sand. Cover the storage trench with mulch to keep it from freezing.

Finally, bring bulbs out of cold storage and ease them into the light and warmth over a seven-to-ten-day period in the same way you would ease a tender bedding plant out into the cold and windy world. The first shoots of hyacinth, for instance, may have developed, but will be blanched. Direct light and 60° to 65 °F. temperatures will be the final destination.

Bulbs coaxed into winter blooming are well aclimatized to cool homes, and the fragrance of many varieties is spring perfume for snowbound days.

AUGUST

MONDAY   AUG. 26
Sun Rises 06:35
Sun Sets 19:50
Moon Rises 17:59
Moon Sets 02:23

MOON IN CAPRICORN

Guillaume Appollinaire 1880   Christopher Isherwood 1904
Albert Sabin 1906   David Begelman 1921

1857: National Teachers Association founded (Philadelphia).
1883: Krakatoa, mightiest volcano ever witnessed by
humans, erupts with violent explosion. **1965:** Hayneville, Ala.
deputy sheriff guns down 2 white clergymen.

Do not be always witty,
even though you should be so
happily gifted as to need the
caution. To outshine others
on every occasion is the
surest road to unpopularity.

Collier's Cyclopedia, 1882

TUESDAY   AUG. 27
Sun Rises 06:36
Sun Sets 19:48
Moon Rises 18:44
Moon Sets 03:28

MOON ENTERS AQUARIUS 06:31

moon oppos venus-05:09. moon square pluto-11:04.
VENUS ENTERS LEO-20:39.
moon conj jupiter-23:02.

Theodore Dreiser 1871   Sam Goldwyn 1882
Mother Teresa 1910   Martha Raye 1916
Ira Levin 1929   Tuesday Weld 1943

55bc: Julius Caesar and 8000 Roman soldiers land in
England. **1660:** John Milton's books burned. **1965:** Elvis
Presley hosts Beatles at his Beverly Hills home. **1967:** Brian
Epstein, record producer, dies at age 33 in London, England
of "accidental death through sleeping tablets." **1976:** M.I.T.
scientists construct first synthetic gene.

*Tomorrow morning, Mars,
Mercury and Venus, will be
aligned above the Eastern Horizon.
Get out and see 'em!*

WEDNESDAY   AUG. 28
Sun Rises 06:36
Sun Sets 19:46
Moon Rises 19:20
Moon Sets 04:35

MOON IN AQUARIUS

moon oppos mercury-13:48. moon square saturn-19:39.
moon square saturn-23:19. moon oppos mars-23:30.

Goethe 1749   Leo Tolstoy 1828
Charles Boyer 1899   Donald O'Connor 1925
Ben Gazzara 1930   Lou Piniella 1943

1784: U.S. trading ship arrives in China. **1863:** 200,000
emancipated slaves and whites hold rally in Washington, D.C.
—largest gathering ever for a redress of grievances. **1938:**
Northwestern Univ. awards Charlie McCarthy an honorary
degree—"Master of Innuendo and Snappy Comeback."

Standing still in the middle of a river is one
thing; standing still in the tide of human
affairs is another.

Japanese Proverb

THURSDAY   AUG. 29
Sun Rises 06:37
Sun Sets 19:44
Moon Rises 19:51
Moon Sets 05:42

MOON ENTERS PISCES 13:25

moon trine pluto-18:15.

Oliver Wendell Holmes 1809   Richard Attenborough 1923
Dinah Washington 1924   Elliot Gould 1938
William Friedkin 1939   Michael Jackson 1958

1831: Michael Faraday discovers electromagnetic induction.
1957: All-time filibuster record set by Sen. Strom Thurmond,
Dem., S.C. —24 hours, 19 minutes, during debate on Civil
Rights Bill. **1965:** Astronaut Gordon Cooper communicates
from space to Scott Carpenter, who is in Sealab 2 205 ft
under the surface of Pacific Ocean.

Everybody wants to be a celebrity. But you
know what happens to old celebrities? They
die or go to Vegas.

Carrie Fisher

FRIDAY   AUG. 30
Sun Rises 06:38
Sun Sets 19:42
Moon Rises 20:17
Moon Sets 06:46

MOON IN PISCES

venus square pluto-01:09. sun oppos moon-02:27.
mercury at asc node-15:24. moon square uranus-15:48.

FULL MOON 02:27

Correggio 1494   Mary Shelley 1797
Maria Montessori 1870   Raymond Massey 1896
Shirley Booth 1907   Fred MacMurray 1908
Ted Williams 1918   Kitty Wells 1918
Geoffrey Beene 1927   Timothy Bottoms 1951

1830: Baltimore & Ohio Railroad abandons horse-drawn
coach. **1957:** Federal judge orders implementation of public
school integration plan in Little Rock, Ark. **1963:** U.S.—
U.S.S.R. hot line goes into operation. **1979:** Comet strikes the
Sun—first time astronomers able to record such an event.
1983: Guion Bluford becomes first black U.S. astronaut.

3-DAY WEEKEND

SATURDAY   AUG. 31
Sun Rises 06:39
Sun Sets 19:40
Moon Rises 20:41
Moon Sets 07:48

MOON ENTERS ARIES 22:42

moon trine saturn-08:13.

Arthur Godfrey 1903   William Saroyan 1908
James Coburn 1928   Eldridge Cleaver 1935

1886: First major earthquake recorded in U.S. **1895:** First
professional football game (Latrobe, Penn.). **1965:** Mutilation
of draft card becomes federal offense—penalty is $10,000
fine or 5 years in jail.

A society which comes to fear its children is
effete. A sniveling, hand-wringing power
structure deserves the violent rebellion it
encourages.

Spiro Agnew

CELESTIAL EVENTS

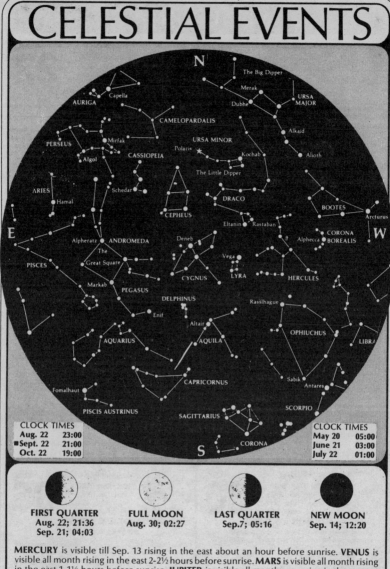

CLOCK TIMES

Aug. 22	23:00
Sept. 22	21:00
Oct. 22	19:00

CLOCK TIMES

May 20	05:00
June 21	03:00
July 22	01:00

FIRST QUARTER
Aug. 22; 21:36
Sep. 21; 04:03

FULL MOON
Aug. 30; 02:27

LAST QUARTER
Sep.7; 05:16

NEW MOON
Sep. 14; 12:20

MERCURY is visible till Sep. 13 rising in the east about an hour before sunrise. **VENUS** is visible all month rising in the east 2-2½ hours before sunrise. **MARS** is visible all month rising in the east 1-1½ hours before sunrise. **JUPITER** is visible all month appearing in the eastern sky at sunset, then setting in the west shortly before sunrise. **SATURN** is visible all month appearing west of midsky at sunset, then setting about midnight. **Aug. 22:** Saturn 3° N. of waxing crescent Moon (evening sky). **Aug. 23:** Venus 7° S. of *Pollux* (morning sky). **Aug. 27:** Jupiter 4° N. of waxing gibbous Moon (night sky). **Aug. 28:** Mercury at gr. elong. W.(18°). **Sep. 04:** Mercury 0.01° S. of Mars (morning sky). **Sep. 06:** Mercury 1.0° N. of *Regulus* (morning sky). **Sep. 08:** Mars 0.8° N. of *Regulus* (morning sky). **Sep. 12:** Venus 5° S. of waning crescent Moon (morning sky). **Sep. 13:** Mars 4° S. of waning crescent Moon (morning sky). **Sep. 18:** Saturn 3° N. of waxing crescent Moon (evening sky). **Sep. 21:** Venus 0.4° N. of *Regulus* (morning sky).

SEPTEMBER

SUNDAY — SEP. 01
Sun Rises 06:40
Sun Sets 19:39
Moon Rises 21:04
Moon Sets 08:47

MOON IN ARIES
moon square neptune-00:25. moon trine venus-09:14.
mercury square saturn-22:49.

Johann Pachelbel 1653   Engelbert Humperdinck 1854
Edgar Rice Burroughs 1875   Yvonne De Carlo 1922
Vittorio Gassman 1922   Rocky Marciano 1923
Seiji Ozawa 1935   Lily Tomlin 1936

1807: Aaron Burr acquitted of treason. 1836: Chop Suey concocted and served for first time in U.S. 1907: First night court session. 1914: Martha, the last passenger pigeon, dies in her cage at the Cincinnati Zoo. 1983: U.S.S.R. fighter shoots down Korean Airlines Flight 007—269 people die.

> A book is a mirror—if an ass peers into it, you can't expect an apostle to peer out.
> *George Lichtenberg*

MONDAY — SEP. 02
Sun Rises 06:41
Sun Sets 19:38
Moon Rises 21:26
Moon Sets 09: 46

MOON IN ARIES
moon trine uranus-02:20. moon trine mercury-22:34.

Allen Drury 1918   Jimmy Connors 1952

1666: Great Fire of London. 1752: Great Britain adopts Gregorian Calendar.

LABOR DAY

TUESDAY — SEP. 03
Sun Rises 06:42
Sun Sets 19:36
Moon Rises 21:50
Moon Sets 10:44

MOON ENTERS TAURUS 10:28
moon trine mars-01:52. moon trine neptune-12:13.
moon oppos pluto-15:58. venus at asc node-17:00.
venus oppos jupiter-23:23.

Sarah Orne Jewett 1849   Ferdinand Porsche 1875
Dixie Lee Ray 1914   Kitty Carlisle 1914
Anne Jackson 1926   Richard Castellano 1934
Eileen Brennan 1935   Valerie Perrine 1943

1609: Henry Hudson discovers Manhattan Island in his ship, the Half Moon. 1752: 11 days lost (Sept. 3 through 13) when England and its colonies switch from the Julian to the Gregorian Calendar. 1875: At multiple hanging in Fort Smith, Ark., 6 convicted criminals are executed in front of 5,000 onlookers—event became known as "The Dance of Death," and judge responsible for the sentences earned the nickname of "Hanging" Parker.

WEDNESDAY — SEP. 04
Sun Rises 06:42
Sun Sets 19:34
Moon Rises 22:17
Moon Sets 11:42

MOON IN TAURUS
moon square jupiter-03:36. moon square venus-04:07.
sun trine moon-11:07. mercury conj mars-13:56.
moon at apogee-14:00.

Chateaubriand 1768   Mary Renault 1905
Richard Wright 1908   Paul Harvey 1918
Jennifer Salt 1944   Tom Watson 1949

1781: Los Angeles founded by 44 settlers—26 were of African descent. 1886: Geronimo surrenders. 1952: New Orleans' Catholics peacefully integrate parochial schools. 1957: Initial attempt to integrate Central High School in Little Rock, Ark. repelled by Arkansas National Guard under orders of Gov. Orville Faubus. 1958: Ford Motor Co. introduces the Edsel. 1979: Soviet officials remove 44 books from U.S. display at 2nd Moscow International Book Fair.

HO HUM

THURSDAY — SEP. 05
Sun Rises 06:43
Sun Sets 19:33
Moon Rises 22:47
Moon Sets 12:42

MOON ENTERS GEMINI 23:27
moon at asc node-08:14. moon moon oppos saturn-08:55.
moon square mars-18:17. moon square mercury-21:11.

Arthur Nielson 1897   Arthur Koestler 1905
John Cage 1912   John Mitchell 1913
Jack Valenti 1921   Bob Newhart 1929
John Danforth 1936   William Devane 1937
Billy Kilmer 1939   Loudon Wainright III 1946

1877: Crazy Horse assassinated. 1939: U.S. proclaims neutrality in European war. 1972: 2 members of Israeli Olympic team die during an attack by members of Black September terrorists on their dormitory in Munich, West Germany—the next day, during shootout with authorities, 5 terrorists die along with 9 more Israeli athletes being held as hostages. 1975: Squeaky Fromme arrested for assassination attempt on Pres. Ford.

FRIDAY — SEP. 06
Sun Rises 06:43
Sun Sets 19:32
Moon Rises 23:23
Moon Sets 13:42

MOON IN GEMINI
sun square uranus-10:30.
MERCURY ENTERS VIRGO-12:39.
moon trine jupiter-16:05.

Billy Rose 1899   Jane Curtin 1947

1847: Henry David Thoreau moves away from Walden Pond. 1909: World receives news that 5 months earlier (April 6) Peary had reached the North Pole. 1971: 2 lightning bolts each kill 4 tobacco workers in Kentucky and Tennessee.

> I think the self-interview is the essence of creativity. Asking yourself questions and trying to find answers. The writer is just answering a series of unuttered questions.
> *Jim Morrison*

FORECAST

BY NAN DE GROVE

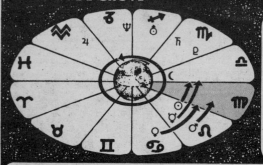

VIRGO

LONGITUDE OF THE PLANETS
21:36 PDT; 08/22/85

Sun 00°00' Virgo
Moon 29°58' Scorpio
Mercury 13°33' Leo
Venus 24°08' Cancer
Mars 18°38' Leo
Jupiter 09°41' Aquarius R
Saturn 22°06' Scorpio
Uranus 13°58' Sagittarius
Nept 00°58' Capricorn R
Pluto 02°25' Scorpio

Virgo, like its opposite sign Pisces, is a point of reorientation in the Zodiac, a phase of harvest, introspection, refinement, and reassessment. We now see the results of processes set in motion around the Spring Equinox and make necessary adjustments to insure further growth. Preparation for more intense involvement with others next month, is also a theme.

This month's good intentions need to be combined with practicality, originality, focus, and foresight. This is a time for putting ideas and ideals to work, for experimenting with different methods and techniques until we find the right one.

Certain compromises and sacrifices may be necessary to accommodate physical reality, but, in most cases, the end result will be worth the effort, and if it isn't...well, back to the drawing board.

Unexpected obstacles, disputes, and sudden changes of plans will upset routines during the first two weeks of September when the Sun and Mercury square Uranus. A critical, irritable attitude could alienate others and undermine group efforts and cooperation that are crucial to success. Nervous strain may result in health problems and, in order to avoid a mishap, caution is advised when using tools or machinery.

EARTH SIGNS are harvesting the results of past labors while cultivating new prospects.

Taurus: you may be reacting to a stressful domestic situation. Take actions necessary to create the stable condition desired. Problems in relationships are probably due to lack of communication.

Virgo: you begin this new cycle with mixed feelings—trying to move ahead, but feeling mired in the past. A sense of purpose and motivation will return around September 10th.

Capricorn: be prepared for a challenge to your authority and expertise. Ease tensions with an attitude that conveys willingness to learn.

AIR SIGNS can benefit through networking, sharing skills and resources. Cooperation is the key to getting things done.

Gemini: ease back into the social life after that period of introspection. Try to defend ideas without being aggressive. Focus on home base and personal foundations; avoid overextending.

Libra: you may have communication problems with someone who is uncompromising. Avoid taking on too many new projects now; this is a gestation time.

Aquarius: you can expect heavy demands and challenges coming from others. Yet, this could be a time of reaping the results of past mistakes in business and relationships. Trust and honesty are the important issues.

WATER SIGNS may be worrying excessively about money or security issues and need to circulate and communicate to get a new perspective.

Cancer: don't waste time worrying over money, but focus instead on making contacts and mobilizing creative and educational resources.

Scorpio: you face professional challenges; avoid being defensive, paranoid, or playing a martyr role.

Pisces: find the time to retreat and sort things out. Understanding how others influence values and behavior is a major concern. Watch nerves and health; try to moderate extremes.

FIRE SIGNS are impatient and may feel others are holding them back.

Aries: be inspired, creatively impassioned, and romantic, if you must, but take a step back and sort things out before plunging in.

Leo: avoid creating problems due to impulsive, self-centered behavior. This is a good time for sharing resources and values.

Sagittarius: reconcile your ideals and grandiose plans with practical considerations. Doing more with less is the key. Tensions between your public and private life need mediating.

SEPTEMBER

SATURDAY
SEP. 07
Sun Rises 06:44
Sun Sets 19:31
Moon Rises ----
Moon Sets 14:42

MOON IN GEMINI

mercury trine neptune-00:22. moon oppos uranus-03:46. sun square moon-05:16.

LAST QUARTER MOON 05:16

Taylor Caldwell 1900
James Van Allen 1914
Donny Allison 1939

Elia Kazan 1909
Buddy Holly 1936
Chrissie Hynde 1952

1908: National Esperanto Club formed. **1967:** *The Flying Nun* arrives on TV. **1970:** 2 die when lightning hits huddle on football field (St. Petersburgh, Fla.).

American audiences don't give a hang whether they are discerning or not. They want to be entertained. I'm not sure if I admire one more than I do the other.
John Huston

SUNDAY
SEP. 08
Sun Rises 06:45
Sun Sets 19:29
Moon Rises 00:05
Moon Sets 15:40

MOON ENTERS CANCER 11:10

moon oppos neptune-12:49. venus trine uranus-15:58. moon trine pluto-16:43.

Richard The "Lionhearted" 1157
Claude Pepper 1900
Grace Metalious 1924
Nguyen Cao Ky 1930

Antonin Dvorak 1841
Sid Caesar 1922
Denise Darcel 1925
Peter Davies 1934

70: Jerusalem surrenders to Roman forces. **1900:** Galveston, Texas is hit by hurricane, between 6,000 and 7,000 people lose their lives. **1935:** The Hoboken Four, with Frank Sinatra, appear on *Major Bowes' Amateur Hour.* **1944:** First German V-2 rocket hits England, near London, at 6:40 p.m.—it kills 2 people. **1953:** No-transfer bus service begins between New York and San Francisco. **1966:** *Star Trek's* TV debut. **1974:** Evel Knievel almost jumps over Snake River on rocket-powered motorcycle (Idaho).

SPORTIN'

MONDAY
SEP. 09
Sun Rises 06:46
Sun Sets 19:27
Moon Rises 00:56
Moon Sets 16:33

MOON IN CANCER

MARS ENTERS VIRGO-18:32.

Galvani 1737
Alf Landon 1887
Paul Goodman 1911
Joe Theisman 1949

Leo Tolstoy 1828
Colonel Sanders 1890
Jimmy The Greek 1918
Kristy McNichol 1962

1776: "United States" become official. **1894:** Sun Yat-sen leads first attempt at revolution in China. **1951:** *Love of Life* premieres on TV. **1971:** Attica prison riot begins. **1976:** Mao Tse-Tung, Chairman of Chinese Communist Party, dies of undisclosed illness at age 82 (Peking).

Literature is an occupation in which you have to keep proving your talent to people who have none.
Jules Renard

TUESDAY
SEP. 10
Sun Rises 06:47
Sun Sets 19:26
Moon Rises 01:55
Moon Sets 17:21

MOON ENTERS LEO 19:27

moon trine saturn-07:01.

Edmond O'Brien 1915
Jose Feliciano 1945

Charles Kuralt 1934
Margaret Trudeau 1948

WEDNESDAY
SEP. 11
Sun Rises 06:48
Sun Sets 19:25
Moon Rises 03:01
Moon Sets 18:02

MOON IN LEO

moon square pluto-00:45. mars trine neptune-02:40. moon oppos jupiter-09:34. moon trine uranus-20:35.

O. Henry 1862
Voinoba Bhave 1895

D.H. Lawrence 1885
Jessica Mitford 1917

Yes, we are a mighty nation. We know it and they know it. We covet no one's territory. We seek to dominate no people. We know it and they know it. That is why you gain nothing from bravado; that is why you gain nothing from rattling your rockets and bluffing with your bombs. That is why you get nowhere by saying you'll lob one into the men's room in the Kremlin.
Lyndon Johnson

THURSDAY
SEP. 12
Sun Rises 06:49
Sun Sets 19:23
Moon Rises 04:10
Moon Sets 18:38

MOON ENTERS VIRGO 23:52

neptune directs-02:16. moon conj venus-03:49. moon square saturn-12:31.

H.L. Mencken 1880
Jesse Owens 1913
Linda Gray 1941

Alfred A. Knopf 1892
George Jones 1931
Maria Muldaur 1942

1846: Robert Browning and Elizabeth Barrett marry. **1953:** John Kennedy marries Jackie.

Simple Cheeses

By John Lehndorff

Cheese is probably the oldest processed food known to man. It is eaten in most countries. The first wine and cheese party probably took place circa 5,000 b.c., and the first records of cheesemaking date from 2000 b.c. The Greek historian, Xenophon, wrote about a delicious goat cheese that had been famous for hundreds of years — in 349 b.c.

Some would say that the essential character of a nation can be revealed by studying the quality and variety of its cheeses. "How can you conceive of a one-party system in a country that has over 200 varieties of cheeses?" President Charles De Gaulle exclaimed about France.

According to legend, the first cheese was made by accident. As the story goes, an ancient traveler filled his water sack (made from an animal stomach) with fresh goat milk early one morning. After the day's journey, he opened the sack for supper only to discover a solid mass of white curds submerged in a clear liquid.

Since he had nothing else to eat, he finally summoned the courage to taste the "spoiled" milk. To his surprise and delight, he found that it was quite delicious. And thus, was cheese born.

Although the methods are now a bit more sanitary, the same basic procedure is used to make the 100,000 or so unique varieties of cheeses available today.

Until 1900, almost all cheese in the U.S. was home-made in small batches. By 1984, more than 90 percent was commercially produced, and more than half of that was "American" cheese. Few cooks make their own cheese, probably due to its unearned reputation for being difficult. Although some types require special ingredients or equipment, most cheeses are no more complicated to make than good bread, once you understand the basic process. And the immense pleasure you can experience upon tasting your own home-made cheese is well worth the effort.

Only two special items are needed for the simple cheese recipes which follow. One is real cheesecloth. You should only need one layer to drain the curds; then it can be washed, sterilized, and re-used. Cheesecloth is usually available at fine food stores and hardware stores. You will also need a stainless steel food thermometer to measure milk temperatures accurately. The dairy products you use should be fresh and exposed to air as little as possible.

Most home cheesemaking fails because of dirty equipment. One should wash and rinse the equipment thoroughly each time it is used. This cannot be overemphasized. Everything that comes in contact with the milk or cheese must be clean. Cheese is made by specific bacteria; foreign bacteria, which is present in the air and on every container and utensil, can alter or destroy the cheesemaking process.

Once all of the equipment is as clean as possible, it also needs to be sterilized to eliminate contamination by extraneous bacteria. Immerse everything in boiling water for at least two minutes, longer for wooden utensils. Plastic equipment should be sterilized in a mild chlorine solution, 2 tablespoons bleach to 1 gallon water (here too, rinsing thoroughly is critical because any bleach residue will kill the cheesemaking bacteria). If possible, use equipment made of enamel, glass, or stainless steel; milk becomes acidic as it turns into cheese and will dissolve metal ions out of iron and aluminum. This makes for foul tasting cheese.

The first step in cheesemaking is to curdle warm milk. This is done with an acidic substance such as lemon juice or a bacterial starter which turns the milk sugar into lactic acid. The lactic acid in turn coagulates the milk protein. Firm, long-lasting cheeses require particular bacteria and rennet, an enzyme derived from either vegetable sources or animal stomachs. The type of curdling agent, the milk, and the processes used, will determine whether the cheese ends up as a spreadable Brie, a hard Romano, or a meltable Mozzarella.

Lemon Cheese

INGREDIENTS
- 1 pint homogenized milk
- 1 pint heavy cream
- Juice of 2 large lemons
- Salt, herbs, spices

METHOD
Heat the milk and cream in a double boiler until the mixture reaches 100 degrees F. Add the lemon juice and stir very thoroughly. Turn off the heat and let the milk set for 20

FRIDAY SEP. 13

Sun Rises 06:49
Sun Sets 19:21
Moon Rises 05:22
Moon Sets 19:10

MOON IN VIRGO

moon trine neptune-01:18. moon conj mars-03:29.
moon conj mercury-22:50. moon square uranus-23:35.

Arnold Schoenberg 1874   Sherwood Anderson 1876
Claudette Colbert 1905   Barbara Bain 1934
Fred Silverman 1937   Jacqueline Bisset 1944

1321: Dante dies. **1899:** Henry Bliss, age 68, becomes first
pedestrian to be killed by an automobile in U.S.—car driven
by Arthur Smith hit Mr. Bliss near corner of 74th Street and
Central Park West in New York City. **1916:** Mary, a circus
elephant, is hanged in Erwin, Tenn., in punishment for killing
3 men—the lynching was accomplished on the 2nd try with
steel cable attached to railroad derrick, 5,000 people
watched.

**You look at everything with a black attitude
and it's all black.**

Paul McCartney

SATURDAY SEP. 14

Sun Rises 06:50
Sun Sets 19:20
Moon Rises 06:35
Moon Sets 19:39

MOON IN VIRGO

mercury square uranus-04:39. sun conj moon-12:20.

NEW MOON 12:20

Margaret Sanger 1883   Hal Wallis 1898
Eric Bentley 1916   Kay Medford 1920
Hughes Rudd 1921   Bud Palmer 1923
Kate Millett 1934   Joey Heatherton 1944

1741: Handel finishes the **Messiah**. **1834:** First patent
granted to a black man, for a corn-planting machine. **1835:**
Ralph Waldo Emerson marries. **1928:** Isadora Duncan is
strangled when her scarf becomes entangled in a Bugatti
wheel (Nice, France). **1964:** Univ. of Calif. Berkeley
administrators ban political activities from campus.

RUTABAGA

SUNDAY SEP. 15

Sun Rises 06:51
Sun Sets 19:18
Moon Rises 07:47
Moon Sets 20:07

MOON ENTERS LIBRA 01:34

moon square neptune-02:57. moon trine jupiter-13:57.

James Fenimore Cooper 1789
Agatha Christie 1891
Kathryn Murray 1906
Robert Benchley 1889
Gaylord Perry 1938
Merlin Olsen 1940
Roy Acuff 1903

1963: 4 young girls die
at the 16th Street Baptist
Church in Birmingham,
Ala. when bomb explodes
during Sunday services.

MONDAY SEP. 16

Sun Rises 06:52
Sun Sets 19:17
Moon Rises 09:00
Moon Sets 20:36

MOON IN LIBRA

moon at perigee-12:00. mercury square saturn-14:14.

Allen Funt 1914   Lauren Bacall 1924
John Knowles 1926   Peter Falk 1927

1920: Bomb explosion in Wall Street kills 35 (New York City).
1972: The Bob Newhart Show begins on TV.

**Young people are naturally prone to seek
the company of those they love; and as their
impulses are often at such times impatient of
control, etiquette prescribes cautionary
rules for the purpose of averting the mischief
that unchecked intercourse and incautious
familiarity might give rise to.**

Collier's Cyclopedia, 1882

ROSH HASHANAH

TUESDAY SEP. 17

Sun Rises 06:53
Sun Sets 19:15
Moon Rises 10:14
Moon Sets 21:08

MOON ENTERS SCORPIO 02:17

moon conj pluto-07:24. moon square jupiter-14:32.

William Carlos Williams 1883   J. Willard Marriott 1900
Hank Williams 1923   Roddy McDowell 1928
Anne Bancroft 1931   Maureen Connolly 1934
Ken Kesey 1935   John Ritter 1948

1683: First drawings of micro-organisms published by Anton
von Leeuwenhoek. **1908:** Thomas Selfridge, a lieutenant in
U.S. Signal Corps, becomes the first person to die in an
airplane crash when a plane piloted by Orville Wright with
Selfridge as observor crashes in Fort Meyer, Florida—Orville
escaped death, but sustained injuries.

**An orange might be an apple's idea
of heaven.**   *Dr. Carrot*

WEDNESDAY SEP. 18

Sun Rises 06:53
Sun Sets 19:13
Moon Rises 11:29
Moon Sets 21:44

MOON IN SCORPIO

moon conj saturn-17:22. moon at desc node-18:32.
moon square venus-21:45.

Samuel Johnson 1709   Elmer Maytag 1883
Greta Garbo 1905   Eddie Rochester 1905
Jack Warden 1920   Frankie Avalon 1940

1850: Fugitive Slave Act passed. **1895:** First treatment of a
patient by a chiropractor. **1927:** CBS hits the airways. **1948:**
Ted Mack's Original Amateur Hour debuts on radio. **1970:**
Jimi Hendrix, musician, dies at age 28, in London—cause of
death..."inhalation of vomit due to barbituate intoxication."

minutes.

Line a colander or strainer with cheese-cloth and ladle the curdled milk in. Tie the corners of the cloth together to form a bag and hang it up to drain for about 2 hours, or until all of the whey has drained out. Untie the bag and scrape the cheese off. It should be creamy and spreadable. It will taste lemony and can be used to replace ricotta cheese in cooking. Add salt, pepper, herbs, and spices to make a tasty spread. Refrigerated, Lemon Cheese stays fresh for 3 or 4 days.

Queso Blanco Cheese
INGREDIENTS
- ½ gallon homogenized milk
- ⅛ cup vinegar (preferably cider or red wine vinegar)

METHOD

Heat the milk in a pan directly over a low flame until the temperature reaches 190 degrees F. Stir constantly to keep from burning. Very slowly, add the vinegar and keep stirring until the curds separate from the whey.

Line a colander or strainer with cheese-cloth and ladle the curds in. Tie the corners of the cloth together to form a bag and hang it up to drain for about 3 hours, or until the bag stops dripping. Untie the bag and remove the solid mass of cheese. Very firm and slightly rubbery, the cheese will have a bland taste. Refrigerate. Queso Blanco stays fresh for about a week. It is frequently used in soups and with sauteed dishes because it does not melt; it substitutes well for tofu.

FEDERAL FOOD FILTH STANDARDS

by John Lehndorff

According to the United States Food and Drug Administration, it is acceptable for you to consume rodent hairs and pellets, thrips, mites, decomposed fish, insect heads, worms, mold, fly eggs, and aphids as long as you don't overdo it.

The Public Health Service has developed standards for food "defect levels" in order to determine whether a product is safe for human consumption. Black pepper, for instance, is considered acceptable if not more than one percent is insect-infested or moldy.

As long as there is not more than one milligram of insect excreta per pound, of pepper, that's considered just hunky-dory too. If this sounds a bit unappetizing, consider the fact that standards in the United States are among the highest in the world. (Bear in mind that insects are a good source of protein and their presence in a food probably indicates an absence of insecticides.)

The list below is a sampling of the most recent federal food filth standards established by the U.S. Health Department. Any product at or below the levels listed here, is considered edible, and safe for human consumption. Bon appetit!

□ □ □

Tomato Sauce — 30 fly eggs, or 15 eggs and 1 larva, or 2 larvae, or a mold count of 40% in a 100 gram sample.

Hops — Average of 2,500 aphids per 100 grams.

Fig Paste — Thirteen insect heads in two 100 gram samples.

Chocolate — Up to 60 microscopic insect fragments per 100 gram sample, or up to 100 fragments in one sample, or an average of 1.5 rodent hairs in each sample, or up to 4 hairs in any one sample.

Strawberries (frozen) — Mold count of 55% in half the samples.

Asparagus (canned or frozen) — 10% infested with 6 asparagus beetle eggs; either 40 thrips or five insects in a 100 gram sample.

Popcorn — In six 10 ounce samples, either one rodent pellet or one rodent hair per sample; two rodent hairs or 20 gnawed grains per pound with hairs in 50% of the samples.

Coffee beans — 10% insect-infested, damaged or molded.

Fish (fresh frozen) — 5% of fillets with definite odor of decomposition over 25% of the fish area, or 20% of the fillets with a slight odor of decomposition over 25% of the fish area.

THURSDAY — SEP. 19
Sun Rises 06:54
Sun Sets 19:11
Moon Rises 12:44
Moon Sets 22:27

MOON ENTERS SAGITTARIUS 03:40
moon square mars-14:06.

William Golding 1911
Harold Brown 1927
Brook Benton 1931
Brian Epstein 1934

Duke Snyder 1926
Adam West 1929
Mike Royko 1932
Paul Williams 1940

1928: Mickey Mouse debuts in **Steamboat Willie** (Colony Theater, New York City).

It's so sad when people expect fame to be so glamorous and great and then it's a zero. People want that to be something and it's nothing. Fame's not fun. Something else is fun, but that's not it.

Teri Garr

FRIDAY — SEP. 20
Sun Rises 06:55
Sun Sets 19:10
Moon Rises 13:56
Moon Sets 23:17

MOON IN SAGITTARIUS
moon conj uranus-03:48.

Upton Sinclair 1878
Jelly Roll Morton 1885
Pia Lindstrom 1938

Maxwell Perkins 1884
Sophia Loren 1934
Guy Lafleur 1951

1519: Magellan begins global voyage to find western passage to the Indies. **1830:** First national convention of blacks (Philadelphia). **1965:** Bolivian military junta declares national state-of-seige. **1973:** Jim Croce, composer and musician, dies at age 30 in plane crash near Natchitoches Municipal Airport in Louisiana.

SATURDAY — SEP. 21
Sun Rises 06:56
Sun Sets 19:09
Moon Rises 15:02
Moon Sets ----

MOON ENTERS CAPRICORN 06:49
moon square mercury-01:44. sun square moon-04:03.
moon trine venus-05:33. moon conj neptune-08:20.
VENUS ENTERS VIRGO-19:53.
moon trine mars-20:12.

FIRST QUARTER MOON 04:03

H.G. Wells 1866
Leonard Cohen 1934
Bill Murray 1950
Joseph Valachi 1904
Tom Lasorda 1927

Larry Hagman 1931
Fannie Flagg 1944
John Houseman 1902
Richard C. Hottelet 1917
Joan Jett 1960

There are no dirty words. Except "not enough salt."

Dudley Moore

A Season For Rimbaud
by Jeff Kelley

Spun in the atmosphere
forged in a slow crease
down the chameleon folds of earth
I am born into a time
where tail meets head
and all color succumbs
by exposing itself

Where every thing becomes
separate and unique
transcending the ubiquitous
with a wry and colorful grin
rolling like a sun
overlapping the splash of death

The Return Of The Comet

by Larry C. Sessions

Astronomers at California's Palomar Observatory first saw it coming back on October 16, 1982, but by the end of 1985, anyone with a pair of binoculars will be able to spot the great Comet Halley. This cosmic specter of tenuous gases and ice has intrigued, mystified, and terrified skywatchers throughout the world for thousands of years.

The Chinese, in the year 240 b.c., were the first to record their observations of it, although it most certainly was viewed with awe and wonder by cultures long before that. The comet has been seen on each successive 76-year orbit of the sun ever since. The last spectacular appearance occurred in 1910.

This time around, Halley's Comet won't be as magnificent as it was in its last appearance, due primarily to its orbital geometry. Nonetheless, it will likely turn out to be the most intensely investigated celestial object in history other than the sun and moon.

Funding cuts have prevented NASA from sending a probe to Comet Halley, but NASA probes already in space will view it from afar. The Russians, Japanese, and Europeans are planning missions to fly close to the comet. The European Space Agency's *Giotto* probe, which is scheduled for launch this July (1985) from French Guiana, is designed to fly right, through the comet's tail in March, 1986.

If you want to see Halley's Comet this year, you'll need a telescope or pair of binoculars. Amateur telescopes should provide a view by September, and good binoculars should do the trick starting about mid-October.

Below is a short ephemeris for observers, but your local planetarium or observatory should be able to supply you with more complete instructions on where to look. The comet will be at its brightest in the early part of 1986. Next year's *Daily Planet Almanac* will provide more detailed information and suggestions, but we'll give you a hint now: if you are really gung ho about viewing Halley's Comet, plan ahead for a trip to the southern hemisphere in March, 1986. Good luck!

COMET HALLEY EPHEMERIS

DATE	RIGHT ASCENSION	DECLINATION	MAGNITUDE	CONSTELLATION
09/21	06 hours, 13 min	+19 deg 43 min	12.0	Orion
09/25	06 hours, 13 min	+19 deg 49 min	11.8	Orion
09/30	06 hours, 12 min	+19 deg 58 min	11.5	Orion
10/05	06 hours, 10 min	+20 deg 09 min	11.1	Orion
10/10	06 hours, 06 min	+20 deg 21 min	10.8	Orion
10/15	06 hours, 01 min	+20 deg 37 min	10.4	Orion
10/20	05 hours, 54 min	+20 deg 55 min	10.0	Orion
10/25	05 hours, 44 min	+21 deg 15 min	09.5	Taurus
10/30	05 hours, 30 min	+21 deg 38 min	09.1	Taurus
11/05	05 hours, 05 min	+22 deg 03 min	08.5	Taurus
11/10	04 hours, 37 min	+22 deg 13 min	08.0	Taurus
11/15	03 hours, 58 min	+21 deg 55 min	07.4	Taurus
11/20	03 hours, 10 min	+20 deg 42 min	07.0	Aries
11/25	02 hours, 14 min	+18 deg 12 min	06.6	Aries
11/30	01 hours, 17 min	+14 deg 32 min	06.3	Pisces
12/05	00 hours, 28 min	+10 deg 28 min	06.1	Pisces
12/10	23 hours, 48 min	+06 deg 45 min	06.0	Pisces
12/15	23 hours, 17 min	+03 deg 42 min	05.9	Pisces
12/20	22 hours, 54 min	+01 deg 20 min	05.8	Pisces
12/25	22 hours, 35 min	–00 deg 31 min	05.7	Aquarius
12/30	22 hours, 21 min	–10 deg 59 min	05.5	Aquarius

Times are midnight Universal Time, which is actually the evening of the previous day for observers in the United States. See About Time **in this issue for conversion to your local time.**

(Ephemeris adapted from NASA documents.)

SEPTEMBER

LIBRA

September 22 — October 22

SUNDAY   SEP. **22**
Sun Rises 06:57
Sun Sets 19:07
Moon Rises 15:58
Moon Sets 00:16

MOON IN CAPRICORN

sun conj mercury-12:50. venus trine neptune-13:14.
MERCURY ENTERS LIBRA-16:13.

Sun Enters Libra 19:07
AUTUMNAL EQUINOX

1789: *Postal service established.* **1881:** *Amp, volt, ohm, farad, and coulomb standardized for international use.* **1961:** *ICC orders end to racial discrimination against bus travelers.* **1965:** *U.N. negotiates India-Pakistan cease-fire.* **1975:** *Sarah Jane Moore arrested for assassination attempt on Pres. Ford.* **1980:** *Iraq and Iran open war over disputed territory.*

This will never be a civilized country until we expend more money for books than we do for chewing gum.

Elbert Hubbard

MONDAY   SEP. **23**
Sun Rises 06:58
Sun Sets 19:06
Moon Rises 16:44
Moon Sets 01:20

MOON ENTERS AQUARIUS 12:11

mercury square neptune-03:56. sun trine moon-13:33.
moon trine mercury-15:22. sun square neptune-16:52.
moon square pluto-18:19.

Euripides 480bc
Walter Pidgeon 1898
Paul Petersen 1944

Walter Lippman 1889
George Jackson 1941
Bruce Springsteen 1949

1952: *Nixon makes "Checkers" speech on national TV— claims his wife has "respectable Republican cloth coat."*

TUESDAY   SEP. **24**
Sun Rises 06:59
Sun Sets 19:04
Moon Rises 17:22
Moon Sets 02:26

MOON IN AQUARIUS

moon conj jupiter-01:26.

Wallenstein 1583
F. Scott Fitzgerald 1896
Sheila MacRae 1924

John Marshall 1755
Joseph Montoya 1915
Anthony Newley 1931

1788: *Department of Justice established.* **1869:** *"Black Friday" on Wall Street.* **1930:** *German counsel admits that undercover agents had infected horses and mules in U.S. cities with anthrax in 1915 and 1916.* **1947:** *Japanese experts announce increased yields of crops in Nagasaki after bombing—50 to 300 ¢ more.* **1960:** *Last Howdy Doody Show on TV.*

Money is a nuisance. We'd all be much better off it if had never been invented.

Doctor Doolittle

NATIVE AMERICAN DAY

WEDNESDAY   SEP. **25**
Sun Rises 07:00
Sun Sets 19:02
Moon Rises 17:54
Moon Sets 03:32

MOON ENTERS PISCES 19:50

moon square saturn-09:14.

William Faulkner 1897
Dimitri Shostakovich 1906
Aldo Ray 1926
Michael Douglas 1944

Mark Rothko 1903
David Muldoon 1921
Glenn Herbert Gould 1932
Mark Hamill 1951

1775: *Ethan Allen taken captive in Montreal.* **1926:** *Ford Motor Co. establishes an 8-hr day, 5-day week.*

Words wound. But as a veteran of twelve years in the United States Senate, I happily attest that they do not kill.

Lyndon Johnson

YOM KIPPUR

GROWING
BY LIZ CAILE

Ginger & Exotica

For the home or greenhouse, you can grow fresh ginger in a ginger pot, if winter room temperatures aren't too cold. *Zingiber officinale* is a tropical plant from southern Asia, and even winter house temperatures may be too cool for it to thrive. But in a warm setting, a piece of ginger root from the market can become an interesting and flavorful houseplant.

Nestle the root horizontally in a rich soil that drains well. Keep it watered and in bright but not direct light.

The root is actually a rhizome, or underground stem. Fibrous roots will sprout from the rhizome into the soil and leaf stalks will grow up from it. The rhizome will add new buds, or joints, which can be sliced off of the original ginger root and used fresh.

Start with a large pot — the leaf stalks may be five feet tall in time. The leaves are narrow and grasslike and smell like ginger. Shorter flower stalks will bear orchid-like purple and yellow flowers, at least they do in the wild.

In subtropical gardens the ginger root can be coaxed along in a rich and partially shaded location. Start the ginger plant from the eyes of the rhizome. Nourish it with liquid compost and harvest it in late fall.

Using Fresh Ginger

Grate fresh ginger on a fine-holed grater and use it in teriyaki sauce and in many oriental dishes, in chutney, marmalade and curry. Or, simply boil it gently in water for ginger tea; or combine it with cardamon, cinnamon bark, and cloves or peppercorns for "yogi tea." Black tea leaves can be steeped in the water after boiling, if you like a caffeine tea — sweeten with honey and milk.

Goldenseal & Ginseng

Two respected folk remedies come from the extensive open woodland of the eastern United States. Both ginseng and goldenseal had a wide application in medicine and both are used today by modern herbalists.

Today, wild goldenseal and American ginseng are rare. The open woods where they grew in the filtered light of tall hardwood species have fallen to waves of agricultural pioneers. And the wild plants were collected by woodsmen, or wildcrafters, who could make a modest living from them.

Because it was the root that was valued, it was a custom to plant the ripe berries to replace the harvested plant. Ecological pressures have taken their toll on these species, however.

To grow goldenseal or ginseng, you must invest in the future, as the valuable roots are not matured in one season. The key to their culture is to duplicate the rich but light and well drained soil of the forest and the filtered light, or partial shade. Rotted leaves or applications of fine ground raw bonemeal are recommended also, as a protective mulch in winter that is removed in the spring.

Tropical Native

Sweet potatoes are native to tropical America and have been a staple food in these area. Most sweet potatoes for marketing in the mainland states are grown in North Carolina, Louisiana, Texas, Mississippi, Georgia and Alabama. The part we eat is actually a stem tuber.

To grow sweet potatoes, you need a season of approximately 150 frost-free days and three months with an average temperature above 68° F. The many different varieties of sweet potatoes, from dark-fleshed, red-skinned to light fleshed, yellow skinned are all *Ipomoea batatas*, a member of the morning glory family. They are rambling vines that in the right environment will be self-propagating, sprouting new roots and vines from vine tips.

Sweet potatoes need to be cured by drying at a warm temperature to develop sweetness. Let tubers lie on the ground to dry after harvesting and cure indoors at around 85° F. for about 10 days. Store at 50° to 55° F.

THURSDAY — SEP. 26

Sun Rises 07:01
Sun Sets 19:01
Moon Rises 18:21
Moon Sets 04:37

MOON IN PISCES

moon trine pluto-02:23. moon oppos venus-06:05.
moon oppos mars-16:14. mercury trine jupiter-16:53.
moon square uranus-23:31.

T.S. Eliot 1888
George Raft 1895
Jack Lalanne 1914
Dave Casper 1951
J. Frank Dobie 1888
Pope Paul 1897
Lynn Anderson 1947
Melissa Sue Anderson 1962

1945: Bela Bartok, Hungarian composer, dies (New York City). **1955:** Last Euler's flycatcher dies.

Far from being the thief of Time, procrastination is the king of it.

Ogden Nash

FRIDAY — SEP. 27

Sun Rises 07:02
Sun Sets 18:59
Moon Rises 18:45
Moon Sets 05:38

MOON IN PISCES

moon trine saturn-19:07.

Sam Adams 1722
Jayne Meadows 1923
Kathy Whitworth 1939
Arthur Penn 1922
Sada Thompson 1929
Shaun Cassidy 1958

1066: William the Conqueror sets sail from France. **1892:** Book matches patented. **1964:** *Warren Report* published. **1965:** 2 American servicemen executed by Vietcong firing squad.

UH-HUH

Life, n. A spiritual pickle preserving the body from decay. We live in daily apprehension of its loss; yet when lost it is not missed.

The Devil's Dictionary

SATURDAY — SEP. 28

Sun Rises 07:03
Sun Sets 18:58
Moon Rises 19:08
Moon Sets 06:38

MOON ENTERS ARIES 05:42

moon square neptune-07:31. sun oppos moon-17:08.

FULL MOON 17:08

Friedrich Engels 1820
Avery Brundage 1887
Tom Harmon 1919
Brigitte Bardot 1934
Georges Clemenceau 1841
Ed Sullivan 1902
Marcello Mastroianni 1924
Ben E. King 1938

1904: Woman arrested for smoking a cigarette in a car on Fifth Avenue in New York City. **1970:** Gamal Abdel Nasser, age 52, President of Egypt, dies from heart attack (Cairo).

Its tough to play piano and chase cars at the same time.

Ralph the Dog

SUNDAY — SEP. 29

Sun Rises 07:04
Sun Sets 18:56
Moon Rises 19:30
Moon Sets 07:36

MOON IN ARIES

moon oppos mercury-04:26. moon trine uranus-10:33.

MONDAY — SEP. 30

Sun Rises 07:04
Sun Sets 18:55
Moon Rises 19:53
Moon Sets 08:35

MOON ENTERS TAURUS 17:35

sun trine jupiter-01:47. moon trine neptune-19:29.

Freddie King 1934
Nancy Ames 1937
Johnny Mathis 1935
Jody Powell 1943

1955: James Dean, actor, dies at age 24 near Paso Robles, Calif.—he was driving over 80 mph in a Porsche Spyder when it collided with another auto at intersection of Route 466 and Route 41. Driver of other car received minor injuries and Dean's passenger was also injured, while force of the crash almost severed Dean's head from his body. **1964:** Univ. of Calif. Berkeley officials initiate disciplinary action against students who have defied ban against "illegal politics" on campus—in response, hundreds of students stage sit-in at administration building. **1965:** All-white jury acquits Deputy Thomas Coleman of shotgun killing of clergyman Richard Daniels in Hayneville. Ala.

SUCCOTH

TUESDAY — OCT. 01

Sun Rises 07:05
Sun Sets 18:54
Moon Rises 20:18
Moon Sets 09:33

MOON IN TAURUS

moon oppos pluto-00:56. moon square jupiter-08:01.
moon trine venus-18:12. moon trine mars-22:01.

Annie Besant 1847
Vladimir Horowitz 1904
Walter Matthau 1920
Jimmy Carter 1924
Laurence Harvey 1928
Edward Villella 1936
Louis Untermeyer 1885
Bonnie Parker 1910
James Whitmore 1921
Roger Williams 1926
George Peppard 1928
Donny Hathaway 1945

1847: Maria Mitchell discovers comet—awarded medal by King of Denmark. **1871:** Brigham Young arrested by U.S. troops for cohabitation with 16 women. **1946:** Nuremberg Tribunal finds 19 of 22 guilty. **1964:** An arrest is thwarted as hundreds of students surround police car and prevent it from leaving Sproul Plaza (Univ. of Calif. Berkeley)—after a rally, second sit-in is staged.

CELESTIAL EVENTS

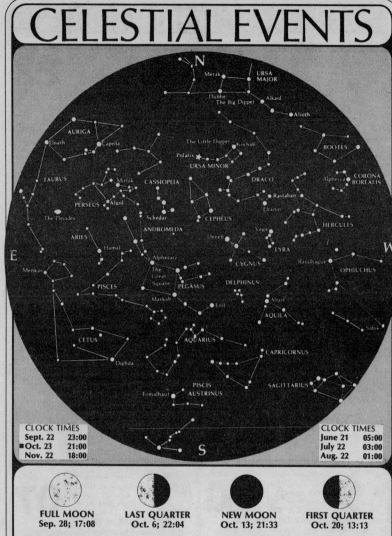

CLOCK TIMES
Sept. 22   23:00
■Oct. 23   21:00
Nov. 22   18:00

CLOCK TIMES
June 21   05:00
July 22   03:00
Aug. 22   01:00

FULL MOON
Sep. 28; 17:08

LAST QUARTER
Oct. 6; 22:04

NEW MOON
Oct. 13; 21:33

FIRST QUARTER
Oct. 20; 13:13

MERCURY comes to superior conjunction Sep. 22 , then becomes visible after Oct. 10 appearing in the western sky at sunset, and setting 1 hour later. **VENUS** is visible all month rising in the east 1½-2 hours before sunrise. **MARS** is visible all month rising in the east near Venus, 1½-2 hours before sunrise. **JUPITER** is visible all month appearing east of midsky at sunset, then setting in the west 2-3 before sunrise. **SATURN** is visible all month appearing in the western sky at sunset, then setting 2-3 hours later. **Sep. 22:** AUTUMNAL EQUINOX, first day of Fall. **Sep. 25:** Jupiter 4° N. of waxing gibbous Moon (night sky). **Oct. 04:** Venus 0.1° N. of Mars (morning sky). **Oct. 11:** Mars 3° S. of waning crescent Moon (morning sky); Venus 3° S. of waning crescent Moon (morning sky). **Oct. 14:** Mercury 1.3° S. of waxing crescent Moon-OCCULTATION-(evening sky). **Oct. 16:** Saturn 4° N. of waxing crescent Moon (evening sky). **Oct. 21:** Jupiter 5° N. of waxing gibbous Moon (night sky).

OCTOBER

WEDNESDAY   OCT. 02
Sun Rises 07:06
Sun Sets 18:52
Moon Rises 20:47
Moon Sets 10:33

MOON IN TAURUS
moon at apogee-06:00. moon at asc node-12:34. moon oppos saturn-20:32. mars square uranus-23:36.

Lord Chesterfield 1694
Wallace Stevens 1879
Bud Abbott 1895
Gore Vidal 1925
Moses Gunn 1929
Rex Reed 1938
Don McLean 1945
John Sinclair 1941
Maury Wills 1932
Sting 1951

Mohandas Gandhi 1869
Groucho Marx 1895
Graham Greene 1904
Spanky MacFarland 1928

Never trust anyone under thirty.

Abbie Hoffman, 1983

THURSDAY   OCT. 03
Sun Rises 07:07
Sun Sets 18:50
Moon Rises 21:20
Moon Sets 11:33

MOON ENTERS GEMINI 06:36
jupiter directs-01:16. venus square uranus-20:37. moon trine jupiter-21:05.

Jerry Apodaca 1934   Dave Winfield 1951

1955: *Mickey Mouse Club* debuts on TV. **1964:** After continued occupation of administration building on Univ. of Calif. Berkeley campus, coalition of campus political groups forms Free Speech Movement (Free Speech Movement)— University officials call hundreds of police to campus.

FRIDAY   OCT. 04
Sun Rises 07:08
Sun Sets 18:48
Moon Rises 21:59
Moon Sets 12:32

MOON IN GEMINI
sun trine moon-05:23. moon oppos uranus-12:29. moon square venus-14:15. moon square mars-14:25. venus conj mars-17:34.

Damon Runyan 1884
Charlton Heston 1924

Buster Keaton 1895
Susan Sarandon 1946

1930: British Airship R-101 crashes in France, killing 47 people aboard, including Secretary of State for Air and Director of Civil Aviation—the disaster dooms further development of airship in Great Britain. **1957:** USSR launches first satellite—Sputnik I. **1970:** Janis Joplin, singer, dies of apparent heroin overdose at age 27 in Hollywood.

One moon landing doesn't make a new heaven and a new earth, but it has dramatized the possibilities of doing so.

James Reston

SATURDAY   OCT. 05
Sun Rises 07:09
Sun Sets 18:46
Moon Rises 22:46
Moon Sets 13:30

MOON ENTERS CANCER 18:59
moon trine mercury-01:46. moon oppos neptune-20:58.

Denis Diderot 1713
Joshua Logan 1908
Bill Dana 1924

Karl Barth 1886
Allan Ludden 1917
Steve Miller 1943

1892: Dalton Gang almost destroyed during bank raid in Coffeyville, Kansas, 4 gang members and 4 town residents are killed. **1983:** Lech Walesa, founder of Solidarity, is announced as recipient of Nobel Peace Prize.

SUNDAY   OCT. 06
Sun Rises 07:10
Sun Sets 18:45
Moon Rises 23:40
Moon Sets 14:25

MOON IN CANCER
moon trine pluto-02:30. sun square moon-22:04.

LAST QUARTER MOON 22:04

Janet Gaynor 1906
Thor Heyerdahl 1914

Carole Lombard 1908
Shana Alexander 1925

1780: First American jailed in Tower of London. **1863:** First Turkish bath opens in U.S. (Brooklyn, N.Y.). **1890:** Mormons renounce polygamy. **1966:** Calif. statute outlawing LSD takes effect—Haight-Ashbury inhabitants respond with "Love Pageant Rally" on same day, precursor of the Be-Ins which followed. **1967:** "Death of Hippie" celebrated as final event of Haight-Ashbury's "Love Generation" (San Francisco).

We live in an age that reads too much to be wise.

Oscar Wilde

MONDAY   OCT. 07
Sun Rises 07:11
Sun Sets 18:44
Moon Rises ----
Moon Sets 15:14

MOON IN CANCER
moon trine saturn-20:15. moon square mercury-20:49. mercury at desc node-23:51.

James Whitcomb Riley 1849
Andy Devine 1905
R.D. Laing 1927

Elijah Muhammad 1897
Helen MacInnes 1907
Al Martino 1927

DRACONID METEOR SHOWER. This could be a very special show, or a washout. Up to 30,000 meteors per hour have fallen from this shower on years such as this when the source comet swings near earth only a few days before the shower date. Best viewing between sunset and moonrise around midnight. Try on the next few nights. Get out and see 'em!.

FORECAST
BY NAN DE GROVE

LIBRA

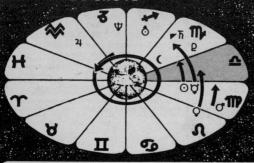

LONGITUDE OF THE PLANETS
19:07 PDT; 09/22/85
Sun 00°00′ Libra
Moon 20°31′ Capricorn
Mercury 00°12′ Libra
Venus 01°10′ Virgo
Mars 08°15′ Virgo
Jupiter 07°18′ Aquarius R
Saturn 24°09′ Scorpio
Uranus 14°22′ Sagittarius
Neptune 00°53′ Capricorn
Pluto 03°20′ Scorpio

A mood of inclusiveness and cooperation creates a favorable atmosphere for reducing tensions and conflicts now, both individually and in the arena of international relations. Aggression is tempered by love, or at least by the desire to be loved. Polarities can be neutralized, as awareness grows that uncompromising, isolationist attitudes are not serving anyone's best interests.

Contracts and resolutions coming out of this period will be generally positive. For many, it is a time of receiving benefits from past efforts; unexpected boons could appear around the first week of October.

The wheel of fortune is turning and, for most of us, this means positive trends and auspicious new beginnings. It could be a time of reckoning and comeuppance, however, for both those whose methods and motives have been selfish and harmful to others, and those who have refused to temper ego drives over the last two months.

Peace can be restored around the New Moon with greater respect for individual differences and a more realistic sense of mutual goals and benefits.

AIR SIGNS are making beneficial connections and getting wind of new directions.

Gemini: use your energy reserves for creative work, romantic pursuits, and successful communications. But practical matters and emotional conflicts need also attention.

Libra: that private something you're involved in is likely to come out in the open around the first week of October. The Full Moon brings good fortune; confusion will clear after October 17th.

Aquarius: you may have to make a few concessions in order to gain support, but they will be mainly a matter of observing social protocol. Be careful not to blow it during the first week of October.

WATER SIGNS can settle misunderstandings and forget old grudges now, in the interest of fairness; attachment to the past may be holding you back.

Cancer: you need private time to resolve an inner conflict; the resolution could involve domestic changes or new sources of nourishment and security.

Scorpio: you may also need to retreat to recognize the changes creating your new beginnings. Around October 12th, is the time for important communications and decisions.

Pisces: you are faced with major decisions concerning finances and values, relationships and career. Acknowledge the need to set limits and make transitions.

FIRE SIGNS have others rallying to their causes now, offering advice and support.

Aries: concentrate on sharing, listening, and being receptive to others; trying to do it all yourself will invite failure. Romance is favored around the Full Moon.

Leo: concern yourself with communications, travel, and connections with others. Increased energy and resources are now likely.

Sagittarius: decisions involving career, relationships, and personal freedom need your attention. Getting and giving support are key issues; avoid overextending.

EARTH SIGNS have magnetism and influence promoting success. Take the initiative in making contacts and communications.

Taurus: take advantage of that exciting new artistic or romantic prospect; something or someone will emerge to shake you out of old routines. A chance encounter could become serious.

Virgo: you could also may be enticed out of your dreary routines by some unpredictable and exciting romantic potential. Watch health and nerves; avoid making promises that can't be kept.

Capricorn: Avoid being overly serious. Connect with others who can provide inspiration and motivation. A new professional role may require a new self image.

TUESDAY   OCT.
08
Sun Rises 07:12
Sun Sets 18:42
Moon Rises 00:42
Moon Sets 15:56

MOON ENTERS LEO 04:33

moon square pluto-11:47. moon oppos jupiter-17:45.

Eddie Rickenbacker 1890	Frank Herbert 1920
Christiaan Barnard 1922	Jesse Jackson 1941
Chevy Chase 1943	Dennis Kucinich 1946

1871: Great Chicago Fire started—250 die in blaze, not including 7 men shot to death next day as they attempt to start new fires (apparently to create looting opportunities), and one person stoned to death by a mob. 1871: Great Pestigo Fire, (Wisc.)—huge forest fire, covering 6 counties, kills 1,182 people, but is virtually ignored by press due to catastrophe in Chicago.

The difference between journalism and literature is that journalism is unreadable and literature is not read.

Oscar Wilde

WEDNESDAY   OCT.
09
Sun Rises 07:13
Sun Sets 18:40
Moon Rises 01:48
Moon Sets 16:33

MOON IN LEO

moon trine uranus-07:42.

E. Howard Hunt 1918	John Lennon 1940
John Entwistle 1944	Jackson Browne 1948
Verdi 1813	Ivan Bunin 1870
Thelonius Monk 1917	James Clavell 1924
Greg Lake 1947	Tanya Tucker 1958

1826: Ralph Waldo Emerson receives license to preach. 1886: Monkey suits introduced in Tuxedo Park, N.Y. 1933: Laundry detergent goes on sale for first time in U.S. 1973: Vice Pres. Agnew resigns and pleads "nolo contendere" to charges of income tax evasion.

There's no sense in meeting our troubles half way.

Doctor Doolittle

THURSDAY   OCT.
10
Sun Rises 07:14
Sun Sets 18:39
Moon Rises 02:58
Moon Sets 17:06

MOON ENTERS VIRGO 10:09

moon square saturn-02:51.
MERCURY ENTERS SCORPIO-11:50.
moon trine neptune-12:00.

FRIDAY   OCT.
11
Sun Rises 07:15
Sun Sets 18:38
Moon Rises 04:09
Moon Sets 17:36

MOON IN VIRGO

moon square uranus-11:32. moon conj mars-20:16.

Eleanor Roosevelt 1884	Joseph Alsop 1910
Jerome Robbins 1918	Daryl Hall 1949

1890: Daughters of American Revolution organized. 1910:

**Great fleas have little fleas upon their backs to bite 'em,
And little fleas have lesser fleas,
And so ad infinitum.
And the great fleas themselves, in turn, have greater fleas to go on;
While these again have greater still, and greater still, and so on.**

De Morgan

3-DAY WEEKEND

SATURDAY   OCT.
12
Sun Rises 07:16
Sun Sets 18:36
Moon Rises 05:21
Moon Sets 18:04

MOON ENTERS LIBRA 12:12

moon conj venus-03:57. moon square neptune-13:59.
moon trine jupiter-23:58.

Aleister Crowley 1875	Dick Gregory 1932
Luciano Pavarotti 1935	Joan Rivers 1935

1492: Native Americans discover Christopher Columbus, a European, lost on their shores. 1945: Medal of Honor awarded to conscientious objector. 1965: U.S. Senate passes Ladybird Johnson's Highway Beautification bill.

HOWDY

The uncreative mind can spot wrong answers, but it takes a creative mind to spot wrong questions.

Antony Jay

SUNDAY   OCT.
13
Sun Rises 07:17
Sun Sets 18:35
Moon Rises 06:35
Moon Sets 18:33

MOON IN LIBRA

mercury conj pluto-03:20. sun conj moon-21:33.

NEW MOON 21:33

Virgil 70bc	Cornel Wilde 1915
Burr Tillstrom 1917	Laraine Day 1917
Lenny Bruce 1925	Eddie Mathews 1931

1886: Great Quebec Fire.

They say violence is immoral. In painting, artists deal with grotesque images constantly. Crucifixions are pretty grotesque, yet painters have painted them for centuries. If those painters were around now, they'd be putting them in movies.

Brian de Palma

The Birth Of The Pencil
by Micki Magyar

The lowly pencil is another commonplace item with a long and interesting history. Today we can buy pencils in a huge variety of sizes, colors, and types. There are thick, fat, and brightly colored pencils made especially for beginning writers. There are instruments that most of us would hardly recognize, designed for designers and technical users. And then there's everything in-between.

In the Middle Ages the scribes used a brush, called a "pencillus" — a "little tail" — and this is where we get our word for the writing tool. And in the early 16th century, the famous artist, Albrecht Durer was using a "silverpoint tool" for his drawing. This was a rod made of a lead and tin alloy. To erase the marks, he would use bread.

But the modern pencil, a thin tube of graphite or some other marking compound encased in wood, only became possible when an unusually pure deposit of graphite was found in Cumberland, England. At first, chunks of this material were used as marking stones.

Later, sticks of graphite were wrapped with string, and the string unrolled as it was used up. Pieces were also pushed into tubes, and the tubes held in metal pincers, somewhat like the modern mechanical pencil. At first, people believed that graphite was a type of lead, and pencils are still often called "lead" pencils. But later, it was discovered to be a form of carbon, and it was called "graphite," from the Greek word for "writing."

As the deposit in England ran out, a great effort was made to find others, and to develop alternative compounds. In 1662, Kaspar Faber developed the first graphite composition pencil, with the writing compound glued to fir or cedar.

Manufacture of this type of pencil was begun in England in 1789, and in the United States in 1827 by a man named Joseph Dixon. By 1876, pencils with round, instead of square, leads were being produced by machinery. Later developments have improved bonding of the lead to the wood, allowing for better quality control and for the multitude of special use pencils now available.

LIFE ON MARS
by Linda Joan Strand

It's time to investigate why the American scientific community has been misleading the public about the findings from the "Viking" mission to Mars. NASA sent two orbiters, as well as two probes which landed on the planet's surface in 1976 — all to search and test for Martian life. What most people do not know, however, is that the results of these experiments were far from the categorical "negative" which the scientific community would have us believe.

It's true that the photographs taken of Mars from both the orbiters and the probes did not reveal Martian lizards nibbling on the cameras. But then, thousands of pictures returned by the mission have not even been thoroughly analyzed. It is possible that any archaeological evidence of a dead civilization — from happier climatic days — was overlooked in the mass of Viking photographs.

Before the Viking mission, scientists were well aware that the Martian environment represented extremely inhospitable conditions for supporting life as we know it. They knew that Mars lacked an ozone layer which, on Earth, shielded life from lethal ultraviolet radiation. Obviously, any organism that we might recognize on the planet would NOT be found sunbathing on the Martian desert sands.

Secondly, they knew that the atmospheric pressure at the Martian surface was far too low for water to exist, except as water vapor or ice. Therefore, anything that might be called "living" on Mars, could not be dependent on liquid water for its survival.

And, thirdly, they knew that Mars is, by our standards, a very cold place indeed.

In spite of this knowledge, the Viking biology experiments were designed almost exclusively to operate under Earth-like conditions — conditions, which are very different from those on Mars.

It is widely accepted by astronomers that Mars was once covered by an ocean and subsequently underwent a drastic climatic change. If this change occurred slowly enough, then any martian organisms which adapted and survived, would have evolved to depend on the conditions now prevalent on the planet. If so, any such organisms might have been killed by the process of Viking's search for life.

The scientists' negative conclusions were drawn from their search for Earth-like organic compounds. However, the instrument which searched for these organics

OCTOBER

MONDAY   OCT. 14

Sun Rises 07:18
Sun Sets 18:34
Moon Rises 07:50
Moon Sets 19:04

MOON ENTERS SCORPIO 12:13

moon at perigee-18:00. moon conj pluto-18:49.
moon conj mercury-23:07. moon square jupiter-23:53.

Katherine Mansfield 1888   Dwight D. Eisenhower 1890
e.e. cummings 1894   Lillian Gish 1896
Le Duc Tho 1911   Roger Moore 1927
Ralph Lauren 1939   Cliff Richard 1940

1947: Charles Yeager breaks speed of sound in Glamorous
Glennie, a Bell X-1 rocket-powered plane.

COLUMBUS DAY
CANADIAN THANKSGIVING

TUESDAY   OCT. 15

Sun Rises 07:19
Sun Sets 18:32
Moon Rises 09:07
Moon Sets 19:39

MOON IN SCORPIO

mercury square jupiter-07:01.

Friedrich Nietzsche 1844   P.G. Wodehouse 1881
S.S. Van Dine 1888   C.P. Snow 1905
John Kenneth Galbraith 1908   Arthur Schlesinger, Jr. 1917
Mario Puzo 1920   Italo Calvino 1923

1917: Mata Hari, exotic dancer, is executed by firing squad
after being convicted of spying (Vincennes, France)—12
members of firing squad plus an officer shot at her, but
autopsy indicated only 4 bullets hit body. 1965: First co-
ordinated mass protests against Vietnam War nationwide—
"Weekend of Protest" includes 14,000 parading in New York
City and 2,000 at Oakland Army base, as well as
demonstrations in Boston, San Francisco, Madison, and Ann
Arbor. 1965: David Miller publicly burns his draft card at New
York City demonstration becoming first person arrested
under newly enacted law that makes mutilation of a draft
card a federal offense.

WEDNESDAY   OCT. 16

Sun Rises 07:20
Sun Sets 18:31
Moon Rises 10:25
Moon Sets 20:20

MOON ENTERS SAGITTARIUS 12:05

moon at desc node-02:50.
VENUS ENTERS LIBRA-06:04.
moon conj saturn-06:18.

Horace Walpole 1717   Noah Webster 1758
Oscar Wilde 1854   Eugene O'Neill 1888
Paul Strand 1890   Louise Day Hicks 1919
Linda Darnell 1921   Gunter Grass 1927
Bob Weir 1947   Suzanne Somers 1948

1793: Marie Antoinette, deposed Queen of France, loses her
head on guillotine (Paris). 1829: First hotel with bathroom
opens (Tremont House in Boston). 1965: First San Francisco
rock concert—produced by Family Dog, Longshoreman's
Hall.

**The road to ignorance is paved with good
editions.**

George Bernard Shaw

THURSDAY   OCT. 17

Sun Rises 07:21
Sun Sets 18:30
Moon Rises 11:42
Moon Sets 21:09

MOON IN SAGITTARIUS

venus square neptune-05:02. moon conj uranus-12:57.

A.S. Neill 1883   Isak Dinesen 1885
Nathanael West 1904   Arthur Miller 1915
Montgomery Clift 1920   Alfred Kahn 1927
Jimmy Breslin 1930   Margot Kidder 1948

1707: J.S. Bach marries. 1814: Rupture in brewery tank in
London sends 3,500 barrels of beer flooding through densely
populated area, killing 9. 1937: Bella Duck splits—leaves
Huey, Dewey, and Louie with Uncle Donald Duck. 1965:
Closing day of New York World's Fair. 1965: 12,000 black
students boycott Chicago schools to protest segregation.

**If you get something for nothing, it's pretty
hard to turn it down.**

Ted Turner

FRIDAY   OCT. 18

Sun Rises 07:22
Sun Sets 18:29
Moon Rises 12:52
Moon Sets 22:07

MOON ENTERS CAPRICORN 13:35

moon square mars-03:53. moon conj neptune-15:38.
moon square venus-18:55.

D.T. Suzuki 1870   Laura Nyro 1947
Pam Dawber 1951   Martina Navratilova 1956

SATURDAY   OCT. 19

Sun Rises 07:23
Sun Sets 18:27
Moon Rises 13:53
Moon Sets 23:11

MOON IN CAPRICORN

Alfred Dreyfus 1859   Jack Anderson 1922
John Le Carre 1931   Peter Max 1937
Peter Tosh 1944   Jeannie C. Riley 1945

1747: Earl of Sandwich says that sandwiches should be
eaten with "a civilized swallow and not a barborous bolt."
(London).

FOREVER

The ocean is my teacher, my mother. But the
forest is the next stage somehow. I mean, it's
the green, all the trees, the green chlorophyll of life.

Kim Novak

would have yielded equally negative results in the Mojave Desert on our own planet. Its limit of resolution was far too low to detect anything but the richest life forms.

The three biology experiments were equally inadequate. The initial positive results of the first two were quickly reversed, perhaps indicating only that scientists had succeeded in drowning the poor little Martians with the water used in the experiments.

The phase of the second experiment designed to eliminate any "false positive" results, only confirmed that the positives were indeed positive, and not coincidental. Curiously, Viking scientists ignored these positive results anyway, and explained them away as the consequence of some "exotic chemistry" caused by the ultraviolet radiation saturating the martian surface. So why didn't they think about that *before*?

The third experiment was very carefully designed to screen out non-biological reactions. It was also the only biological experiment which made any serious attempt to perform the tests under conditions duplicating the Martian environment. The rigorous and careful design of this experiment makes its results especially interesting. The fact is, in seven out of nine trials, it yielded FIRMLY POSITIVE RESULTS. The results of this experiment are the most difficult of all to blame on non-biological processes.

The search for life on Mars, initiated almost a decade ago by the Viking mission, has degenerated into a frantic quest to find some way — ANY way — of dismissing the results as "negative," due to the influence of non-biological factors. Yet in all this time, scientists have been unable to duplicate these results in the laboratory. The obvious strategy at this point is to send a return mission to Mars and redesign the ill-conceived experiments.

The unwillingness of the scientific community to admit that these results may indeed have been positive, leads one to ask: What will it take for them to concede that there may be life on Mars? How obvious will the evidence have to be?

Would they notice if life were STARING THEM IN THE FACE?

NUTRITIOUS RECIPES FOR LUNCH by Jacqueline Weller

For natural and nutritious workplace snacks, try these bite-size munchables: grapes, apricots, plums, cherries, hard-boiled eggs, chicken wings, slices of cheese, dill pickles, wholegrain muffins, rolls, and crackers.

Have you tried Japanese rice cakes? Made from compressed puffed rice, they contain only thirty-five calories per cake. Take enough for your boss or colleagues and you can all avoid another morning coffee-break pastry.

Roasted soybeans are very cheap when you make them yourself. Boil the beans halfway, then finish by roasting them in the oven with a little oil. Sprinkle with tamari, onion, and garlic powder.

Everyone has munched on carrot and celery sticks, but have you tried sliced jicama, chayote squash, fennel, celeriac, or Jerusalem artichoke? Raw turnip has a pleasant peppery taste.

Surprise your foreman with cold potatoes, delicious dipped in homemade mayonnaise. Yams are so sweet, they're almost like candy.

Feeling sophisticated? Bring fresh crab legs, cracked, with lemon wedges on the side. Or giant prawns in the shell.

And for the nibblers: raw almonds and raisins or carob chips and dry roasted peanuts. Try sharing with the maintenance staff or the gals at the front desk.

Mix your own fruit yogurt and save money while avoiding stabilizers, sweeteners, and colorings. Especially good are fresh strawberries, blueberries, and peaches. For variety, try applesauce, raisins, and cinnamon; a few tablespoons of frozen orange, grape, or apple juice concentrate; vanilla and honey; shredded coconut and crushed pineapple; chopped, dried fruits and nuts; apple or apricot butter; granola.

And for lunch, there is a world of nutritious possibilities. In cold weather, pack a thermos full of hot and wholesome soup. If you have chutzpah, keep some simmering all day in a crockpot small enough to fit inside a desk drawer or locker. Try split pea, lentil, miso, beef and barley, or cream of mushroom.

Do you have access to a toaster oven or microwave at the plant or office? Make open-face toasted cheese sandwiches or pizzas on halved English muffins. Treat your co-workers to real nachos made with oven-baked, unsalted corn tortillas; fresh guacamole; undyed, natural cheese; chopped tomatoes; scallions and jalapeño peppers.

How about fresh wholegrain cookies? Mix up the batch at home, rolling the dough into a cylindrical roll. Cover with wax paper and refrigerate or freeze. Bring a few inches of the roll to your workplace, slice into flat cookies, and bake in the toaster oven. If they're really tasty, offer some to the vice-president in charge of personnel.

OCTOBER

SUNDAY — OCT. 20

Sun Rises 07:24
Sun Sets 18:26
Moon Rises 14:44
Moon Sets ----

MOON ENTERS AQUARIUS 17:54

moon trine mars-10:08. sun square moon-13:13.

FIRST QUARTER MOON 13:13

Arthur Rimbaud 1854	John Dewey 1859
Jomo Kenyatta 1891	Wayne Morse 1900
Ellery Queen 1905	Arlene Francis 1908
Roy Ash 1918	Art Buchwald 1925

1964: Herbert Hoover, 30th Pres. of U.S., dies at his home in New York City at age 90 years and 71 days, after a long illness—cause of death was bleeding from upper gastrointestinal tract and a strained vascular system.

ORIONID METEOR SHOWER A good shower for the early birds; best viewed before dawn. This shower should climax on the 21st. Get out and see 'em!

MONDAY — OCT. 21

Sun Rises 07:25
Sun Sets 18:25
Moon Rises 15:24
Moon Sets 00:18

MOON IN AQUARIUS

moon square pluto-01:52. moon trine venus-05:02.
moon conj jupiter-07:48.

Samuel Taylor Coleridge 1772	Alfred Nobel 1833
Ursula Le Guin 1929	Carrie Fisher 1956

1969: Jack Kerouac dies. **1979:** First bomb-sniffing dog in New York City is retired after 8 years on the job.

You can say you're not always doing what you want to do, but actually you are every moment. That is a great source of pain to me. The fear of doing what I want to do and the potential of being rejected and abandoned. That's life.

Dudley Moore

TUESDAY — OCT. 22

Sun Rises 07:26
Sun Sets 18:23
Moon Rises 15:58
Moon Sets 01:25

MOON IN AQUARIUS

moon square mercury-01:35. venus trine jupiter-11:47. moon square saturn-19:59.

Constance Bennett 1904	Jimmie Foxx 1907
Doris Lessing 1919	Timothy Leary 1920
Annette Funicello 1942	Catherine Deneuve 1943

1911: First airplanes used in war (Italo-Turkish War, Tripoli). **1934:** Charles Arthur "Pretty Boy" Floyd, Public Enemy Number One, dies in cornfield near East Liverpool, Ohio, after being shot 8 times by FBI agents—he was 33 years old. **1965:** Hayneville, Ala. jury acquits 3 Klansmen in slaying of civil rights worker, Mrs. Viola Liuzzo, in Selma.

You can't make chicken salad out of chicken manure.

Ted Turner

Citrus Sorbet — John Lehndorff

A light, refreshing sherbet or "ice" to serve as dessert or to cleanse the palate between courses of a meal, the citrus sorbet is especially delicious with chicken or duck.

INGREDIENTS
- 1 cup white sugar
- juice of one lime and one lemon
- 4 cups orange juice, frozen-reconstituted or fresh-squeezed
- 3 tablespoons triple sec, Cointreau, or Gran Marnier liqueur
- 3 tablespoons finely grated lemon and lime peel
- pinch:salt

Place all ingredients in a blender or a food processor with a metal blade. Blend for 20 seconds. (Blend in two batches if necessary.) Pour the mixture into 3 ice cube trays and freeze until solid, usually overnight.

Don't complete the sorbet until you are ready to serve it. At that time, place the frozen cubes, a few at a time, in the blender or processor. Turn machine on and off rapidly until a lump-free ice forms. Serve immediately.

VARIATIONS
Replace 2 cups of the orange juice with 2 cups of tangerine, grapefruit, and/or pineapple juice. Replace one cup of the orange juice with one cup of pureed fresh or frozen fruit, e.g. peaches, nectarines, or kiwi fruit. Replace the orange liqueur with melon or raspberry liqueur.

Cabbage Trivia Quiz

by Judith Hiatt and Bruce Burkhart

There are a number of interesting facts about this underestimated vegetable that you may or may not know. Test yourself on the following questions. . . .

1. What stands on one leg and has its heart in its head?
2. Who said, "Training is everything. The peach was once a bitter almond; cauliflower is nothing but cabbage with a college education."
3. Where did the term "cole slaw" originate?
4. Who first brought cabbage to North America from Europe?
5. What is "liberty cabbage"?
6. What is the main nutritional element of raw cabbage?
7. Who first introduced cabbage into France from Italy?
8. How did Captain Cook prevent scurvy on board his ship during his three world voyages?
9. Where does the expression "by cabbages swear I" come from?
10. In France, what do they say is born under a cabbage?
11. What garden companions are beneficial to cabbage and should be planted nearby? (name at least one)
12. What does the term "cabbage leaf" mean?
13. Who rides on cabbage stalks like witches do on brooms?
14. In what country do they eat cabbage on New Year's Day to bring good luck for the year?
15. What does the expression "to cabbage onto something" mean?
16. What great classical composer wrote a violin concerto based on a German folktune entitled "Beets and Cabbages Make Me Fart"?
17. How did the man in the moon get there?
18. Who tried to hybridize cabbage but found nature had already transformed it into broccoli, cauliflower, kohlrabi, Brussels sprouts, collards, etc., and he could take it no further?
19. Which plants should not be grown near cabbages? (name at least one)
20. Where did Mr. McGregor find Peter Rabbit?

ANSWERS

1. Cabbage.
2. Mark Twain.
3. From the Dutch "kool sla," meaning cabbage salad.
4. Jacques Cartier in 1541.
5. The term for sauerkraut during World War II, to avoid using a German name.
6. Vitamin C, by weight as much as orange juice.
7. Catherine de Medici, the Italian-born Queen of French King Henri II, around 1533.
8. By supplying 1 pound of sauerkraut a week to each sailor.
9. 5th century B.C. Ionia, a colony of ancient Greece, where the cabbage was sacred.
10. Boys are born under cabbages, girls under cauliflowers.
11. Camomile, marigolds, thyme, sage, mint and rosemary.
12. A cheap cigar.
13. Fairies.
14. Ireland.
15. To grab, snatch or steal something.
16. Beethoven, Violin Concerto in D minor.
17. He was banished to the moon as punishment for stealing a cabbage on Christmas Eve.
18. Luther Burbank.
19. Grapes, strawberries, tomatoes, pole beans and rue.
20. In the cabbage patch.

SCORE

20-17 . . . Congratulations! Bona fide cabbagehead
16-13 . . . Excellent, mon petit chou
12-9 . . . . Good. You deserve a pound of sauerkraut a week
8-5 . . . . . Fair. Try eating more cabbage
4-0 . . . . . You're banished to the moon

OCTOBER

SCORPIO

October 23 – November 21

WEDNESDAY   OCT. **23**

Sun Rises 07:27
Sun Sets 18:22
Moon Rises 16:26
Moon Sets 02:29

MOON ENTERS PISCES 01:27

sun trine moon-01:12. moon trine pluto-10:03.

Sun Enters Scorpio 04:22

Johnny Carson 1925   William P. Clark 1931
Pele 1940   Michael Crichton 1942

1915: *First National Horseshoe Tournament.* 1915: *25,000 women march demanding right to vote (New York City).* 1950: *Al Jolson, comedian, dies of heart attack while playing cards at St. Francis Hotel in San Francisco.* 1956: *Hungarian Revolution begins.*

Storytelling will not really cure us. The best novel will not change things. Still, when I write I am able to forget for a while the so-called human condition.

Isaac Bashevis Singer

THURSDAY   OCT. **24**

Sun Rises 07:28
Sun Sets 18:21
Moon Rises 16:50
Moon Sets 03:31

MOON IN SCORPIO

moon square uranus-07:24. moon trine mercury-18:16.

Sonny Terry 1911   Y.A. Tittle 1926
George Crumb 1929   The Big Bopper 1930
David Nelson 1936   Bill Wyman 1941

1871: *During a vicious riot in Chinatown section of Los Angeles, mob kills about 25 Chinese residents by beating, stabbing, and hanging—nobody was ever tried or convicted for these crimes, but public pressure eventually forced city officials to change name of main street in Chinese section from Nigger Alley to Los Angeles Street.*

I'm not a very religious man, but I know there's an Old Man Upstairs. I can't help but see him that way.   *Willem de Kooning*

UNITED NATIONS' DAY

FRIDAY   OCT. **25**

Sun Rises 07:29
Sun Sets 18:20
Moon Rises 17:13
Moon Sets 04:31

MOON ENTERS ARIES 11:47

moon trine saturn-06:37. moon oppos mars-09:22.
moon square neptune-14:29.

Georges Bizet 1838   Pablo Picasso 1881
Henry Steele Commager 1902   Norman O. Brown 1913
Hannah Gray 1930   Russell Schweikart 1935
Bobby Knight 1940   Helen Reddy 1941

1954: *U.S. Air Force concludes that flying saucers are illusions or explainable as "conventional phenomena."* 1957: *Albert Anastasia, Lord High Executioner of Murder, Inc., is murdered by 2 unknown gunmen in barber shop of Park Sheraton Hotel in New York City.*

If you take a jackass and put him through medical school, you'll just have an educated jackass.

Dr. Lloyd Moglen

SATURDAY   OCT. **26**

Sun Rises 07:30
Sun Sets 18:19
Moon Rises 17:35
Moon Sets 05:30

MOON IN ARIES

moon oppos venus-13:17. moon trine uranus-19:04.

Ralph Bakshi 1938   Jaclyn Smith 1947

1785: *Mules imported into U.S.* 1965: *Selective Service announces that married men will henceforth be drafted.*

GROWING
BY LIZ CAILE

NOW'S THE TIME — Southwest: Indeterminate tomatoes will keep bearing until frost. Wild watercress is available in mountain canyons. **Mountain States, Midwest, Northeast:** To end the garden year, here's an old fashioned recipe for a garden dressing: layer manure, compost, wood ashes and bonemeal over emptied garden plot. Turning over the soil before winter will expose grubs of insects to freezing. Remember that valuable potash washes out of wood ashes if they've been left out in the rain before placing on garden soil. Also, if large quantities of newsprint and especially of colored papers have been burned with wood, the percentage of heavy metal contamination may be significant. **Midwest:** Harvest native tallgrass seeds to naturalize on vacant land. Cellar shelves are lined with winter squash and other produce. **Southeast:** You may use easy-to-come-by leaf mulch to protect salad crops through frost before harvest. Store sweet potatoes, winter squash, and pumpkins. in cool, dry place. Clean debris from yard and garden. **Northwest:** Pull perennial weeds now to prevent strong growth in spring, but if you don't get to it, remember weeds are green manure, too. Turn them under in the spring. Leeks, horseradish, kale, parsley, and salsify may be left in the garden for winter harvest, if protected by a clean mulch.

Tomato Follow-Up

Tomato seeds are notoriously hardy. The story has been told of a man who fertilized his lawn with processed sludge from a nearby sewage treatment plant and found he had inadvertently planted a crop of tomatoes. If you have grown an open-pollinated tomato variety in your garden and found it to be very satisfactory there, you can save seeds for next year's crop.

You'll want to collect the seeds and dry them out completely, separating them from any pulp. Several sources suggest fermenting the juicy pulp and seeds at room temperature for about three days before drying out the seeds. This will kill seed-born diseases. Pick very ripe or overripe fruits for seed saving.

Seeds can be stored in film cans, or in paper envelopes or waxed or plastic sandwich bags inside a coffee can with a tight-fitting lid, or in small jars in the refrigerator. Keep seeds dry and cool.

Hopefully, you have planted several tomato varieties in the garden to cover all bases — early bearers, late bearers, plum tomatoes for sauce, big fruits for sandwiches and a variety to endure whatever vagaries the summer may have brought.in terms of insects and weather.

You will want to save and ripen those last fine fruits from the vine before the first frost. Traditional storing techniques include layering the tomatoes in newspaper and storing in a cool garage or basement, or pulling the whole vine and hanging it upside down where it is dark as well as cool. A sunny windowsill works fine for ripening fruits and promotes the formation of vitamin C. Or, try putting the fruits in a bag along with an ethylene-exuding apple or pear to hasten sweet ripening.

There seems to be a breaking point between hard green tomatoes that won't ever ripen after separation from the vine, and those with a touch of color or a slight fade from the green stage, that promises a flavorful post-frost fruit.

Natural Storing

Cool season crops should be stored at cool temperatures, and warm season crops at higher temperatures. Fruits and vegetables with a high water content — apples, for example — need to be stored in relatively humid air. Most stored fruits and vegetables should be kept in the dark.

Garlic, onions, pumpkins and winter squash can be stored at relatively low humidity — 70 to 75 percent. Net bags are available from some seed companies and can be used to hang these edibles from basement rafters. Remember that basement and cellar temperatures will vary considerable from floor to ceiling.

Stored fruits and vegetables should be checked periodically for spoilage. No bruised or damaged produce should be stored.

Apples can be wrapped individually in newspaper and stored in plastic garbage cans at temperatures as low as 32° F. When past their eating prime, use them up as applesauce, baked apples, and in pies. This avoids a lot of work in the fall. Even if you don't have an apple tree or orchard to harvest, you can benefit from low market prices and greater variety in the fall.

Avacados should be stored at 40° to 45° F. or above. Store citrus fruits as follows: grapefruit, 50° F.; lemon, 52° to 55° F.; oranges, 38° F. Low temperatures reduce respiration and ethylene production — metabolic functions that are part of ripening.

In lieu of a root cellar, apples, carrots, turnips and many other vegetables can be stored in insulating layers of sawdust in a box or barrel, even in unheated rooms where temperatures drop below freezing.

SUNDAY — OCT. 27

Sun Rises 06:31
Sun Sets 17:17
Moon Rises 16:58
Moon Sets 05:27

MOON IN ARIES
MARS ENTERS LIBRA-07:16.
sun conj pluto-20:12.

James Cook 1728	Isaac Singer 1811
Theodore Roosevelt 1858	Dylan Thomas 1914
Ruby Dee 1924	Cleo Laine 1927
Kyle Rote 1928	Sylvia Plath 1932
Floyd Cramer 1933	Jayne Kennedy 1951

1867: Garibaldi marches on Rome. **1904:** First subway opens in New York City.

DAYLIGHT SAVINGS TIME ENDS
Set Clocks Back 1 Hour

MONDAY — OCT. 28

Sun Rises 06:32
Sun Sets 17:16
Moon Rises 17:22
Moon Sets 06:26

MOON ENTERS TAURUS 15:51
moon trine neptune-01:52. moon oppos pluto-08:32.
sun oppos moon-09:38. moon square jupiter-15:36.

FULL MOON 09:38

Howard Hanson 1896	Evelyn Waugh 1903
Jonas Salk 1914	Harvey Swados 1920
Bowie Kuhn 1926	Bruce Jenner 1949

1862: First battle by black troops in Civil War—1st Kansas Colored Volunteers drives off large force of Confederates (Island Mound, Mo.) **1893:** Carter Harrison, mayor of Chicago, is assassinated.

People don't understand how the press works. People don't understand that the press, they just use you to sell papers.
Bob Dylan

TUESDAY — OCT. 29

Sun Rises 06:33
Sun Sets 17:15
Moon Rises 17:49
Moon Sets 07:25

MOON IN TAURUS
moon at apogee-14:00. mars square neptune-15:03.
mercury conj saturn-17:39. moon at asc node-18:28.

James Boswell 1740	Bill Mauldin 1921
Melba Moore 1945	Kate Jackson 1949

1940: First peacetime compulsory military service instituted in U.S. **1971:** Duane Allman, musician, dies at age 25 (Macon, Ga.) after hours of surgery following motorcycle crash.

THURSDAY — OCT. 31

Sun Rises 06:36
Sun Sets 17:12
Moon Rises 18:57
Moon Sets 09:25

MOON IN GEMINI
moon trine jupiter-05:03.
MERCURY ENTERS SAGITTARIUS-08:44.
sun square jupiter-14:24. moon oppos uranus-20:17.

Tom Paxton 1937	Jane Pauley 1950

1880: In Denver, Colo., angry mob lynches Chinese man from lamppost at height of Chinese Riot—many other Chinese were attacked and killed in other cities during wave of anti-Chinese sentiment. During this period, Henry Ward Beecher said, "We have clubbed them, stoned them, burned their houses and murdered some of them; yet they refuse to be converted. I do not know any way, except to blow them up with nitroglycerin, if we are ever to get them to Heaven." **1965:** American B-52 pilots exonerated of killing 48 Vietnamese civilians in De Duc by mistake. **1966:** "The Acid Graduation", final "Acid Test" held by Ken Kesey and Merry Pranksters.

HALLOWEEN

WEDNESDAY — OCT. 30

Sun Rises 06:35
Sun Sets 17:13
Moon Rises 18:20
Moon Sets 08:25

MOON ENTERS GEMINI 11:59
moon oppos saturn-07:51. moon oppos mercury-09:27.
moon trine mars-16:17.

Christopher Columbus 1451	Paul Valery 1771
Ezra Pound 1885	Charles Atlas 1893
Ruth Gordon 1896	Harold Pinter 1930
Louis Malle 1932	Amiri Baraka 1934
Grace Slick 1943	Henry Winkler 1945

1888: Ball point pen patented. **1912:** James Sherman, candidate for Vice Pres., dies of uremic poisoning a few days before election—3,484,980 votes are cast for a dead man. **1938:** Orson Welles' radio broadcast of War of the Worlds panics the nation. **1965:** U.S. B-52s mistakenly bomb friendly South Vietnamesee village of De Duc, killing 48 civilians and wounding 55. **1965:** 25,000 demonstrators march in New York City in support of Vietnam War.

FRIDAY — NOV. 01

Sun Rises 06:37
Sun Sets 17:11
Moon Rises 19:41
Moon Sets 10:24

MOON IN GEMINI
moon trine venus-04:10.

Stephen Crane 1871	Sholem Asch 1880
Grantland Rice 1880	James Kilpatrick 1920
Betsy Palmer 1926	Larry Flynt 1942

1870: U.S. Weather Bureau makes its first official observations. **1952:** U.S. explodes first hydrogen bomb. **1966:** LBJ tells cheering U.S. troops in Korea that his great-grandfather died at the Alamo—a bald-faced lie.

Whatever philosophy may determine of material nature, it is certainly true of intellectual nature, that it abhors a vacuum: our minds cannot be empty.
Samuel Johnson

CELESTIAL EVENTS

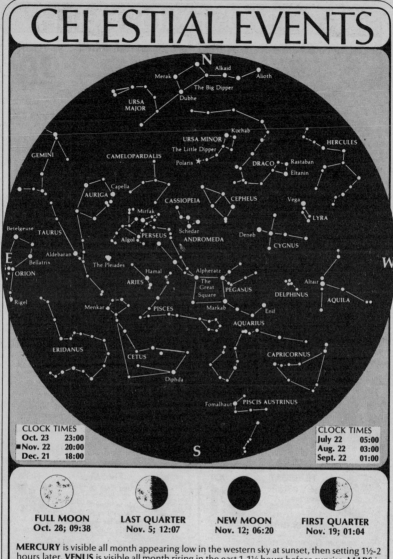

CLOCK TIMES

Oct. 23	23:00
■Nov. 22	20:00
Dec. 21	18:00

CLOCK TIMES

July 22	05:00
Aug. 22	03:00
Sept. 22	01:00

FULL MOON
Oct. 28; 09:38

LAST QUARTER
Nov. 5; 12:07

NEW MOON
Nov. 12; 06:20

FIRST QUARTER
Nov. 19; 01:04

MERCURY is visible all month appearing low in the western sky at sunset, then setting 1½-2 hours later. **VENUS** is visible all month rising in the east 1-1½ hours before sunrise. **MARS** is visible all month rising in the east 2-3 hours before sunrise. **JUPITER** is visible all month appearing near midsky at sunset, then setting about midnight. **SATURN** is visible till Nov. 10, appearing low in the western sky at sunset, then setting about 1 hour later. **Oct. 28:** TOTAL ECLIPSE OF THE MOON (not visible from N. America). **Oct. 30:** Mercury 4° S. of Saturn (evening sky). **Nov. 03:** Venus 4° N. of *Spica* (morning sky). **Nov. 08:** Mercury at gr. elong. E.(23°); Mercury 1.8° N. of *Antares* (evening sky). **Nov. 09:** Mars 1.7° S. of waning crescent Moon (morning sky). **Nov. 11:** Venus 0.8° N. of waning crescent Moon-OCCULTATION-(morning sky). **Nov. 12:** TOTAL ECLIPSE OF THE SUN (visible from Antarctica and southern S. America. **Nov. 13:** Mercury 0.5° N. of waxing crescent Moon-OCCULTATION-(evening sky). **Nov. 17:** Jupiter 5° N. of waxing crescent Moon (evening sky).

NOVEMBER

SATURDAY NOV. 02

Sun Rises 06:38
Sun Sets 17:09
Moon Rises 20:32
Moon Sets 11:19

MOON ENTERS CANCER 00:31

moon oppos neptune-03:36. moon square mars-08:02.
moon trine pluto-10:17. sun trine moon-21:48.

James Polk 1795
Burt Lancaster 1913
Dave Stockton 1941

Harlow Shapley 1885
Ken Rosewall 1934
Stefanie Powers 1942

1950: George Bernard Shaw, English playwright, dies in England at age 94—he was suffering from kidney infection and was weak from a fall suffered on Sept. 11. The broken bone that resulted from fall prompted him to say, "When one is very old your legs give in before your head does." 1965: Norman Morrison, Quaker, dies from burns suffered when he set himself on fire outside window of Defense Secretary Robert McNamara's office at Pentagon in Washington, D.C.—event was planned as protest of U.S. involvement in Vietnam.

SUNDAY NOV. 03

Sun Rises 06:39
Sun Sets 17:08
Moon Rises 21:30
Moon Sets 12:09

MOON IN CANCER

moon square venus-22:12.

Larry Holmes 1949   Adam Ant 1954

1883: Treasure Island published. 1957: Russia sends first dog into space. 1982: Pope John Paul II confesses publicly that the Inquisition, the 3 century reign of terror which burned thousands of "heretics" at the stake, was mistake of Catholic church.

MONDAY NOV. 04

Sun Rises 06:40
Sun Sets 17:07
Moon Rises 22:33
Moon Sets 12:53

MOON ENTERS LEO 11:03

moon trine saturn-08:17. moon square pluto-20:32.
moon trine mercury-21:27.

Will Rogers 1879
Walter Cronkite 1916
Loretta Swit 1939
Clark Graebner 1943

Pauline Trigere 1912
Art Carney 1918
Delbert McClinton 1940
Andrea McArdle 1963

1952: Winner of U.S. presidential election is correctly projected for first time by a computer.

Being in a stable situation is probably conducive to producing nicely balanced work. But not the really good stuff. That comes from pain, not comfort. Pain is essential. If you have not got pain, then you had better go and get some.
Sting

TUESDAY NOV. 05

Sun Rises 06:41
Sun Sets 17:06
Moon Rises 23:40
Moon Sets 13:31

MOON IN LEO

moon oppos jupiter-03:48. sun square moon-12:07.
moon trine uranus-17:20.

LAST QUARTER MOON 12:07

Will Durant 1885
Vivien Leigh 1913
Bill Walton 1952

Joel McCrea 1905
Clifford Irving 1930
Tatum O'Neal 1963

1872: Susan B. Anthony arrested for attempting to vote. 1955: First stereo radio broadcast.

I always wanted to be famous because I thought that if I couldn't be good I'd be famous.
Cher

GENERAL ELECTION DAY

WEDNESDAY NOV. 06

Sun Rises 06:42
Sun Sets 17:05
Moon Rises ----
Moon Sets 14:04

MOON ENTERS VIRGO 18:18

moon square saturn-16:11. moon trine neptune-22:17.

John Phillip Sousa 1854
Edsel Ford 1893
James Jones 1921
Jean Shrimpton 1942

Walter P. Johnson 1887
Ray Conniff 1916
Mike Nichols 1931
Sally Field 1946

THURSDAY NOV. 07

Sun Rises 06:43
Sun Sets 17:04
Moon Rises 00:48
Moon Sets 14:34

MOON IN VIRGO

moon square mercury-08:44. moon square uranus-22:46.

Marie Curie 1867
Billy Graham 1918
Joan Sutherland 1926
Johnny Rivers 1942

Albert Camus 1913
Al Hirt 1922
Mary Travers 1937
Joni Mitchell 1943

1811: Gen. Harrison defeats Chief Tecumseh's Shawnees at Battle of Tippecanoe. 1874: Thomas Nast creates cartoon of Republican Party elephant. 1922: Tutankhamen's inner tomb opened. 1962: Eleanor Roosevelt, "First Lady of World," dies from effects of lung infection and anemia at age 78 in her home in New York City.

CHECK OUT

FORECAST

SCORPIO

LONGITUDE OF THE PLANETS
04:22 PDT; 10/23/85

Sun 00°00′ **Scorpio**
Moon 01°29′ **Pisces**
Mercury 18°53′ **Scorpio**
Venus 08°36′ **Libra**
Mars 27°23′ **Virgo**
Jupiter 07°47′ **Aquarius**
Saturn 27°09′ **Scorpio**
Uranus 15°30′ **Sagittarius**
Neptune 01°18′ **Capricorn**
Pluto 04°30′ **Scorpio**

A chain of major celestial events makes this a dynamic, destiny-shaping month: the Sun joins Pluto in Scorpio on the 27th of October; eclipses fall on both the Full Moon and the New Moon; Saturn enters Sagittarius on November 17th, and Mercury turns retrograde on the 18th. A new cycle begins now, collectively and individually.

Many of us will experience events that have major impact on our lives and values. Whether we feel ourselves to be victims of fate or assume an active role in creating our reality, we will feel the purifying, regenerating energy of Scorpio. Changes we have been delaying become urgent, and old identities crumble as egos are unmasked. Unconscious motives, secrets, and betrayals are revealed; power and trust become vital concerns in all relationships.

Beliefs, ideals, and goals are in flux for many. Saturn's entry into Sagittarius is a collective event of the utmost importance, but it will have a major impact on individual lives also. Saturn's previous 2½-year transit of Scorpio involved concern with a cycle of focusing on deep emotions, our capacity for destruction, and issues of power and sharing.

Now, as Saturn enters Sagittarius for the next 2½ years, we can expect that changes recognized as being vital to our survival during the Scorpio transit, will be incorporated into society through restructuring of law, religion, education, and social welfare.

WATERS SIGNS are especially sensitive to emotional currents and experience significant turning points this month.

Cancer: you'll likely find yourself concerned with children, self-expression, and romantic involvements. Emphasis is on releasing the past.

Scorpio: time to begin a new chapter, assimilating inner changes of the past two years. Your energies are potent for good or ill; take it easy around the Full Moon.

Pisces: realizing how changing beliefs are affecting your life, you will begin to feel an increasing need to define your role in the world.

FIRE SIGNS must deal with unconscious factors and unfinished issues from the past. A new sense of destiny and purpose is emerging.

Aries: you have important developments concerning resources, values, investments, and debts. Pay attention to details.

Leo: you may be planning a family or thinking seriously about a new creative venture. Your new identity is emerging.

Sagittarius: express that urgent need to define life goals and actualize convictions. But take it easy and unwind around Full Moon.

EARTH SIGNS are introspective; emotional dynamics of relationships are a primary concern.

Taurus: you have significant decisions and turning points this month; inner values and outer reality are both in flux. Take it easy around Full Moon.

Virgo: your security base is changing. Avoid making decisions or drawing conclusions until after December 8th.

Capricorn: as you emerge from a period of deep metamorphosis, seek to connect with others in a new way. A mood of cautious optimism prevails.

AIR SIGNS are subject to emotional extremes.

Gemini: avoid overcommitting or making too many promises; sudden changes and reversals occur throughout this month. Watch health and seek some seclusion to restore sanity.

Libra: you are preoccupied with finances; focus on underlying values and use of resources. Self-sufficiency may be the primary issue.

Aquarius: you have a turning point involving career, goals, and public image. A setback could be a benefit in the long run. Lighten up.

NOVEMBER

FRIDAY   NOV. 08

Sun Rises 06:44
Sun Sets 17:03
Moon Rises 01:57
Moon Sets 15:02

MOON ENTERS LIBRA 21:52

Edmund Halley 1656	Hermann Rorschach 1884
Margaret Mitchell 1900	Katharine Hepburn 1909
Morley Safer 1931	Alain Delon 1935
Bonnie Raitt 1949	Rickie Lee Jones 1954

1887: *"Doc" Holliday, dentist, dies at age 35 in sanitarium in Glenwood Springs, Colo., after drinking glass of whiskey and saying, "I'll be damned!"—he had been suffering from tuberculosis for many years.* **1966:** *An actor, Ronald Reagan, is elected governor of California.* **1974:** *National Guardsmen acquitted in Kent State killings.*

SATURDAY   NOV. 09

Sun Rises 06:45
Sun Sets 17:02
Moon Rises 03:08
Moon Sets 15:30

MOON IN LIBRA
moon square neptune-00:44.
VENUS ENTERS SCORPIO-07:08.
moon conj mars-11:28. moon trine jupiter-13:17.

Ivan Turgenev 1818	Marie Dressler 1868
Muggsy Spanier 1906	Spiro Agnew 1918
Dorothy Dandridge 1922	Bob Gibson 1931
Carl Sagan 1934	Tom Weiskopf 1942

1953: *Dylan Thomas dies of alcohol and drug overdose.* **1977:** *U.S. Army admits it gave LSD to witting and unwitting subjects to interrogate them and test security training.*

> There never has been one like me before, and there never will be one like me again.
> *Howard Cosell*

SUNDAY   NOV. 10

Sun Rises 06:46
Sun Sets 17:01
Moon Rises 04:20
Moon Sets 15:59

MOON ENTERS SCORPIO 22:31

Martin Luther 1483	William Hogarth 1697
Johann Von Schiller 1759	Claude Raines 1889
J.P. Marquand 1893	Karl Shapiro 1913
Mackenzie Phillips 1959	

1871: *Stanley finds Livingstone.* **1951:** *First direct-dial phone service coast-to-coast.* **1965:** *Pacifist Roger LaPorte immolates himself in front of U.N. to protest Vietnam War.*

ARG!

My job is to work and have a responsible public image—not to have people saying, "That flake is saying this," but saying, "That responsible person is doing this."
Donald Sutherland

MONDAY   NOV. 11

Sun Rises 06:47
Sun Sets 17:00
Moon Rises 05:36
Moon Sets 16:31

MOON IN SCORPIO
moon conj venus-02:04. moon conj pluto-06:52.
moon square jupiter-13:43. mars trine jupiter-15:31.

Howard Fast 1914	Kurt Vonnegut 1922

1831: *Nat Turner is hanged (Jerusalem, Va.).* **1938:** *Typhoid Mary dies while under detention on N. Brother Is. on East R. (New York City)—there were 7 separate typhoid epidemics directly attributed to her, and estimates of epidemic ranged from a few hundred to over 1,000.* **1945:** *Jerome Kern, composer, dies in hospital in New York City—he had been unconscious for several days after collapsing on corner of 57th Street and Park Avenue. Oscar Hammerstein attempted to revive his friend, without success, by singing "Ol' Man River" in his ear.*

VETERAN'S DAY
REMEMBRANCE DAY

TUESDAY   NOV. 12

Sun Rises 06:48
Sun Sets 17:00
Moon Rises 06:55
Moon Sets 17:09

MOON ENTERS SAGITTARIUS 21:52
moon at perigee-05:00. sun conj moon-06:20.
moon at desc node-13:06. moon conj saturn-21:09.

NEW MOON 06:20

Jack Oakie 1903	Grace Kelly 1929
Charles Manson 1934	Neil Young 1945

1936: *San Francisco-Oakland Bay Bridge opens.* **1974:** *First salmon caught in Thames River since 1840s (London).* **1975:** *Justice William O. Douglas resigns after longest term on Supreme Court.*

WEDNESDAY   NOV. 13

Sun Rises 06:49
Sun Sets 16:59
Moon Rises 08:15
Moon Sets 17:55

MOON IN SAGITTARIUS
venus conj pluto-13:49. moon conj mercury-19:26.

St. Augustine 354	Robert Louis Stevenson 1850
Nathaniel Benchley 1915	Jack Elam 1916
Charles Bronson 1922	Paul Simon 1942

1839: *Liberty Party organized—first antislavery political party (Warsaw, N.Y.)* **1939:** *First Sadie Hawkins Day celebrated in Dogpatch.* **1958:** *Supreme Court rules segregation on public buses is unconstitutional.* **1982:** *Vietnam Veteran's Memorial dedicated (Washington, D.C.).*

Curses and Charms

by Kathleen Cain

Curses and charms are harder to find these days than they were even 100 years ago. The encyclopedia, that old reliable of the reference world, has, for the most part, forsaken the space between "Curry powder" and "Cursor Mundi" that was once occupied by the word "Curse." Charms are easier to find, though not much.

While cursing has not gone out of style, the style itself has changed. Richard Nixon & Company gave it a new twist, but "(expletive deleted) you!" is about as creative or intricate as the contemporary curser gets. There are always the old standbys like "Go to hell!" or "Damn you!" or "Up yours!" or "Your mama!" but, let's face it, none of these can hold a candle to the kind of verve or flare found in a phrase like, "May the fleas of a thousand camels come to find a home in your armpits!"

It's not that cursing has come to a standstill. Not at all. It's still a powerful force in the world, especially in cultures where *belief* in it is powerful. But, with few exceptions, cursing in the U.S. has been reduced to swearing and obscenities. In a time of near-nuclear holocaust and herpes, all we have by way of words to fling are leftovers from the elaborate exclamations that once abounded.

A curse is the calling down of evil, bad luck, or misfortune upon a person, place, or thing. There are lots of different ways to lay on a curse. It can be complicated. Some curses depend on words alone. In others, the words must be said in a certain order, or follow a formula. Still others are extemporaneous, allowing the curser to make them up as he goes, but, note, the body position might be important, as in the "one hand, one foot, one eye" curse from Ireland. For this particular curse to be effective, the curser had to stand on one foot, hold one hand behind the back, and close one eye.

Sometimes the place the curse is uttered from counts. Maybe a tangible object had to be involved. This could range from the well-known image of the victim with pins stuck in it to a mere wisp of straw from a field. Or it could be something as common as salt or a penny.

Charms, on the other hand, could be used to work both sides of the supernatural fence. Most often, though, they are thought of in much the same way as blessings: for good luck, protection, an enchantment. Love potions are charms.

The word "gesundheit" (God Bless You) is an old charm for protection, as it was once thought that at the moment you sneezed, the spirit could leave the body and evil enter in. Our modern view of someone "charming" is a person who can convince or sway others easily.

Curses and charms often use the same technique, sometimes even the same substance, to work their effects. Here are a few that have something in common. Remember, however, what Patrick Power, collector of curses, says: "Unjust malediction is seldom successful."

CURSES

With good reason, ALCOHOLISM has long been known as the "Curse of the Irish."

Here's one for stamp collectors: burn the paper that has the head of a dog and the head of a buffalo on it. Mix the ASHES with some sacred ashes (you have to find these yourself) and put them in your enemy's tea.

To curse a house, enter it BACKWARDS while cleaning a boot.

In ancient Ireland, the BLACKSMITH was most powerful. The anvil of a smith could be turned against the sun (counter-clockwise) to effect a curse.

If a FEATHER falls on your hair, it means an angry day is ahead.

Evil comes when you FIND: a white collar button, anything black, rags, a silk ribbon, a nest of snakes, needles, a comb, or an empty peanut shell.

If you meet an ass at the start of a JOURNEY, there will be trouble.

In the Orkney Islands, a woman confessed to having made a man impotent by tying nine KNOTS in a blue thread.

Burning old love LETTERS brings evil.

St. Adelbert had a special curse for

NOVEMBER

THURSDAY — NOV. 14
Sun Rises 06:50
Sun Sets 16:58
Moon Rises 09:31
Moon Sets 18:51

MOON ENTERS CAPRICORN 21:53
moon conj uranus-00:18.

Leopold Mozart 1719
Claude Monet 1840
Mamie Eisenhower 1896
Louise Brooks 1900
Barbara Hutton 1912
Brian Keith 1921
Edward H. White 1930

Robert Fulton 1765
Henry Sell 1889
Aaron Copland 1900
Dick Powell 1904
Veronica Lake 1919
Johnny Desmond 1921
Mclean Stevenson 1930

O, Sovereign Owners and Princely Players, masters of amortization, tax shelters, bonuses and deferred compensation, go back to work. You have been entrusted with the serious work of play, and your season of responsibility has come.

A. Bartlett Giamatti

FRIDAY — NOV. 15
Sun Rises 06:51
Sun Sets 16:58
Moon Rises 10:40
Moon Sets 19:55

MOON IN CAPRICORN
moon conj neptune-01:01. moon square mars-17:59.

William Herschel 1738
Georgia O'Keeffe 1887
Averill Harriman 1891

Felix Frankfurter 1882
Erwin Rommel 1891
Yaphet Kotto 1937

1907: *Mutt and Jeff* appear in comics for first time. **1945:** Censorship Office dissolved. **1959:** Clutter family are murdered "In Cold Blood" near Holcomb, Kansas, by Richard Hickock and Perry Smith, who are caught, tried, and hanged in April, 1965. **1969:** 400,000 peacefully protest Vietnam War (Washington, D.C.).

I divide all readers into two classes; those who read to remember and those who read to forget.

William Lyon Phelps

SATURDAY — NOV. 16
Sun Rises 06:52
Sun Sets 16:57
Moon Rises 11:37
Moon Sets 21:03

MOON IN CAPRICORN
SATURN ENTERS SAGITTARIUS-18:13.

Tiberius 42bc
Burgess Meredith 1908

John Philip Sousa 1854
Martine Van Hamel 1945

1907: Land which was to have been Indian territory forever is proclaimed as the state of Oklahoma. **1982:** National Football League players reach accord with owners—longest strike in history of sports ends.

SUNDAY — NOV. 17
Sun Rises 06:53
Sun Sets 16:56
Moon Rises 12:23
Moon Sets 22:13

MOON ENTERS AQUARIUS 00:25
moon square pluto-10:05. venus square jupiter-13:41. moon conj jupiter-18:46. moon square venus-19:15.

August Mobius 1790
Bob Mathias 1930
Gordon Lightfoot 1938

Lee Strasberg 1901
Peter Cook 1937
Lauren Hutton 1943

1973: Nixon says he is not a crook.

Well, people make mistakes, but you don't fire a guy for a mistake, do you?

Richard Nixon

MONDAY — NOV. 18
Sun Rises 06:54
Sun Sets 16:56
Moon Rises 12:59
Moon Sets 23:20

MOON IN AQUARIUS
moon trine mars-00:31. mercury retrogrades-08:16.

Sir William Gilbert 1836
George Gallup 1901
Johnny Mercer 1909

Brooks Atkinson 1894
Imogene Coca 1908
Linda Evans 1942

1247: Mythical hero Robin Hood dies. **1307:** William Tell shoots an apple off his son's head, according to legend. **1886:** Chester A. Arthur, 21st Pres. of U.S., dies in New York City, at age 57 years and 44 days—he died of cerebral hemorrhage and was suffering from Bright's disease. **1966:** Last meatless Friday for Roman Catholics—end of 1,000-year-old tradition.

No matter how thin you slice it, it's still baloney.

Rube Goldberg

TUESDAY — NOV. 19
Sun Rises 06:55
Sun Sets 16:55
Moon Rises 13:29
Moon Sets ----

MOON ENTERS PISCES 06:42
sun square moon-01:04. moon square saturn-07:16. moon trine pluto-17:16.

FIRST QUARTER MOON 01:04

Tommy Dorsey 1905
Ted Turner 1938
Dan Haggerty 1941

Dick Cavett 1936
Garrick Utley 1939
Jodie Foster 1962

1828: Franz Schubert, composer, dies from effects of typhoid fever—he is buried next to Beethoven. **1850:** Richard Johnson, former Vice Pres., dies of stroke, although local papers reported he had been suffering from "an attack of dementia." **1975:** Franco dies (Spain).

FESS UP

burglars, using a bell, a book, and a candle. As the LIGHT from the candle went out, these words were said: "And as the candle, which is thrown out of my hand here, is put out, so let their works and their souls be quenched in the stench of hell-fire, except they restore that which they have stolen. . . ."

To get rid of bad luck, throw a PENNY over your shoulder. The bad luck will pass to whomever picks it up.

The use of PRAYER to bring about evil was recorded by Lisiansky in his *Voyage Round the World*. He found a religious cult in the Sandwich Islands that conducted a "homicide litany" and prayed people to death.

If you could put SALT and pepper into someone's house secretly, you could curse them.

In some places, a medicine man could throw a SPIDER'S WEB at an enemy from a distance and kill him.

SPITTING once on the ground in front of your enemy will bring him bad luck.

WRITE your enemy's name on a stone, drop it in a well, and you have a curse.

CHARMS

An old charm against ALCOHOLISM was to place an egg, unseen, in someone's coffin. As the egg rots, so does the harmful habit. (Albeit a little late for the dearly departed).

This is an easy one for smokers: carry a little bag of ASHES in your pocket to prevent accidents or diseases. (It doesn't say if this will ward off lung cancer.)

Going upstairs BACKWARDS will change your luck.

The water used by the BLACKSMITH to cool the red-hot metal was especially potent for healing.

It is lucky to carry pigeon FEATHERS in your pocket (unless you live in Philadelphia), as it will keep others from working their will on you.

When you find something, if you say this, all will be well: "I do not pick up (name the object); I pick up good luck, which may never abandon me."

If you eat a bean before you start a JOURNEY, you will have good luck.

In Worcestershire, England, a cord with nine KNOTS tied around the neck was used to cure whooping cough.

As far as LETTERS go, it was once thought to be good luck, before the days of the U.S. Postal Service (and the airplane), to carry on a train a mail sack that had survived an accident. If you were a postal clerk and carried a piece of such a mail sack, you would never be in a wreck yourself.

Used by peasants as well as the princely, LIGHT has long been a way to dispel darkness and evil. It rids the night of spirits. Our modern version is the mercury-vapor streetlamp. Even Emerson said, "Light is the best policeman."

Some used to think it was lucky to keep or carry PENNIES taken from the eyes of a corpse.

The use of PRAYER to attempt to bring about good is widely known and hardly needs discussion.

A little SALT thrown over the left shoulder will keep evil away.

In Ireland, a SPIDER'S WEB kept in a little bag and worn around the neck cured whooping cough.

If you SPIT three times when you come upon your enemies, they'll cease being your enemies.

WRITE "be-doon" on an article, and it will keep you from harm by land and water. **BE-DOON. . . .**

Fingernail Clip Guide

"Cut them on Monday, cut them for news.
Cut them on Tuesday, a pair of new shoes.
Cut them on Wednesday, cut them for health.
Cut them on Thursday, cut them for wealth.
Cut them on Friday, cut them for woe.
Cut them on Saturday, a journey to go."

Lousy Votes

"At Hardenburg, in Sweden...the mode of choosing a burgomaster is this: The persons eligible sit around with their beards upon a table. A louse is put on the table in the middle, and the one in whose beard the insect first seeks shelter is the magistrate for the ensuing year."

Encyclopedia of Superstitions, 1903

Hold the Salt

In a bizarre twist of fate, nature has turned the tables on Salt Lake City, Utah. This city, named for the heavily saline lake which is its neighbor, has never had a problem getting the salt it needs to keep its roads ice-free in winter. Unfortunately, the weather in 1983 changed this situation.

Record amounts of precipitation have raised the level of the lake to its highest level ever, causing an overflow into the ponds that are normally used to evaporate the water, leaving behind the salt. In addition, the salinity of the lake has been diluted by the new influx of water from melting snow and rain, plus the extra snow has blocked access to the ponds, and hidden the salt that was already collected. The result: Salt Lake City has been buying salt from other locations and shipping it into town.

WEDNESDAY   **NOV.** **20**

Sun Rises 06:56
Sun Sets 16:54
Moon Rises 13:55
Moon Sets 00:24

MOON IN PISCES

moon trine venus-09:09. moon square mercury-10:36.
moon square uranus-15:14.

Norman Thomas 1884
Robert Kennedy 1925
Richard Dawson 1932

Alistair Cooke 1908
Estelle Parsons 1927
Duane Allman 1946

THURSDAY   **NOV.** **21**

Sun Rises 06:58
Sun Sets 16:54
Moon Rises 14:18
Moon Sets 01:25

MOON ENTERS ARIES 16:42

sun trine moon-15:58. moon trine saturn-17:53.
moon square neptune-20:57.

Voltaire 1694
Coleman Hawkins 1904
Stan Musial 1920
Marlo Thomas 1938
Earl Monroe 1944

Rene Magritte 1898
Eleanor Powell 1912
Howard Pawley 1934
Larry Mahan 1943
Goldie Hawn 1945

1718: Edward "Blackbeard the Pirate" Teach, dies near Ocracoke Island, N.C., after intense struggle in which he was shot 5 times and cut 25 times by a cutlass—fight ended when someone hit him from behind with a sword, severing his head. 1945: Robert Benchley, actor, humorist, critic, dies at age 56 (New York City).

PIPE DOWN

Know What Know How

by Dawn I. Brett

Machines are not yet conscious in the prevailing human sense, but what if people began to think like computers? Science fiction writers such as Arthur C. Clarke point out that the survivors of our species may be largely silicon: machine repositories of the contents of the mind, including consciousness.

There are portents of this today. Telecommunication advances make compunication, or computer to computer communication, an increasingly common phenomenon in government, industry, and education. Computers use program logic, not feeling. Computer programmers are known to prefer long hours of work with machines to the often unpredictable relationships with people. Is this compurosis? Or should we give that name to the fear of computer logic?

Then there are people who think only in tandem with the television, the telephone, and the computer, and from there, recognize error only with machine assistance. These are humanoids whose lives are machine-dependent and machine-mediated. The humanoid understands and is excited by computer engineering, the "know how." It is, as Norbert Wiener pointed out, the "know what" that is troublesome.

A very successful electronic thief in Los Angeles who was "forgiven" his crimes so that he could teach banks and industries to protect themselves from people like himself said, with a smile, "They still won't know if I am stealing from them." Logical consistency requires only that we know how to fit the pieces together, not that we be honest or realistic. Those, after all, are human qualities.

The mainframe computer is now so complicated that it is best described as steered rather than run. A billion binary operations in a second may be within its reach. The question is: *who* is steering? Peter Drucker once said that the main impact of the computer has been to provide unlimited jobs for clerks. The speed of our mental operations has been eclipsed by machine performance. Furthermore, machines do not demand or promise. They solve problems antiseptically, teaching you what you want to know when you want to learn it.

Machines have much to learn about confidentiality, and we have much to discover about the "know what" in our relationships with the machinery rolling into place around us. Perhaps, like the banking industry, we should be concerned with MTBBU(maximum time before belly up) so that we do not disappear by electronic default.

Can We be Intelligent about Intelligence?

Thrive and Survive Rx

by Robert McFarland, M.D.

In the long standing debate about intelligence — what is it and can it be measured—the life and work of Sir Cyril Burt stands out as unique. Burt was the first English psychologist to be knighted — for his research in educational testing programs. He was widely respected, and when he died in 1971 at the age of eighty-eight, he was the most prominent man in his field.

But a few years later, his critics discovered that he'd made up much of his scientific data. His most famous study was his comparison of identical twins who had been separated and raised in different environments. In several papers he reported that their intelligence was almost the same, just as if they'd been raised together. This supported the belief that heredity was much more important than environment in determining intelligence. When it was found that he had no data to back up his claims and that he may have made up the entire twin study, the old debate was revived.

One of his friends and collaborators, Arthur R. Jensen of the University of California, attacked Burt's detractors in 1977 by writing: "The charges, as they presently stand, must be judged as the sheer surmise and conjecture, and perhaps wishful thinking, of a few intensely ideological psychologists whose antipathy for Burt's hereditarian position in the so-called IQ controversy is already well known." However, by 1981, Jensen had changed his opinion. This time he wrote, "All of his massive purported data on inheritance of mental ability is suspect and must now be treated as worthless."

That will not be easy to do. Burt's ideas have been in textbooks for fifty years, and have influenced our whole approach to the study of intelligence. Jensen, who may be the best known psychologist in this field since Burt, has yet to change his attitude about the relative importance of heredity and environment. Since the expose of Burt's various scams, more recent research tends to show heredity is less important than was once believed, and even Jensen may yet modify his position.

Meanwhile, people realize intelligence may not necessarily be what is measured by intelligence tests. In fact, reaction time is correlated very closely with intelligence as measured by standard IQ tests. We understand this relationship intuitively; we often use "quick" as one synonym for intelligent. We also use words such as bright, clever, smart, and sharp. The dual meaning of these words indicates we are not always completely comfortable with intelligent people. Quick, after all, can also mean impatient or hot-tempered; clever comes from a word meaning claws or talons; sharp means the ability to cut easily; and smart also means physical pain.

One wonders if, in the long run, it makes any sense to argue whether intelligence is primarily inherited or if it can be significantly influenced by environment. The argument quickly becomes political. People who favor the status quo in society claim that class differences in rank, prestige, and wealth are related largely to intelligence; and since intelligence is mainly inherited, nothing much can be done to change things. Their favorite argument is that if all the world's wealth were somehow divided evenly, within a few short years a very small minority would again have the lion's share, just as they do now.

People who are the underdogs of society and who do not have wealth, prestige, and power believe that IQ tests are designed to explain and maintain the status quo in society, and thus, they cause more harm than good. If these complicated tests were replaced by a machine to measure reaction time, there would probably be less voodoo and more validity in their application.

According to Burt's very sympathetic and compassionate biographer, L.S. Hearnshaw, Burt was a person who had a great need to win arguments. In his reference to this sad story, Arthur Jensen wrote, "Unfortunately, it is not an extremely rare thing in science for bold falsehoods to be promulgated."

Perhaps we can learn a great deal from Sir Cyril Burt in his studies of twins if we question science and scientists. Even more dangerous than scientific falsehood is our present tendency to treat science as our religion or to reject it completely when science cannot solve our many problems. Rather than simply distrusting scientists, we might try modifying their education and training. If we keep them in the mainstream of society rather than confining them to laboratories or placing them on special pedestals, we might be more satisfied with their efforts.

NOVEMBER

SAGITTARIUS

November 22 – December 21

FRIDAY — NOV. 22

Sun Rises 06:59
Sun Sets 16:54
Moon Rises 14:40
Moon Sets 02:23

MOON IN ARIES

sun conj saturn-17:45. moon trine mercury-19:21.

Sun Enters Sagittarius 00:51

Charles de Gaulle 1890 — Wiley Post 1899
Claiborne Pell 1918 — Rodney Dangerfield 1921
Geraldine Page 1924 — Jamie Lee Curtis 1958

*1963: Pres. John F. Kennedy assassinated (Dallas, Tex.).
1963: Aldous Huxley, writer, dies of throat cancer in Santa Barbara, Calif.—with his doctor's consent, he was under influence of LSD.*

DREAM

Rather cold tea and cold rice than cold words and cold looks.

Japanese Proverb

SATURDAY — NOV. 23

Sun Rises 07:00
Sun Sets 16:53
Moon Rises 15:03
Moon Sets 03:21

MOON IN ARIES

moon oppos mars-02:15. moon trine uranus-03:07.

Harpo Marx 1888 — Charles Berlitz 1914

1876: Intercollegiate Football Assoc. formed. 1945: Food rationing in the U.S. ends.

A human body cannot endure under unrelenting, artificial excitement and stimulation—it will burn itself out. Likewise, a body politic, such as our constitutional republic, cannot forever withstand continual carnival on the streets of its cities and the campuses of the nation.

Spiro Agnew

SUNDAY — NOV. 24

Sun Rises 07:00
Sun Sets 16:53
Moon Rises 15:26
Moon Sets 04:19

MOON ENTERS TAURUS 05:07

moon trine neptune-09:38. moon oppos pluto-16:53.

Baruch Spinoza 1632 — Scott Joplin 1868
Dale Carnegie 1888 — Geraldine Fitzgerald 1914
Howard Duff 1917 — Percy Sutton 1920
John V. Lindsay 1921 — William F. Buckley, Jr. 1925

1871: National Rifle Assoc. incorporated. 1963: Jack Ruby murders Lee Harvey Oswald.

I think that for any generation to assert itself as an aware human entity, it has to break with the past, so obviously the kids that are coming along next are not going to have much in common with what we feel.

Jim Morrison

MONDAY — NOV. 25

Sun Rises 07:01
Sun Sets 16:53
Moon Rises 15:52
Moon Sets 05:17

MOON IN TAURUS

moon square jupiter-04:27. moon at apogee-14:00.
moon oppos venus-23:43. moon at asc node-23:45.

Carry Nation 1846 — Anastas Mikoyan 1895
Helen Gahagan Douglas 1900 — Etta Jones 1928

2348bc: The Great Flood, according to biblical scholars. 1944: German V-2 rocket lands on Woolworth's store on New Cross Road in Deptford, London, England, killing 160 shoppers and store personnel.

GROWING
BY LIZ CAILE

NOW'S THE TIME — South, Southwest: As the rest of the country turns indoors and away from outdoor growing, you may still be planting. In some southern lattitudes sowing cool weather mustards and alliums is in order. Fruit trees, berries, nut trees, and hardy flower plants can be set outdoors. In more northern latitudes, start cool weather plants and salad greens in the cold frame. Utilize greenhouse and sunporches for starting tender plants and cultivating potted ornamentals. **Northwest:** Begin winter pruning on deciduous trees. Potted fuscias, geraniums, tuberous begonias have been moved indoors to airy locations that are too warm. Berry pruning can be done — protect canes from wind as well as cold, especially canes of the more tender blackberries. **Mountain States:** It's not too late to pot paperwhite narcissus bulbs in attractive bowls or planters. Used bookstores have good values on gifts for gardeners; prints and books of botanical illustrations please growers as well. Begin to plant a rock garden for one corner of your world. **Northeast, Midwest:** Use evergreen boughs to protect perennials and hold leaf mulches in place. You can shovel early snows over perennial beds for added protection. Try to keep salt from roads and sidewalks away from plants and the garden.

When Snow Comes

Where snow is an expected part of the winter scene, a dry winter is disturbing. The frozen ground and dry grasses are exposed to fierce, biting winds. No wonder landscape plantings need extra protection and deep watering, when temperatures are warm enough.

Where snow is expected, nothing is more pleasing than for the permanent snowbanks to fill in early in the season, insulating the house and plumbing, burying plants and land under a cold but gentle layer. Even the compost pile seems to benefit from the snow's protection. If you want to add to it through the winter, stick a pole into the middle of it and mark where winter wastes begin. Include layers of dirt and ashes as well as kitchen wastes.

In the spring, the snow pulls back from a rested, fruitful land — ideally. In fact, with acid precipitation measured in many parts of the country, the grower should be aware that the acid migrates through snow banks and is concentrated in spring run-off and where snow has lain the deepest.

In the high mountains of the West, as the snowbanks recede, the avalanche lily comes into bloom almost as if it has been sowed by the winter. Known as dogtooth violet in the East, where it is more persistant on wooded slopes just below timberline, this clear yellow-flowered lily reminds us of the transience of summer and the growing season.

Growing takes time. We can pull on plants to grow one way or another, but they'll ultimately respond to their own clocks. Gardening well also takes time. Finding this one essential ingredient, *Time*, is all it really takes to learn to garden well.

To begin with, we can't compare the gardening and growing time scale with the time and money scale that so relentlessly rules our day-to-day lives. But in time, our growing efforts are more rewarding — while our labor remains constant, the fruits of our labor increase dramatically.

We build up the soil to sustainable productivity. We learn how to deal with set backs in the garden. We learn what crops and combinations will fill our individual needs most efficiently. We provide our families with not only sustenance, but fruits and vegetables that are no longer available in the market, are ridiculously expensive, or insipidly flavored.

Eventually we will discover that the quality of home-grown produce, and of the value of the gardening experience (shaping not in man's image, but being shaped by the image of the multitude of living things) compete successfully on the time-money scale as well.

Garden Gifts

●Canned peaches, marmalades, chutney, jams.

●Potted herbs for windowsills, with recipes to match.

●A collection of homegrown, hand-collected vegetable and flower seeds.

●Potted divisions from amaryllis lilies, aloe vera, and other houseplants, including a card explaining all you know about the care, history and use of the plant.

●Sachets of lavender, rose petals, other fragrant homegrown flowers — use orris root, from an iris species, to hold the scent.

●Ornamental hot pepper plants started from seed last spring and raised on the patio or apartment porch during summer.

The process of growing high-value food in small plots produces more true wealth with fewer inputs of energy than any other widely available kind of work.

—*Robert Rodale*

TUESDAY — NOV. 26

Sun Rises 07:02
Sun Sets 16:52
Moon Rises 16:22
Moon Sets 06:17

MOON ENTERS GEMINI 18:08

mercury at asc node-13:36. moon oppos saturn-20:34.

Samuel Reshevsky 1911
Eugene Ionesco 1912
Charles Schulz 1922
Robert Goulet 1933
Tina Turner 1941

Eric Sevareid 1912
Frederik Pohl 1919
Michael Butler 1926
Rich Little 1938
Wendy Turnbull 1952

1970: Native American National Day of Mourning held by Indians to counter festivities commemorating Pilgrim Fathers' 350th Thanksgiving (Plymouth, Mass.)

WEDNESDAY — NOV. 27

Sun Rises 07:03
Sun Sets 16:52
Moon Rises 16:57
Moon Sets 07:18

MOON IN GEMINI

sun oppos moon-04:42. moon oppos mercury-10:40. moon trine jupiter-18:06.

FULL MOON 04:42

Sprague de Camp 1907
David Merrick 1912
Jimi Hendrix 1942

James Agee 1909
Buffalo Bob Smith 1917
Eddie Rabbitt 1944

1868: Custer attacks peaceful camp of Cheyenne Indians— over 100 Indians killed (Washita River). 1934: George "Baby Face" Nelson, Public Enemy, dies at age 26 from effects of 17 bullet wounds from FBI agents during gun battle in ditch near Barrington, Il. 1965: 35,000 demonstrators march against Vietnam War in Washington, D.C.

HOW?

THURSDAY — NOV. 28

Sun Rises 07:04
Sun Sets 16:52
Moon Rises 17:39
Moon Sets 08:17

MOON IN GEMINI

moon oppos uranus-05:24. moon trine mars-10:36. sun conj mercury-13:56.

William Blake 1757
Berry Gordy, Jr. 1929
Gary Hart 1937

Anton Rubinstein 1829
Hope Lange 1933
Randy Newman 1943

1925: Grand Ol' Opry begins. 1942: Coconut Grove fire—481 killed (Boston).

On the one hand, I like to see things preserved. On the other, I hate to think of everything being a national park. We're just running short of world, that's all. It's running out on us.

John Huston

THANKSGIVING DAY

FRIDAY — NOV. 29

Sun Rises 07:05
Sun Sets 16:52
Moon Rises 18:28
Moon Sets 09:14

MOON ENTERS CANCER 06:23

moon oppos neptune-11:08. moon trine pluto-18:12.

Robert Devereux 1566
Louisa May Alcott 1832
Frank Reynolds 1923
James Rosenquist 1933
Chuck Mangione 1940

John Ray 1627
C.S. Lewis 1898
John Gary 1932
Willie Morris 1934
Felix Cavaliere 1944

1864: 900 U.S. Cavalrymen massacre 500 Cheyenne and Arapaho men, women, and children (Sand Creek). 1870: Production of paper from pulpwood begins in New England. 1890: First Army-Navy football game.

If we encounter a man of rare intellect, we should ask him what books he reads.

Ralph Waldo Emerson

SATURDAY — NOV. 30

Sun Rises 07:06
Sun Sets 16:51
Moon Rises 19:24
Moon Sets 10:06

MOON IN CANCER

Jonathan Swift 1667
Winston Churchill 1874
Brownie McGee 1915
Rex Reason 1928
Paul Stookey 1937

Mark Twain 1835
Clytford Still 1904
Efrem Zimbalist Jr. 1923
Abbie Hoffman 1936
Robert Guillaume 1937

1954: First known impact between a meteorite and a human being—Elizabeth Hodges struck by 8 1/2 lb stone which fell through her roof (Sylacauga, Ala).

SUNDAY — DEC. 01

Sun Rises 07:07
Sun Sets 16:51
Moon Rises 20:25
Moon Sets 10:52

MOON ENTERS LEO 16:59

moon square mars-00:57. moon trine venus-12:58. moon trine saturn-20:25. moon trine mercury-21:30.

Rex Stout 1886
Walter Alston 1911
Mary Martin 1913

Cyril Richard 1898
Minoru Yamasaki 1912
Woody Allen 1935

1955: Mrs. Rosa Parks, a black seamstress from Montgomery, Ala., is arrested as she refuses to give up her seat in the front of a bus when a white man could sit down—beginning of the Civil Rights Movement in the U.S. 1956: U.S. Army announces plans to deactivate last combat mule outfit. 1970: Divorce approved in Italy.

In literature, as in love, we are astonished at what is chosen by others.

Andre Maurois

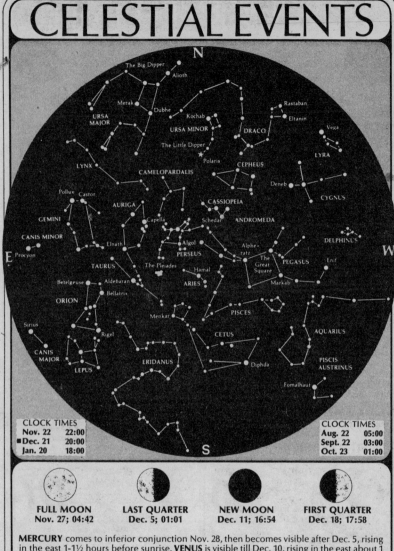

N

The Big Dipper
Alioth
Merak
Dubhe
Kochab
Rastaban
Eltanin
Vega
URSA MAJOR
URSA MINOR
DRACO
The Little Dipper
LYRA
Polaris
CAMELOPARDALIS
CEPHEUS
LYNX
Deneb
Pollux Castor
CASSIOPEIA
CYGNUS
AURIGA
Schedar
ANDROMEDA
Capella
GEMINI
DELPHINUS
CANIS MINOR
Elnath
Alphe-
ratz
E Procyon
PERSEUS
Algol
The Great Square
PEGASUS
Enif
TAURUS
The Pleiades
Hamal
Markab
W
Betelgeuse Aldebaran
ARIES
Bellatrix
ORION
Menkar
PISCES
Sirius
Rigel
CETUS
AQUARIUS
CANIS MAJOR
Diphda
PISCIS AUSTRINUS
LEPUS
ERIDANUS
Fomalhaut

S

CLOCK TIMES	
Nov. 22	22:00
■Dec. 21	20:00
Jan. 20	18:00

CLOCK TIMES	
Aug. 22	05:00
Sept. 22	03:00
Oct. 23	01:00

FULL MOON
Nov. 27; 04:42

LAST QUARTER
Dec. 5; 01:01

NEW MOON
Dec. 11; 16:54

FIRST QUARTER
Dec. 18; 17:58

MERCURY comes to inferior conjunction Nov. 28, then becomes visible after Dec. 5, rising in the east 1-1½ hours before sunrise. **VENUS** is visible till Dec. 10, rising in the east about 1 hour before sunrise. **MARS** is visible all month rising in the east 3-4 hours before sunrise, then fading east of midsky with morning twilight. **JUPITER** is visible all month appearing west of midsky at sunset, and setting 3-5 hours later. **SATURN** comes to conjunction Nov. 22, then becomes visible after Dec. 5, rising in the east 1-2 hours before sunrise. **Dec. 02:** Mars 3° N. of *Spica* (morning sky). **Dec. 03:** Mercury 1.6° N. of Venus (morning sky). **Dec. 05:** Venus 1.1° S. of Saturn (morning sky). **Dec. 08:** Mars 0.01° S. of waning crescent Moon-OCCULTATION-(morning sky). **Dec. 10:** Mercury 5° N. of waning crescent Moon (morning sky); Saturn 4° N. of waning crescent Moon (morning sky). **Dec. 15:** Jupiter 5° N. of waxing crescent Moon (evening sky). **Dec. 16:** Mercury 0.5° N. of Saturn (morning sky); Mercury at gr. elong. W. (21°). **Dec. 21:** Mercury 6° N. of *Antares* (morning sky).

DECEMBER

MONDAY   DEC. 02

Sun Rises 07:08
Sun Sets 16:51
Moon Rises 21:30
Moon Sets 11:31

MOON IN LEO

moon square pluto-04:33. mercury conj saturn-08:31.
sun trine moon-13:15. moon oppos jupiter-17:04.

Charles Ringling 1863   Randolph Hearst 1915
Julie Harris 1925   Tracy Austin 1962

1964: *Free Speech Movement continues to defy ban on politics with sit-ins and rallies—thousands rally in Sproul Plaza (Univ. of Calif. Berkeley); more than 800 spend the night.* **1965:** *Blacks in Bogalusa, La. win federal court order barring Ku Klux Klan from interfering with their civil rights.* **1982:** *Barney Clark, retired dentist, receives world's first artificial heart (Salt Lake City).*

Question: How come everyone gets mad if I leave my used cigar butts in the ashtray? Answer: I'll bet you don't flush the toilet either.
The Cigar Almanac

TUESDAY   DEC. 03

Sun Rises 07:09
Sun Sets 16:51
Moon Rises 22:36
Moon Sets 12:05

MOON IN LEO

moon trine uranus-02:39.
VENUS ENTERS SAGITTARIUS-05:00.
mercury conj venus-16:25.

Joseph Conrad 1857   Anton Von Webern 1883
Anna Freud 1895   Maria Callas 1923
Ferlin Husky 1927   Jean-Luc Godard 1930
Andy Williams 1930   Bobby Allison 1937

1910: *Mary Baker Eddy, founder of Christian Science, dies while battling cold which she thought caused by evil forces,—she had stated that no disease could hurt her.* **1964:** *Calif. governor Pat Brown dispatches over 600 police to Univ. of Calif. Berkeley campus to quell Free Speech Movement demonstrations— arrests of 814 students continue for more than 12 hours. Faculty/student strike cancels classes.* **1965:** *3 Klansmen, convicted under federal conspiracy charges of killing Mrs. Violet Liuzzo, are given 10 year sentences—they were acquitted in state court earlier.*

WEDNESDAY   DEC. 04

Sun Rises 07:10
Sun Sets 16:51
Moon Rises 23:42
Moon Sets 12:35

MOON ENTERS VIRGO 01:14

moon square mercury-01:46. moon square venus-03:22.
moon square saturn-05:01. moon trine neptune-05:54.
MERCURY ENTERS SCORPIO-12:16.
venus conj saturn-22:11.

Wassily Kandinsky 1866   Rainer Maria-Rilke 1875
Francisco Franco 1892   Pappy Boyington 1912
Deanna Durbin 1922   Stewart Mott 1937
Southside Johnny 1948   Jeff Bridges 1949

1956: *U.S. Army announces it will no longer use messenger pigeons—18 pigeons that had saved lives will be sent to zoos.* **1969:** *Fred Hampton and Mark Clark, Black Panther Party leaders, die from gunshot wounds during police raid in Chicago.*

DOWN UNDER

THURSDAY   DEC. 05

Sun Rises 07:11
Sun Sets 16:50
Moon Rises ----
Moon Sets 13:02

MOON IN VIRGO

sun square moon-01:01. moon square uranus-09:27.

LAST QUARTER MOON 01:01

Lawrence Sterne 1713   Christina Rossetti 1830
George Custer 1839   Fritz Lang 1890
Philip Wrigley 1894   Walt Disney 1901
Werner Heisenberg 1901   Otto Preminger 1906
Joan Didion 1934   J. J. Cale 1938
Jose Carreras 1946   Jim Messina 1947

1791: *Mozart dies.* **1876:** *Brooklyn Theater in New York City burns, killing 289 people—survey done at that time reported that 1 out of every 4 theaters burned within 4 years after being built.* **1929:** *National League for Nudists organized.* **1955:** *Martin Luther King Jr. leads blacks in boycott of city buses to protest the arrest of Rosa Parks (Montgomery, Ala.).*

FRIDAY   DEC. 06

Sun Rises 07:12
Sun Sets 16:50
Moon Rises 00:49
Moon Sets 13:29

MOON ENTERS LIBRA 06:33

moon square neptune-11:06.

Joyce Kilmer 1886   Lynn Fontanne 1887
Ira Gershwin 1896   Alfred Eisenstaedt 1898
Agnes Moorehead 1906   Wardell Pomeroy 1913
Richard Speck 1941   Dwight Stone 1953

1876: *First body incinerated in a crematorium in U.S. (Washington, Pa).* **1957:** *AFL-CIO ousts Teamsters Union.* **1965:** *Bill Graham produces his first rock concert at San Francisco's Fillmore Auditorium.* **1965:** *McCone Report on causes of Watts riot released—denies charges of police brutality.*

The man who does not read good books has no advantage over the man who can't read them.
Mark Twain

SATURDAY   DEC. 07

Sun Rises 07:13
Sun Sets 16:50
Moon Rises 01:58
Moon Sets 13:56

MOON IN LIBRA

moon trine jupiter-05:29.

Theodor Schwann 1810   Willa Cather 1873
Joyce Cary 1888   Eli Wallach 1915
Ted Knight 1923   Tom Waits 1949

FORECAST SAGITTARIUS
BY NAN DE GROVE

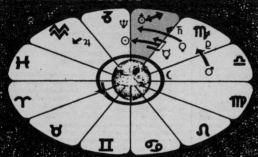

LONGITUDE OF THE PLANETS
00:51 PST; 11/22/85

Sun *00°00′* Sagittarius
Moon *04°04′* Aries
Merc *13°50′* Sagittarius R
Venus *15°57′* Scorpio
Mars *16°05′* Libra
Jupiter *10°59′* Aquarius
Saturn *00°37′* Sagittarius
Uranus *17°06′* Sagittarius
Neptune *02°11′* Capricorn
Pluto *05°41′* Scorpio

This will be a mentally, socially, and spiritually stimulating month. A reflective and philosophical mood prevails after the emotional turmoil of Scorpio, and with Saturn's entrance into Sagittarius, we are questioning some basic beliefs and values in light of recent experience.

Practical idealism is a key concept. Saturn's austerity and seriousness may tone down the expansiveness and careless optimism of Sagittarius, but there is a potential for more clearly defined, realistic goals. Ideals and aspirations will have to be realized as well as imagined. We should be mindful of our goals because with effort, we will probably attain them over the next couple of years.

With fire and air signs predominating this month, minds are strongly activated and communications are lively. The pursuit of knowledge and the social status it may confer is a concern, especially around the Full Moon at the end of November. Many will be making plans to upgrade their social or professional status through furthering their education.

Venus joins Saturn in Sagittarius on December 5th; this combination emphasizes social connections established on the basis of shared knowledge and beliefs, perhaps in a teacher-student context. There is a tendency to be romantically attracted to one who appears as an intellectual authority or a spiritual guide.

FIRE SIGNS begin a new cycle with increased self-discipline, maturity, and focus.

Aries: you have opportunities in travel, education, and spiritual growth and may be involved with a teacher or mentor. Tensions erupt in the last week of the month; keep your cool.

Leo: with a stronger self-image now, allow yourself to feel a sense of accomplishment and unburdening.

Sagittarius: try to begin this new cycle with increased seriousness and commitment in all areas. This is a time for clearing out the non-essential elements of your life and establishing priorities.

EARTH SIGNS have opportunities to learn new skills and techniques while expanding their sphere of influence.

Taurus: be prepared for a spiritual and/or emotional crisis that involves the dynamics of sharing. You may need to revise some relationships.

Virgo: your foundations are shifting. Assess personal needs, values, and goals; eliminate energy drains.

Capricorn: you may need to expand and update your belief system to accommodate new experience and psychological insights.

AIR SIGNS are back in circulation after a low point last month.

Gemini: time to review commitments, and reconsider issues of responsibility in relationships. Realize that you can't be all things to all people without losing your identity.

Libra: connect with others who inspire initiative and action; but you may need to be more definite and assertive in dealing with strong personalities.

Aquarius: you begin to feel a sense of relief and increased freedom. A long struggle may be ending; you are beginning to get support rather than opposition from others.

WATER SIGNS may feel fragmented and irritated as this month's fire and air energies seem inimical to their natures.

Cancer: try not to let work pressures and that growing list of unfinished tasks get you down. Watch health and heed intuition.

Scorpio: you need to re-examine your values and beliefs about physical reality. Time to mobilize your unused resources.

Pisces: become aware of the need to restructure your professional life and goals. New educational opportunities are presenting themselves. Release an old self-image.

SUNDAY DEC. 08

Sun Rises 07:14
Sun Sets 16:50
Moon Rises 03:10
Moon Sets 14:25

MOON ENTERS SCORPIO 08:56

moon conj mars-02:29. mercury directs-03:33.
moon conj pluto-19:10.

Horace 65bc	Joel Chandler Harris 1848
Jean Sibelius 1865	James Thurber 1894
Flip Wilson 1933	David Carradine 1936
James Galway 1939	Jim Morrison 1943

1886: *American Federation of Labor founded.* **1941:** *U.S. declares war on Japan.* **1980:** *John Lennon murdered (New York City).* **1982:** *Michigan court declares Jimmy Hoffa legally dead as of July 30, 1982, exactly 7 years after his disappearance.*

The multitude of books is making us ignorant.

Voltaire

HANUKKAH

MONDAY DEC. 09

Sun Rises 07:15
Sun Sets 16:50
Moon Rises 04:25
Moon Sets 14:59

MOON IN SCORPIO

moon square jupiter-07:22. moon at desc node-23:06.
sun conj uranus-23:47.

King Gustavus Adolphus 1594	John Milton 1608
Margaret Hamilton 1902	Dalton Trumbo 1905
Tip O'Neill 1912	Kirk Douglas 1916
Red Foxx 1922	Willie Hartack 1932
Beau Bridges 1941	Dick Butkus 1942
Joan Armatrading 1950	Donny Osmond 1957

1884: *Ball bearing roller skates patented.* **1941:** *China declares war on Japan, Germany, and Italy.* **1958:** *John Birch Society founded by retired candy manufacturer Robert Welch.*

Just because you're getting older, doesn't mean you're doing it better. But you can't stop, either, or you'll be lost.

Willem de Kooning

TUESDAY DEC. 10

Sun Rises 07:16
Sun Sets 16:50
Moon Rises 05:43
Moon Sets 15:41

MOON ENTERS SAGITTARIUS 09:13

moon conj mercury-07:53. moon conj saturn-13:42.
moon at perigee-17:00.

Emily Dickinson 1830	Rumer Godden 1907
Professor Longhair 1918	Susan Dey 1952

1898: *Spanish-American War ends—Spain gives the U.S. Guam, Puerto Rico, Philippines and gives up its claim to Cuba.* **1965:** *3 white men are acquitted in Selma, Ala. of murder of Rev. James Reebe.*

Mercury visible above the Eastern Horizon just before morning twilight. Most people have never seen it. You can get out and see it!

WEDNESDAY DEC. 11

Sun Rises 07:17
Sun Sets 16:50
Moon Rises 07:01
Moon Sets 16:31

MOON IN SAGITTARIUS

moon conj venus-00:51. moon conj uranus-14:17.
sun conj moon-16:54.

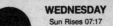

NEW MOON 16:54

Hector Berlioz 1803	Fiorello La Guardia 1882
Gilbert Roland 1905	Carlo Ponti 1913
Rita Moreno 1931	Donna Mills 1943
Booker T. Jones 1944	Bess Armstrong 1953

1844: *Nitrous Oxide first used during tooth extraction.* **1964:** *Sam Cooke, singer, dies at age 29, in motel room in Los Angeles after being shot 3 times by a woman who described him as an assailant.*

The best time for planning a book is while you're doing the dishes.

Agatha Christie

THURSDAY DEC. 12

Sun Rises 07:18
Sun Sets 16:50
Moon Rises 08:16
Moon Sets 17:32

MOON ENTERS CAPRICORN 08:59

MERCURY ENTERS SAGITTARIUS-03:04.
moon conj neptune-13:36.

Gustave Flaubert 1821	Edvard Munch 1863
Jules Dassin 1911	Karl Carstens 1914
Edward Koch 1924	Helen Frankenthaler 1928
John Osborne 1929	Madrid Hurtado 1934
Tom Hayden 1940	Cathy Rigby 1952

1872: *Last Labrador duck dies (Long Island, N.Y.).* **1917:** *Worst train wreck ever—543 die in Modane, France.* **1976:** *Jack Cassidy, actor, dies at age 49 in Los Angeles—he was burned beyond recognition in fire that destroyed his apartment... identification was accomplished through dental records.*

GRAND SLAM

FRIDAY DEC. 13

Sun Rises 07:18
Sun Sets 16:50
Moon Rises 09:20
Moon Sets 18:40

MOON IN CAPRICORN

Heinrich Heine 1797
Carlos Montoya 1903
Johannes Vorster 1915
Drew Pearson 1897
Ross MacDonald 1915

Tom Smith by Jane Brakhage

Tom Smith died on November 2, 1870 at the age of forty. It was Moses Miles did it, chopped his head up with an ax.

Abilene was a great cow town. Abilene was the end of the Chisholm Trail and all the other cow trails. Abilene was where the Texas Longhorns could be put on the train and sold in New York City. Any other route to the East was blocked off by law because wherever the Texas Longhorns went, every other kind of cow died. It was decades before anyone realized it was the ticks that fell off the Longhorns that killed the other cattle. Longhorns were immune to them, so state after state barred them from coming through and there was no way for them left but the train.

Joe McCoy figured it all out. He saw how Texas was more or less ruined after the Civil War, the Longhorns weren't kept care of at all — just for hides, shiploads of hides, no meat to speak of between hide and bone, Longhorns just running wild around Texas, cowboys occasionally rounded up some for hides. Joe McCoy saw all that and he saw the train tracks building through Kansas and he went out to Kansas and made Abilene.

Not that the town wasn't there before he arrived, it was. It was twelve log huts with sod roofs, one was the saloon, one was the general store, one was the county seat and the other nine residential. This was the spring of 1867 and the Kansas Pacific Railroad had just passed through and was going on toward Salina. Mrs. Hersey had named the town, she was already reading *The Bible* to everyone," Lysanias the tetrarch of Abilene ," it said, *Luke, Chapter 3, Verse 1*, so she named the town Abilene.

By three years later, the place had become a roaring Boom Town with several hotels, banks, vast stockyards, a Mayor, quantities of saloons and dance halls, a large and thriving red-light district, hundreds of Texas cowboys slavering for any kind of excitement they could rustle up, each one with a loaded gun on his hip. The Texans came north with no feeling of kindness for the people of Kansas. The South had only just lost the War, the feeling was still strong in their minds that the people of Kansas were the enemy. Guns blazed day and night, people were beaten, robbed, murdered, made to dance the jig with bullets flashing around their feet. Clearly, it was time for the town to invest in a marshal. "Hell is in session in Abilene," was one newspaper statement.

Another was more erudite. "Gathered together in Abilene and its environs is the greatest collection of Texas cowboys, rascals, desperadoes and adventuresses the United States has ever known. There is no law, no restraint in this seething cauldron of vice and depravity."

In the spring of 1870, a cook for one of the Texas outfits went through town threatening people, shooting out street lights, and generally disturbing what peace there was. When he was locked up in the basement of the mayor's office, twenty Texans broke into the place, shooting off locks, ripping up curtains, breaking furniture. Finding not enough scope in the mayor's office, they expanded to the town, shooting out more street lights, breaking windows, galloping around in the night, whooping and hollering and shooting and smashing things.

Mayor T.C. Henry, five years later to be known as "The Wheat King of Kansas," shored himself up in his mutilated office with half a dozen armed men wondering if they'd see the next day, wondering what the hell could be done about this insane community. T.C. Henry was trembling. The cowboys finally roared out of town in triumph.

The next afternoon, Tom Smith rode into town on his big gray mare, Silverheels. He rode directly to the mayor's office, hitched Silverheels to the hitching post, and walked in.

He was tall, wiry, broad-shouldered and solid. His stance was straight, and athletic. He was soft-spoken, polite, clean and respectful. "I'm interested in the job of marshal," he said.

"You better look the town over," said T.C. Henry, the Mayor. "You might change your mind."

"I've looked the town over," said Tom Smith. "It's about what I expected."

T.C. Henry reached backward with his hand for the arm of his chair and lowered himself carefully to a seat. "Then you'll take the job?" he queried. "You think you can control the town?" It seemed an idiotic question. Obviously, nobody could control that town.

"That's what I'm here for, Mr. Henry," said Tom Smith. "I believe I can control it."

Ed Masterson got $75 a month for being marshal of Dodge City. In Wichita, Wyatt Earp got $60 a month. T.C. Henry offered Tom Smith $150 a month plus $2 extra for every arrest.

The first thing Tom Smith did as marshal was to put up signs all over town prohibiting the carrying of guns. Naturally, the next thing that happened was that the signs were defaced or torn down. Tom Smith rode around town on Silverheels, his brace of pistols hidden in shoulder holsters under his coat. The people of Abilene couldn't figure him out. But Tom Smith had a secret weapon. It didn't take a day for Abilene to discover it. What it was, he knew how to use his fists.

He saw a cowpuncher tearing down one of his signs, leaped off Silverheels, socked him in the jaw, knocked him cold, threw him over his shoulder, hauled him off to the pokey, got back on Silverheels and went out

DECEMBER

SATURDAY — DEC. 14
Sun Rises 07:19
Sun Sets 16:51
Moon Rises 10:13
Moon Sets 19:53

MOON ENTERS AQUARIUS 10:15
moon square mars-10:13.
MARS ENTERS SCORPIO-10:59.
moon square pluto-21:15.

Michael de Nostradamus 1503　　Tycho Brahe 1546
Morey Amsterdam 1912　　James Aubrey 1918
Shirley Jackson 1919　　Charlie Rich 1932
Stewart Brand 1938　　Patty Duke 1946

1799: George Washington dies after being bled by physicians trying to cure his laryngitis—he was 67 years and 295 days old. His last words were, "It is well." 1911: Roald Amundsen reaches the South Pole.

SUNDAY — DEC. 15
Sun Rises 07:20
Sun Sets 16:51
Moon Rises 10:55
Moon Sets 21:04

MOON IN AQUARIUS
moon conj jupiter-12:00.

Maxwell Anderson 1888　　J. Paul Getty 1892
John Hammond, Sr. 1910　　Dave Clark 1942

1890: Sitting Bull and his son Crowfoot assassinated by Indian police. 1961: Adolph Eichmann sentenced to death. 1973: Kidnappers release J.Paul Getty III after family pays $2.8 million ransom.

GEMINID METEOR SHOWER An all night show, best past midnight. Get out and see 'em!

MONDAY — DEC. 16
Sun Rises 07:20
Sun Sets 16:51
Moon Rises 11:29
Moon Sets 22:11

MOON ENTERS PISCES 14:50
mercury conj saturn-12:02. moon trine mars-17:23.
moon square saturn-21:19. moon square mercury-22:00.

Jane Austen 1775　　George Santayana 1863
Noel Coward 1899　　Margaret Mead 1901
Arthur C. Clarke 1917　　Lesley Stahl 1941

1903: New York City's first female ushers hired at Majestic Theater. 1916: Grigori Rasputin, mystic and advisor to Russian royal family, dies at hands of his enemies—he was poisoned with potassium cyanide, shot in back, shot twice in front, beaten, and shoved through a hole in ice of river in St. Petersburg. 1965: Historic rendezvous between 2 Gemini spacecraft is effected 180 miles in space.

GRANDIOSE

TUESDAY — DEC. 17
Sun Rises 07:21
Sun Sets 16:51
Moon Rises 11:57
Moon Sets 23:15

MOON IN PISCES
moon trine pluto-02:51.

John Greenleaf Whittier 1807　　Ford Madox Ford 1873
Arthur Fiedler 1894　　Erskine Caldwell 1903
Paul Cadmus 1904　　Paul Butterfield 1942

63: Lazarus dies for the second time. 1830: Simon Bolivar dies. 1903: Wilbur and Orville Wright make the first manned airplane flight. 1925: Billy Mitchell court-martialed.

What difference does it make if you make friends with a snake? If all your friends are human friends, it's like looking in a mirror. What can you learn?

Kim Novak

WEDNESDAY — DEC. 18
Sun Rises 07:21
Sun Sets 16:52
Moon Rises 12:22
Moon Sets ----

MOON ENTERS ARIES 23:36
venus conj uranus-01:33. moon square uranus-01:43.
moon square venus-01:45. sun square moon-17:58.

FIRST QUARTER MOON 17:58

Saki 1870　　Ty Cobb 1886
Christopher Fry 1907　　Ossie Davis 1917
Anita O'Day 1919　　Ramsey Clark 1927
Roger Smith 1932　　Keith Richards 1943

1963: 500 African students riot in Moscow's Red Square—protesting racial discrimination. 1965: B-52s begin bombing Ho Chi Minh trail in Laos.

I would never read a book if it were possible for me to talk half an hour with the man who wrote it.

Woodrow Wilson

THURSDAY — DEC. 19
Sun Rises 07:22
Sun Sets 16:52
Moon Rises 12:44
Moon Sets 00:15

MOON IN ARIES
moon square neptune-05:44. moon trine saturn-07:06.
moon trine mercury-12:55.

Albert Michelson 1852　　Fritz Reiner 1888
Jean Genet 1910　　Edith Piaf 1915
Al Kaline 1934　　Cicely Tyson 1939
Phil Ochs 1940　　Stan Smith 1946

1732: Ben Franklin publishes Poor Richard's Almanac. 1965: Renewed fighting breaks out in Dominican Republic.

Why do people always expect authors to answer questions? I am an author because I want to ask questions. If I had answers I'd be a politician.

Eugene Ionesco

to do it again. He caught several that day and for several days, always replacing the signs. He had plenty of signs. In the meantime, he was talking to managers of stores, saloons, and hotels, getting their support, setting up gun racks in prominent places all over town. And he not only defended his signs, he enforced the gun ordinance. Some people didn't like that.

Like Big Hank. "No way," said Big Hank, "is that little bastard gonna get my gun." And that first Saturday night, he came into town, walked up to Marshal Tom Smith. "What're ya gonna do about that gun ordinance?" he said. Dozens of cowboys were gathered around to see how this would come out.

"See that it's enforced," said Tom Smith in his soft voice. "I'll trouble you to hand me yours."

"Like hell I will," said Big Hank.

"Hand me your gun, sir," said the marshal.

"Over your grandmother's ass, sir," said Big Hank.

With one fluid movement, Tom Smith leaped forward, swung a mighty blow at Big Hank's jaw and over he went. Quickly, the marshal grabbed Big Hank's pistol, pointed it at him and as Hank slowly rose to his feet, ordered him to go back to his camp. Hank left.

Within an hour or so the whole town knew, all the outfits camped outside of town knew. But they didn't know what to do about his technique. "We don't know no more about fist fightin'," said the Texans, "than a hog knows about a sidesaddle."

Another champion for the cause of guns was sought. Out on Chapman Creek, Wyoming Frank laid bets to make it worth his while and in the morning he arrived in Abilene, gun in prominent display on his hip. Massive shoulders, bulging muscles, swagger, more bets, people gathering 'round.

The marshal arrived eventually, ambling on Silverheels down the middle of the street. He saw Wyoming Frank and his gun and his swagger and he slipped off of Silverheels' back. Wyoming Frank began his conversation with a few general insults. Tom Smith demanded Frank's gun and walked toward him. Wyoming Frank backed up to keep out of the range of the marshal's fist. The marshal followed. Pretty soon Wyoming Frank had backed through the swinging doors of the Lone Star Saloon and up against the bar. When Frank drew his gun, Tom Smith socked him a good one, wrenched his gun away, pistol whipped him and sent him out of town.

A few days later, the marshal went into The Old Fruit Saloon to arrest a cowboy. The cowboy's friends lined up in front of him, one threw a kerosene lamp at the marshal, others shot at him point blank. Tom Smith, unhurt, boxed his way to the cowboy and carried him over his shoulder to the hoosegow.

1870 was a peaceful and law-abiding summer in Abilene. In August, the Board of Trustees voted to raise Tom Smith's salary to the unimaginable heights of $225 a month. The man never killed anyone in Abilene, never drank, swore, gambled, or, as Mayor T.C. Henry delicately put it, "was in the least dissolute otherwise." Though the Texans called such folks as Hickock, Earp and the Mastersons "fighting pimps," they wouldn't call Tom Smith that. He wasn't. He was a Nineteenth Century New York Irish cop.

Born in New York City of Irish immigrant parents, Thomas James Smith was raised a Catholic and a gentleman in the traditional Irish manner. But he didn't stay in the New York police department long. In 1857, in Utah, he was left for dead in the Mountain Meadows Massacre. Later, in Wyoming, he fought like a hero in the Bear River Riot and it was as "Bear River Tom Smith" that he began working on the construction of the Union Pacific Railroad.

He cared more about justice than law. In a town slapped together by the Union Pacific as it slowly built its way across Colorado, a friend of Tom's was tossed into jail on trumped-up charges and landed in a cell with three vicious unprincipled murderers. Tom tried every legal channel he could to get his friend out and when that didn't work, he got a gang together from the construction crew and raided the town, fought a fierce battle with vigilantes, was badly wounded, but managed to save his friend. It was after that, that the Union Pacific hired Bear River Tom as marshal for the construction towns along the way west.

As has been mentioned, the summer of 1870 was a quiet one in Abilene. By late October, the Texans had gone back to Texas, the whores had packed up for St. Louis to spend the winter, the town was down to the few hundred year-round residents.

Then Andrew McConnell up Chapman Creek shot and killed John Shea for letting his cattle walk on McConnell's land. Andrew McConnell's friend, Moses Miles, testified that John Shea had shot first but his gun hadn't gone off. So they let McConnell out — until the neighbors raised a fuss, showing evidence that Moses Miles was lying. The county sheriff knew that Andrew McConnell and Moses Miles were dangerous and although it was a good way outside of the marshal's jurisdiction, the sheriff asked Tom Smith to go with one of the sheriff's deputies and bring back Andrew McConnell.

Moses Miles was out chopping wood when the two of them arrived. Tom Smith went to Andrew McConnell's dugout with his gun drawn and left the deputy outside with a bead on Moses Miles. Two shots went off in the dugout. Now, what the deputy should have done was not what he did. What he did was, when he heard the shots he lit out of there toward Abilene. So he didn't see Tom Smith and Andrew McConnell wrest-

DECEMBER

FRIDAY   **DEC.**

Sun Rises 07:22
Sun Sets 16:53
Moon Rises 13:07
Moon Sets 01:13

20

MOON IN ARIES
moon trine uranus-13:04. moon trine venus-19:47.

Susanne Langer 1895   Robert Van de Graaf 1901
Max Lerner 1902   Irene Dunne 1904
Hortense Calisher 1911   Harry Byrd Jr. 1914

SATURDAY   **DEC.**

Sun Rises 07:23
Sun Sets 16:53
Moon Rises 13:30
Moon Sets 02:11

21

MOON ENTERS TAURUS 11:40
sun trine moon-11:27. moon trine neptune-18:13.
moon oppos mars-20:58.

Sun Enters Capricorn 14:08
WINTER SOLSTICE

TOM SMITH continued

ling and grappling together out the door of the dugout, blood dripping from Andrew McConnell's now useless gun hand, a red spot growing on Tom Smith's chest, didn't see Moses Miles run with his ax just as Tom Smith hauled out the handcuffs, didn't see the ax fall on Tom Smith's head. And as Tom Smith rolled and sagged off of Andrew McConnell's back, Moses Miles raised his ax and struck Tom Smith again, and then again with a third blow chopped his head off, all but a strip of skin on the back of his neck.

The posse caught 'em all right over Clay Center way and they got long prison terms, which didn't satisfy the people of the town at all because Tom Smith had been the best thing that had ever happened to Abilene. The whole town turned out for the funeral. Silverheels was saddled and bridled and covered with branches and flowers. Tom Smith's brace of pearl-handled pistols were hanging from the pommel. Everyone wore black crepe. And the next spring Wild Bill Hickock came into town.

Spiders   by Marilyn Auer

Most of us are not impartial to spiders. Even when we respect their work and honor their unique role in the balance of life, we do not want them crawling up our legs.

But a spider's web always captures my gaze as it does its prey. As a spider finishes the scaffolding for its web, the outside framework spokes into the hub. Spiral strands circle around and around from the center to the frame. Now begins the next stage: retracing steps, cutting away the first strands and replacing them with adhesive silk.

When the spider is finished with its web, it will step aside to watch and wait. The net has been cast into a sea of air, from which the spider will extract the day's sustenance.

Their Latin name is *Arachnoidea*, after the Greek weaver Arachne, who had the misfortune of being a better weaver and spinner than the goddess Athena.

But Arachne is a minor character compared to other weavers of mythology. The human recognition of, and respect for, a spider's intelligence and skill is common to many cultures and traditions. The Hopi Earth Mother is Kokyanwuhti, Spider Woman, companion of Tawa, Lord of Light.

From Tawa's thoughts, Kokyanwuhti created clay forms and instilled them with life. Men and women were made in their images. When creation was complete, she divided men and women into tribes and had each tribe follow another creature — deer, puma, snake, eagle, antelope — to learn where to build their homes. Kokyanwuhti taught the Hopi to spin and weave, and she remained the dispenser of knowledge from

her underground kiva thereafter.

According to Cherokee legend, Kanane'ski amai'yehi, Water Spider, played a role similar to that of the Greek Prometheus. It happened that the Thunders, "who live above in the sky," realized that earth's creatures had no heat or light, so they sent a bolt of lightning to a sycamore tree on an island. All the creatures could see the fire, but none, except for Water Spider, could retrieve it. To do this, Kanane'ski amai'yehi spun a bowl from her silk called a tusti bowl, and strapped it to her back. She then skimmed across the water to the island, placed a live coal in the bowl, and brought it back to mankind.

There are real aquatic, pontooned dancers that live for long periods of time under the water of mountain streams — although they, like all spiders, are air-breathers. Their aquatic survival involves weaving a web under water and attaching it to plants. When this is complete, the spider resurfaces, traps air bubbles between its abdomen and legs, then returns to the underwater web. The spider releases the air bubbles into the net, where it remains trapped, providing an ingenious air supply. This allows the spider to remain safe underwater for extended periods of time.

The canny intelligence of these animals and the symbolism of their myths share much common ground. And whether or not we are willing to acknowledge the power of spiders on the psyche's level, we must at least respect their instincts and craftsmanship.

Pet Geriatrics
by Pat Wagner

Are you prepared to take care of your favorite pet another five years? Ten years? FIFTEEN YEARS? Medical advances and increased public awareness about vaccination and nutrition make the 20-year-old dog or cat less of a novelty every year. But, as in human geriatrics, the issues of dealing with an aging pet are not limited to taking care of the physical health of the patient; the emotional health of the entire family must also be considered if the final years of a pet are to be rewarding for both animal and owner.

PREVENTIVE MEDICINE

You can add years to your pet's life by paying attention to the same factors you attend to in your own lifestyle: diet, stress, exercise, genetics, family life, medical advances. Beware of the same confusion in making decisions, however; the leading authorities on cat and dog care contradict each other as often as do their human health counterparts.

CHECK-UPS

Cats and dogs over ten years old should have check-ups at six-month intervals. Blood pressure can be monitored, diet checked, and, if nothing else, claws can be trimmed and ears cleaned. A vet who gets to know your pet might well be able to catch changes in behavior and appearance that you won't see living with it every day.

Larger breeds of dogs should have more frequent examinations than other pets, because size is apparantly linked to the rate of aging in dogs. If your pet's breed has a history with a certain ailment, it might also be wise to get a recommendation from your local breeder of a vet experienced with the particular breed.

A sad fact is that thousands of older pets die every year because the veterinarian was not brought in until it was too late. Cats, for example, will stop eating when ill and dehydrate rapidly. A younger animal might survive a few days in this condition, but the older pet has less of a margin to work with.

One important part of the examination will be checking for lumps — as in most animals, cancer is a disease mainly of the elderly. For many pet owners, there is emotional agony in discovering that a beloved companion has a tumor. One vet reports that the majority of her clients will immediately ask that the animal be killed, even in cases where a cure is assured. As with humans, the majority of masses are not malignant tumors. If you are checking your own pet for lumps and masses, this is important to know. Some pet owners will find a lump or growth and become so terrified that they refuse to take the animal in for a biopsy.

Another purpose for the regular check-ups is to keep the animal current on vaccinations. An older animal can catch rabies or distemper, even after a lifetime of care, if the vaccinations are allowed to lapse.

DENTAL CARE

Abscesses, loose, or cracked teeth, gum infections, and mouth injuries can destroy the health of an older pet. Not only does nutrition suffer, but the constant pain and infection can stress the entire system. The weakened animal might succumb to some other ailment, all because of neglected teeth.

Animals that only eat soft food seem more prone to gum disease, so hard, crunchy food should be part of the diet (even an older pet with missing teeth can eat hard food with little discomfort, but each case should be checked first with your vet).

NUTRITION

An elaborate diet is not necessarily the best thing for your pet. A survey of elderly cats by one of the country's leading pet magazines was unable to show any correlation between specific diet factors and longevity. Admittedly, the survey was not scientific, but it indicates the importance of individuality in diet in animals.

With your vet's help, you can design a diet plan for your pet that deals with the pet's specific problems — low-sodium for the dog with heart disease, or high salt for the cat with kidney problems. Some of these menus are available ready-made, others need to be developed by your vet.

Although there are some fine pet care books with good information on diet, an owner should check with a vet before attempting the diagnosis and cure of a pet via nutritional therapy. There are veterinarians who use vitamin therapy and homeopathic treatments in their practice; others are willing to work with an owner on trying new ideas.

ENVIRONMENT

All the rules of pet care you have followed faithfully during its younger years will be even more important as it grows older. In particular, make sure your pet has a warm, dry place to sleep, is kept clean, protected from over-heating in the summer, and has a bookkeeping (no matter how rudimentary). Without a basic knowledge of sales, building revenues becomes an overwhelming task. And understanding financial management is essential to survival.

9. Have I ever been fired? Most small business owners have been fired, or they resigned just before their jobs were terminated. Why? Reread the discussion under question 6. While many companies look for creativity and a high degree of initiative in their prospective employees, almost as many organizations have difficulties when their employees' inventiveness is contrary to corporate policy.

10. Why do I want to start a business? The motivations for wanting to start a business are summed up by the following statements: "I want to help people"; "I think I can perform better on my own";"I want more freedom to set my own schedule"; or "I want to make more money." Successful business owners give a combination response — money and helping others, or money and improved productivity — to this question. Regardless of the answers, money is the primary impetus. Increased efficiency and usefulness to others is viewed as the necessary (and ethical) path to increased prosperity.

Now that you have completed the questions and checked your responses with the explanations given, is small business the pursuit for you? Is it a bad idea? Or do you need to do some thinking before you take the plunge?

YES, NO, OR LATER?

If five or less of your responses agreed with the answers above, owning a business probably is not the pursuit for you. However, the situation is not hopeless. A small business can be a wonderful working environment.

The atmosphere is usually more informal than a larger corporation. Employees in a small business can get a wider variety of work experience. Large organizations can afford specialization of tasks. For a small business, with its few employees, generalists are more valuable.

If your answers corresponded with between six or seven of the responses, cheer up. A business of your own could be a possibility in the future. You probably have some learning to do first. It might be taking an assertiveness class, working in a small business, or learning bookkeeping. Depending on the business that interests you, a partner might hasten the process.

If your responses concurred with eight or more of the discussion items, owning a small business may be your kind of excitement. You may want to brush up on rusty skills. Researching your chosen business endeavor might be advisable. Reviewing all the necessary steps for your new venture with a friend or relative who has owned a business would be sensible.

Working for yourself can be the most thrilling, exhilarating experience imaginable. Each day is different. You test all your abilities to the maximum. The opportunity for learning and growth is limited only by your eagerness to meet each new challenge.

True, sleep becomes a concept whose meaning is lost now and then. Finding time for children and a mate can be well nigh impossible. Scheduling much-needed quiet time just to think can become one of your most creative functions.

Like anything else, business ownership is only for some people. Within the universe of work, it is one of several paths. For you, the wisdom of starting a business depends on how much you know about yourself and the outside environment. The choice is yours.

THE AMAZING BLINTZ

by Pat Wagner

In my earliest childhood memories, I am returning home, entering our kitchen on a frigid Midwest winter day, after an afternoon of sledding and snowball fights. There, my grandmother Fagel, a stately white-haired woman wearing a flowered apron, would be orchestrating dinner amid a cloud of steam. While I stood blinking the melted frost from my eyes, Fagel would unwrap the many layers of sweaters and scarves that bound me, clucking over my red nose. Once I was whittled down to normal size, she would lift me up and let me stand on a chair in front of the stove.

The air was thick with the carrot-sweet scent of chicken soup, simmering under a thin layer of yellow fat, and the earthy odor of chopped chicken liver, speckled with egg and onion. But my attention was fixed on the bowl of batter and the skillet sizzling with hot butter; my favorite pastime was about to begin: blintz-making.

Fagel would guide my hand as I dipped a ladle into the liquid and poured it into the skillet. She would then deftly tilt the skillet until the batter covered the bottom; as I watched, it became the golden pancake known in White Russian Jewish families as the blintz.

We would wait a few magical seconds, then Fagel would produce a spatula and flip the thin blintz over. The air trapped inside the batter would begin to expand and the blintz would heave and rock like something alive. A few more seconds, and Fagel's spatula would transfer the blintz to a plate near the stove to keep warm.

Eight blintzes — always eight — would come from the bowl. The first one was usually too limp with butter to be aesthetically acceptable for the dinner table; this greasy treat, smeared with jam, would be my reward for helping. The other seven would be saved for dessert.

After dinner, each member of our family would slide a buttery blintz from the steaming stack to their plate. Then, we would each roll our blintz around a simple filling of cottage cheese and sour cream. My mother would have opened one of those little sugar-laden frozen packages of strawberries, or, if she was feeling very extravagant, we would have frozen raspberries instead.

The adults would carve the blintz apart like a sausage, but I would take the long roll into my mouth, the bottom folded to keep the filling from running down my arm. Naturally, I would have tucked the sweet fruit sauce inside.

Years later, after leaving home, I discovered, to my horror, that the mighty blintz was often folded into a little package, stuffed with baked filling, for God's sake, and frequently contained raisins! These assembly-line pastries made me suddenly aware of life's harsh realities. Oh, where was that rich interplay of golden, warm blintz with cold tart filling from my idyllic childhood? What would poor Fagel, bless her soul, say of such things?

If I know Fagel, she would probably suggest that you try her recipe for authentic blintzes.

FAGEL'S BLINTZES
(Enough for four hungry adults)

INGREDIENTS

- One cup unbleached white flour
- Three large eggs
- One cup milk
- One tablespoon sugar or honey
- Four tablespoons butter
- One pinch salt

EQUIPMENT

One or two large **skillets** or **frying pans**, at least 8".

One large fireproof **bowl**, ceramic is good. A metal bowl is likely to allow the batter to cook and thicken before it is ladled, not so good.

One **ladle**, ¼ cup size. You can also fill a measuring cup with the batter and measure out about ¼ cup at a time.

One large **serving plate**.

A metal **spatula** or your favorite pancake flipper.

Some small **dish** to put the butter in (it will need to hold melted butter, since by the time you are done, that is what you will have).

Extras: Sour cream, yoghurt, cottage cheese, fruit or berries in sauce. The simpler, the better, unless you want to impress someone.

PREPARATION

Sift the cup of flour into your large mixing bowl. Make a depression in the top of the flour, and slowly pour in the milk, stirring with a fork. This method helps reduce lumping. When the cup of milk and the cup of flour are well mixed, add the three eggs (which have been waiting in a bowl, slightly beaten.) Mix the batter vigorously until well blended. The batter can now sit for a few minutes while you get organized at the stove.

You will need to have the bowl of batter, the hot skillet, and the serving plate fairly close together, so plan accordingly.

This can get a little hot; make sure you have plenty of pot holders handy.

Melt two tablespoons of the butter into the skillet. Heat the skillet slowly, until it is pancake hot — just under the temperature needed to scorch the butter.

READY, SET, GO

1. Pour the excess butter from the skillet into the batter and stir quickly.
2. Measure about ¼ cup of batter into the ladle or cup.
3. While you hold the skillet by the handle with one hand, pour the batter into the skillet with the other, and immediately begin tilting the pan until all parts of the skillet bottom are covered. As you watch, the batter should turn from a rich cream to yellow. This can happen quickly, so get your spatula ready.
4. When the blintz has set and the edges are starting to turn brown, carefully lift it on the spatula and flip it over. This first try will tell you much about your blintz batter and the temperature of the skillet. Experience will teach you whether the skillet needs to be hotter or if the batter needs to be adjusted with a smidgen of milk or water. Don't worry if the first one isn't perfect; as long as it is cooked through, it will still taste wonderful.
5. The air trapped by your skillful swirling of the batter may bulge your blintz and cause it to swell and rock. Don't be afraid, but watch for overheated patches on the bottom — lift and peek, if you must. The blintz will be done when the smooth yellow surface is slightly browned (or the button-sized brown air bubbles are dark brown). The longer you cook the blintz, the stiffer it becomes; too long, and it will more resemble a dinner plate than a soft crepe. Part of the fun of blintz-making is piercing the bubbles so the blintz lies flat (I am sure you will find this very therapeutic).
6. When you are satisfied with its condition, remove the blintz from the pan and place it on a large serving plate. Immediately add a touch of fresh butter to the pan and start again from step 2.

While you are watching the magic, you can butter the top of the finished blintz on the plate. By the time you get to the last blintz, the batter might have become too thick if you were not stirring it once in a while during the cooking process. If so, turn down the heat on this last blintz, so it can cook longer at a lower heat.

SERVING

Once the blintzes are done, they can be kept in a warm oven until serving time. Assemble your fillings — and let you guests indulge. Often, people will wait for you to show them the "right" way to proceed — by all means, encourage them to experiment.

What do you serve with a blintz? I often make it a main course with water-packed fruit or a wine sauce to complement the filling. A fancy salad with cheese and ham or a seafood plate is a nice first course; you might want to add a clear soup. However, if you are not watching your waistline, or have a family of hungry children to fill up at dinnertime, the amazing blintz is still the best dessert in the world.

Fantastic Facts by Larry C. Sessions

Nature encompasses many incredible phenomena, but perhaps the most awesome and unbelievable facts come from the science of astronomy. The truth is, many of the fascinating facts of astronomy are so stupendous that they are almost incomprehensible. So I'll try to present some of these astounding facts in more understandable terms.

First, how big is a star? Our Sun, which is slightly below average in size, is about 865,000 miles in diameter (109 times the diameter of the Earth) and 2,717,478 miles in circumference. That sounds huge, but can you really conceive of just how big that is? Well, if we could fly around the Sun in a jetliner at 600 miles per hour, the trip would take just a little more than six months of constant flight. In the trusty family car cruising at 55 mph, we would face a hot, nonstop trip of five-and-a-half years!

Since the Sun is 93 million miles away, a cruise to our nearby star at the 55 mph speed limit would take several lifetimes (actually, 193 years), while at the speed of a jetliner, the voyage would still take a generation (18 years). Even at the average speed of an Apollo spacecraft hurtling toward the Moon (25,000 mph), a straight-line flight to the Sun would require more than five months.

The Sun, of course, is the closest star; the next nearest is so far that a journey at one million miles per hour would take 29,000 years. Even at the maximum speed possible (186,282.397 miles per *second* — the speed of light), the trip would take more than four years. To cross our Milky Way galaxy at the speed of light would take 100,000 years, or roughly 15 times the age of civilization.

If our entire solar system, from the Sun out to Pluto's farthest reaches, could fit on the face of a quarter, the spiral-shaped Milky Way would be about the size of India. The nearest star would be almost a block away and the nearest major galaxy (the one in Andromeda) would drift slowly 38,000 miles out in space, one-sixth the distance to the moon!

In the Milky Way there are about 100 billion stars like the Sun, but just how many is a billion? In American terminology, a "billion" is one thousand million, or one thousand times one thousand times one thousand!

Let's imagine that the stars in the galaxy are all sugar cubes one-half inch to the side. One million of these sugar cube stars would fit snugly into a box four feet, two inches high, wide and deep. One *billion* sugar cube stars would need a thousand such boxes, or a single box 41 feet, 8 inches to a side. In other words, a large three-story house would hold about one billion sugar cube stars. At least one hundred large houses could hold as many sugar cubes as there are stars in the Milky Way.

Is your brain boggled yet? Well, that's just the beginning. Astronomers know of literally "billions" of other galaxies, all averaging about 100 billion stars equivalent to the Sun.

Stars give off a phenomenal amount of energy. If we could somehow collect and store all the energy the Sun emits in just one second, we would have enough to last the United States, at the current rate of consumption, for 13 million years. Of course, only a small fraction of the Sun's energy reaches the Earth, but even that is extremely impressive.

Each day about four *trillion* (one thousand *billion*) megawatt-hours of solar energy reaches the outer atmosphere of our planet (one megawatt-hour is enough to light 10,000 100-watt light bulbs for an hour). Less than half of that ever reaches the surface, but even that amounts to about 28,000 times the level of energy consumed on our planet for all commercial purposes. The sunlight that falls each day on U.S. roads alone contains twice as much energy as is expended in fossil fuels throughout the world in the same period!

All this sunlight not only has energy, it has weight, too. On a clear day, 5,423 tons of sunlight falls on the United States at any given moment — we don't feel it because it is spread out over more than 3.5 million square miles.

And some stars give off a lot more energy than our puny Sun. "Supergiants" are so large that more than a million suns could fit inside. More than a trillion planets the size of Earth could do the same.

On the other hand, some stars are incredibly small. A white dwarf, for instance, may be no larger than Earth and yet it may outweigh the Sun. And then there are "neutron" stars only 20 miles across which have such prodigious gravity that a 150-pound-person (Earth weight) would tip the scales at 40 trillion pounds on the star's surface. Neutron stars have so much pent-up energy that a BB dropped onto the surface would release the power of the atom bomb exploded over Hiroshima.

And what about those mysterious "black holes"? A black hole is actually a star that has collapsed in on itself, shrunk to a tiny miniature of its former self. The black hole shrinks, but it doesn't lose any mass, so the smaller it shrinks, the "heavier" it feels.

Soon the star doesn't have the power to resist any longer and not even the light from the star has the energy to escape. Since the light from the star can't radiate outward from the star, we can't see it — it has become a black hole!

Because of the immense gravity of a black hole, anything that comes too close to it will be pulled in, down into the whirlpool of darkness with no hope of escape.

All sorts of bizarre things could happen near a black hole, such as time apparently standing still and possibly even a "warpage" in the fabric of space itself through which a spacecraft might, repeat *might*, be able to travel lightyears across space in a fraction of a second!

The size of a black hole will vary according to how large it was as a normal star and how much matter it has pulled in as a black hole. In theory it can be miles across or it can be microscopic. In order to become a black hole, the sun would have to shrink to about four miles in diameter, or about twice the width of Manhatten Island!

Our 8,000-mile-diameter Earth would shrink to about the size of the sugar cubes we discussed earlier before it would become a black hole. But don't worry, there is no reason to believe that either the sun or the Earth will ever become a black hole. We hope.

Scentsory Delights

Judith Hiatt

Modern perfumes and cosmetics, aside from costing a small fortune, are often neither pleasant-smelling nor natural. So-called "floral scents" rarely contain oils derived from the actual flowers, but, instead, are a compound of numerous chemical ingredients: preservatives, coloring agents, and artificial fragrances. It is possible to buy several lines of cosmetics labeled "fragrance free" if you have sensitive skin which reacts to chemically perfumed products. However, these retail at two to three times the cost of the average brands.

There are ways to "smell like a rose," that won't drain either your pocketbook or the natural oils from your skin. With a small amount of space in which to grow flowers and herbs, you can make a number of scented lotions, creams, oils, and pomades for a fraction of the cost of the commercial products.

The most precious ingredient is your time, for you must grow, gather, and prepare your herbs and flowers. If you can't grow your own, you can buy them fresh. However, make certain they have not been treated with harmful chemicals.

Some of the best flowers and herbs are those that are good for the skin: rose, lavender, marigold, mint, sage, basil, and thyme. They should be gathered before full bloom. Harvest them early in the day just after all dew has evaporated.

Roses top the list of flowers that help the skin. They cleanse, and help to prevent acne, blackheads, and wrinkles. Roses also soothe sunburn.

Lavender not only has a long-lasting, sweetly pungent aroma, but is also good for treating eczema, acne, burns, and insect bites.

Marigolds are used for treating acne, rashes, eczema, warts, boils, and corns. They are especially beneficial for eye problems. They grow profusely and have a somewhat unpleasant odor, but a small quantity added to rose and lavender is quite pleasing.

Mint is refreshing and cool to the skin. It helps reduce swelling, heal bruises, and treat infections.

Sage increases blood circulation and is, therefore, stimulating to the skin. It also reduces dandruff.

Thyme is from the same family (Labiatae) as sage, mint, rosemary, marjoram, and basil. It is used for burns and bruises, and to help increase circulation to the skin.

Basil, likewise, is good for burns, inflammations, and bruises, and cools like mint. Basil and mint make a nice combination.

Scented rubbing alcohol is great to cool the skin on hot days or especially luxurious to rub onto hot and tired feet. To make it, take flower petals or herbs and bruise them using a mortar and pestle. Fill a bottle one quarter full with them and top off with rubbing alcohol. Cap tightly and leave in a warm place for two to three weeks. (You can periodically add more flowers for a stronger odor). Strain the pulp from the liquid and seal tightly. Mint and basil are especially refreshing. Lotions made with lavender soothe mosquito bites.

Astringents help close pores and eliminate oil on the face. Scented rubbing alcohol can be used as an astringent or you can make another from vinegar. Using good white or red wine vinegar or leftover dry wine, add one part bruised herbs or petals to three parts vinegar. Cork, leave two weeks in a warm place, and strain. This same vinegar solution doubles as a douche when mixed in one part to two parts warm water.

Floral or herbal rinses provide a nice finale to a thorough skin cleansing when used as a face rinse or added to bathwater. Boil petals or herbs in distilled water for a few minutes, then strain. Make only enough to use at one time; it has no preservatives to make it last. This liquid can also be mixed with milk or buttermilk for a rinse to make an especially soothing sunburn treatment. (Though consuming excessive amounts of dairy products is said to be unhealthy for the complexion, it seems milk makes a rich external treatment for the skin.) It is especially good when scented with rose water. Add as much rose milk as you can afford to a warm (not hot) tub of water. For conjunctivitis or other eye problems, a rinse made from marigolds can be soothing.

Scented oil is excellent for dry skin care. You can rub it directly onto your wet skin after a shower or add about a tablespoon to your bathwater. It is simple to make and stores well. Virgin olive oil is excellent to use. Other good oils include almond, safflower, sesame, and mineral. Bruise the herbs or flowers. Put one or two handfuls into a ceramic crock or a glass jar. Add one cup of oil, rubbing some around the rim, and place a piece of paper on top to seal it. Leave it for two to three weeks in a warm place.

Heat the oil on the stove until the bubbling ceases and all the liquid has evaporated. Remove it immediately from the heat. Strain and store in dark glass bottles (corked beer bottles work wonderfully). A shortcut to scenting your oil is to purchase the essence of the herb or flower you desire. It will only take a drop or two to make a cup of scented oil. Essences of rose, lavender, lilac, mint, eucalyptus, jasmine, etc. are available in most grocery, drug, or health food stores.

Eye cream and lip pomade can be made with petroleum jelly which is one of the best moisturizers. It tends to be greasy but, when applied in a thin sheen, adds a sparkle to the eyes and lips and softens dry cuticles and calloused feet. Heat petroleum jelly in a saucepan over very low heat until liquid. Turn off the heat and let it cool but not jell. Add one handful of bruised leaves or petals (if they start to fry, it is still too hot). Leave in a

warm place for a few weeks. Reheat the mixture until liquid and strain. While still liquid, pour into small containers (35mm film canisters work well). For a harder lip gloss, one part beeswax can be added to ten parts petroleum jelly when reheated and the liquid then poured into used lipstick tubes.

These natural products are mild and don't normally cause a skin reaction. However, should a rash appear from using them or any other cosmetics, the following recipe may provide relief and can be easily concocted from ordinary kitchen supplies:

For **allergic reaction**, fill a pint jar with crushed ice. Add two teaspoons salt and one cup milk or buttermilk. Shake it well. Soak a clean washcloth in the mixture and apply to the affected area. Repeat several times for up to ten to fifteen minutes.

You can experiment with many different things such as flowers, herbs, citrus fruit peels, vanilla, etc., to create a variety of unusual scents. Not only will your perfumes be unique but you'll have the satisfaction of knowing you have made them and that they're 100 percent natural.

"A tree cannot grow in the sky."
— *Lucretius, On the Nature of Things.*

HANGING GARDENS
by George Nash

Beneath the dense canopy of a tropical rain forest, a diverse plant community competes in a habitat characterized by scarce nutrients, dim light, and extremely high humidity — conditions that give rise to some rather strange adaptive mechanisms. Rain forest flora is noted for large waxy leaves (a means of increasing light absorption and diffusion), rapid growth rates (which help plants outdistance the competition), exotic flowers (to attract pollinators), and many other novel features. Because water cannot readily evaporate in the still humid air of the forest floor, many tropical plants are equipped with special cells that "sweat" excess water.

An interesting strategy that has evolved in many groups of plants including orchids, spanish moss, christmas cacti, and several vines, ferns, and bromeliads, is to grow upon other plants. They are called epiphytes. These plants spend all or part of their lives off the ground, usually on the trunks or branches of trees. Most are not, as one might suppose, parasitic. They live on the tree, not off of it. In taking to the treetops, epiphytes are able to exploit a niche unavailable to their ground dwelling competitors.

This is such an attractive alternative that fully 10 percent of all vascular plants are considered to be epiphytic. High up in the understory, the light is more intense and there is more air movement to speed evaporation. There is far less competition for nutrients (there are, however, less nutrients available) and there is freedom from predation by grazing animals. The adjustment of plants and animals to these microclimatic differences is so finely tuned that often only a single species will inhabit a particular level, or sometimes only a certain

side of a tree, at a certain height.

Life in the treetops may be more spacious but it is not necessarily easier. Indeed, it poses its own set of rigors. Terrestrial plants absorb soil nutrients through a network of delicate root hairs. Lacking a protective soilblanket, the naked roots of an epiphyte are sheathed with a thick layer of cells to prevent dehydration, and too much nutrient uptake. These coarse adventitious roots serve mainly to anchor the plant to its substrate. What little absorption they are capable of occurs at the interface of the plant and its host.

Some species of orchids that inhabit fog-shrouded uplands send out dense clumps of upward growing "air roots" that are able to absorb moisture and carbon dioxide directly from the air and also trap nutrient-rich debris. One reason why epiphytes are found predominantly in tropic and temperate environments is the vulnerability of these exposed roots to frost.

Epiphytes exhibit an architecture designed to capture and store water and debris. The leaf sweat from the tree canopy, loaded with dissolved nutrients, either drips directly down, or is carried by rainwater runoff along the limbs into the basket-shaped leaves and spongy root mass of the plant. Here it is held until the nutrients are extracted. For this reason, the texture and composition of the bark to which the epiphyte is attached can be a very important feature of its habitat. Rough bark holds and channels water. Bark also contains a potpourri of potential nutrients and other substances which leach into the rainwater runoff. Some of these promote growth and others discourage it. Many epiphytes seem to favor a particular type of bark. Yet others show no preference. For some, the texture rather than the composition of the substrate is more important.

Some species have evolved a symbiotic relationship with ants. The ants find a home in hollow swellings called pseudobulbs, possibly attracted by the moisture stored in these structures or drawn by the nectar they secrete. The ants repay their hosts' hospitality by leaving their debris and droppings, and for some species, by warding off carpenter bees which damage flowers. In any case, ants seem to be desirable tenants since the orchid must expend considerable energy to provide the nectar banquet.

Even under the best of circumstances, an airy niche offers only a marginal habitat. Debris may not always be found in readily digestible form and the light level may still be too low for adequate photosynthesis. The plant may suffer from chronic malnutrition. Some orchids offer an amazing example of the subtleties of adaptation. These plants are intimately associated with fungi. What may initially have been a parasitic attack has evolved into a symbiotic relationship. Mycorhizal fungi break down debris and other organic matter such as cellulose, i.e. bark, into forms useable by the epiphyte. In turn, the moist root mass of the plant offers a more hospitable environment to the fungus than a bare branch. Some orchids have become so dependent on their fungal partners that they have taken on many of the same features, dispensing altogether with food producing leaves and chlorophyll pigment. Many orchids have seeds so small that they cannot store enough food to survive until they are established.

But a fungus that invades the seed coat in turn supplies field rations to the embryonic plant. This balance is so delicate that if the fungus dies, the young orchid dies with it. Likewise, an attempted invasion by the "wrong" sort of fungus is repulsed by a fungicide secreted by the seed. The relationship between fungi and epiphytes is so complicated and various that it is almost impossible to decide whether fungal byproducts, photosynthate, or leach water contributes more to the larder. The menu may change from meal to meal.

Another variation on the theme of flexible response is shown by the vanilla vine orchid. As a seedling, it is rooted in the ground, and sends tendrils up a tree. Once firmly ensconced, it pulls up its roots to become a true epiphyte. The strangler fig does just the opposite, and sends down roots which become so dense and entangled that they often overwhelm the unfortunate host tree.

Most epiphytes, if placed in soil, will develop true roots. In fact, they tend to flourish as never before, especially if the new surroundings are a greenhouse pot. Nature is, above all, economical; few species work any harder than they have to. So who can blame the hard-pressed epiphyte for accepting a better job opportunity?

FORGOTTEN MEASURES

by Ed Quillen

If Acts of Congress meant anything, we'd be measuring in meters this year, thanks to the Metric Conversion Act of 1975, which gave us a decade to convert. As it turns out, we're probably closer to universal peace and the abolition of hunger than we are to adopting the metric system. We Americans have somehow resisted all the alleged advantages of metrification.

One purported reason to go metric is that the United States is the only industrial nation on earth that hasn't gone metric. So, to keep up with the Joneses of this planet, we're supposed to follow their example. If the United States were the only nation with trial by jury, or freedom of religion and expression, should we abandon our cherished rights merely because most other nations prefer to manufacture evidence and torture dissenters?

The metric system is reputed to be simpler. Instead of learning that four quarts make a gallon, our children are now taught that 1,000 *milliliters* make a *liter*, and that 1,000 liters make not a kiloliter, but a *stere*. Have you ever seen a stere? Has anyone you know ever seen a stere?

Instead of learning that 640 acres make a square mile, they must recite that 100 *centimeters* make a *meter*, 10 meters make a *dekameter*, and a *square dekameter* is an *are*. Just how much simpler is that? When someone refers to ares, is he measuring land, discussing intransitive verbs, or explaining his astrological portents?

Further, no one seems to know just what to call this farrago of *joules*, *ares*, *steres*, *Kelvens*, and *moles*. We commonly call it, when we call it something printable, the *Metric system*. Various other aliases include the *Scientific System*, the *SI System*, the *International System of Units*, and the *Systeme International d'Unites*.

Just how international is it? We call the weight of one milliliter of distilled water at 4° C. a *gram*. In France or England, that's a *gramme*. What the British sometimes call a *long ton* is in this nation a *metric ton* and in much of the world a *tonne*. According to universal metric standards, it should be a called *megagram*, which is universally used nowhere. Despite its glaring faults, the metric invasion just might succeed. Perhaps that is because we have ignored so much of our conventional system. We have dozens, perhaps scores, of neglected measuring units.

For instance, we measure liquid volumes with a handy binary system, easy for any beginning cook to master. Two **tablespoons** equal a **fluid ounce**. Two fluid ounces equal a **wineglassful**. Two wineglassfuls equal a **gill**. Two gills equal a **cup**. Two cups equal a *pint*. Two pints equal a **quart**. But what do two quarts equal? Four quarts make a **gallon**, but it seems absurd that we'd go all the way by twos, and then mysteriously switch to multipling by four.

We have neglected the **pottle**, equal to two quarts or half of a gallon. Armed with this knowledge, you can drop by the store and pick up a quart, pottle, or gallon of milk, depending on your needs and budget.

While other practical units haven't exactly been neglected, they have been appropriated by certain activities and excluded from general use. For example, a **furlong** is an eighth of a mile, about the length of a long city block. It's ideal for distances too long for yards and too short for miles. But if you don't hang out at the racetrack, you'll never hear of distances measured in furlongs. Horse breeders have also usurped another good measure, the **hand**, equal to four inches.

Hands and furlongs aren't the only units of distance we've ignored. There's the **iron**, one forty-eighth of an inch, still used by some leather workers and merchants. Less arcane is the **barleycorn**; there are three to the inch. More handy is the **digit**, ¾ of an inch. Then comes the **nail**, equal to 2¼ inches, followed by the **ell**, a cloth measure equal to 45 inches. The needle trades have others; 24 heers make a **spindle** — a **heer** is 600 **yards**. In yarn, a **thread** is 1½ yards; 80 threads make a **lea**, and seven leas make a

hank.

When figuring areas, we might resurrect the **oxgang** or the **bovate**. Each is 15 **acres**, and eight of them make a **carucate**. That 120-acre area can also be called a **sulung** or **hide**, and can be divided into four **jugums** or **yokes**.

As for volumes, we need not stick to pints and pottles. There's the **peck**, which seems to survive only as what Peter Piper picked in the tongue twister. A peck is two **bodges**, or half a **firlot**. Four firlots make a **boll**, and 16 bolls are a **chalder**. A peck is also one-quarter of a **bushel**. There's also the **puncheon** or **pipe**, which is two **hogsheads**. A hogshead holds 63 gallons, or two **barrels**.

Long before a drinker works up to barrels though, he can imbibe of more ancient measures, starting with the **baby**, ⅛ of a traditional wine bottle, and the **nip**, a quarter of a bottle. The **bottle** holds 26 and two-thirds fluid ounces; a double size bottle is a **magnum**. Four bottles equal a **jeroboam**; six a **rehoboam**; eight a **methuselah**. A **salmanazar** holds 12 regular bottles, a **balthazar** 16, and a **nebuchadnezzar** 20, or just over four gallons. That should be enough for even a Babylonian bash.

All these humble measures come from English and Scots tradition. Every culture has something to contribute, from the **abdat** of Egypt, about four inches, to the Arabian **zudda**, about two gallons, or to be precise, 8 **nusfiah**.

In between are delights like the **xylon** of Greece, 55 inches long; the Estonian **sagene**, 7 feet or 3 **arshins**; the Assyrian **qasab**, 12.6 feet; the **mkono** of east Africa, 1.5 feet the Russian **loof**, equal to 592 **tchasts** or 1.84 bushels. Most versatile, perhaps, is the **fanega**, once common throughout Latin America. It varies from 2.75 bushels in Chile to 8.81 acres in Mexico.

These measures have evolved for centuries to fit each culture, and indeed, each profession in that culture. Jewelers purchase gold by the **pennyweight** and sell stones by the **carat**. Firewood comes in **cords**, and lumber in **board-feet**. Printers measure type in **picas** and **points**, and newspapers sell advertising by the **column-inch** and **agate line**. Surveyors lay out **links**, **rods**, and **chains** to delineate **acres**, **sections**, and **townships**. Water rights in arid states are sold in **cusecs** and **acre-feet**. **Bolts** of cloth are 40 yards long, and bolts of wallpaper are 16 yards long. Beer fills 31½ gallon barrels and crude oil fills 42-gallon barrels.

Our world is a big and diverse place; too big and diverse for any single system to accomodate, no matter how universal or scientific that system pretends to be.

The National Headache

by Ken Freed

Everyone gets headaches. Some people have chronic headaches; others, only occasional ones. More than half of all doctor visits each year are made because of this malady. Indeed, headaches may be the chief health complaint in the United States today. Perhaps this situation is a sign of our times, but the drug companies are certainly raising no objections.

Americans spent close to a $1.5 billion in 1983 for over-the-counter pain killers. This was up from $635 million in 1973, a 235 percent increase in ten years. Prescription analgesics earned $3.7 billion in gross sales for the pharmaceutical industry during 1983, reflecting a similar percentage increase. With retail and prescription medicines combined accounting for almost one quarter of all pharmaceutical sales, drug manufacturers collect over $5.2 billion per year from our collective national headache.

The dependence on analgesics to treat headaches is a relatively recent phenomenon. In prehistoric times, neolithic medicine men apparently believed such pains were caused by evil spirits. Evidence has been found that these headache demons by were sometimes released by trepanning, drilling or chipping a hole (an inch in diameter or more) in the patient's skulls.

In the first century after Christ, the top physician of Nero's armies used torpedo fish, a less potent cousin of the electric eel, on headache sufferers. This surgeon, Pedanius Dioscorides, also prescribed Indian hemp (marijuana) to relieve headaches.

Medical treatments had not advanced much further by the start of the 20th Century. Electric headbands and tinctures of cannibis were advertised in the many almanacs published by patent medicine manufacturers. The assorted headache powders and elixirs sold through these journals generally relied upon opium for their effectiveness.

The first modern breakthrough in the treatment of headaches came in 1899 with the introduction of aspirin into medical practice by Hermann Dresser in Germany. A derivative of the salicylic acid found naturally in wintergreen leaves, sweet birch bark, tulips, hyacinths, violets, grapes, strawberries, and other fruits, aspirin quickly became the treatment of choice by most physicians.

Past reliance on herbal remedies for headaches was broken almost single-handedly by aspirin. When salicylic acid preparations were made publicly available in the early 1900s, the retail medicine manufacturers experienced their first real burst of public acceptance. This credibility waxed and waned over the following decades while over-the-counter sales grew.

With the advent of television advertising in the fifties and sixties, sales of headache remedies accelerated dramatically, outselling all other over-the-counter medicines. Americans consumed 40 billion aspirin tablets in 1963, enough to form a strip three feet wide along the length of U.S. Highway 40 from the Boardwalk in Atlantic City to Fishermen's Wharf in San Francisco. That strip of aspirin would be almost four feet wide today, and all of the retail headache tablets and capsules combined would completely blanket the highway.

The pharmaceutical industry has encouraged dependence upon over-the-counter and prescription products. Their advertisements have created a climate of easy acceptability for using drugs to solve everyday problems. At the same time, they have carefully and skillfully induced practicing physicians to view prescription medicines in the best possible light.

This situation prompted President Nixon to comment in 1971, "We have produced an environment in which people come naturally to expect they can take a pill for every problem — that they can find satisfaction and health and happiness in a handful of tablets or a few grains of powder." A sharper commentary about the central role of drugs in our society came from Kurt Vonnegut, Jr. In one of his novels, the author wrote, "The hand that stocks the drug stores rules the world."

Ever since Sir Francis Bacon pulled a few political strings to help London apothecaries gain the King's charter in 1614, the pharmaceutical industry has been gathering strength. Only in this century, however, has the industry emerged as exclusive source of medicines, especially do-it-yourself medications, and the efficacy and quality of these retail preparations are rarely doubted.

Yet these products do constitute a significant health risk. As just one example, excessive amounts of aspirin can cause gastrointestinal bleeding, hearing damage, cardiac difficulties, a severe drop in blood sugar among diabetics, fetal hemorrhaging among pregnant women, and failure of the body's blood clotting mechanism. Among children, aspirin overdose is one of the leading causes of death.

Considering these health risks, are there any viable alternatives for treating headaches? The answer is "yes." But taking advantage of these options requires a willingness to take responsibility for one's health, and a working knowledge of how and why headaches occur.

What hurts in a headache is neither the brain nor the skull; both of these are without pain receptors. The sensitive areas exist outside the cranium — the scalp, muscles, veins, and especially the arteries. A headache is the result of pressure or tension on or in at least one of these areas.

Researchers have identified at least 15 different types of headaches. Best known and least understood are migraine headaches. These feature swollen blood vessels, loss of appetite and nausea. A frequent type of migraine is the cluster headache, lasting from 20 minutes to a few hours, where the pain is concentrated in one eye and along one side of the head. Migraine headaches generally are chronic conditions.

The most common type are tension headaches. In such cases, a muscle group at the back of the head or along the forehead contracts painfully. Because these headaches are usually caused by stress, they can last for hours, days, weeks, months, or years.

Tension headaches are frequently found in conjunction with migraines — a double whammy.

Other types of headaches include those caused by sinus congestion, diseases such as the flu, poor vision or improperly adjusted eye wear, neck sprains, upper spinal cord injuries, concussions, facial nerve damage, some types of dental infections, monosodium glutamate (MSG), too many cigarettes, withdrawal from too much coffee, and a few too many trips to the bar.

Physicians like to emphasize that headaches are only a symptom of some ailment, not a disease in and of itself. A headache is a painful sensation that serves as a warning that something inside the organism is wrong. Using over-the-counter or prescription headache remedies only masks the symptoms. These drugs do not address the cause of the pain.

When the source of a headache is some medical disorder, treating the injury or disease is the best way to end the headache. This same applies when the problem is eye strain. When headaches are caused by MSG, cigarettes, coffee, or alcohol, eliminating those substances from the diet will likewise eliminate the headaches.

Stopping migraine or tension headaches, however, requires more deliberate effort. The first step is to identify the source of the internal disorder. This might involve examining one's values to look for inner conflicts regarding a career or a relationship, resolving some source of worry and doubt, or working through emotional blocks born out of past experiences. Professional or peer counseling often helps effect a self-cure.

Meanwhile, a variety of drug-free techniques exist for coping with the physiological side of headaches. These include spending a few moments to quiet the mind and calm the body, taking a hot bath, soaking the hands in warm water (especially good for migraines, although doctors are not sure why), relaxation training, biofeedback, self-hypnosis, acupuncture, mild electrical stimulation, and operant conditioning.

EVERYDAY WONDERS

Birth of Margarine

by Micki Magyar

We usually think that margarine was invented during WWII, as a substitute for scarce butter. It was invented during a war, but a much earlier one. Napoleon III had offered a prize for a substitute "to replace butter for the Navy and the less prosperous classes." M.H. Mege-Mouries of Paris won the prize in 1869.

A factory for the manufacture of margarine was first set up in Holland in 1871. The name comes from the fancied resemblance to pearls, at one stage in the manufacture. The inventor called it after the Greek "margarites," meaning "pearl."

In the United States, a law had been passed forbidding the addition of color to margarine. Without the color, it was white and looked like lard. Only the very patriotic or very hungry would buy it. It wasn't until this law was no longer enforced that margarine could find a market.

TABLES &
CHARTS

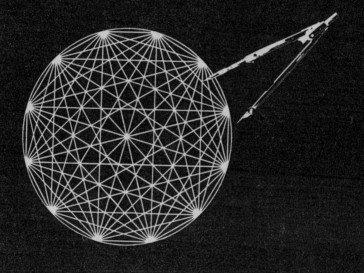

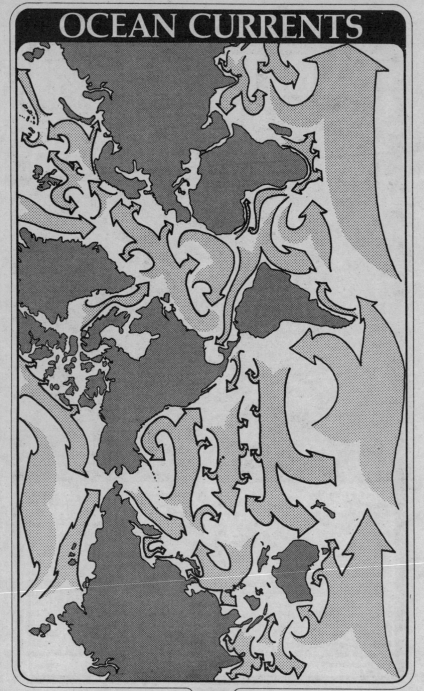

MAGNETIC DECLINATION

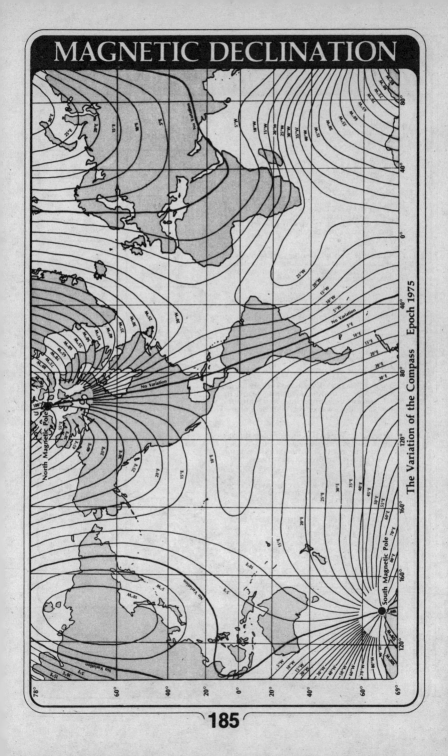

The Variation of the Compass   Epoch 1975

North Magnetic Pole

South Magnetic Pole

BEAUFORT FORCE SCALE OF WIND VELOCITY

0   1 MPH 1 KT Calm; Smoke rises vertically, sea like mirror

1   1-3 MPH 1-3 KT Light air, Wind direction shown by smoke drift but not wind vanes, sea surface appears scaly

2   4-7 MPH 4-6 KT Light breeze; Wind felt on face; leaves rustle; ordinary vane moved by wind; sea forms small wavelets with glassy crests, not breaking

3   8-12 MPH 7-10 KT Gentle breeze; Leaves and small twigs in constant motion; wind extends light flag. Sea forms large wavelets, some white caps

4   13-18 MPH 11-16 KT Moderate breeze; Raises dust and loose paper, small branches moved; numerous white caps at sea

5   19-24 MPH 17-21 KT Fresh breeze; Small trees in leaf begin to sway; moderate waves of greater length; many whitecaps; some spray

6   25-31 MPH 22-27 KT Strong breeze; Large branches in motion; whistling heard in telegraph wires; umbrellas used with difficulty; larger waves at sea; whitecaps numerous, much spray

7   32-38 MPH 28-33 KT Moderate gale; Whole trees in motion; resistance felt walking against the wind; seas heap up; streaks of foam blown from breaking waves

8   39-46 MPH 34-40 KT Fresh gale; Twigs break off trees; fairly high waves of greater length, well marked streaks of foam

9   47-54 MPH 41-47 KT Strong gale; Slight structural damage (chimney pots and shingles removed); high waves with sea beginning to roll, dense streaks of foam with spray blown high into the air, visibility may be reduced

10   55-63 MPH 48-55 KT Whole gale; Seldom experienced inland, trees uprooted, considerable structural damage; sea is white with foam; waves with overhanging crests reduced visibility

11   64-72 MPH 56-63 KT Whole gale; Very rarely experienced inland, widespread damage; sea covered with foam, waves exceptionally high

12-17   73-136 MPH 64-118 KT Hurricane; Maximum wind damage; sea completely covered with spray, air filled with foam, greatly reduced visibility

WIND CHILL

Wind chill chart gives equivalent temperatures experienced by exposed skin or other moist objects.　　　　　　To estimate wind speed, see *Beaufort Scale* p. 186.

Wind Speed (mph)	calm	TEMPERATURE (°F.)									
		50	40	30	20	10	0	−10	−20	−30	−40
5		48	37	27	16	6	−5	−15	−26	−36	−47
10		40	28	16	4	−9	−21	−33	−46	−58	−70
15		36	22	9	−5	−18	−32	−45	−58	−72	−85
20		32	18	4	−10	−25	−39	−53	−67	−82	−96
25		30	16	0	−15	−29	−44	−59	−74	−88	−104
30		28	13	−2	−18	−33	−48	−63	−79	−94	−109
35		27	11	−4	−20	−35	−51	−67	−82	−98	−113
40		26	10	−6	−21	−37	−53	−69	−85	−100	−116

Little Danger　　　　Moderate Danger　　　　Great Danger

The TIDES
Tidal Differences From San Francisco

Using the Tables

To determine times and heights of the tides at the locations listed below: add, subtract or multiply, as indicated, the time and height values given in the tide forecast tables by the correction values given in the Tidal Differences table.

Station	Times		Heights	
	high water	low water	high water	low water
San Diego	−232	−210	−0.1	−0.2
La Jolla	−235	−214	−0.6	−0.2
Los Angeles	−227	−209	−0.4	−0.2
Santa Barbara	−204	−148	−0.5	−0.1
Avalon	−222	−202	−0.5	−0.2
Monterey	−116	−058	−0.5	0.0
Santa Cruz	−119	−104	−0.5	0.0
San Francisco	000	000	0.0	0.0
Bodega Hbr. entr.	−042	−022	−0.1	+0.1
Humboldt Bay	+018	+041	+0.6	+0.1
Coos Bay	+148	+209	+1.6	0.0
Newport	+031	+053	+2.2	+0.2
Astoria	+136	+218	+2.4	0.0
Willapa	+056	+113	+2.4	+0.2
Aberdeen	+133	+156	*1.84	*1.36
Cape Flattery	+047	+110	*1.41	*1.27
Seattle	+517	+547	*2.04	*2.55
Bellingham	+523	+557	*1.53	*2.36

*Ratio.

The TIDES

SAN FRANCISCO · PACIFIC STANDARD TIME

JANUARY

Day	Time (h m)	Ht (ft)	Day	Time (h m)	Ht (ft)
1 Tu	0013	2.4	16 W	0021	2.6
	0659	5.7		0706	6.6
	1357	1.0		1406	-0.2
	2054	3.7		2123	4.4
2 W	0105	2.8	17 Th	0127	3.0
	0735	5.9		0756	6.8
	1439	0.4		1502	-0.6
	2159	4.1		2225	4.7
3 Th	0154	3.1	18 F	0229	3.2
	0813	6.1		0848	6.9
	1519	0.0		1550	-0.9
	2249	4.4		2314	5.0
4 F	0240	3.3	19 Sa	0325	3.2
	0852	6.3		0937	6.9
	1557	-0.4		1635	-1.0
	2330	4.6		2359	5.1
5 Sa	0325	3.5	20 Su	0415	3.1
	0932	6.5		1023	6.8
	1634	-0.8		1715	-1.0
6 Su	0009	4.8	21 M	0038	5.1
	0404	3.5		0502	3.0
	1013	6.7		1105	6.5
	1711	-1.0		1753	-0.9
7 M	0045	4.9	22 Tu	0116	5.1
	0449	3.4		0547	2.9
	1051	6.7		1147	6.2
	1748	-1.2		1829	-0.6
8 Tu	0123	4.9	23 W	0152	5.0
	0532	3.3		0633	2.8
	1133	6.6		1226	5.8
	1831	-1.2		1905	-0.3
9 W	0202	5.0	24 Th	0224	5.0
	0620	3.2		0716	2.7
	1222	6.4		1305	5.3
	1913	-1.0		1937	0.1
10 Th	0239	5.1	25 F	0256	5.0
	0715	3.0		0809	2.6
	1311	5.9		1347	4.8
	1953	-0.7		2012	0.6
11 F	0318	5.3	26 Sa	0323	5.0
	0817	2.7		0905	2.4
	1408	5.4		1438	4.2
	2038	-0.1		2048	1.2
12 Sa	0358	5.5	27 Su	0355	5.1
	0930	2.3		1005	2.2
	1516	4.7		1539	3.8
	2124	0.5		2123	1.9
13 Su	0440	5.8	28 M	0428	5.2
	1045	1.7		1111	1.8
	1642	4.2		1714	3.4
	2217	1.3		2211	2.5
14 M	0526	6.1	29 Tu	0509	5.4
	1158	1.1		1215	1.4
	1825	3.9		1916	3.5
	2319	2.0		2310	3.0
15 Tu	0613	6.3	30 W	0554	5.6
	1306	0.4		1312	1.0
	2007	4.0		2055	3.8
			31 Th	0023	3.3
				0645	5.8
				1404	0.5
				2151	4.2

FEBRUARY

Day	Time (h m)	Ht (ft)	Day	Time (h m)	Ht (ft)
1 F	0125	3.5	16 Sa	0232	3.1
	0737	6.0		0837	6.4
	1450	0.0		1537	-0.6
	2230	4.4		2255	5.0
2 Sa	0221	3.5	17 Su	0326	2.9
	0823	6.3		0929	6.4
	1532	-0.5		1619	-0.6
	2305	4.7		2332	5.1
3 Su	0307	3.4	18 M	0411	2.6
	0912	6.5		1014	6.2
	1610	-0.9		1657	-0.6
	2337	4.8			
4 M	0353	3.1	19 Tu	0004	5.1
	0957	6.6		0455	2.3
	1649	-1.1		1056	6.0
				1729	-0.5
5 Tu	0009	4.9	20 W	0036	5.0
	0436	2.8		0532	2.1
	1043	6.7		1135	5.7
	1729	-1.2		1801	-0.2
6 W	0044	5.1	21 Th	0102	5.0
	0521	2.5		0609	1.9
	1131	6.5		1213	5.3
	1807	-1.1		1830	0.2
7 Th	0116	5.2	22 F	0124	4.9
	0608	2.1		0648	1.8
	1220	6.2		1252	4.9
	1846	-0.8		1858	0.6
8 F	0148	5.4	23 Sa	0148	5.0
	0703	1.7		0731	1.6
	1313	5.7		1334	4.5
	1925	-0.2		1927	1.2
9 Sa	0227	5.6	24 Su	0214	5.0
	0801	1.4		0813	1.5
	1411	5.1		1422	4.1
	2007	0.5		1958	1.8
10 Su	0306	5.8	25 M	0243	5.1
	0904	1.1		0904	1.4
	1523	4.5		1527	3.7
	2053	1.3		2030	2.4
11 M	0349	6.0	26 Tu	0316	5.2
	1016	0.8		1001	1.3
	1655	4.0		1700	3.5
	2148	2.1		2109	3.0
12 Tu	0439	6.1	27 W	0401	5.3
	1135	0.5		1110	1.1
	1841	3.9		1911	3.6
	2253	2.8		2221	3.4
13 W	0536	6.2	28 Th	0454	5.3
	1245	0.2		1219	0.8
	2015	4.2		2037	3.9
				2357	3.6
14 Th	0013	3.2			
	0639	6.3			
	1354	-0.1			
	2121	4.6			
15 F	0127	3.3			
	0741	6.4			
	1450	-0.4			
	2212	4.8			

MARCH

Day	Time (h m)	Ht (ft)	Day	Time (h m)	Ht (ft)
1 F	0559	5.5	16 Sa	0133	3.0
	1321	0.4		0725	5.7
	2122	4.2		1426	-0.2
				2143	4.9
2 Sa	0106	3.5	17 Su	0231	2.6
	0702	5.7		0824	5.7
	1412	-0.1		1511	-0.2
	2154	4.5		2219	5.0
3 Su	0204	3.2	18 M	0319	2.2
	0757	5.9		0921	5.6
	1500	-0.5		1552	-0.2
	2226	4.7		2251	5.0
4 M	0253	2.8	19 Tu	0402	1.8
	0853	6.1		1006	5.4
	1542	-0.8		1626	-0.1
	2254	4.8		2320	5.0
5 Tu	0339	2.3	20 W	0438	1.4
	0945	6.3		1048	5.2
	1621	-1.0		1656	0.1
	2326	5.0		2345	5.0
6 W	0421	1.7	21 Th	0513	1.1
	1034	6.2		1130	5.0
	1700	-0.9		1721	0.5
	2355	5.3			
7 Th	0508	1.2	22 F	0006	5.0
	1126	6.1		0548	0.9
	1739	-0.6		1208	4.7
				1753	0.9
8 F	0027	5.5	23 Sa	0026	5.0
	0555	0.7		0620	0.7
	1218	5.7		1247	4.4
	1815	-0.1		1818	1.4
9 Sa	0102	5.7	24 Su	0048	5.1
	0647	0.3		0655	0.6
	1317	5.2		1334	4.2
	1857	0.6		1847	1.9
10 Su	0137	5.9	25 M	0113	5.2
	0734	0.1		0734	0.6
	1421	4.7		1427	4.0
	1938	1.4		1915	2.5
11 M	0217	6.1	26 Tu	0142	5.2
	0842	0.0		0820	0.6
	1538	4.3		1533	3.8
	2027	2.2		1947	3.0
12 Tu	0304	6.0	27 W	0217	5.2
	0951	0.0		0912	0.6
	1710	4.1		1705	3.7
	2129	2.8		2030	3.4
13 W	0400	6.0	28 Th	0304	5.1
	1107	0.1		1017	0.6
	1847	4.2		1842	3.8
	2248	3.2		2152	3.6
14 Th	0504	5.8	29 F	0404	5.1
	1221	0.0		1127	0.4
	2005	4.5		1954	4.1
				2336	3.6
15 F	0021	3.3	30 Sa	0517	5.1
	0616	5.7		1234	0.2
	1330	0.0		2033	4.3
	2058	4.7			
			31 Su	0051	3.3
				0629	5.2
				1332	-0.2
				2105	4.5

PACIFIC STANDARD TIME. TIME MERIDIAN 120°W, BETWEEN APRIL 28 AND OCTOBER 27 ADD 1 HOUR FOR DAYLIGHT TIME.
0000 IS MIDNIGHT. 1200 IS NOON
HEIGHTS ARE RECKONED FROM THE DATUM OF SOUNDINGS ON CHARTS OF THE LOCALITY WHICH IS MEAN LOWER LOW WATER.

The TIDES

SAN FRANCISCO — *PACIFIC STANDARD TIME*

APRIL

Day	Time (h m)	Ht (ft)	Day	Time (h m)	Ht (ft)
1 M	0146	2.7	16 Tu	0305	1.5
	0738	5.4		0908	4.7
	1418	-0.5		1510	0.4
	2137	4.8		2202	5.1
2 Tu	0237	2.0	17 W	0344	1.0
	0837	5.5		0958	4.6
	1503	-0.6		1545	0.6
	2205	5.0		2227	5.1
3 W	0323	1.3	18 Th	0419	0.6
	0934	5.6		1043	4.5
	1545	-0.5		1617	0.9
	2234	5.3		2251	5.1
4 Th	0409	0.5	19 F	0451	0.3
	1032	5.5		1128	4.4
	1624	-0.2		1642	1.3
	2306	5.6		2310	5.2
5 F	0454	-0.2	20 Sa	0525	0.0
	1128	5.4		1212	4.3
	1706	0.3		1714	1.8
	2339	5.9		2333	5.3
6 Sa	0540	-0.7	21 Su	0557	-0.1
	1225	5.2		1257	4.2
	1745	0.9		1743	2.3
				2356	5.3
7 Su	0015	6.1	22 M	0630	-0.2
	0632	-0.9		1345	4.1
	1326	4.9		1811	2.7
	1827	1.6			
8 M	0054	6.2	23 Tu	0025	5.4
	0724	-1.0		0708	-0.2
	1434	4.6		1440	4.0
	1913	2.3		1843	3.1
9 Tu	0137	6.2	24 W	0057	5.3
	0820	-0.8		0751	-0.1
	1549	4.4		1541	4.0
	2011	2.9		1925	3.4
10 W	0227	5.9	25 Th	0136	5.2
	0925	-0.5		0843	-0.1
	1712	4.4		1657	4.0
	2127	3.2		2021	3.6
11 Th	0329	5.6	26 F	0226	5.1
	1037	-0.2		0939	0.0
	1830	4.5		1803	4.1
	2257	3.4		2149	3.6
12 F	0438	5.3	27 Sa	0329	4.9
	1147	0.0		1044	0.0
	1933	4.7		1855	4.3
				2323	3.4
13 Sa	0022	3.0	28 Su	0444	4.8
	0557	5.1		1147	-0.1
	1256	0.1		1933	4.5
	2023	4.8			
14 Su	0127	2.5	29 M	0030	2.8
	0707	4.9		0600	4.7
	1347	0.1		1244	-0.2
	2101	5.0		2009	4.8
15 M	0223	2.0	30 Tu	0130	2.1
	0810	4.8		0714	4.7
	1431	0.2		1335	-0.1
	2134	5.0		2041	5.1

MAY

Day	Time (h m)	Ht (ft)	Day	Time (h m)	Ht (ft)
1 W	0219	1.2	16 Th	0324	0.5
	0826	4.8		0951	4.0
	1421	0.1		1457	1.5
	2113	5.5		2133	5.4
2 Th	0308	0.3	17 F	0359	0.0
	0932	4.8		1045	4.0
	1506	0.4		1535	1.9
	2145	5.8		2156	5.5
3 F	0353	-0.5	18 Sa	0432	-0.3
	1035	4.9		1133	4.1
	1548	0.9		1607	2.3
	2221	6.2		2221	5.6
4 Sa	0441	-1.2	19 Su	0503	-0.5
	1135	4.9		1220	4.2
	1630	1.4		1638	2.7
	2257	6.4		2249	5.7
5 Su	0527	-1.6	20 M	0536	-0.7
	1236	4.8		1305	4.2
	1719	2.0		1710	3.0
	2337	6.5		2318	5.7
6 M	0616	-1.7	21 Tu	0611	-0.7
	1336	4.8		1355	4.3
	1804	2.5		1746	3.3
				2351	5.7
7 Tu	0020	6.4	22 W	0650	-0.7
	0708	-1.5		1440	4.3
	1442	4.7		1824	3.5
	1900	2.9			
8 W	0106	6.2	23 Th	0030	5.6
	0801	-1.2		0732	-0.7
	1548	4.7		1534	4.3
	2006	3.2		1915	3.6
9 Th	0201	5.8	24 F	0112	5.4
	0900	-0.8		0817	-0.6
	1653	4.7		1624	4.4
	2122	3.3		2018	3.6
10 F	0300	5.4	25 Sa	0201	5.2
	1003	-0.4		0910	-0.5
	1756	4.7		1713	4.5
	2249	3.1		2139	3.4
11 Sa	0409	4.9	26 Su	0304	4.9
	1106	0.0		1006	-0.3
	1848	4.9		1755	4.7
				2300	3.0
12 Su	0006	2.7	27 M	0413	4.5
	0522	4.5		1102	-0.1
	1203	0.3		1834	5.0
	1933	5.0			
13 M	0112	2.2	28 Tu	0009	2.3
	0639	4.2		0538	4.3
	1257	0.5		1157	0.2
	2011	5.1		1912	5.3
14 Tu	0203	1.6	29 W	0108	1.4
	0750	4.0		0704	4.1
	1342	0.8		1249	0.6
	2041	5.2		1947	5.7
15 W	0245	1.0	30 Th	0202	0.5
	0854	4.0		0825	4.2
	1421	1.1		1339	1.0
	2108	5.3		2026	6.1
			31 F	0252	-0.4
				0938	4.3
				1427	1.5
				2105	6.4

JUNE

Day	Time (h m)	Ht (ft)	Day	Time (h m)	Ht (ft)
1 Sa	0341	-1.1	16 Su	0409	-0.4
	1044	4.5		1133	4.2
	1519	2.0		1534	3.0
	2143	6.7		2143	6.0
2 Su	0427	-1.6	17 M	0442	-0.7
	1143	4.7		1218	4.4
	1608	2.4		1613	3.2
	2227	6.8		2218	6.0
3 M	0515	-1.8	18 Tu	0517	-0.8
	1242	4.8		1300	4.5
	1657	2.8		1649	3.4
	2312	6.8		2254	6.1
4 Tu	0604	-1.8	19 W	0555	-0.9
	1338	4.9		1342	4.5
	1751	3.0		1730	3.5
	2355	6.6		2332	6.0
5 W	0653	-1.6	20 Th	0631	-1.0
	1433	4.9		1421	4.6
	1846	3.2		1815	3.5
6 Th	0047	6.7	21 F	0012	5.9
	0744	-1.2		0713	-1.0
	1525	4.9		1502	4.6
	1951	3.3		1904	3.4
7 F	0136	5.7	22 Sa	0057	5.7
	0835	-0.8		0756	-0.7
	1621	4.9		1541	4.8
	2104	3.2		2008	3.3
8 Sa	0231	5.2	23 Su	0149	5.3
	0925	-0.3		0842	-0.6
	1710	4.9		1621	4.9
	2218	2.9		2118	3.0
9 Su	0333	4.6	24 M	0248	4.8
	1018	0.2		0928	-0.2
	1755	5.0		1659	5.2
	2334	2.5		2231	2.4
10 M	0443	4.1	25 Tu	0403	4.3
	1109	0.6		1019	0.3
	1834	5.1		1741	5.5
				2343	1.7
11 Tu	0039	2.4	26 W	0530	3.9
	0605	3.7		1111	0.9
	1157	1.1		1820	5.9
	1909	5.2			
12 W	0132	1.4	27 Th	0049	0.9
	0728	3.5		0706	3.8
	1246	1.5		1210	1.5
	1941	5.4		1904	6.2
13 Th	0217	0.8	28 F	0145	0.0
	0844	3.6		0836	4.0
	1331	2.0		1306	2.1
	2010	5.5		1947	6.6
14 F	0257	0.3	29 Sa	0240	-0.7
	0951	3.8		0950	4.3
	1413	2.4		1405	2.5
	2039	5.7		2034	6.8
15 Sa	0334	-0.1	30 Su	0329	-1.2
	1047	4.0		1052	4.6
	1456	2.7		1500	2.8
	2111	5.9		2121	7.0

The TIDES

SAN FRANCISCO — *PACIFIC STANDARD TIME*

JULY

Day	Time (h m)	Ht (ft)		Day	Time (h m)	Ht (ft)
1 M	0418	-1.5		16 Tu	0422	-0.6
	1148	4.8			1159	4.6
	1553	3.0			1554	3.4
	2209	7.0			2157	6.3
2 Tu	0507	-1.6		17 W	0459	-0.8
	1236	5.0			1231	4.7
	1648	3.1			1636	3.3
	2257	6.8			2239	6.4
3 W	0551	-1.5		18 Th	0535	-1.0
	1321	5.2			1307	4.8
	1740	3.1			1719	3.2
	2342	6.6			2320	6.3
4 Th	0636	-1.3		19 F	0610	-1.0
	1408	5.0			1339	4.8
	1833	3.1			1801	3.0
5 F	0028	6.1		20 Sa	0006	6.1
	0718	-0.9			0649	-0.9
	1453	5.0			1414	5.0
	1929	3.0			1851	2.8
6 Sa	0117	5.6		21 Su	0051	5.8
	0801	-0.5			0729	-0.7
	1532	5.0			1449	5.1
	2030	2.8			1950	2.5
7 Su	0206	5.0		22 M	0143	5.3
	0843	0.0			0811	-0.2
	1613	5.0			1525	5.4
	2139	2.6			2056	2.1
8 M	0258	4.4		23 Tu	0246	4.7
	0927	0.6			0854	0.5
	1648	5.1			1607	5.7
	2247	2.3			2205	1.7
9 Tu	0403	3.9		24 W	0403	4.2
	1012	1.2			0943	1.2
	1724	5.2			1649	5.9
	2353	1.9			2318	1.1
10 W	0528	3.5		25 Th	0541	3.9
	1054	1.8			1039	1.9
	1759	5.3			1735	6.2
11 Th	0049	1.4		26 F	0027	0.5
	0711	3.4			0722	3.9
	1147	2.3			1141	2.5
	1836	5.5			1827	6.5
12 F	0138	0.9		27 Sa	0133	-0.1
	0841	3.6			0849	4.2
	1242	2.8			1250	3.0
	1912	5.7			1921	6.7
13 Sa	0226	0.4		28 Su	0228	-0.6
	0950	3.9			0957	4.6
	1338	3.1			1356	3.1
	1954	5.9			2015	6.8
14 Su	0305	0.0		29 M	0322	-0.9
	1039	4.2			1047	4.8
	1428	3.3			1455	3.1
	2036	6.1			2111	6.9
15 M	0344	-0.3		30 Tu	0409	-1.1
	1121	4.4			1133	5.0
	1515	3.4			1550	3.0
	2116	6.2			2200	6.8
				31 W	0454	-1.1
					1215	5.1
					1641	2.8
					2248	6.6

AUGUST

Day	Time (h m)	Ht (ft)		Day	Time (h m)	Ht (ft)
1 Th	0534	-1.0		16 F	0508	-0.9
	1252	5.1			1218	5.0
	1727	2.7			1702	2.4
	2331	6.3			2312	6.3
2 F	0613	-0.7		17 Sa	0544	-0.8
	1329	5.1			1251	5.2
	1813	2.5			1747	2.0
3 Sa	0014	5.9		18 Su	0000	6.0
	0648	-0.4			0619	-0.5
	1403	5.0			1324	5.4
	1902	2.4			1835	1.7
4 Su	0058	5.4		19 M	0049	5.6
	0724	0.1			0658	0.0
	1434	5.0			1357	5.6
	1952	2.3			1932	1.3
5 M	0140	4.8		20 Tu	0148	5.1
	0759	0.7			0737	0.7
	1504	5.1			1435	5.8
	2046	2.1			2030	1.1
6 Tu	0233	4.3		21 W	0254	4.6
	0834	1.3			0822	1.4
	1533	5.1			1515	6.0
	2145	1.9			2139	0.8
7 W	0336	3.8		22 Th	0418	4.2
	0913	1.9			0914	2.2
	1609	5.2			1601	6.2
	2247	1.7			2252	0.5
8 Th	0507	3.5		23 F	0602	4.1
	0958	2.6			1020	2.9
	1648	5.4			1700	6.3
	2353	1.4				
9 F	0706	3.6		24 Sa	0005	0.2
	1101	3.1			0738	4.3
	1733	5.5			1139	3.3
					1803	6.4
10 Sa	0052	1.0		25 Su	0114	-0.1
	0839	3.9			0847	4.6
	1213	3.4			1255	3.3
	1825	5.7			1907	6.4
11 Su	0147	0.6		26 M	0216	-0.3
	0935	4.2			0943	4.9
	1319	3.5			1402	3.2
	1916	5.9			2007	6.5
12 M	0233	0.2		27 Tu	0308	-0.5
	1017	4.4			1022	5.1
	1411	3.5			1458	2.9
	2007	6.1			2105	6.5
13 Tu	0315	-0.2		28 W	0354	-0.6
	1049	4.6			1104	5.2
	1457	3.3			1548	2.5
	2055	6.3			2154	6.4
14 W	0354	-0.5		29 Th	0433	-0.5
	1121	4.8			1139	5.2
	1537	3.1			1630	2.2
	2141	6.4			2240	6.1
15 Th	0433	-0.8		30 F	0509	-0.3
	1149	4.9			1210	5.2
	1619	2.8			1712	1.9
	2226	6.4			2322	5.8
				31 Sa	0541	0.0
					1239	5.1
					1754	1.7

SEPTEMBER

Day	Time (h m)	Ht (ft)		Day	Time (h m)	Ht (ft)
1 Su	0004	5.4		16 M	0547	0.3
	0613	0.4			1231	5.9
	1304	5.1			1820	0.3
	1833	1.6				
2 M	0047	5.0		17 Tu	0054	5.3
	0642	0.9			0627	1.0
	1329	5.1			1305	6.1
	1914	1.5			1913	0.1
3 Tu	0131	4.6		18 W	0157	5.1
	0713	1.5			0708	1.7
	1355	5.2			1344	6.2
	1957	1.4			2009	0.0
4 W	0223	4.2		19 Th	0310	4.6
	0745	2.1			0757	2.5
	1421	5.2			1430	6.3
	2046	1.4			2114	0.0
5 Th	0326	3.9		20 F	0434	4.4
	0820	2.7			0856	3.1
	1459	5.3			1523	6.2
	2145	1.3			2227	0.1
6 F	0501	3.8		21 Sa	0612	4.5
	0906	3.3			1018	3.5
	1539	5.3			1632	6.1
	2252	1.2			2343	0.1
7 Sa	0701	3.9		22 Su	0733	4.7
	1018	3.6			1149	3.6
	1637	5.3			1743	6.0
8 Su	0824	4.2		23 M	0055	0.0
	1154	3.8			0827	5.0
	1738	5.4			1306	3.2
					1856	5.9
9 M	0102	0.7		24 Tu	0155	0.0
	0906	4.4			0913	5.2
	1304	3.6			1405	2.7
	1842	5.6			2002	5.9
10 Tu	0154	0.3		25 W	0244	-0.1
	0934	4.6			0951	5.3
	1356	3.3			1457	2.3
	1941	5.8			2057	5.8
11 W	0239	-0.1		26 Th	0323	0.0
	1003	4.8			1023	5.4
	1440	2.9			1542	1.8
	2034	6.0			2142	5.6
12 Th	0319	-0.4		27 F	0401	0.2
	1031	5.0			1053	5.4
	1522	2.4			1621	1.4
	2125	6.1			2234	5.4
13 F	0357	-0.5		28 Sa	0434	0.4
	1100	5.1			1121	5.4
	1604	1.8			1659	1.1
	2214	6.1			2316	5.2
14 Sa	0433	-0.5		29 Su	0505	0.8
	1128	5.4			1143	5.3
	1646	1.3			1732	0.8
	2306	6.0				
15 Su	0512	-0.2		30 M	0002	4.9
	1157	5.6			0533	1.5
	1732	0.8			1205	5.4
	2358	5.7			1804	0.7

PACIFIC STANDARD TIME. TIME MERIDIAN 120°W, BETWEEN APRIL 28 AND OCTOBER 27 ADD 1 HOUR FOR DAYLIGHT TIME.
0000 IS MIDNIGHT. 1200 IS NOON
HEIGHTS ARE RECKONED FROM THE DATUM OF SOUNDINGS ON CHARTS OF THE LOCALITY WHICH IS MEAN LOWER LOW WATER.

The TIDES

SAN FRANCISCO — PACIFIC STANDARD TIME

OCTOBER

Day	Time h m	Ht ft	Day	Time h m	Ht ft
1 Tu	0044	4.6	16 W	0103	5.1
	0602	1.8		0557	2.0
	1227	5.4		1223	6.6
	1839	0.6		1854	-0.9
2 W	0131	4.4	17 Th	0207	4.9
	0631	2.4		0644	2.7
	1250	5.4		1305	6.6
	1918	0.6		1950	-0.8
3 Th	0224	4.2	18 F	0322	4.8
	0702	2.9		0741	3.2
	1321	5.4		1355	6.4
	2003	0.7		2052	-0.5
4 F	0330	4.1	19 Sa	0439	4.8
	0734	3.4		0851	3.6
	1357	5.3		1454	6.1
	2055	0.8		2201	-0.2
5 Sa	0505	4.1	20 Su	0557	4.9
	0825	3.8		1021	3.6
	1442	5.2		1605	5.7
	2155	0.8		2313	0.0
6 Su	0639	4.2	21 M	0702	5.0
	0954	4.0		1153	3.3
	1544	5.3		1722	5.4
	2305	0.8			
7 M	0738	4.4	22 Tu	0021	0.2
	1140	3.9		0752	5.2
	1657	5.1		1304	2.8
				1840	5.2
8 Tu	0013	0.6	23 W	0117	0.3
	0812	4.6		0834	5.4
	1248	3.5		1359	2.2
	1806	5.2		1949	5.1
9 W	0108	0.3	24 Th	0205	0.5
	0842	4.8		0907	5.5
	1336	3.0		1448	1.6
	1912	5.3		2049	5.0
10 Th	0154	0.1	25 F	0245	0.7
	0909	5.0		0939	5.6
	1420	2.3		1527	1.1
	2015	5.4		2142	4.9
11 F	0237	0.0	26 Sa	0322	1.0
	0939	5.3		1005	5.6
	1506	1.5		1606	0.7
	2113	5.5		2233	4.7
12 Sa	0319	0.0	27 Su	0354	1.4
	1007	5.6		1028	5.6
	1545	0.8		1638	0.3
	2209	5.5		2319	4.6
13 Su	0357	0.3	28 M	0426	1.8
	1037	5.9		1051	5.7
	1631	0.1		1710	0.1
	2304	5.5			
14 M	0436	0.8	29 Tu	0005	4.6
	1109	6.2		0454	2.3
	1716	-0.5		1114	5.7
				1741	0.0
15 Tu	0002	5.3	30 W	0051	4.5
	0515	1.4		0526	2.7
	1144	6.5		1135	5.7
	1805	-0.8		1817	0.0
			31 Th	0140	4.4
				0558	3.2
				1201	5.7
				1852	0.0

NOVEMBER

Day	Time h m	Ht ft	Day	Time h m	Ht ft
1 F	0232	4.4	16 Sa	0318	5.0
	0628	3.5		0729	3.5
	1233	5.6		1331	6.4
	1931	0.1		2033	-0.8
2 Sa	0331	4.3	17 Su	0423	5.0
	0705	3.8		0843	3.6
	1314	5.5		1433	5.9
	2020	0.2		2133	-0.3
3 Su	0444	4.4	18 M	0526	5.1
	0806	4.0		1013	3.5
	1400	5.3		1539	5.4
	2115	0.3		2235	0.1
4 M	0546	4.5	19 Tu	0621	5.2
	0939	4.0		1136	3.0
	1502	5.1		1655	4.9
	2217	0.4		2335	0.4
5 Tu	0635	4.6	20 W	0707	5.4
	1110	3.8		1249	2.5
	1614	4.9		1814	4.5
	2320	0.3			
6 W	0714	4.9	21 Th	0030	0.8
	1221	3.2		0745	5.5
	1730	4.7		1344	1.8
				1930	4.3
7 Th	0016	0.3	22 F	0119	1.1
	0744	5.1		0820	5.7
	1313	2.5		1430	1.2
	1847	4.7		2039	4.3
8 F	0106	0.4	23 Sa	0201	1.5
	0814	5.4		0849	5.8
	1403	1.6		1511	0.7
	2002	4.8		2142	4.3
9 Sa	0152	0.6	24 Su	0239	1.9
	0846	5.8		0914	5.9
	1445	0.7		1546	0.2
	2108	4.9		2235	4.4
10 Su	0236	0.9	25 M	0318	2.3
	0918	6.2		0942	5.9
	1530	-0.2		1619	-0.1
	2211	5.0		2326	4.4
11 M	0320	1.4	26 Tu	0353	2.7
	0952	6.6		1007	6.0
	1617	-0.9		1651	-0.3
	2312	5.1			
12 Tu	0404	1.9	27 W	0014	4.5
	1029	6.8		0429	3.1
	1703	-1.4		1033	6.0
				1723	-0.4
13 W	0011	5.1	28 Th	0055	4.6
	0449	2.4		0501	3.4
	1108	7.0		1102	6.0
	1750	-1.6		1757	-0.4
14 Th	0113	5.1	29 F	0142	4.6
	0535	2.9		0536	3.6
	1151	7.0		1135	6.0
	1839	-1.5		1833	-0.4
15 F	0214	5.1	30 Sa	0227	4.6
	0627	3.3		0612	3.8
	1239	6.8		1210	5.9
	1934	-1.2		1912	-0.3

DECEMBER

Day	Time h m	Ht ft	Day	Time h m	Ht ft
1 Su	0315	4.6	16 M	0348	5.2
	0654	3.9		0827	3.3
	1249	5.7		1408	5.7
	1957	-0.2		2101	-0.3
2 M	0400	4.6	17 Tu	0437	5.2
	0753	3.9		0944	3.1
	1337	5.4		-1507	5.0
	2043	-0.1		2151	0.3
3 Tu	0447	4.7	18 W	0525	5.3
	0908	3.8		1100	2.7
	1430	5.1		1619	4.4
	2136	0.1		2243	0.8
4 W	0529	4.9	19 Th	0608	5.4
	1032	3.4		1213	2.2
	1539	4.7		1742	3.9
	2228	0.3		2334	1.3
5 Th	0609	5.2	20 F	0646	5.6
	1145	2.8		1315	1.6
	1701	4.4		1915	3.8
	2321	0.6			
6 F	0643	5.5	21 Sa	0026	1.9
	1245	1.9		0722	5.7
	1831	4.2		1404	1.1
				2037	3.8
7 Sa	0017	1.0	22 Su	0115	2.3
	0720	5.9		0754	5.9
	1340	1.4		1446	0.6
	1956	4.2		2146	4.1
8 Su	0109	1.5	23 M	0200	2.7
	0759	6.3		0826	6.0
	1429	0.1		1525	0.2
	2115	4.4		2241	4.3
9 M	0200	2.0	24 Tu	0249	3.1
	0836	6.7		0858	6.1
	1517	-0.7		1600	-0.2
	2220	4.7		2327	4.5
10 Tu	0249	2.4	25 W	0328	3.3
	0917	7.0		0933	6.2
	1603	-1.3		1635	-0.4
	2322	4.9			
−11 W	0341	2.8	26 Th	0009	4.7
	1000	7.3		0407	3.5
	1652	-1.7		1009	6.3
				1707	-0.5
12 Th	0018	5.1	27 F	0047	4.7
	0430	3.0		0445	3.6
	1045	7.3		1044	6.3
	1741	-1.7		1743	-0.6
13 F	0111	5.2	28 Sa	0123	4.8
	0522	3.2		0521	3.6
	1132	7.2		1119	6.2
	1829	-1.6		1818	-0.7
14 Sa	0203	5.2	29 Su	0158	4.8
	0617	3.3		0601	3.8
	1223	6.8		1156	6.1
	1919	-1.2		1853	-0.7
15 Su	0254	5.2	30 M	0237	4.8
	0718	3.4		0644	3.5
	1313	6.3		1238	5.8
	2009	-0.8		1932	-0.5
			31 Tu	0312	4.9
				0737	3.4
				1322	5.5
				2011	-0.3

PACIFIC STANDARD TIME. TIME MERIDIAN 120°W, BETWEEN APRIL 28 AND OCTOBER 27 ADD 1 HOUR FOR DAYLIGHT TIME.
0000 IS MIDNIGHT. 1200 IS NOON
HEIGHTS ARE RECKONED FROM THE DATUM OF SOUNDINGS ON CHARTS OF THE LOCALITY WHICH IS MEAN LOWER LOW WATER.

MOON Rise and Set

LOCAL MEAN TIME at MERIDIAN OF GREENWICH. To obtain CLOCK TIME, see *About Time* p. 8

	30°N		40°N		50°N			30°N		40°N		50°N	
	Rise	Set	Rise	Set	Rise	Set		Rise	Set	Rise	Set	Rise	Set
	h m	h m	h m	h m	h m	h m		h m	h m	h m	h m	h m	h m
Dec. 21	5 47	16 09	6 17	15 38	7 00	14 54	Mar. 1	12 09	1 58	11 36	2 30	10 48	3 17
22	6 54	17 04	7 27	16 04	8 15	15 41	2	13 04	2 56	12 31	3 30	11 41	4 19
23	7 55	18 04	8 28	17 31	9 17	16 42	3	14 06	3 51	13 35	4 24	12 48	5 11
24	8 48	19 06	9 19	18 36	10 04	17 52	4	15 14	4 42	14 46	5 11	14 08	5 52
25	9 34	20 07	10 01	19 42	10 39	19 06	5	16 23	5 28	16 02	5 51	15 33	6 23
26	10 13	21 06	10 34	20 47	11 04	20 20	6	17 33	6 09	17 20	6 25	17 01	6 47
27	10 46	22 03	11 02	21 50	11 24	21 31	7	18 42	6 47	18 37	6 55	18 29	7 07
28	11 16	22 57	11 26	22 50	11 40	22 40	8	19 51	7 22	19 54	7 23	19 57	7 25
29	11 44	23 50	11 48	23 49	11 54	23 47	9	21 00	7 57	21 10	7 51	21 24	7 43
30	12 11	....	12 09	....	12 07	....	10	22 09	8 33	22 27	8 20	22 52	8 01
31	12 38	0 43	12 30	0 47	12 21	0 53	11	23 18	9 12	23 43	8 51	....	8 23
Jan. 1	13 06	1 36	12 53	1 46	12 36	2 01	12	....	9 55	....	9 28	0 18	8 51
2	13 37	2 31	13 19	2 47	12 53	3 10	13	0 26	10 43	0 56	10 12	1 40	9 26
3	14 13	3 28	13 49	3 50	13 15	4 22	14	1 30	11 37	2 04	11 03	2 54	10 13
4	14 55	4 27	14 26	4 55	13 45	5 34	15	2 29	12 35	3 03	12 01	3 53	11 12
5	15 43	5 28	15 11	6 00	14 24	6 46	16	3 21	13 35	3 53	13 05	4 39	12 20
6	16 39	6 28	16 06	7 02	15 17	7 50	17	4 06	14 35	4 33	14 09	5 13	13 32
7	17 42	7 25	17 10	7 58	16 25	8 44	18	4 44	15 34	5 06	15 14	5 37	14 45
8	18 48	8 17	18 21	8 46	17 42	9 26	19	5 17	16 31	5 34	16 17	5 57	15 57
9	19 56	9 03	19 35	9 26	19 05	9 58	20	5 47	17 26	5 58	17 18	6 12	17 06
10	21 03	9 43	20 49	10 00	20 29	10 23	21	6 15	18 19	6 20	18 17	6 26	18 14
11	22 08	10 19	22 01	10 29	21 52	10 42	22	6 41	19 12	6 40	19 16	6 39	19 22
12	23 13	10 53	23 13	10 56	23 14	11 00	23	7 08	20 05	7 01	20 15	6 52	20 29
13	....	11 26	....	11 22	....	11 17	24	7 36	20 59	7 23	21 15	7 06	21 37
14	0 17	12 00	0 25	11 49	0 35	11 34	25	8 05	21 54	7 47	22 16	7 22	22 47
15	1 22	12 36	1 37	12 18	1 57	11 54	26	8 39	22 51	8 15	23 18	7 42	23 57
16	2 28	13 16	2 50	12 52	3 20	12 18	27	9 17	23 48	8 48	....	8 07	....
17	3 34	14 01	4 02	13 32	4 42	12 50	28	10 01	....	9 29	0 20	8 42	1 06
18	4 40	14 53	5 12	14 20	5 59	13 32	29	10 52	0 46	10 18	1 20	9 28	2 09
19	5 42	15 50	6 15	15 16	7 05	14 27	30	11 50	1 41	11 16	2 15	10 28	3 04
20	6 38	16 50	7 10	16 19	7 57	15 33	31	12 53	2 32	12 23	3 03	11 40	3 48
21	7 26	17 52	7 55	17 25	8 36	16 45	Apr. 1	14 00	3 19	13 35	3 45	13 01	4 22
22	8 08	18 53	8 32	18 31	9 05	18 00	2	15 08	4 01	14 51	4 21	14 27	4 48
23	8 44	19 51	9 02	19 35	9 27	19 13	3	16 17	4 39	16 07	4 52	15 54	5 09
24	9 15	20 47	9 28	20 37	9 44	20 23	4	17 26	5 15	17 24	5 20	17 22	5 27
25	9 44	21 41	9 50	21 37	9 59	21 32	5	18 36	5 50	18 42	5 48	18 51	5 45
26	10 11	22 33	10 12	22 35	10 13	22 39	6	19 47	6 26	20 01	6 16	20 21	6 03
27	10 38	23 26	10 33	23 34	10 26	23 45	7	20 58	7 04	21 20	6 47	21 51	6 23
28	11 05	....	10 54	....	10 40	....	8	22 10	7 47	22 39	7 22	23 20	6 48
29	11 35	0 20	11 18	0 34	10 56	0 53	9	23 19	8 35	23 52	8 04	....	7 21
30	12 08	1 15	11 46	1 35	11 15	2 03	10	....	9 28	....	8 55	0 41	8 05
31	12 46	2 13	12 19	2 38	11 41	3 14	11	0 22	10 27	0 57	9 52	1 48	9 01
Feb. 1	13 31	3 12	13 00	3 42	12 15	4 26	12	1 18	11 28	1 51	10 56	2 40	10 08
2	14 23	4 12	13 50	4 45	13 01	5 33	13	2 06	12 29	2 35	12 01	3 17	11 21
3	15 23	5 11	14 50	5 44	14 02	6 33	14	2 46	13 29	3 10	13 06	3 44	12 35
4	16 29	6 05	15 59	6 36	15 17	7 20	15	3 21	14 26	3 39	14 10	4 05	13 47
5	17 38	6 54	17 14	7 20	16 40	7 56	16	3 51	15 21	4 04	15 11	4 21	14 57
6	18 47	7 38	18 30	7 57	18 07	8 24	17	4 19	16 14	4 26	16 10	4 35	16 05
7	19 56	8 17	19 46	8 29	19 33	8 46	18	4 45	17 07	4 46	17 09	4 48	17 12
8	21 02	8 52	21 00	8 58	20 58	9 05	19	5 12	18 00	5 07	18 08	5 00	18 19
9	22 09	9 26	22 14	9 24	22 22	9 22	20	5 39	18 53	5 28	19 08	5 13	19 27
10	23 15	10 00	23 28	9 51	23 46	9 39	21	6 08	19 48	5 51	20 09	5 29	20 37
11	....	10 36	....	10 20	....	9 59	22	6 40	20 45	6 18	21 11	5 47	21 47
12	0 21	11 15	0 41	10 53	1 09	10 21	23	7 16	21 42	6 49	22 13	6 10	22 57
13	1 28	11 58	1 54	11 30	2 32	10 51	24	7 58	22 40	7 27	23 13	6 41	....
14	2 33	12 48	3 04	12 15	3 50	11 29	25	8 46	23 35	8 12	....	7 23	0 03
15	3 35	13 42	4 09	13 08	4 59	12 19	26	9 41	....	9 07	0 09	8 17	1 00
16	4 32	14 41	5 05	14 08	5 54	13 20	27	10 41	0 27	10 09	0 59	9 23	1 46
17	5 22	15 42	5 53	15 12	6 36	14 30	28	11 44	1 14	11 17	1 42	10 39	2 23
18	6 05	16 42	6 31	16 18	7 08	15 44	29	12 50	1 56	12 29	2 19	12 00	2 50
19	6 43	17 41	7 03	17 23	7 31	16 57	30	13 56	2 34	13 43	2 50	13 24	3 12
20	7 15	18 37	7 30	18 25	7 50	18 09	May 1	15 03	3 10	14 57	3 19	14 49	3 31
21	7 45	19 32	7 53	19 26	8 05	19 18	2	16 11	3 44	16 13	3 46	16 15	3 48
22	8 12	20 25	8 15	20 25	8 19	20 25	3	17 20	4 18	17 30	4 13	17 44	4 05
23	8 39	21 18	8 36	21 24	8 32	21 32	4	18 32	4 55	18 50	4 42	19 15	4 24
24	9 06	22 11	8 57	22 23	8 45	22 40	5	19 45	5 35	20 10	5 14	20 47	4 46
25	9 34	23 05	9 19	23 23	9 00	23 48	6	20 57	6 21	21 29	5 54	22 15	5 15
26	10 05	....	9 45	....	9 17	....	7	22 06	7 14	22 41	6 41	23 32	5 54
27	10 40	0 01	10 15	0 25	9 39	0 59	8	23 08	8 12	23 42	7 37	....	6 46
28	11 21	0 59	10 51	1 28	10 09	2 09	9	....	9 15	....	8 41	0 32	7 51

MOON Rise and Set

LOCAL MEAN TIME at MERIDIAN OF GREENWICH. To obtain CLOCK TIME, see *About Time* p. 8

	30°N Rise	30°N Set	40°N Rise	40°N Set	50°N Rise	50°N Set
	h m	h m	h m	h m	h m	h m
May 10	0 00	10 18	0 32	9 48	1 17	9 05
11	0 45	11 20	1 11	10 55	1 48	10 21
12	1 22	12 19	1 42	12 01	2 11	11 35
13	1 54	13 15	2 09	13 03	2 29	12 46
14	2 23	14 09	2 31	14 03	2 43	13 55
15	2 49	15 02	2 52	15 02	2 56	15 02
16	3 16	15 55	3 13	16 01	3 09	16 09
17	3 42	16 48	3 33	17 00	3 21	17 17
18	4 10	17 43	3 56	18 01	3 36	18 26
19	4 41	18 39	4 21	19 03	3 53	19 37
20	5 17	19 37	4 51	20 06	4 15	20 48
21	5 57	20 35	5 27	21 07	4 43	21 55
22	6 43	21 31	6 10	22 05	5 21	22 56
23	7 36	22 24	7 02	22 57	6 11	23 46
24	8 34	23 12	8 02	23 42	7 14	....
25	9 36	23 55	9 08	....	8 27	0 25
26	10 40	....	10 17	0 20	9 45	0 54
27	11 44	0 33	11 28	0 52	11 06	1 17
28	12 48	1 09	12 39	1 20	12 27	1 36
29	13 53	1 42	13 52	1 47	13 50	1 53
30	14 59	2 15	15 06	2 12	15 14	2 09
31	16 08	2 49	16 22	2 39	16 42	2 26
June 1	17 19	3 26	17 41	3 09	18 11	2 46
2	18 32	4 08	19 00	3 44	19 41	3 11
3	19 43	4 57	20 17	4 27	21 06	3 44
4	20 50	5 54	21 25	5 20	22 16	4 30
5	21 48	6 56	22 21	6 21	23 09	5 30
6	22 38	8 01	23 06	7 29	23 47	6 42
7	23 19	9 05	23 42	8 38	....	8 00
8	23 54	10 07	....	9 47	0 14	9 17
9	....	11 06	0 11	10 52	0 34	10 31
10	0 24	12 02	0 35	11 54	0 50	11 42
11	0 52	12 56	0 57	12 54	1 03	12 51
12	1 18	13 48	1 17	13 52	1 16	13 58
13	1 45	14 41	1 38	14 51	1 29	15 05
14	2 12	15 35	2 00	15 52	1 43	16 14
15	2 42	16 31	2 24	16 53	1 59	17 24
16	3 16	17 29	2 52	17 56	2 19	18 35
17	3 55	18 27	3 26	18 59	2 45	19 45
18	4 39	19 25	4 07	19 59	3 19	20 49
19	5 31	20 20	4 57	20 53	4 06	21 43
20	6 28	21 10	5 55	21 41	5 06	22 26
21	7 30	21 55	7 00	22 21	6 17	22 58
22	8 33	22 35	8 09	22 55	7 34	23 23
23	9 37	23 10	9 19	23 24	8 54	23 43
24	10 41	23 43	10 30	23 50	10 15	....
25	11 44	....	11 41	....	11 36	0 00
26	12 48	0 15	12 52	0 15	12 57	0 15
27	13 54	0 48	14 05	0 41	14 20	0 31
28	15 01	1 23	15 20	1 08	15 46	0 49
29	16 11	2 01	16 37	1 40	17 14	1 11
30	17 22	2 46	17 53	2 18	18 39	1 39
July 1	18 30	3 38	19 05	3 05	19 56	2 18
2	19 33	4 37	20 07	4 02	20 57	3 11
3	20 27	5 41	20 57	5 08	21 42	4 18
4	21 12	6 47	21 38	6 18	22 13	5 35
5	21 50	7 52	22 10	7 28	22 37	6 54
6	22 23	8 53	22 36	8 36	22 54	8 12
7	22 52	9 51	22 59	9 40	23 09	9 25
8	23 19	10 46	23 21	10 42	23 22	10 36
9	23 46	11 40	23 41	11 42	23 35	11 44
10	....	12 33	....	12 41	23 48	12 52
11	0 13	13 27	0 02	13 41	....	14 00
12	0 42	14 22	0 26	14 42	0 03	15 10
13	1 14	15 18	0 52	15 44	0 22	16 20
14	1 51	16 16	1 23	16 47	0 45	17 31
15	2 33	17 15	2 02	17 48	1 16	18 37
16	3 22	18 11	2 48	18 46	1 59	19 36
17	4 18	19 04	3 44	19 36	2 54	20 23
18	5 20	19 52	4 48	20 20	4 03	20 59

	30°N Rise	30°N Set	40°N Rise	40°N Set	50°N Rise	50°N Set
	h m	h m	h m	h m	h m	h m
July 19	6 24	20 34	5 58	20 56	5 20	21 27
20	7 29	21 11	7 09	21 27	6 41	21 48
21	8 34	21 45	8 21	21 54	8 03	22 06
22	9 38	22 18	9 32	22 20	9 25	22 22
23	10 42	22 50	10 43	22 45	10 46	22 38
24	11 46	23 23	11 55	23 11	12 08	22 55
25	12 52	....	13 08	23 41	13 31	23 14
26	14 00	0 00	14 23	....	14 57	23 39
27	15 09	0 41	15 38	0 16	16 21	....
28	16 16	1 29	16 50	0 58	17 40	0 13
29	17 20	2 24	17 54	1 50	18 46	0 59
30	18 16	3 25	18 49	2 51	19 36	2 00
31	19 05	4 30	19 33	3 59	20 12	3 13
Aug. 1	19 45	5 35	20 08	5 09	20 38	4 31
2	20 20	6 38	20 36	6 18	20 58	5 50
3	20 51	7 38	21 01	7 25	21 14	7 06
4	21 19	8 35	21 23	8 28	21 28	8 19
5	21 46	9 30	21 44	9 29	21 40	9 29
6	22 13	10 24	22 05	10 29	21 53	10 37
7	22 41	11 17	22 27	11 29	22 08	11 45
8	23 12	12 12	22 52	12 29	22 24	12 54
9	23 46	13 07	23 21	13 31	22 45	14 05
10	....	14 05	23 56	14 33	23 13	15 15
11	0 26	15 03	....	15 35	23 50	16 23
12	1 12	16 00	0 38	16 34	....	17 25
13	2 05	16 54	1 30	17 28	0 40	18 17
14	3 04	17 44	2 32	18 14	1 43	18 57
15	4 09	18 29	3 40	18 54	2 58	19 28
16	5 15	19 09	4 52	19 27	4 20	19 52
17	6 21	19 45	6 06	19 56	5 44	20 11
18	7 27	20 18	7 19	20 22	7 08	20 28
19	8 33	20 51	8 32	20 48	8 31	20 44
20	9 38	21 24	9 45	21 14	9 55	21 00
21	10 45	22 00	10 59	21 43	11 19	21 19
22	11 52	22 40	12 14	22 16	12 45	21 42
23	13 01	23 26	13 29	22 56	14 10	22 13
24	14 09	....	14 42	23 44	15 30	22 54
25	15 12	0 18	15 47	....	16 39	23 49
26	16 10	1 16	16 44	0 41	17 33	....
27	17 00	2 19	17 30	1 46	18 13	0 57
28	17 43	3 23	18 07	2 54	18 42	2 13
29	18 19	4 26	18 38	4 03	19 03	3 32
30	18 51	5 26	19 03	5 10	19 20	4 48
31	19 20	6 24	19 26	6 15	19 34	6 02
Sept. 1	19 47	7 20	19 47	7 17	19 47	7 13
2	20 14	8 14	20 08	8 18	19 59	8 22
3	20 41	9 08	20 29	9 18	20 13	9 31
4	21 11	10 02	20 53	10 18	20 28	10 40
5	21 43	10 58	21 19	11 19	20 47	11 50
6	22 20	11 54	21 51	12 21	21 11	13 00
7	23 03	12 51	22 30	13 23	21 43	14 09
8	23 52	13 48	23 17	14 22	22 26	15 13
9	....	14 43	....	15 18	23 23	16 09
10	0 48	15 34	0 14	16 06	....	16 53
11	1 50	16 21	1 18	16 48	0 33	17 27
12	2 55	17 02	2 29	17 24	1 52	17 54
13	4 02	17 40	3 42	17 55	3 16	18 15
14	5 09	18 15	4 57	18 22	4 41	18 32
15	6 16	18 48	6 12	18 49	6 07	18 49
16	7 23	19 22	7 27	19 15	7 33	19 05
17	8 32	19 58	8 43	19 43	9 00	19 23
18	9 41	20 37	10 01	20 15	10 28	19 45
19	10 52	21 22	11 18	20 53	11 57	20 13
20	12 01	22 13	12 33	21 40	13 21	20 51
21	13 07	23 10	13 42	22 35	14 34	21 42
22	14 07	....	14 42	23 37	15 33	22 47
23	14 59	0 12	15 30	....	16 16	....
24	15 43	1 15	16 09	0 45	16 47	0 01
25	16 20	2 18	16 41	1 53	17 09	1 18
26	16 53	3 18	17 07	3 00	17 27	2 34

MOON Rise and Set

LOCAL MEAN TIME at MERIDIAN OF GREENWICH. To obtain CLOCK TIME, see *About Time* p. 8

	30°N Rise	30°N Set	40°N Rise	40°N Set	50°N Rise	50°N Set
	h m	h m	h m	h m	h m	h m
Sept. 27	17 22	4 17	17 30	4 05	17 41	3 48
28	17 49	5 12	17 51	5 07	17 54	5 00
29	18 16	6 07	18 12	6 08	18 06	6 09
30	18 43	7 01	18 33	7 08	18 19	7 18
Oct. 1	19 11	7 55	18 55	8 08	18 34	8 27
2	19 42	8 49	19 21	9 09	18 51	9 37
3	20 17	9 45	19 50	10 11	19 12	10 47
4	20 57	10 42	20 26	11 13	19 40	11 57
5	21 43	11 39	21 09	12 13	20 18	13 02
6	22 36	12 34	22 01	13 09	21 09	14 01
7	23 34	13 25	23 00	13 59	22 12	14 49
8	....	14 13	....	14 43	23 26	15 26
9	0 36	14 55	0 07	15 20	....	15 55
10	1 40	15 34	1 18	15 52	0 46	16 17
11	2 46	16 09	2 31	16 21	2 09	16 36
12	3 53	16 43	3 45	16 47	3 34	16 52
13	5 00	17 17	5 00	17 13	5 00	17 08
14	6 09	17 52	6 17	17 41	6 28	17 25
15	7 20	18 30	7 36	18 11	7 58	17 45
16	8 33	19 14	8 57	18 48	9 31	18 11
17	9 46	20 04	10 16	19 32	11 01	18 46
18	10 56	21 01	11 31	20 26	12 22	19 34
19	12 00	22 03	12 36	21 28	13 29	20 36
20	12 56	23 07	13 29	22 36	14 17	21 49
21	13 43	....	14 11	23 45	14 52	23 06
22	14 22	0 11	14 45	....	15 16	....
23	14 56	1 13	15 13	0 52	15 35	0 23
24	15 26	2 11	15 36	1 57	15 50	1 38
25	15 53	3 07	15 57	3 00	16 03	2 49
26	16 20	4 01	16 18	4 00	16 15	3 59
27	16 46	4 55	16 38	5 00	16 27	5 07
28	17 14	5 49	17 00	6 00	16 41	6 16
29	17 44	6 43	17 24	7 01	16 57	7 25
30	18 17	7 39	17 52	8 02	17 16	8 36
31	18 55	8 35	18 25	9 04	17 42	9 46
Nov. 1	19 39	9 32	19 05	10 05	18 16	10 53
2	20 29	10 28	19 54	11 03	19 02	11 54
3	21 24	11 20	20 50	11 55	19 59	12 46
4	22 23	12 08	21 52	12 40	21 08	13 26
5	23 25	12 51	23 00	13 18	22 23	13 57
6	....	13 30	....	13 51	23 43	14 20
7	0 28	14 05	0 09	14 20	....	14 40
8	1 32	14 38	1 20	14 46	1 04	14 56

	30°N Rise	30°N Set	40°N Rise	40°N Set	50°N Rise	50°N Set
	h m	h m	h m	h m	h m	h m
Nov. 9	2 37	15 11	2 33	15 11	2 27	15 12
10	3 44	15 44	3 47	15 37	3 52	15 28
11	4 53	16 21	5 04	16 06	5 20	15 46
12	6 05	17 02	6 25	16 39	6 52	16 08
13	7 20	17 49	7 47	17 20	8 26	16 38
14	8 34	18 45	9 07	18 11	9 56	17 21
15	9 44	19 47	10 20	19 12	11 13	18 18
16	10 46	20 54	11 21	20 20	12 11	19 30
17	11 38	22 00	12 09	21 31	12 52	20 50
18	12 22	23 04	12 46	22 41	13 21	22 09
19	12 58	....	13 16	23 49	13 42	23 26
20	13 29	0 05	13 41	....	13 58	....
21	13 57	1 02	14 03	0 52	14 11	0 39
22	14 24	1 57	14 24	1 54	14 24	1 49
23	14 50	2 50	14 44	2 53	14 36	2 58
24	15 17	3 43	15 05	3 53	14 49	4 06
25	15 46	4 37	15 28	4 53	15 04	5 15
26	16 18	5 33	15 55	5 54	15 22	6 25
27	16 55	6 29	16 26	6 56	15 45	7 35
28	17 37	7 26	17 04	7 58	16 17	8 44
29	18 25	8 23	17 50	8 57	16 59	9 48
30	19 19	9 16	18 44	9 51	17 53	10 43
Dec. 1	20 17	10 05	19 45	10 38	18 58	11 26
2	21 17	10 50	20 50	11 18	20 11	11 59
3	22 18	11 29	21 57	11 52	21 28	12 25
4	23 20	12 04	23 06	12 12	22 46	12 45
5	....	12 37	....	12 47	....	13 01
6	0 22	13 08	0 15	13 12	0 05	13 16
7	1 25	13 40	1 25	13 36	1 25	13 31
8	2 30	14 13	2 38	14 02	2 49	13 48
9	3 39	14 51	3 54	14 32	4 16	14 07
10	4 51	15 34	5 14	15 08	5 47	14 32
11	6 05	16 25	6 35	15 53	7 19	15 08
12	7 18	17 25	7 53	16 50	8 45	15 57
13	8 28	18 31	9 02	17 56	9 54	17 04
14	9 25	19 40	9 58	19 09	10 45	18 23
15	10 14	20 48	10 42	20 23	11 20	19 46
16	10 55	21 52	11 16	21 34	11 45	21 07
17	11 29	22 52	11 43	22 41	12 03	22 24
18	11 59	23 49	12 07	23 44	12 18	23 37
19	12 26	....	12 28	....	12 31	....
20	12 53	0 44	12 49	0 45	12 43	0 46
21	13 19	1 37	13 09	1 45	12 56	1 55

MOON Phases

GREENWICH MEAN TIME. To obtain CLOCK TIME, see *About Time* p. 8

Lunation	New Moon d h m	First Quarter d h m	Full Moon d h m	Last Quarter d h m
767	Dec. 22 11 47	Dec. 30 05 27	Jan. 7 02 16	Jan. 13 23 27
768	Jan. 21 02 28	Jan. 29 03 29	Feb. 5 15 19	Feb. 12 07 57
769	Feb. 19 18 43	Feb. 27 23 41	Mar. 7 02 13	Mar. 13 17 34
770	Mar. 21 11 59	Mar. 29 16 11	Apr. 5 11 32	Apr. 12 04 41
771	Apr. 20 05 22	Apr. 28 04 25	May 4 19 53	May 11 17 34
772	May 19 21 41	May 27 12 56	June 3 03 50	June 10 08 19
773	June 18 11 58	June 25 18 53	July 2 12 08	July 10 00 49
774	July 17 23 56	July 24 23 39	July 31 21 41	Aug. 8 18 29
775	Aug. 16 10 06	Aug. 23 04 36	Aug. 30 09 27	Sept. 7 12 16
776	Sept. 14 19 20	Sept. 21 11 03	Sept. 29 00 08	Oct. 7 05 04
777	Oct. 14 04 33	Oct. 20 20 13	Oct. 28 17 38	Nov 5 20 07
778	Nov. 12 14 20	Nov. 19 09 04	Nov. 27 12 42	Dec. 5 09 01
779	Dec. 12 00 54	Dec. 19 01 58		

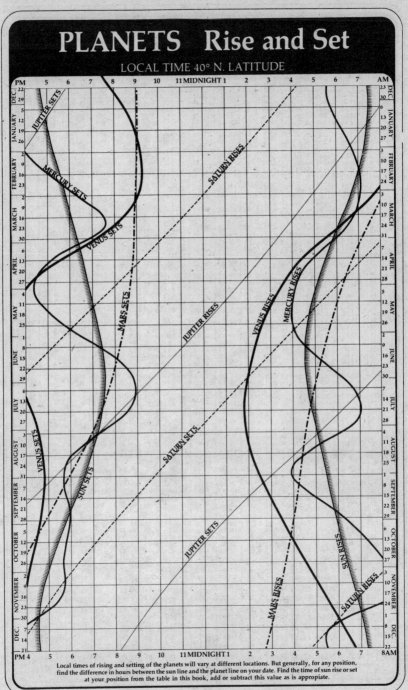

PLANETS Rise and Set
LOCAL TIME 40° N. LATITUDE

Local times of rising and setting of the planets will vary at different locations. But generally, for any position, find the difference in hours between the sun line and the planet line on your date. Find the time of sun rise or set at your position from the table in this book, add or subtract this value as is appropiate.

SUN Rise and Set

	25°N Rise	25°N Set	30°N Rise	30°N Set	34°N Rise	34°N Set	38°N Rise	38°N Set	42°N Rise	42°N Set	46°N Rise	46°N Set	50°N Rise	50°N Set
	h. m.	h. m.	h. m.	h. m.	h. m.	h. m.	h. m.	h. m.	h. m.	h. m.	h. m.	h. m.	h. m.	h. m.
Dec. 21	6 41	17 16	6 52	17 05	7 02	16 54	7 13	16 43	7 25	16 31	7 39	16 17	8 06	15 50
26	6 43	17 18	6 54	17 07	7 04	16 57	7 15	16 46	7 27	16 34	7 41	16 20	8 08	15 54
31	6 45	17 21	6 56	17 10	7 06	17 00	7 17	16 49	7 28	16 38	7 42	16 24	8 08	15 58
Jan. 1	6 45	17 22	6 56	17 11	7 06	17 02	7 16	16 51	7 28	16 39	7 42	16 25	7 59	16 09
6	6 46	17 26	6 57	17 15	7 06	17 06	7 17	16 56	7 28	16 44	7 42	16 30	7 58	16 14
11	6 47	17 29	6 57	17 19	7 05	17 10	7 16	17 00	7 27	16 49	7 40	16 36	7 56	16 21
16	6 47	17 33	6 57	17 23	7 05	17 15	7 15	17 05	7 25	16 55	7 38	16 42	7 52	16 28
21	6 46	17 37	6 55	17 28	7 04	17 20	7 12	17 11	7 22	17 01	7 34	16 49	7 48	16 36
26	6 45	17 41	6 54	17 32	7 01	17 25	7 09	17 16	7 19	17 07	7 30	16 56	7 42	16 44
31	6 43	17 44	6 51	17 36	6 58	17 29	7 06	17 22	7 14	17 13	7 24	17 04	7 35	16 52
Feb. 5	6 41	17 48	6 48	17 41	6 54	17 34	7 01	17 27	7 09	17 20	7 18	17 11	7 28	17 01
10	6 38	17 51	6 44	17 45	6 50	17 39	6 56	17 33	7 03	17 26	7 11	17 18	7 20	17 09
15	6 35	17 54	6 40	17 49	6 45	17 44	6 50	17 39	6 56	17 33	7 03	17 26	7 11	17 18
20	6 31	17 57	6 36	17 53	6 40	17 48	6 44	17 44	6 49	17 39	6 55	17 33	7 02	17 27
25	6 27	18 00	6 31	17 56	6 34	17 53	6 38	17 49	6 42	17 45	6 47	17 40	6 52	17 35
Mar. 2	6 22	18 03	6 25	18 00	6 28	17 57	6 31	17 54	6 34	17 51	6 38	17 48	6 42	17 43
7	6 18	18 05	6 20	18 03	6 22	18 01	6 24	17 59	6 26	17 57	6 29	17 55	6 32	17 52
12	6 13	18 08	6 14	18 06	6 15	18 05	6 16	18 04	6 18	18 03	6 19	18 01	6 21	18 00
17	6 08	18 10	6 08	18 10	6 09	18 09	6 09	18 09	6 09	18 09	6 10	18 08	6 10	18 08
22	6 02	18 12	6 02	18 13	6 01	18 13	6 01	18 14	6 01	18 14	6 00	18 15	5 59	18 16
27	5 57	18 14	5 56	18 16	5 55	18 17	5 53	18 18	5 52	18 20	5 50	18 22	5 48	18 24
Apr. 1	5 52	18 16	5 50	18 19	5 48	18 21	5 46	18 23	5 43	18 25	5 41	18 28	5 37	18 32
6	5 47	18 18	5 44	18 22	5 41	18 24	5 38	18 27	5 35	18 31	5 31	18 35	5 27	18 39
11	5 42	18 21	5 38	18 25	5 35	18 28	5 31	18 32	5 27	18 36	5 22	18 41	5 16	18 47
16	5 37	18 23	5 33	18 28	5 28	18 32	5 24	18 37	5 19	18 42	5 13	18 48	5 06	18 55
21	5 33	18 25	5 27	18 31	5 22	18 36	5 17	18 41	5 11	18 48	5 04	18 55	4 56	19 03
26	5 28	18 28	5 22	18 34	5 17	18 40	5 10	18 46	5 03	18 53	4 55	19 01	4 46	19 11
May 1	5 25	18 30	5 17	18 37	5 11	18 43	5 04	18 51	4 56	18 58	4 47	19 08	4 37	19 18
6	5 21	18 33	5 13	18 40	5 06	18 47	4 59	18 55	4 50	19 04	4 40	19 14	4 28	19 26
11	5 18	18 35	5 09	18 44	5 02	18 51	4 54	19 00	4 44	19 09	4 33	19 20	4 20	19 33
16	5 15	18 38	5 06	18 47	4 58	18 55	4 49	19 04	4 39	19 14	4 27	19 26	4 13	19 40
21	5 13	18 40	5 03	18 50	4 55	18 59	4 45	19 08	4 34	19 19	4 22	19 32	4 07	19 47
26	5 11	18 43	5 01	18 53	4 52	19 02	4 42	19 12	4 31	19 24	4 17	19 37	4 01	19 53
31	5 10	18 45	5 00	18 56	4 50	19 05	4 40	19 16	4 28	19 28	4 14	19 42	3 57	19 59
June 5	5 10	18 47	4 59	18 58	4 49	19 08	4 38	19 19	4 25	19 32	4 11	19 46	3 53	20 04
10	5 10	18 49	4 58	19 01	4 48	19 11	4 37	19 22	4 24	19 37	4 09	19 50	3 51	20 08
15	5 10	18 51	4 58	19 02	4 48	19 14	4 37	19 24	4 24	19 39	4 09	19 52	3 50	20 11
20	5 11	18 52	4 59	19 04	4 49	19 14	4 37	19 26	4 24	19 39	4 09	19 54	3 50	20 13
25	5 12	18 53	5 00	19 05	4 51	19 15	4 38	19 26	4 25	19 40	4 10	19 55	3 52	20 13
30	5 13	18 54	5 02	19 05	4 52	19 15	4 40	19 27	4 27	19 40	4 12	19 55	3 54	20 13
July 5	5 15	18 54	5 04	19 05	4 54	19 15	4 43	19 26	4 30	19 39	4 15	19 53	3 58	20 11
10	5 17	18 53	5 06	19 04	4 57	19 14	4 46	19 25	4 33	19 37	4 19	19 51	4 02	20 08
15	5 19	18 52	5 09	19 03	5 00	19 12	4 49	19 22	4 37	19 34	4 24	19 48	4 07	20 04
20	5 22	18 51	5 12	19 01	5 03	19 10	4 53	19 19	4 41	19 31	4 28	19 44	4 13	19 59
25	5 24	18 49	5 15	18 58	5 06	19 06	4 57	19 16	4 46	19 26	4 34	19 38	4 19	19 53
30	5 26	18 46	5 18	18 55	5 10	19 03	5 01	19 11	4 51	19 21	4 40	19 32	4 26	19 46
Aug. 4	5 29	18 43	5 20	18 51	5 13	18 58	5 05	19 06	4 56	19 15	4 46	19 26	4 33	19 38
9	5 31	18 40	5 24	18 47	5 17	18 54	5 09	19 01	5 01	19 09	4 52	19 19	4 40	19 30
14	5 33	18 36	5 27	18 42	5 21	18 48	5 14	18 55	5 06	19 02	4 58	19 11	4 48	19 21
19	5 35	18 31	5 29	18 37	5 24	18 43	5 18	18 48	5 12	18 55	5 04	19 02	4 55	19 11
24	5 38	18 27	5 32	18 32	5 28	18 37	5 23	18 42	5 17	18 47	5 10	18 54	5 02	19 01
29	5 40	18 22	5 35	18 26	5 31	18 30	5 27	18 34	5 22	18 39	5 16	18 45	5 10	18 51
Sept. 3	5 42	18 17	5 38	18 21	5 35	18 24	5 31	18 27	5 27	18 31	5 23	18 35	5 17	18 40
8	5 43	18 12	5 41	18 14	5 38	18 17	5 35	18 19	5 32	18 22	5 29	18 26	5 25	18 30
13	5 45	18 07	5 43	18 08	5 42	18 10	5 40	18 12	5 38	18 14	5 35	18 16	5 32	18 19
18	5 47	18 01	5 46	18 02	5 45	18 03	5 44	18 04	5 43	18 05	5 41	18 06	5 40	18 08
23	5 49	17 56	5 49	17 56	5 49	17 56	5 48	17 56	5 48	17 56	5 48	17 56	5 47	17 57
28	5 51	17 50	5 51	17 50	5 52	17 49	5 53	17 48	5 53	17 47	5 54	17 47	5 55	17 46
Oct. 3	5 53	17 45	5 54	17 43	5 56	17 42	5 57	17 41	5 59	17 39	6 01	17 37	6 03	17 35
8	5 55	17 40	5 57	17 38	5 59	17 35	6 02	17 33	6 04	17 30	6 07	17 27	6 10	17 24
13	5 57	17 35	6 00	17 32	6 03	17 29	6 06	17 25	6 10	17 22	6 14	17 18	6 18	17 14
18	6 00	17 31	6 04	17 26	6 07	17 23	6 11	17 19	6 16	17 14	6 20	17 09	6 26	17 04
23	6 02	17 26	6 07	17 21	6 11	17 17	6 16	17 12	6 21	17 07	6 27	17 01	6 34	16 54
28	6 05	17 22	6 11	17 17	6 16	17 12	6 21	17 06	6 27	17 00	6 34	16 53	6 43	16 44
Nov. 2	6 08	17 19	6 14	17 12	6 20	17 07	6 26	17 00	6 34	16 53	6 42	16 45	6 51	16 36
7	6 11	17 16	6 18	17 09	6 25	17 02	6 32	16 55	6 40	16 47	6 49	16 38	6 59	16 28
12	6 14	17 14	6 22	17 06	6 29	16 59	6 37	16 51	6 46	16 42	6 56	16 32	7 08	16 20
17	6 18	17 12	6 26	17 03	6 34	16 56	6 43	16 47	6 52	16 38	7 03	16 27	7 16	16 14
22	6 21	17 11	6 31	17 01	6 39	16 53	6 48	16 44	6 58	16 34	7 10	16 22	7 24	16 08
27	6 25	17 10	6 35	17 00	6 44	16 51	6 53	16 42	7 04	16 31	7 16	16 19	7 31	16 04
Dec. 2	6 29	17 10	6 39	17 00	6 48	16 51	6 58	16 41	7 09	16 29	7 22	16 16	7 38	16 01
7	6 32	17 11	6 43	17 00	6 52	16 51	7 02	16 40	7 14	16 29	7 28	16 15	7 44	15 59
12	6 35	17 12	6 46	17 01	6 56	16 52	7 07	16 41	7 19	16 29	7 33	16 15	7 49	15 58
17	6 38	17 14	6 49	17 03	6 59	16 53	7 10	16 42	7 22	16 30	7 36	16 16	7 53	15 59

SUN Right Ascension & Declination

Date	R.A. (h m)	Dec. (° ')	Date	R.A. (h m)	Dec. (° ')	Date	R.A. (h m)	Dec. (° ')	Date	R.A. (h m)	Dec. (° ')	Date	R.A. (h m)	Dec. (° ')
21	17 56	-23 26	4	22 58	-6 32	May 16	3 30	+19 02	28	8 28	+19 03	9	12 57	-6 09
22	18 01	23 26	5	23 02	6 09	17	3 34	19 16	29	8 32	18 49	10	13 01	6 32
23	18 05	23 26	6	23 06	5 46	18	3 38	19 29	30	8 36	18 34	11	13 04	6 54
24	18 10	23 25	7	23 09	5 22	19	3 42	19 42	31	8 40	18 20	12	13 08	7 17
25	18 14	23 23	8	23 13	4 59	20	3 46	19 55	Aug. 1	8 44	18 05	13	13 12	7 40
26	18 19	-23 22	9	23 17	-4 36	21	3 50	+20 07	2	8 48	+17 50	14	13 16	-8 02
27	18 23	23 19	10	23 20	4 12	22	3 54	20 19	3	8 52	17 34	15	13 19	8 24
28	18 28	23 17	11	23 24	3 49	23	3 58	20 31	4	8 56	17 19	16	13 23	8 47
29	18 32	23 13	12	23 28	3 25	24	4 02	20 43	5	8 59	17 03	17	13 27	9 09
30	18 36	23 10	13	23 31	3 01	25	4 06	20 54	6	9 03	16 46	18	13 30	9 31
31	18 41	-23 06	14	23 35	-2 38	26	4 10	+21 04	7	9 07	+16 30	19	13 34	-9 52
Jan. 1	18 45	23 01	15	23 39	2 14	27	4 15	21 15	8	9 11	16 13	20	13 38	10 14
2	18 50	22 56	16	23 42	1 50	28	4 19	21 25	9	9 15	15 56	21	13 42	10 35
3	18 54	22 50	17	23 46	1 27	29	4 23	21 34	10	9 19	15 38	22	13 46	10 57
4	18 58	22 45	18	23 50	1 03	30	4 27	21 43	11	9 22	15 21	23	13 49	11 18
5	19 03	-22 38	19	23 53	-0 39	31	4 31	+21 52	12	9 26	+15 03	24	13 53	-11 39
6	19 07	22 31	20	23 57	-0 16	June 1	4 35	22 01	13	9 30	14 45	25	13 57	12 00
7	19 12	22 24	21	0 01	+0 07	2	4 39	22 09	14	9 34	14 27	26	14 01	12 20
8	19 16	22 16	22	0 04	0 31	3	4 43	22 16	15	9 37	14 08	27	14 05	12 41
9	19 20	22 08	23	0 08	0 55	4	4 47	22 24	16	9 41	13 49	28	14 08	13 01
10	19 25	-21 59	24	0 12	+1 18	5	4 51	+22 31	17	9 45	+13 30	29	14 12	-13 21
11	19 29	21 50	25	0 15	1 42	6	4 55	22 37	18	9 49	13 11	30	14 16	13 41
12	19 33	21 41	26	0 19	2 05	7	5 00	22 43	19	9 52	12 52	31	14 20	14 01
13	19 38	21 31	27	0 23	2 29	8	5 04	22 49	20	9 56	12 32	Nov. 1	14 24	14 20
14	19 42	21 21	28	0 26	2 52	9	5 08	22 54	21	10 00	12 12	2	14 28	14 39
15	19 46	-21 10	29	0 30	+3 16	10	5 12	+22 59	22	10 03	+11 52	3	14 32	-14 58
16	19 51	20 59	30	0 33	3 39	11	5 16	23 04	23	10 07	11 32	4	14 36	15 17
17	19 55	20 47	31	0 37	4 03	12	5 20	23 08	24	10 11	11 11	5	14 40	15 35
18	19 59	20 35	Apr. 1	0 41	4 26	13	5 24	23 11	25	10 15	10 51	6	14 44	15 53
19	20 03	20 23	2	0 44	4 49	14	5 29	23 15	26	10 18	10 30	7	14 48	16 11
20	20 08	-20 10	3	0 48	+5 12	15	5 33	+23 17	27	10 22	+10 09	8	14 52	-16 29
21	20 12	19 57	4	0 52	5 35	16	5 37	23 20	28	10 25	9 48	9	14 56	16 46
22	20 16	19 44	5	0 55	5 58	17	5 41	23 22	29	10 29	9 27	10	15 00	17 03
23	20 20	19 30	6	0 59	6 20	18	5 45	23 24	30	10 33	9 06	11	15 04	17 20
24	20 25	19 16	7	1 03	6 43	19	5 49	23 25	31	10 36	8 44	12	15 08	17 37
25	20 29	-19 01	8	1 06	+7 06	20	5 53	+23 26	Sept. 1	10 40	+8 22	13	15 12	-17 53
26	20 33	18 46	9	1 10	7 28	21	5 58	23 26	2	10 44	8 01	14	15 16	18 09
27	20 37	18 31	10	1 14	7 50	22	6 02	23 26	3	10 47	7 39	15	15 20	18 24
28	20 41	18 16	11	1 17	8 12	23	6 06	23 26	4	10 51	7 17	16	15 24	18 40
29	20 45	18 00	12	1 21	8 34	24	6 10	23 25	5	10 55	6 55	17	15 28	18 55
30	20 49	-17 43	13	1 25	+8 56	25	6 14	+23 23	6	10 58	+6 32	18	15 33	-19 09
31	20 54	17 27	14	1 28	9 18	26	6 18	23 22	7	11 02	6 10	19	15 37	19 23
Feb. 1	20 58	17 10	15	1 32	9 40	27	6 23	23 20	8	11 05	5 47	20	15 41	19 37
2	21 02	16 53	16	1 36	10 01	28	6 27	23 17	9	11 09	5 25	21	15 45	19 51
3	21 06	16 35	17	1 39	10 22	29	6 31	23 14	10	11 13	5 02	22	15 49	20 04
4	21 10	-16 18	18	1 43	+10 43	30	6 35	+23 11	11	11 16	+4 39	23	15 53	-20 17
5	21 14	16 00	19	1 47	11 04	July 1	6 39	23 07	12	11 20	4 17	24	15 58	20 29
6	21 18	15 41	20	1 51	11 25	2	6 43	23 03	13	11 23	3 54	25	16 02	20 41
7	21 22	15 23	21	1 54	11 45	3	6 47	22 59	14	11 27	3 31	26	16 06	20 53
8	21 26	15 04	22	1 58	12 06	4	6 52	22 54	15	11 30	3 08	27	16 10	21 04
9	21 30	-14 45	23	2 02	+12 26	5	6 56	+22 48	16	11 34	+2 45	28	16 15	-21 15
10	21 34	14 26	24	2 06	12 46	6	7 00	22 43	17	11 38	2 21	29	16 19	21 25
11	21 38	14 06	25	2 09	13 06	7	7 04	22 37	18	11 41	1 58	30	16 23	21 36
12	21 42	13 46	26	2 13	13 25	8	7 08	22 30	19	11 45	1 35	Dec. 1	16 28	21 45
13	21 46	13 26	27	2 17	13 44	9	7 12	22 23	20	11 48	1 12	2	16 32	21 54
14	21 50	-13 06	28	2 21	+14 03	10	7 16	+22 16	21	11 52	+0 48	3	16 36	-22 03
15	21 53	12 46	29	2 24	14 22	11	7 20	22 08	22	11 56	0 25	4	16 41	22 12
16	21 57	12 25	30	2 28	14 41	12	7 24	22 00	23	11 59	+0 02	5	16 45	22 20
17	22 01	12 04	May 1	2 32	14 59	13	7 28	21 52	24	12 03	-0 21	6	16 49	22 27
18	22 05	11 43	2	2 36	15 17	14	7 32	21 43	25	12 06	0 44	7	16 54	22 34
19	22 09	-11 22	3	2 40	+15 35	15	7 37	+21 34	26	12 10	-1 08	8	16 58	-22 41
20	22 13	11 00	4	2 44	15 53	16	7 41	21 24	27	12 14	1 31	9	17 02	22 47
21	22 17	10 39	5	2 47	16 10	17	7 45	21 14	28	12 17	1 54	10	17 07	22 53
22	22 20	10 17	6	2 51	16 27	18	7 49	21 04	29	12 21	2 18	11	17 11	22 58
23	22 24	9 55	7	2 55	16 44	19	7 53	20 53	30	12 24	2 41	12	17 16	23 03
24	22 28	-9 33	8	2 59	+17 00	20	7 57	+20 43	Oct. 1	12 28	-3 04	13	17 20	-23 07
25	22 32	9 11	9	3 03	17 17	21	8 01	20 31	2	12 32	3 27	14	17 24	23 11
26	22 36	8 49	10	3 07	17 32	22	8 05	20 20	3	12 35	3 51	15	17 29	23 15
27	22 39	8 26	11	3 11	17 48	23	8 09	20 08	4	12 39	4 14	16	17 33	23 18
28	22 43	8 03	12	3 15	18 03	24	8 13	19 55	5	12 43	4 37	17	17 38	23 20
Mar. 1	22 47	-7 41	13	3 19	+18 18	25	8 17	+19 42	6	12 46	-5 00	18	17 42	-23 22
2	22 51	7 18	14	3 23	18 33	26	8 21	19 29	7	12 50	5 23	19	17 47	23 24
3	22 54	6 55	15	3 26	18 48	27	8 24	19 16	8	12 53	5 46	20	17 51	23 25

THE PLANETS

	MERCURY	VENUS	EARTH	MARS	JUPITER	SATURN	URANUS	NEPTUNE	PLUTO
Maximum Distance from Sun (Millions of Kilometers)	69.7	109	152.1	249.1	815.7	1,507	3,004	4,537	7399
Minimum Distance from Sun (Millions of Kilometers)	45.9	107.4	147.1	206.7	740.9	1,347	2,735	4,456	4422
Mean Distance from Sun (Millions of Kilometers)	57.9	108.2	149.6	227.9	778.3	1,427	2,869.6	4,496.6	5910
Mean Distance from Sun (Astronomical Units)	.387	.723	1	1.524	5.203	9.539	19.18	30.06	39.53
Period of Revolution	88 d	224.7 d	365.26 d	687 d	11.86 y	29.46 y	84.01 y	164.1 y	248.7 y
Period of Rotation	59 d	243 d Retrograde	23 H 56 m 4 s	24 h 37 m 23 s	9 h 55 m 30 s	10 h 39 m 20 s	23 h 54 m Retrograde	16 h	6 d 9 h 18 m Retrograde
Orbital Velocity (Kilometers per Second)	47.9	35	29.8	24.1	13.1	9.6	6.8	5.4	4.7
Inclination of Axis	2°	3°	23°27'	25°12'	3°05'	26°44'	97°55'	28°48'	65°
Inclination of Orbit to Ecliptic	7°	3.4°	0°	1.9°	1.3°	2.5°	.8°	1.8°	17.2°
Eccentricity of Orbit	.206	.007	.017	.093	.048	.056	.047	.009	.25
Equatorial Diameter (Kilometers)	4,880	12,104	12,756	6,787	142,800	120,400	51,800	49,500	4000
Mass (Earth = 1)	.055	.815	1	.108	317.9	95.2	14.6	17.2	.0024
Volume (Earth = 1)	.06	.88	1	.15	1,316	755	67	57	.03
Density (Water = 1)	5.4	5.2	5.5	3.9	1.3	.7	1.2	1.7	0.5
Atmosphere (Main Components)	None	Carbon Dioxide	Nitrogen, Oxygen	Carbon Dioxide	Hydrogen, Helium	Hydrogen, Helium	Helium, Hydrogen, Methane	Hydrogen, Helium, Methane	Methane
Atmospheric Pressure at Surface (Milibars)	10^{-9}	90,000	1,000	6	?	?	?	?	?
Mean Temperature at Visible Surface (°C) S=Solid, C=Clouds	350(S) Day -170(S)Night	-33 (C) 480 (S)	22 (S)	-23 (S)	-150 (C)	-180 (C)	-210 (C)	-220 (C)	-236?
Known Satellites	0	0	1	2	16	21	5	2	1
Surface Gravity (Earth = 1)	.37	.88	1	.38	2.64	1.15	1.17	1.18	0.024
Escape Velocity (Kilometers/Second)	4.2	10.3	11.2	5.0	61	37	22	25	.98
Stellar Magnitude	-1.2 to 1.1	-4.3 to -3.3	—	-2.8 to 1.6	-2.5 to -1.4	-0.4 to 0.9	5.7 to 5.9	7.7	14.5

The Twenty Five BRIGHTEST STARS

#	Bayer Name	Proper Name	Visual Magnitude	Spectral Type	Effective Temperature °K	Color	Distance Light Years	Declination ° ' "	Right Ascension h m s	Radius x Sun's	Mass x Sun's	Luminosity x Sun's	Notes
1		Sun	-26.73	G2 V	5,800	Yellow	1.5×10^{-5}			1	1	1	
2	α Canis Majoris	Sirius	-1.46	A1 V	10,400	Green	8.7	-16 41 44	06 44 31	1.8	2.4	23	Double
3	α Carinae	Canopus	-0.72	F0 II	7,500	White	98	-52 41 15	06 23 38	30	8	1400	
4	α Bootis	Arcturus	-0.04	K2 IIIp	4,250	Orange	36	+19 15 27	14 14 60	30	4	115	
5	α Lyrae	Vega	+0.03	A0 Va	9,500	Green	26.5	+38 46 11	18 36 27	2.2	3	58	Double
6	α Aurigae	Capella	0.08	G8 III	5,000	Orange	45	+45 59 04	05 16 41	13	4.2	150	Double
7	β Orionis	Rigel	0.12	B8 Ia	11,200	Blue	900	-08 13 04	05 14 32	50	50	57,000	Double
8	α Centauri A	Rigel Kentarus	0.33	G2 V	5,800	Yellow	4.3	-60 46 34	14 38 37	1.1	1.1	1.5	Double
9	α Canis Minoris	Procyon	0.38	F5 IV-V	6,450	White	11.3	+05 15 46	07 38 33	2.2	1.8	6	Double
10	α Eridani	Achernar	0.46	B3 Vp	14,000	Blue	118	-57 18 36	01 37 11	7	6	650	
11	α Orionis	Betelgeuse	0.50	M2 Iab	3,800	Red	520	+07 24 19	05 54 23	920	20	14,000	Var. Dbl.
12	β Centauri	Hadar	0.61	B1 III	22,000	Blue	490	-60 18 13	14 02 48	11	25	3100	Var. Dbl.
13	α Aquilae	Altair	0.77	A7 IV-V	8,250	Green	16.5	+08 49 46	19 50 05	1.4	2	9	Double
14	α Tauri A	Aldebaran	0.85	K5 III	3,900	Orange	68	+16 28 51	04 35 05	40	4	125	Double
15	α Scorpii A	Antares	0.96	M1.5 Iab	3,600	Red	520	-26 24 03	16 28 31	700	20	9,000	Var. Dbl.
16	α Virginis	Spica	0.97	B1 IV	20,000	Blue	220	-11 05 09	13 24 26	8.1	13	2,300	Variable
17	β Geminorum	Pollux	1.14	K0 IIIb	4,100	Orange	35	+28 03 43	07 44 26	8	2.7	35	
18	α Piscis Austrini	Fomalhaut	1.16	A3 V	9,300	Yellow	22.6	-29 41 58	22 56 51	2	2	14	Double
19	β Crucis	Mimosa	1.25	B0.5 III	26,600	Blue	490	-59 36 35	12 46 52	9	12	5,800	
20	α Cygni	Deneb	1.25	A2 Ia	9,500	Yellow	1600	+45 13 41	20 40 56	60	25	60,000	
21	α Leonis A	Regulus	1.35	B7 V	13,000	Blue	84	+12 02 19	10 07 36	5	5	160	Var. Dbl.
22	ε Canis Majoris A	Adara	1.50	B2 II	21,000	Blue	680	-28 57 06	06 58 03	10	31	9,000	
23	α Crucis A	Acrux	1.58	B0.5 IV	18,000	Blue	370	-63 01 08	12 25 47	9	15	3,000	Double
24	λ Scorpii	Shaula	1.63	B1.5 IV	20,000	Blue	200	-37 05 39	17 32 37	11	9	2,200	Double
25	γ Orionis	Bellatrix	1.64	B2 III	21,000	Blue	230	+06 20 14	05 24 21	11	9	2,500	Double

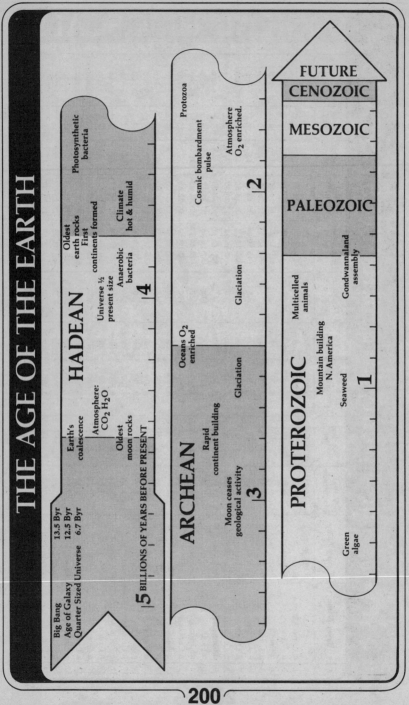

THE AGE OF THE EARTH

Big Bang 13.5 Byr
Age of Galaxy 12.5 Byr
Quarter Sized Universe 6.7 Byr

|5 BILLIONS OF YEARS BEFORE PRESENT

HADEAN

Earth's coalescence

Atmosphere: CO_2 H_2O

Oldest moon rocks

Universe ½ present size

Anaerobic bacteria

Oldest earth rocks
First continents formed

Climate hot & humid

Photosynthetic bacteria

|4

ARCHEAN

Rapid continent building

Oceans O_2 enriched

Moon ceases geological activity

Glaciation

|3

Protozoa

Cosmic bombardment pulse

Atmosphere O_2 enriched.

Glaciation

|2

PROTEROZOIC

Multicelled animals

Mountain building N. America

Green algae

Seaweed

Gondwannaland assembly

|1

PALEOZOIC

MESOZOIC

CENOZOIC

FUTURE

GEOLOGICAL TIME SCALE

ERA	PERIOD	EPOCH	M.Y.*	GEOLOGICAL & CLIMATIC HISTORY	BIOLOGICAL HISTORY
Cenozoic	Quaternary	Holocene	.01	The interglacial interludes of the Pleistocene have ranged between five and ten thousand years. The last glaciation ended ten thousand years ago. We may still be in the Pleistocene!	
		Pleistocene	2	The Great Ice Age. Rapid uplift of Sierra Nevada Mountains. Volcanoes erupt in mountains of western N. America.	Early species of Homo replaced by Homo sapiens. Peak of Mammals followed by widespread extinction.
	Tertiary	Pliocene	5.1	Panama lifted, North and South America reconnected. Mountain building including Pacific Coast Ranges. Climate cools, glaciation begins. Mediterranean refills.	First apemen, Australopithicus, followed by Homo. Large carnivores, horses, cattle roam the plains. Exchange of animals between N. and S. America.
		Miocene	25	Italy collides with Europe pushing up the Alps. Southern Hemisphere glaciation. Mediterranean dries up. Basin and Range, and Rocky Mountains uplifted.	Whales, apes and grazers proliferate. Typical grasses appear and displace forests.
		Oligocene	36	South America and Antarctica split. San Andreas Fault opens Gulf of California. First cooling foretelling the Great Ice Age.	Modern families appear: monkey, cat, dog, elephant. Giant herbivores dominate northern continents.
		Eocene	55	India collides with Eurasia pushing up the Himalayas. Australia and Antarctica split. Cosmic impact forms 100 km crater in USSR.	Significant evolution of birds. Primitive horses, camels and rodents present. Whales appear.
		Paleocene	65	North America and Europe split. Increased seasonality, overall warming. Early uplift of Rocky Mountains.	Dominance of archaic mammals. Diversification of birds, primates and carnivores. First grasses appear.
Mesozoic	Cretaceous		145	Gondwannaland breaks up. Three oceanic anoxic events. Vast inland seas form then retreat.	Extinction of dinosaurs. Angiosperms appear and become dominant plants. Diatoms appear.
	Jurassic		210	N. America and Africa split, Atlantic ocean opens. Climate becomes more stable. Formation of Sierra Nevada granite begins.	Dinosaurs' zenith. Birds appear. Cycads and ferns abundant.
	Triassic		250	Assembly of Asia. Pangaea breakup begins with spreading Tethys Sea.	Dinosaurs, mammals and coccolithophores appear. Forests of gymnosperms and ferns. First flowers.
Paleozoic	Permian		285	Assembly of supercontinent Pangaea. Glaciation of Southern Hemisphere.	Radiation of reptiles replacing amphibians. 96% of marine species become extinct.
	Carboniferous		360	Euramerica hits Gondwannaland then Siberia. Folding and uplift of Appalachians. Glaciation of Southern Hemisphere.	Dominance of amphibians. Reptiles and winged insects appear.
	Devonian		400	Warm and moist. Iapetus Ocean closed. Deposition of Appalachian rocks.	Fishes invade fresh water, dominate the seas. First trees. Amphibians and insects appear.
	Silurian		440	Warm and moist. High sea level produces vast shallow seas.	Invasion of land by vascular plants and arthropods. Jawed fish appear.
	Ordovician		500	Europe collides with North America. Glaciation in Africa then located at South Pole. High sea level.	First land plants. Rise of predators. First vertebrates: jawless fish appear. Dominant animals suspension feeders.
	Cambrian		600	Consolidation of Gondwannaland. Deposition of biogenic carbonates begins.	Hard skeletons evolve; fossils become abundant. Major groups of invertebrates present and dominant. Most animals deposit feeders.

* BEGAN MILLION YEARS BEFORE PRESENT

ELECTRO-MAGNETIC SPECTRUM

Major Bands of the Spectrum

Color	Frequency cycles/sec.	Wavelength meters
Red	4.2×10^{14}	7.1×10^{-7}
Orange	4.8×10^{14}	6.2×10^{-7}
Yellow	5.2×10^{14}	5.7×10^{-7}
Green	5.8×10^{14}	5.2×10^{-7}
Blue	6.2×10^{14}	4.7×10^{-7}
Indigo	6.8×10^{14}	4.4×10^{-7}
Violet	7.3×10^{14}	4.1×10^{-7}

Band	Frequency cycles/sec.	Wavelength meters
Long Wave	$1.0 - 5.3 \times 10^4$	$3.0 - .054 \times 10^4$
AM	$5.3 - 16 \times 10^5$	$5.45 - 1.87 \times 10^2$
Short Wave	$1.6 - 54 \times 10^6$	$1.87 - .055 \times 10^2$
VHF (TV 2-6)	$5.4 - 8.8 \times 10^7$	$5.55 - 3.41 \times 10^0$
FM	$8.8 - 10.8 \times 10^7$	$3.41 - 2.78 \times 10^0$
VHF (TV 7-13)	$1.74 - 2.16 \times 10^8$	$1.72 - 1.39 \times 10^0$
UHF (TV 14-83)	$4.75 - 8.90 \times 10^8$	$6.3 - 3.37 \times 10^{-1}$

Frequency in cycles/sec.
$10^2 \quad 10^3 \quad 10^4 \quad 10^5 \quad 10^6 \quad 10^7 \quad 10^8 \quad 10^9 \quad 10^{10} \quad 10^{11} \quad 10^{12} \quad 10^{13} \quad 10^{14} \quad 10^{15} \quad 10^{16} \quad 10^{17} \quad 10^{18} \quad 10^{19} \quad 10^{20} \quad 10^{21} \quad 10^{22} \quad 10^{23}$

Bands: RADIO — LW — AM — SW — FM — TV — MICROWAVE — INFRARED — VISIBLE — ULTRAVIOLET — X-RAY — GAMMA-RAY

Sources: ELECTRONICS — KLYSTRON — GAS DISCHARGE — INCANDESCENCE — SYNCHROTRON — BREMSSTRAHLUNG — NUCLEAR DECAY

Wavelength in meters
$10^7 \quad 10^6 \quad 10^5 \quad 10^4 \quad 10^3 \quad 10^2 \quad 10^1 \quad 1 \quad 10^{-1} \quad 10^{-2} \quad 10^{-3} \quad 10^{-4} \quad 10^{-5} \quad 10^{-6} \quad 10^{-7} \quad 10^{-8} \quad 10^{-9} \quad 10^{-10} \quad 10^{-11} \quad 10^{-12} \quad 10^{-13} \quad 10^{-14} \quad 10^{-15}$

Photon energy in electron volts
$10^{-13} \quad 10^{-12} \quad 10^{-11} \quad 10^{-10} \quad 10^{-9} \quad 10^{-8} \quad 10^{-7} \quad 10^{-6} \quad 10^{-5} \quad 10^{-4} \quad 10^{-3} \quad 10^{-2} \quad 10^{-1} \quad 1 \quad 10^1 \quad 10^2 \quad 10^3 \quad 10^4 \quad 10^5 \quad 10^6 \quad 10^7 \quad 10^8 \quad 10^9$

Major Sources of Radiation

The source of all electromagnetic radiation is the positive or negative acceleration of charged particles. In most but not all cases, these are electrons.

Bremsstrahlung - Violent deceleration of fast moving free electrons colliding with solids. **Electronic** - Electrons oscillating under the influence of alternating currents in wires. **Gas-Discharge** - Energy transitions of outer electrons of ionized atoms of gases. **Incandescence** - Energy transitions of outer electrons of thermally excited atoms in collision. **Klystron** - Electrons oscillating under the influence of alternating current in cavities. **Nuclear Decay** - Release of excess energy from nuclei or nuclear particles following collision or nuclear decay. Energy represents lost mass. **Synchroton** - Centripital acceleration of free electrons following a circular path at near the speed of light.

PERIODIC TABLE of the ELEMENTS

METALS

TRANSITION METALS

NON METALS

1a	2a	3b	4b	5b	6b	7b	8	8	8	1b	2b	3a	4a	5a	6a	7a	0
H 1 1.00 HYDROGEN																	**He** 2 4.00 HELIUM
Li 3 6.94 LITHIUM	**Be** 4 9.01 BERYLLIUM											**B** 5 10.81 BORON	**C** 6 12.01 CARBON	**N** 7 14.01 NITROGEN	**O** 8 16.00 OXYGEN	**F** 9 19.00 FLUORINE	**Ne** 10 20.18 NEON
Na 11 22.99 SODIUM	**Mg** 12 24.31 MAGNESIUM											**Al** 13 26.98 ALUMINUM	**Si** 14 28.09 SILICON	**P** 15 30.97 PHOSPHORUS	**S** 16 32.06 SULFUR	**Cl** 17 35.45 CHLORINE	**Ar** 18 39.95 ARGON
K 19 39.10 POTASSIUM	**Ca** 20 40.08 CALCIUM	**Sc** 21 44.96 SCANDIUM	**Ti** 22 47.90 TITANIUM	**V** 23 50.94 VANADIUM	**Cr** 24 52.00 CHROMIUM	**Mn** 25 54.94 MANGANESE	**Fe** 26 55.85 IRON	**Co** 27 58.93 COBALT	**Ni** 28 58.71 NICKEL	**Cu** 29 63.55 COPPER	**Zn** 30 65.37 ZINC	**Ga** 31 69.72 GALLIUM	**Ge** 32 72.59 GERMANIUM	**As** 33 74.92 ARSENIC	**Se** 34 78.96 SELENIUM	**Br** 35 79.90 BROMINE	**Kr** 36 83.80 KRYPTON
Rb 37 85.47 RUBIDIUM	**Sr** 38 87.62 STRONTIUM	**Y** 39 88.91 YTTRIUM	**Zr** 40 91.22 ZIRCONIUM	**Nb** 41 92.91 NIOBIUM	**Mo** 42 95.94 MOLYBDENUM	**Tc** 43 145 TECHNETIUM	**Ru** 44 101.03 RUTHENIUM	**Rh** 45 102.91 RHODIUM	**Pd** 46 105.40 PALLADIUM	**Ag** 47 107.87 SILVER	**Cd** 48 112.40 CADMIUM	**In** 49 114.82 INDIUM	**Sn** 50 118.69 TIN	**Sb** 51 121.75 ANTIMONY	**Te** 52 127.60 TELLURIUM	**I** 53 126.90 IODINE	**Xe** 54 131.30 XENON
Cs 55 132.91 CESIUM	**Ba** 56 137.34 BARIUM	**La-Lu** 57-71	**Hf** 72 178.48 HAFNIUM	**Ta** 73 180.95 TANTALUM	**W** 74 183.85 TUNGSTEN	**Re** 75 186.20 RHENIUM	**Os** 76 190.20 OSMIUM	**Ir** 77 192.20 IRIDIUM	**Pt** 78 195.09 PLATINUM	**Au** 79 196.97 GOLD	**Hg** 80 200.59 MERCURY	**Tl** 81 204.37 THALLIUM	**Pb** 82 207.19 LEAD	**Bi** 83 208.98 BISMUTH	**Po** 84 210 POLONIUM	**At** 85 210 ASTATINE	**Rn** 86 222 RADON
Fr 87 223 FRANCIUM	**Ra** 88 226 RADIUM	**Ac-Lw** 89-103	**Ru** 104 261 RUTHERFORDIUM	**Ha** 105 262 HAHNIUM	106 263	107 262	108 400	109 266									

alkali metals · alkali earths · coinage metals · halogens · inert gases

RARE EARTHS

La 57 138.91 LANTHANUM	**Ce** 58 140.12 CERIUM	**Pr** 59 140.91 PRASEODYMIUM	**Nd** 60 144.24 NEODYMIUM	**Pm** 61 145 PROMETHIUM	**Sm** 62 150.35 SAMARIUM	**Eu** 63 151.96 EUROPIUM	**Gd** 64 157.25 GADOLINIUM	**Tb** 65 158.92 TERBIUM	**Dy** 66 162.50 DYSPROSIUM	**Ho** 67 164.93 HOLMIUM	**Er** 68 167.26 ERBIUM	**Tm** 69 168.93 THULIUM	**Yb** 70 173.04 YTTERBIUM	**Lu** 71 174.97 LUTETIUM
Ac 89 227 ACTINIUM	**Th** 90 232.04 THORIUM	**Pa** 91 231 PROTACTINIUM	**U** 92 238.03 URANIUM	**Np** 93 237 NEPTUNIUM	**Pu** 94 242 PLUTONIUM	**Am** 95 243 AMERICIUM	**Cm** 96 245 CURIUM	**Bk** 97 245 BERKELIUM	**Cf** 98 248 CALIFORNIUM	**Es** 99 253 EINSTEINIUM	**Fm** 100 254 FERMIUM	**Md** 101 256 MENDELEVIUM	**No** 102 253 NOBELIUM	**Lw** 103 257 LAWRENCIUM

EARTH'S ROTATION

NAME	OBJECT IN MOTION	RELATIVE TO	DIRECTION	PERIOD	LINEAR VELOCITY	ANGULAR VELOCITY
Day (Mean Solar)	Earth	Sun	West to East	24 hr (86,400 sec)	.46 km/sec at Equator	360.986°/day
Day (Sidereal)	Earth	Stars	West to East	23 hr 56 min 4.091 sec	.46 km/sec at Equator	360°/day
Diurnal Motion	Stars in the Sky	Earth	East to West	23 hr 56 min 4.091 sec	—	15°/hr

Related Phenomena

PRECESSION: 25,735 year cycle. The slow gyration of the Earth's axis which sweeps out a circle in the sky. This motion of the Earth causes a slight but continuous change of the polar positions in the sky. It is caused by the gravitational torque of the Sun and Moon on the Earth's equatorial bulge. This results in a westward motion of the equinoxes along the ecliptic, and the reversal of the seasons over a half cycle.

PROGRESSION OF PERIHELION: 96,000 year cycle. The continual motion of Perihelion (point closest to the Sun) eastward, or in the opposite direction of Precession. Together, these two motions produce a 20,000 year cycle of the equinox relationship to perihelion.

OBLIQUITY OF THE ECLIPTIC: 41,000 year cycle. Gradual change in the inclination of the earth's axis ranging from 21°59' to 24°36'. Presently, the inclination of the earth's axis is 23°27'.

ROTATIONAL DECELERATION: Very slight decrease in the earth's rotational speed, at the rate of 50 seconds per century.

EARTH'S ORBIT

Year (Tropical)	Earth	Sun	West to East	365.2422 solar days	30 km/sec	0.986°/day
Year (Sidereal)	Earth	Stars	West to East	366.2422 solar days	30 km/sec	0.986°/day
Annual Motion	Stars	Earth	East to West	1 sidereal year	—	-4 min rising time/day
Annual Motion	Sun	Zodiac	Direct W to E	1 tropical year	—	30°/mo

Related Phenomena

ECCENTRICITY OF ORBIT: 96,000 year cycle. Gradual elongation of the earth's eliptical orbit from an eccentricity of almost zero (circle) to .06. The eccentricity of the Earth's orbit is presently .02.

CELESTIAL MOTIONS

MOON'S ORBIT

NAME	OBJECT IN MOTION	RELATIVE TO	DIRECTION	PERIOD	LINEAR VELOCITY	ANGULAR VELOCITY
Month (Synodic)	Moon	Earth & Sun	West to East	29.5306 days	1.02 km/sec	13°/day
Month (Sidereal)	Moon	Stars	Direct W to E	27.3217 days	1.02 km/sec	13°/day
	Moon	Zodiac	Direct W to E	27 days	—	-1 hr rising time/day

Related Phenomena

PROGRESSION OF PERIGEE: 8.85 year cycle. The point of perigee moves around the earth with direct (west to east) motion.

NUTATION: 18.61 year cycle. The nodes move along the ecliptic in a retrograde (east to west) direction.

SUN

Galactic Year	Sun	Galactic Center	Towards Cygnus	2.2×10^8 yr	300 km/sec	6×10^5 yr/°
Peculiar Motion	Sun	Nearby Stars	Towards Hercules	—	20 km/sec	—

MILKY WAY GALAXY

Peculiar Motion	Milky Way	Local Group	Towards Andromeda Galaxy	—	80 km/sec	—
Peculiar Motion	Local Group	Greater Universe	Direction of Corvus	—	600 km/sec	—

Combining all applicable motions gives the Earth an AVERAGE NET MOTION relative to the Greater Universe of 400 kilometers per second (900,000 miles per hour) in the direction of Leo.

Universal Conversions

$$°F = \frac{9°C}{5} + 32$$

$$°C = \frac{5}{9}(°F - 32)$$

$$°K = °C + 273.16$$

FOR EXAMPLE

To convert 2 miles to fathoms; first look under "miles" as that is where the direct conversion would be found. Upon finding that this conversion is not given, look under "fathoms." *Note: when the usefulness of a unit does not merit the listing of conversion factors in both directions between it and a more common unit, the conversion given will be listed under the least common unit.* The conversion from fathoms to miles is not to be found there either, however the conversion from fathoms to feet is. And looking back under miles, the conversion from miles to feet is given. With this information proceed. First multiply 2 miles by 5280 to obtain feet.

2 miles x 5280 = 10560 feet

Then since converting from feet to fathoms is the reverse of the conversion given, divide 10560 feet by the factor given.

10560 Feet ÷ 6 = 1760 Fathoms

Thereby 2 miles equals 1760 fathoms.

MULTIPLY	BY	TO FIND
Acres	0.4047	hectares
Acres	10	square chains
Acres	43,560	square feet
Acres	160	square rods
Angstroms	10^{-10}	meters
Astr. units	149,504,000	kilometers
Astr. units	1.580214×10^{-5}	light years
Astr. units	92,897,000	miles
Atmospheres	1.013	bars
Atmospheres	1.013250×10^{6}	dynes/cm²
Atmospheres	33	feet of water
Atmospheres	14.7	pounds/sq.in.
Atomic mass units	$1.66 \cdot 10^{-27}$	kilograms
Bushels	2,150.42	cubic inches
Bushels	4	pecks
Centimeters	.0328	feet
Centimeters	.3937	inches
Chains	100	links
Chains	1.250×10^{-2}	miles
Chaldrons	36	bushels
Cubic centimeters	.0610	cubic inches
Cubic centimeters	.0010	liters
Cubic feet	28,317.0170	cu. centimeters
Cubic feet	1,728	cubic inches
Cubic feet	.0283	cubic meters
Cubic feet	.0370	cubic yards
Cubic feet	7.4805	gallons
Cubic feet	28.3163	liters
Cu.ft. of water	62.4283	pounds
Cubic inches	16.3872	cu. centimeters
Cu.inches	5.787×10^{-4}	cubic feet
Cubic inches	.0164	liters
Cubic meters	10^{6}	cu. centimeters
Cubic meters	35.3145	cubic feet

MULTIPLY	BY	TO FIND
Cu. meters	61,023.3753	cubic inches
Cubic meters	1.3079	cubic yards
Cubic meters	264.1700	gallons
Cubic yards	27	cubic feet
Cubic yards	.7646	cubic meters
Degrees	.0175	radians
Fathoms	6	feet
Fathoms	1.8288	meters
Feet	30.4801	centimeters
Feet	12	inches
Feet	3.0480×10^{-1}	kilometers
Feet	.3048	meters
Feet	.3333	yards
Feet/min	.508	cent./sec
Foot-candles	10.76	lumens/sq.meter
Foot-pounds	.1383	meter-kilogram
Furlong	660	feet
Gallons, imperial	1.2009	gallons, U.S.
Gallons, imperial	4.5459	liters
Gallons, U.S.	3,785.4	cu. centimeters
Gal., U.S.	.8327	imperial gallons
Gal., U.S.	3.7853	liters
Gallons, U.S.	4	quarts
Grams	15.4324	grains
Grams	.0010	kilograms
Grams	1.000	milligrams
Grams	.0353	ounces
Grams	.0022	pounds
Hectares	2.471	acres
Hectares	10,000	square meter
Hectares	1,195.9	square yards
Hogsheads	63	gallons U.S.
Horsepower	33,000	ft.-lbs/min
Horsepower	550	ft.-lbs/sec

MULTIPLY	BY	TO FIND
Horsepower	76.0404	kgm-m/sec
Horsepower	1.0139	metric hspwr.
Hours	3600	seconds
Inches	2.5400	centimeters
Inches	.0833	feet
Kilograms	1,000	grams
Kilograms	35.2740	ounces
Kilograms	2.2046	Pounds
Kilogr./sq.cm.	14.223	lbs/sq inch
Kilometers	3,280.8330	feet
Kilometers	.6214	miles
Kilometers/hr	27.778	centimeters/sec
Kilometers/hr	54.68	feet/min.
Kilometers/hr	.6214	miles/hr
Knots	1.8532	kilometers/hr
Knots	1.1516	miles per hour
Knots	1	nautical mi/hr
Light years	63282.57	Astr. units
Light years	9.461×10^{12}	kilometers
Links	7.92	inches
Liters	1000	cu. centimeters
Liters	1.0567	quarts
Lumens/sq.m.	0.093	foot-candles/sq.ft.
Meters	10^{10}	angstroms
Meters	3.2808	feet
Meters	39.3700	inches
Meters	9.461×10^{-15}	light years
Meters	1.09936	yards
Meter-kilogr.	7.2307	foot-pounds
Meters/min.	1.6667	centimeters/sec
Meters/min.	.0547	feet/sec
Micron	1×10^{-6}	meters
Miles	5,280	feet
Miles	1.6093	kilometers

MULTIPLY	BY	TO FIND
Miles/hr.	.8684	nautical miles
Miles/hr.	1.4667	feet/sec
Miles/hr.	1.6093	kilometers/hr.
Miles/hr.	.4470	meters/sec.
Mills	.0010	inches
Mills	.0254	millimeters
Nautical miles	6,080.20	feet
Nautical mi.	1,853.2486	meters
Nautical miles	1.1516	miles
Nautical miles	1	min. of latitude
Ounces	28.3495	grams
Ounces	2.8349×10^{-2}	kilograms
Ounces	.0625	pounds
Parsec	206,265	astr. units
Parsec	3.08×10^{13}	kilometers
Parsec	3.26	light years
Parsec	1.92×10^{13}	miles
Pecks	8	quarts
Pints	16	fluid ounces
Pints	.5	quarts
Pints fresh water	1.044	pounds
Pounds	453.5924	grams
Pounds	.4536	kilograms
Pounds	16.00	ounces
Pounds/cu.ft.	16.0184	kilogr./cu.met.
Pounds/cu.in.	27.6797	grams/cu.cm.
Pounds/cu.in.	1.7728	pounds/cu.ft.
Pounds/sq.ft.	4.8824	kilogr./sq.met.
Pounds/sq.in.	2.0360	in. of mercury
Quarts	.25	gallons, U.S.
Quarts	.946	liters
Quarts	2	pints
Quarts(dry)	67.20	cubic inches

MULTIPLY	BY	TO FIND
Quart(liquid)	57.75	cubic inches
Radian	57.2958	degrees (arc)
Revolutions	6.2832	radians
Revolutions/min.	.1047	radians/sec
Rods	16.5	feet
Scruples	20	grains
Seconds	3.00×10^{8}	meter's light travel time
Slugs	14.5939029	kilograms
Slugs	32.1740	pounds
Sq. centimeters	.0011	square feet
Sq. ft.	2.29568×10^{-5}	acres
Square feet	.0929	square meters
Square feet	929.0304	sq. centimeters
Square inches	6.4516	sq. centimeters
Square inches	645.1625	sq. millimeters
Sq. kilometers	247.1044	acres
Square kilometers	.3861	square miles
Sq. kilom.	1.196×10^{6}	square yards
Square meters	10.7639	square feet
Square meters	1.1960	square yards
Square miles	640	acres
Square miles	2.59	sq. kilometers
Square yards	8,361.31	sq. centimeters
Square yards	.8361	square meters
Tons, long	2,240	pounds
Tons, metric	1,000	kilograms
Tons, short	2000	pounds
Yards	91.44	centimeters
Yards	.3333	feet
Yards	.9144	meters
Years	8,766.144	hours

COSMIC CONSTANTS

GEOMETRY

Triangle:
Area = ½ base × height

Pythagorean Theorem
$a^2 + b^2 = c^2$

Square:
Area = side²
Circumference = 4 × side

Rectangle:
Area = length × width
Circumference = 2 lengths + 2 widths

Circle:
Area = π × radius²
Circumference = π × diameter

Cone:
Surface = π × R × length of a side
Volume = 3 height × π × radius²

Sphere:
Surface = 4 × radius² × π
Volume = 4 × R³ × π ÷ 3

Cube:
Surface = 6 × side²
Volume = side³

Rectangular solid:
Surface = (2 × length × width) + (2 × width × height) + (2 × height × length)
Volume = length × width × height

Cylinder:
Surface = 2 × radius × π × height
Volume = base × height

Pyramid:
Volume = ⅓ height × area of base
π = 3.14159265358979323384626433
83279502884197169399375ll

MECHANICS

Speed = distance ÷ time
Force = mass × acceleration
Momentum = mass × velocity
Work = force × distance
Kinetic energy = ½ × mass × velocity²

PHYSICS

Boltzman constant: $k = 1.3807 \times 10^{-16}$ erg °K

Avogadro's number: $N_A = 6.0220 \times 10^{23}$ particles/mole

Gas constant: $R = 8.3144$ joule/mole/°K
Volume of ideal gas @ STP: $V_m = 22.4138$ litres/mole

Gas Law: $pV = nRT$
Speed of Sound in Air: 331 m/sec

SUBATOMIC PARTICLES

Electron rest mass: $m_e = 9.1095 \times 10^{-28}$ gram
Electron rest energy: $m_ec^2 = 8.1872 \times 10^{-14}$ joule
$m_ec^2 = 0.51100$ MeV

Proton rest mass: $m_p = 1.6727 \times 10^{-24}$ gram
Proton rest energy: $m_pc^2 = 1.5033 \times 10^{-10}$ joule
$m_pc^2 = 938.28$ MeV

Neutron rest mass: $m_n = 1.6750 \times 10^{-24}$ gram
Neutron rest energy: $m_nc^2 = 1.5054 \times 10^{-10}$ joule
$m_nc^2 = 939.57$ MeV

Elementary charge: $e = 1.6022 \times 10^{-19}$ coulomb

ELECTRICITY

Ohm's law: Amperage = voltage ÷ resistance
Watts = volts × amps

RADIATION

Frequency (cycles/sec) = Speed of light (cm/sec) ÷ Wave length (cm)

Solar constant: 1.940 gram calories/sq cm/min
Speed of light in vacuum: $c = 2.9980 \times 10^8$ m/sec
Planck constant: $h = 6.6262 \times 10^{-27}$ erg sec
Energy of a photon = Planck constant × frequency

GRAVITY

Grav. attraction = G × mass₁ × mass₂ ÷ distance²
Grav. constant: $G = 6.6720 \times 10^8$ cm³/g/sec²
Grav. acceleration (earth): g = 9.807 meters/sec²

CELESTIAL BODIES

Galaxy's mass: 2×10^{11} solar masses
Galaxy's radius: 5×10^4 light years
Galaxy's radius at Sun: 2.89×10^{18} kilometers
Sun's mass: 1.989×10^{30} kilograms
Sun's mean radius: 6.9598×10^5 meters
Sun's luminosity: 3.83×10^{23} kilowatts
Earth's mass: 5.976×10^{24} kilograms
Earth's mean radius: 6.731×10^3 kilometers
Earth's volume: 1.083×10^{27} centimeters³
Earth's surface area: 5.1×10^{18} centimeters²
Earth's mean orbital radius: 1.49×10^8 Km, 1AU
Moon's mass: 7.35×10^{22} kilograms
Moon's mean radius: 1.74×10^3 kilometers
Moon's mean orbital radius: 3.84×10^5 Km

KITCHEN EQUIVALENTS

1 ounce = 28 grams
1 pound = 454 grams
1 kilogram = 35.27 ounces
1 kilogram = 2.2 pounds

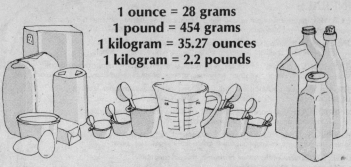

VOLUME MEASURES

TRADITIONAL	TRADITIONAL	TRADITIONAL	METRIC
1 pinch	less than ⅛ tsp.	---	---
60 drops (thick fluid)	1 teaspoon	1/6 fl. oz.	5 ml.
100 drops (thin fluid)	1 teaspoon	1/6 fl. oz.	5 ml.
2 teaspoons	1 dessert spoon	1/3 fl. oz.	10 ml.
3 teaspoons	1 tablespoon	½ fl. oz.	15 ml.
2 tablespoons	----	1 fl. oz.	30 ml.
16 tablespoons	1 cup	8 fl. oz.	236.5 ml.
2 cups	1 pint	16 fl. oz.	473 ml.
2 pints	1 quart	32 fl. oz.	946 ml.
4.24 cups	1.06 quarts	33.8 fl. oz.	1 liter
4 quarts	1 gallon	128 fl. oz.	3.79 liter
2 gallons	1 peck	538 cu. in.	7.57 liter
4 pecks	1 bushel	2,150 cu. in.	30.28 liter
7.48 gallons	.80 bushels	1 cu. ft.	28.32 liter

VOLUME/WEIGHT

1 cup water	8 oz.	3 medium tomatoes	1 lb.
2 tablespoons butter	1 oz.	4 cups grated cheese	1 lb.
3 tablespoons flour	1 oz.	9 medium eggs	1 lb.
3 teaspoons soda	½ oz.	3 large bananas	1 lb.
4 teaspoons baking powder	½ oz.	1 cup nutmeats	5 oz.
3½ cups whole wheat flour	1 lb.	1 cup rice uncooked*	8 oz.
2½ cups wheat flour	1 lb.	4 cups apples (sliced)	1½ lb.
2½ cups buckwheat flour	1 lb.	2 cups ground meat	1 lb.
5 1/3 cups coffee (dry)	1 lb.	2¾ cups brown sugar	6-7 oz.
6½ cups tea (dry)	1 lb.	1 cup granulated sugar	8 oz.
2 cups lard	1 lb.	1 cup confectioner's sugar	4½ oz.
2 cups butter	1 lb.	1 cup honey, molasses,	
2 cups cornmeal	1 lb.	corn syrup	12 oz.
2⅜ cups raisins	1 lb.	*Rice doubles in volume upon	
4 medium potatoes	1 lb.	cooking.	

VITAMIN & MINERAL SOURCES

MINERALS

CALCIUM: Component of bones and teeth, blood clotting, nerve and muscle response.
Milk products, greens, almonds, sesame seeds, soy products, molasses, oats, eggs.

IRON: Hemoglobin components, carrys oxygen, and prevents enemia.
Lean meats, chicken, shellfish, beans, molasses, eggs, whole grain products.

POTASSIUM: Component of muscles and organs, acts with sodium in nerve transmission
Bananas, oranges, avocado, potatoes, tomatoes, greens, peanuts, beans, soy, yeast, molasses, meat.

SODIUM: Component of blood and body fluids, acts with potassium in nerve transmission
Table salt, milk, cheese, eggs, carrots, beets, spinach, celery.

PHOSPHOROUS: Component of basic cell structure and teeth and bones.
Meat, fish, poultry, peas, beans, milk, eggs, whole grain.

MAGNESIUM: Bone, muscle and blood component, nerve response, metabolism.
Bananas, whole grains, beans, milk, dark green leafy vegetables, nuts.

IODINE: Component of thyroxine hormone, thyroid function.
Seafoods, sea weed, iodized table salt.

VITAMINS

VITAMIN A: Good vision, skin and hair, infection resistance, normal growth and development
Milk, butter, margarine, eggs, liver, leafy green and yellow vegetables.

VITAMIN B1 (thiamine): Heart and nervous system function, prevents beriberi.
Cereals, fish, lean meat, liver, milk, poultry, greens, yeast, nuts.

VITAMIN B2 (riboflavin): Builds and maintains tissues, skin; cell respiration.
Eggs, bread, cereals, leafy green vegetables, lean meat, liver, yeast, milk.

VITAMIN B6 - Fat metabolism, brain function, teeth, blood system.
Wheat germ, vegetables, yeast, meat, whole grains, prunes, raisins, eggs.

VITAMIN B12 - Prevents pernicious anemia; growth and development, nervous system.
Liver, kidney, milk, fish, lean meat, eggs.

NIACIN: Prevents pellagra and appetite loss; nervous system, food metabolism.
Lean meats, liver, yeast, cereals and bread, eggs, green vegetables.

VITAMIN C - Prevents scurvy, builds cells and blood vessels, resistance.
Citrus fruits, berries, tomatoes, cabbage, green vegetables.

VITAMIN D - Prevents rickets, aids use of calcium and phosphorous.
Fortified milk, cod liver oil, salmon, tuna, eggs.

VITAMIN E - Prevents infertility, muscular dystrophy; healthy skin.
Vegetable oil, whole grains, peanuts, dark leafy greens.

COMPLETE PROTEIN COMBINATIONS

FOOD COMBINATIONS	USABLE PROTEIN	CALORIES
1 c. RICE & 1/3 c. SESAME SEEDS	16 grams	992
1 c. PEANUT BUTTER & 1½ c. MILK	84	2604
2/3 c. RICE & ¼ c. BEANS	15	645
1 c. RICE & ¼ c. BREWERS YEAST	24	840
¾ c. RICE & 1 c. MILK	17	714
2½ c. RICE & 6 oz. TOFU	37	1961
1 medium POTATOE & 1 c. MILK	9	324
½ c. BEANS & 1 c. MILK	22	528
¾ c. PEANUTS & 1 c. SUNFLOWER SEEDS	55	3025
6 CORN TORTILLAS & ¼ c. BEANS	14	574
2 c. FLOUR & 1 c. MILK	28	952

All quantities refer to uncooked grains and dry beans

FOOD VALUES

MEAT

FOOD		AMT.	CALORIES	GMS. PROTEIN	GMS. FAT
Beef,	chuck	1 lb.	1166	84.8	88.9
	flank	1 lb.	631	98.9	23.1
	t-bone	1 lb.	1596	59.1	149.1
	round	1 lb.	1420	91.6	55.8
	sirloin	1 lb.	1420	76.1	121.1
	ground	1 lb.	812	93.9	45.4
	liver	1 lb.	635	87.0	21.3
Lamb,	leg	1 lb.	948	82.1	66.2
	loin	1 lb.	1252	76.2	102.5
Pork,	loin	1 lb.	1352	77.6	112.9
	bacon	1 sl.	92	4.6	4.8
	ham	1 lb.	1397	39.2	120.7
	ribs	1 lb.	976	39.2	89.7
	roast	1 lb.	1302	70.3	111.1
Veal,	round	1 lb.	744	88.5	41.0
	loin	1 lb.	821	87.1	50.0
Venison		1 lb.	572	95.0	18.0

POULTRY

FOOD		AMT.	CALORIES	GMS. PROTEIN	GMS. FAT
Chicken,	fryer	1 lb.	382	57.4	15.1
	rooster	1 lb.	791	60.3	59.3
	egg	1 lg.	88	7.0	6.2
Duck,	roaster	1 lb.	1213	59.5	106.4
	egg	1 lg.	172	12.0	13.0
Turkey,	roast	1 lb.	722	66.6	48.7
	egg	1 lg.	156	12.0	10.9

SEAFOOD

FOOD		AMT.	CALORIES	GMS. PROTEIN	GMS. FAT
Fish,	bass	1 lb.	422	85.7	2.3
	halibut	1 lb.	454	94.8	5.4
	sole	1 lb.	358	75.8	3.5
	trout	1 lb.	762	83.0	45.4
	tuna, canned	1 lb.	1306	109.8	93.0
Shellfish,	abalone	1 lb.	445	84.8	2.3
	clams	1 lb.	363	50.3	4.1
	crabs	1 lb.	427	78.9	8.5
	lobster	1 lb.	413	76.7	8.6
	oysters	1 lb.	413	48.1	10.0
	scallops	1 lb.	367	69.4	0.9

DAIRY

FOOD		AMT.	CALORIES	GMS. PROTEIN	GMS. CARBO HYDRATES
Milk,	whole	1 c	159	8.5	12.0
	skim	1 c	88	8.8	12.5
	buttermilk	1 c	88	8.8	0.2
	goats	1 c	164	7.8	1.2
Cream		1 lb.	838	5.2	7.4
Cheese,	cheddar	1 lb.	1805	113.4	9.5
	cottage	1 c	172	33.9	5.4
	cream	1 lb.	1696	36.3	9.5
Ice cream		1 c	329	3.8	26.6
Sour cream		1 c	485	7.0	10.0
Yoghurt		1 c	152	7.4	12.0

GRAINS

FOOD		AMT.	CALORIES	GMS. PROTEIN	GMS. CARBO HYDRATES
Bread,	whole wheat	1 lb.	1193	39.5	236.3
	french	1 lb.	1315	41.3	251.3
	rye	1 lb.	1102	41.3	236.3
	white	1 lb.	1225	39.5	229.1
Corn flakes		1 lb.	1751	35.8	389.9
Macaroni		1 lb.	1674	60.3	341.1
Pinto Beans		1 lb.	1583	103.9	288.9
Popcorn		1 lb.	1751	57.6	347.9
Rice,	white	1 lb.	1647	30.4	364.7
	brown	1 lb.	1633	34.0	351.1
Wheat,	bran	1 lb.	966	72.6	280.8
	germ	1 lb.	1647	120.7	211.8
Soy beans		1 lb.	1828	154.7	152.0

STAPLES

FOOD		AMT.	CALORIES	GMS. PROTEIN	GMS. CARBO HYDRATES
Butter		1 lb.	3245	2.7	1.8
Margarine		1 lb.	3266	2.7	1.8
Veg oil		1 cup	1945	0	0
Honey		1 cup	983	1.0	266.0
Sugar,	white	1 lb.	1763	0	451.3
	brown	1 lb.	1692	0	437.3
Molasses		1 c	652	0	168

FRUIT

FOOD	AMT.	CALORIES	GMS. PROTEIN	GMS. CARBO HYDRATES
Apples	1 lb.	242	.8	60.5
Apricots	1 lb.	217	4.3	54.6
Bananas	1 lb.	262	3.4	68.5
Cherries	1 lb.	286	5.3	71.0
Cranberries	1 lb.	200	1.7	47.0
Dates	1 lb.	1243	10.0	330.7
Grapefruit	1 lb.	91	1.1	23.0
Lemon	1 lb.	90	3.3	24.9
Oranges	1 lb.	162	3.3	40.4
Cantaloupe	1 lb.	68	1.6	17.0
Honeydew	1 lb.	94	2.3	22.0
Peaches	1 lb.	150	2.4	38.0
Pears	1 lb.	252	2.9	63.3
Pineapple	1 lb.	123	0.9	32.3
Raisins	1 lb.	1311	11.3	351.1
Strawberries	1 lb.	161	3.0	36.6
Watermelon	1 lb.	54	1.0	13.4

VEGETABLES

FOOD	AMT.	CALORIES	GMS. PROTEIN	GMS. CARBO HYDRATES
Artichokes	1 g.	16	5.3	19.2
Avocado	1 lb.	589	7.6	20.7
Bean sprouts	1 lb.	159	17.2	29.9
Broccoli	1 lb.	113	12.7	20.9
Cabbage	1 lb.	98	5.3	22.0
Carrot	1 lb.	156	4.1	36.1
Celery	1 lb.	58	3.1	13.3
Corn	1 lb.	372	14.1	89.4
Cucumber	1 lb.	65	3.9	14.7
Eggplant	1 lb.	92	4.4	20.6
Green beans	1 lb.	128	7.6	28.3
Lettuce	1 lb.	56	3.9	12.5
Mushrooms	1 lb.	123	11.9	19.4
Onions	1 lb.	157	6.2	35.9
Potatoes	1 lb.	279	7.7	62.8
Tomatoes	1 lb.	100	5.0	21.3

ALCOHOL

FOOD	AMT.	CALORIES	GMS. PROTEIN	GMS. CARBO HYDRATES
Beer	1 c	101	0.7	9.1
Gin	1 c	586	0	0
Wine	1 c	198	0.5	12.0

COMMON	BOTANICAL
Angelica	Angelica Archangelica
Anise	Pimpinella Anisum
Basil, Sweet	Ocimum Basilicum
Bay, Sweet	Laurus nobilis
Bergamot (Bee balm)	Monarda didyma
Blackberry	Rubus spp.
Boneset	Eupatorium perfoliatum
Borage	Borago officinalis
Burdock, Great	Arctium lappa
Burnet, Salad	Sanguisorba minor
Camomile, German	Matricaria Chamomilla
Caraway	Carum Carvi
Catnip	Nepeta Cataria spp.
Chervil	Anthriscus Cerefolium
Chicory	Cichorium intybus
Chives	Allium Schoenoprasum
Comfrey	Symphytum officinale
Coriander	Coriandrum sativum
Costmary	Chrysanthemum Balsamita
Dandelion, Common	Taraxacum officinale
Dill	Anethum graveolens
Fennel, Sweet	Foeniculum officinale
Garlic	Allium sativum
Geranium, Scented	Pelargonium spp.
Germander	Teucrium Chamaedrys
Golden Seal	Hydrastis canadensis
Horehound	Marrubium vulgare
Hyssop (Blue Flower)	Hyssopus officinalis
Lamb's Quarters	Chenopodium album
Lavender	Lavandula spp.
Leek	Allium porrum

HOME & GARDEN HERB CHART

Properties / Uses (columns):

- Drying
- Oils/Shampoos
- Fragrances
- Baking
- Butters
- Confectionery
- Salads
- Sauces
- Soups/Stews
- Teas
- Vinegars
- Antiscorbutic
- Antiseptic
- Antispasmodic
- Aromatic
- Astringent
- Carminative
- Detergent
- Diaphoretic
- Diuretic
- Expectorant
- Febrifuge
- Laxative
- Sedative
- Stimulant
- Stomachic
- Tonic
- Vulnerary

Herbs (rows):

Common Name	Botanical Name
Lemon Balm	*Melissa officinalis*
Lovage	*Levisticum officinale*
Mallow (Marshmallow)	*Althaea officinalis*
Marjoram	*Majorana hortensis*
Mint family	*Mentha spp.*
Mustard	*Brassica spp.*
Nasturtium	*Tropaeolum majus*
Oregano	*Origanum vulgare*
Parsley	*Petroselinum hortense*
Purslane	*Portulace oleracea*
Rosemary	*Rosmarinus officinalis*
Safflower	*Carthamus tinctorius*
Sage	*Salvia officinalis*
Savory	*Satureja spp.*
Shepherd's Purse	*Capsella bursa-pastoris*
Tarragon	*Artemisia Dracunculus*
Thyme	*Thymus spp.*
Valerian	*Valeriana officinalis*
Watercress	*Nasturtium officinale*
Woodruff, Sweet	*Asperula odorata*
Yarrow	*Achillea millefolium*

PARTS OF PLANT TO BE HARVESTED:

- • Berries
- ♡ Bulb
- 88 Flower
- ∅ Leaves
- Root (Whole)
- Seeds
- Stem (Whole)
- Whole Plant

DRILL SIZES

DECIMAL EQUIVALENTS

DRILL SIZE	DECIMAL	DRILL SIZE	DECIMAL	DRILL SIZE	DECIMAL
80	.0135	29	.1360	21/64	.3281
79	.0145	28	.1405	Q	.3320
1/64	.0156	9/64	.1406	R	.3390
78	.0160	27	.1440	11/32	.3437
77	.0180	26	.1470	S	.3480
76	.0200	25	.1495	T	.3580
75	.0210	24	.1520	23/64	.3594
74	.0225	23	.1540	U	.3680
73	.0240	5/32	.1562	3/8	.3750
72	.0250	22	.1570	V	.3770
71	.0260	21	.1590	W	.3860
70	.0280	20	.1610	25/64	.3906
69	.0292	19	.1660	X	.3970
68	.0310	18	.1695	Y	.4040
1/32	.0313	11/64	.1719	13/32	.4062
67	.0320	17	.1730	Z	.4130
66	.0330	16	.1770	27/64	.4219
65	.0350	15	.1800	7/16	.4375
64	.0360	14	.1820	29/64	.4531
63	.0370	13	.1850	15/32	.4687
62	.0380	3/16	.1875	31/64	.4843
61	.0390	12	.1890	1/2	.5000
60	.0400	11	.1910	33/64	.5156
59	.0410	10	.1935	17/32	.5313
58	.0420	9	.1960	35/64	.5469
57	.0430	8	.1990	9/16	.5625
56	.0465	7	.2010	37/64	.5781
3/64	.0469	13/64	.2031	19/32	.5937
55	.0520	6	.2040	39/64	.6094
54	.0550	5	.2055	5/8	.6250
53	.0595	4	.2090	41/64	.6406
1/16	.0625	3	.2130	21/32	.6562
52	.0635	7/32	.2187	43/64	.6719
51	.0670	2	.2210	11/16	.6875
50	.0700	1	.2280	45/64	.7031
49	.0730	A	.2340	23/32	.7187
48	.0760	15/64	.2344	47/64	.7344
5/64	.0781	B	.2380	3/4	.7500
47	.0785	C	.2420	49/64	.7656
46	.0810	D	.2460	25/32	.7812
45	.0820	E 1/4	.2500	51/64	.7969
44	.0860	F	.2570	13/16	.8125
43	.0890	G	.2610	53/64	.8281
42	.0935	17/64	.2656	27/32	.8437
3/32	.0937	H	.2660	55/64	.8594
41	.0960	I	.2720	7/8	.8750
40	.0980	J	.2770	57/64	.8906
39	.0995	K	.2811	29/32	.9062
38	.1015	9/32	.2812	59/64	.9219
37	.1040	L	.2900	15/16	.9375
36	.1065	M	.2950	61/64	.9531
7/64	.1093	19/64	.2968	31/32	.9687
35	.1100	N	.3020	63/64	.9844
34	.1110	5/16	.3125	1	1.000
33	.1130	O	.3160		
32	.1160	P	.3230		
31	.1200				
1/8	.1250				
30	.1285				

TAP DRILLS

THREAD	DRILL
#0—80	3/64
#1—64	No. 53
#1—72	No. 53
#2—56	No. 51
#2—64	No. 50
#3—48	5/64
#3—56	No. 46
#4—40	No. 43
#4—48	No. 42
#5—40	No. 39
#5—44	No. 37
#6—32	No. 36
#6—40	No. 33
#8—32	No. 29
#8—36	No. 29
#10—24	No. 25
#10—32	No. 21
#12—24	No. 17
#12—28	No. 15
1/4—20	No. 8
1/4—28	No. 3
5/16—18	F
5/16—24	I
3/8—16	5/16
3/8—24	Q
7/16—14	U
7/16—20	W
1/2—13	27/64
1/2—20	29/64
9/16—12	31/64
9/16—18	33/64
5/8—11	17/32
5/8—18	37/64
3/4—10	21/32
3/4—16	11/16
7/8—9	49/64
7/8—14	13/16
1—8	7/8
1—14	15/16
1-1/8—7	63/64
1-1/8—12	1-3/64
1-1/4—7	1-7/64
1-1/4—12	1-11/64
1-1/2—6	1-11/32
1-1/2—12	1-27/64

THREADED FASTENERS

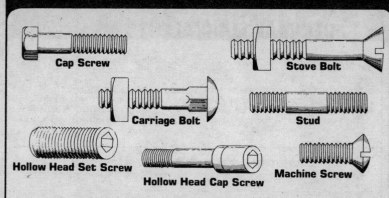

Cap Screw

Stove Bolt

Carriage Bolt

Stud

Hollow Head Set Screw

Hollow Head Cap Screw

Machine Screw

Machine screws and bolts are designated by a pair of numbers. The first number indicates the diameter of the bolt, smaller sizes by an assigned whole number e.g. 2, 10, larger sizes by a fraction of an inch e.g. 1/4, 9/16. The second number is the thread "pitch" and is indicated by the number of threads per inch.

Most bolts fall into one of two series.

COARSE THREAD SERIES (UNC): General use, optimum resistance to stripping of threads therefore required for softer materials. Easy repeated assembly and disassembly.

FINE THREAD SERIES (UNF): For vibration resistance, fine adjustment, or where length of engagement is short. Avoid fine threads in soft or brittle materials.

TORQUE VALUES: All figures are foot-pounds

There is no difference in this chart between the torque figures for fine or coarse threads. The torque figures for a finely-threaded fastener of the same diameter may be slightly higher but hardly worth mentioning.

FASTENER	TYPE	MATERIAL	BODY SIZE OR OUTSIDE DIAMETER OF FASTENER									
			1/4	5/16	3/8	7/16	1/2	9/16	5/8	3/4	7/8	1
	SAE 0-1-2	LOW CARBON STEEL	6	12	20	32	47	69	96	155	206	310
	SAE 5	MEDIUM CARBON HEAT TREAT STEEL	10	19	33	54	78	114	154	257	382	587
	SAE 8	MEDIUM CARBON ALLOY STEEL	14	29	47	78	119	169	230	380	600	700
	HOLLOW HEAD CAP SCREW	HIGH CARBON CASE HARDENED STEEL	16	33	54	84	125	180	250	400	640	970
	HOLLOW HEAD SET SCREW	HIGH CARBON CASE HARDENED STEEL	6	12	18	29	43	63	100	146		

FOOT POUNDS

215

METRIC FASTENERS

Metric fasteners, though not yet completely standardized internationally, use millimeters to describe both diameter and pitch. The ISO system of standards specifies one fine thread pitch, and one course thread pitch for each diameter. The coarse series is generally listed without a pitch designation. e.g. a coarse 8 mm bolt with a standard pitch of 1.25 mm would be listed M8 while an 8 mm fine would be listed M8 x 1.0.

METRIC TAP & DRILL SIZES

TAP SIZE	DRILL SIZE	TAP SIZE	DRILL SIZE
M4 x .7	3.30 mm	M8 x 1.00	7.00 mm
M5 x .8	4.20 mm	M10 x 1.50	8.50 mm
M6 x 1	5.00 mm	M10 x 1.25	8.75 mm
M6 x .75	5.40 mm	M12 x 1.75	10.20 mm
M8 x 1.25	6.75 mm	M12 x 1.25	10.75 mm

PITCHES & HEAD SIZES

BOLT DIAMETER	PITCH FINE	COARSE	HEAD SIZE
4	0.7	0.5	7 mm
5	0.8	0.5	8 mm
6	1.0	.75	10-11 mm
8	1.25	1.0	13-12 mm
10	1.5	1.25	17-14 mm
12	1.75	1.25	19-17 mm

TORQUE VALUES

The condition of your threads, in conjunction with the type and amount of lubricant used will cause variations. Use manufacturers specifications when available.

STEEL GRADE		6mm	8mm	10mm	12mm	14mm	16mm
(5D)	5.6	5 ft-lb	12 ft-lb	23 ft-lb	40 ft-lb	65 ft-lb	100 ft-lb
		6.9 N-m	16.7 N-m	31.4 N-m	53.9 N-m	88.3 N-m	135 N-m
(8G)	8.8	9 ft-lb	21 ft-lb	40 ft-lb	70 ft-lb	110 ft-lb	170 ft-lb
		12.7 N-m	28.4 N-m	53.9 N-m	95.1 N-m	149 N-m	230 N-m
(10K)	10.9	11 ft-lb	26 ft-lb	50 ft-lb	87 ft-lb	135 ft-lb	210 ft-lb
		14.7 N-m	35.3 N-m	67.7 N-m	118 N-m	183 N-m	284 N-m
(12K)	12.9	13 ft-lb	32 ft-lb	60 ft-lb	105 ft-lb	160 ft-lb	250 ft-lb
		17.1 N-m	43.1 N-m	81.4 N-m	142 N-m	217 N-m	338 N-m

Above table header spanned by: **BOLT DIAMETER**

WOOD SCREWS

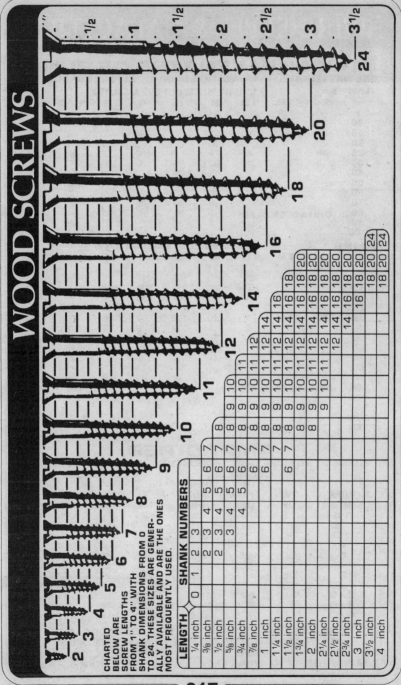

CHARTED BELOW ARE SCREW LENGTHS FROM 1" TO 4" WITH SHANK DIMENSIONS FROM 0 TO 24. THESE SIZES ARE GENERALLY AVAILABLE AND ARE THE ONES MOST FREQUENTLY USED.

LENGTH	SHANK NUMBERS																	
	0	1	2	3	4	5	6	7	8	9	10	11	12	14	16	18	20	24
1/4 inch	0	1	2	3														
3/8 inch			2	3	4	5	6	7										
1/2 inch			2	3	4	5	6	7										
5/8 inch				3	4	5	6	7	8	9	10	11						
3/4 inch					4	5	6	7	8	9	10	11	12					
7/8 inch							6	7	8	9	10	11	12	14				
1 inch							6	7	8	9	10	11	12	14	16			
1 1/4 inch								7	8	9	10	11	12	14	16	18		
1 1/2 inch							6	7	8	9	10	11	12	14	16	18	20	
1 3/4 inch									8	9	10	11	12	14	16	18	20	
2 inch									8	9	10	11	12	14	16	18	20	
2 1/4 inch										9	10	11	12	14	16	18	20	
2 1/2 inch											10	11	12	14	16	18	20	
2 3/4 inch													12	14	16	18	20	
3 inch														14	16	18	20	24
3 1/2 inch															16	18	20	24
4 inch																18	20	24

WIRE TYPES & CAPACITIES

MAXIMUM LENGTHS OF RUNS

ONE WAY LENGTHS   2% VOLTAGE DROP   COPPER CONDUCTORS

WIRE SIZE @ 120 VOLTS

AMPS	14	12	10	8	6	4	2	1/0	2/0
5	90	142	226	360	573	911			
10	45	71	113	180	286	455	704		
15	30	47	75	120	191	304	483	768	965
20	22	36	57	90	143	228	362	576	726
25	18	28	45	72	115	182	290	461	581
30	15	23	38	60	95	152	241	384	494
40		18	32	45	72	114	174	288	363
50			27	36	57	91	145	230	290
60			22	30	48	76	121	192	242
70				26	40	65	104	165	207
80	DISTANCES IN FEET				36	57	90	144	181
90					32	51	80	128	161
100					29	46	72	115	145

WIRE SIZE @ 240 VOLTS

AMPS	14	12	10	8	6	4	2	1/0	2/0
5	179	285	453	720					
10	90	142	226	360	527	911			
15	60	95	151	240	351	607	965		
20	45	71	113	180	264	455	724		
25	36	57	91	144	211	364	579	922	
30	30	50	75	120	176	304	483	768	968
40		41	56	90	132	228	362	576	726
50			45	72	105	182	290	461	581
60				60	88	152	241	384	484
70				50	76	130	207	329	415
80					66	114	181	288	363
90					59	101	161	256	323
100	DISTANCES IN FEET				53	91	145	230	290
125						73	116	184	232
150							97	154	194
175							83	132	166
200								115	145

AMPACITIES

BURIAL OR NO MORE THAN 3 CONDUCTORS IN CONDUIT OR CABLE

WIRE SIZE	COPPER			ALUMINUM		
	T TW UF	THW THWN USE	THHN RHH XHHW	T TW	THW THWN	THHN XHHW
14	15	15	15	—	—	—
12	20	20	20	15	15	15
10	30	30	30	25	25	25
8	40	45	50	30	40	40
6	55	65	70	40	50	55
4	70	85	90	55	65	70
2	95	115	120	75	90	95
1/0	125	150	155	100	120	125
2/0	145	175	185	115	135	145
3/0	165	200	210	130	155	165
4/0	195	230	235	155	180	185

FOR MORE THAN 3 CONDUCTORS IN RACEWAY OR CABLE
DERATE AMPERAGES TO THE FOLLOWING PERCENTAGES

4-6 CONDUCTORS .... 80%   25-42 CONDUCTORS 60%
7-24 CONDUCTORS ...... 70%   43+ CONDUCTORS 50%

GLOSSARY

Capricorn
Aquarius
Pisces
Aries
Taurus
Gemini
Cancer
Leo
Virgo
Libra
Scorpio
Sagittarius

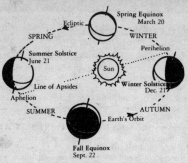

Spring Equinox March 20
Ecliptic
SPRING
WINTER
Summer Solstice June 21
Perihelion
Sun
Line of Apsides
Aphelion
Winter Solstice Dec. 21
SUMMER
AUTUMN
Earth's Orbit
Fall Equinox Sept. 22

REVOLUTION OF THE SEASONS

Sun
Moon
Mercury
Venus
Earth
Mars
Jupiter
Saturn
Uranus
Neptune
Pluto

Albedo: The percentage of light that a planet, moon or other non-radiating celestial body reflects.

Annular Eclipse: An eclipse of the Sun that occurs when the apparent diameter of the Moon is smaller than the apparent diameter of the Sun, leaving a ring of Sunlight around the Moon.

Aphelion: That point in the orbit of a body about the Sun, at which it is positioned farthest from the Sun.

Apogee: That point in the orbit of a body about the Earth, at which point it is positioned farthest from the Earth.

Apparent Magnitude: A measure of the brightness of a star or other celestial body as seen from the Earth.

Ascending Node: The point in the orbit of a planet at which it crosses the ecliptic from south to north.

Asterism: A star group within a constellation.

Astronomical Unit: The mean distance between the Earth and Sun.

Autumn Equinox: The point on the celestial equator where the Sun passes from north to south. The first day of fall.

Biennial: Occurring once every two years. A plant which produces leaves the first year, and then fruits and dies the second year.

Cardinal Points: The four main points of the compass: North, East, South and West.

Celestial Equator: The projection of the Earth's equator onto the sky, that is the line 90° from each pole in the sky.

Celestial Latitude: Distance in degrees North or South of the ecliptic.

Celestial Longitude: Distance in degrees, minutes and seconds East along the ecliptic, from the First Point of Aries.

Celestial Meridian: The great circle through the celestial poles and the observer's zenith.

Celestial Poles: Extension of the Earth's axis onto the sky; points on the celestial sphere, about which the stars seem to rotate daily.

Celsius Temperature Scale: A temperature scale which utilizes the freezing point of water as 0° C. and the boiling point of water as 100° C. (Synonymous with the Centigrade scale.)

Circumpolar Stars: Those stars near the celestial poles which are always either above or below the horizon; this varies with the observer's latitude.

Compounds: Distinct substances formed by chemical union of two or more elements.

Constellation: A configuration of stars that suggest the form of a person, object or animal. Today, a constellation includes a definite area of the sky around such a configuration.

Cosmic Rays: High energy electromagnetic radiation that strikes the Earth from space.

Declination: The smallest angle between a given celestial object and the celestial equator.

Descending Node: The point in the orbit of a body where it crosses the ecliptic passing from north to south.

N. Pole of the Ecliptic   N. Celestial Pole
Declination
Celestial Latitude
Celestial Equator
Celestial Longitude
Ecliptic
Right Ascension
S. Celestial Pole   S. Pole of the Ecliptic

CELESTIAL RECKONING

Eclipse, Lunar: Opposition of the Sun and Moon when the Moon is at its node and thus is temporarily blocked from the Sun's light by the Earth's shadow.

Eclipse, Solar: Conjunction of the Sun and Moon, when the Moon is at its node (on the

more GLOSSARY

ecliptic) and thus obscures the orb of the Sun.

Ecliptic: The plane of the Earth's orbit projected onto the sky. The apparent path of the Sun on the celestial sphere.

Electromagnetic Spectrum: The full array of electromagnetic radiation (radio, infra red, visible light, ultraviolet, x-rays, gamma rays.) A map of the different energy states of the photon.

Element: The simplest form of a substance that cannot be broken down into simpler forms by chemical process.

Equator: A great circle on the Earth lying midway between the two poles.

Era: A portion of the age of the Earth that encompasses a major geological or biological developmental stage in Earth's Evolution. Total planetary change.

Evening Star: A planet which appears in the sky as the Sun sets, then later sets in the West sometime before Sunrise.

First Point of Aries: Point where the ecliptic and the celestial equator intersect, presently in the constellation of Pisces, the Vernal Equinox.

Frequency: The number of waves (cycles) that pass a given point per second.

Galaxy: A fundamental collection of stellar material, usually containing millions to hundreds of billions of stars, and revolving and evolving around a common center.

Gram: The fundamental metric unit of mass.

Gravitation: The mutual force of attraction that masses exert on each other.

Great Circle: A circle on a sphere, such as the Earth, that lies on a plane passing through the center of the sphere. Thus, a circumference of the sphere.

Greatest Elongation: The largest angle of separation between the Sun and Mercury or Venus when viewed from Earth.

Greenwich Meridian: Also called the prime meridian. A great circle on the Earth passing through both poles, and a point in the Royal Greenwich Observatory. Zero degree longitude from which all other longitudes are measured.

Inclination: The angle between the plane of the orbit of a body and its axis of rotation.

Inferior Conjunction: The configuration of Mercury or Venus when the planet is directly between the Earth and the Sun.

International Date Line: A line opposite the prime meridian at approximately 180° longitude. Upon crossing this line, the date is changed by one day.

Ion: An electrically charged particle or group of atoms.

Kelvin Temperature Scale: A temperature scale which begins at absolute zero (-273° Celsius equals 0° Kelvin) with Celsius degree increments rising from this zero base.

Latitude: An angular measure of a point on the Earth indicating its distance north or south of the equator.

Light: Electromagnetic radiation of a frequency that is visible to the eye.

Liter: Metric unit of volume.

Longitude: An angular measure of a point on the Earth indicating its distance east or west of the Greenwich Meridian.

Magnetic Declination: The number of degrees a compass needle reads east or west of true north.

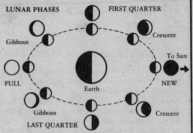

LUNAR PHASES — FIRST QUARTER — Crescent — Gibbous — To Sun — FULL — Earth — NEW — Gibbous — Crescent — LAST QUARTER

Main Sequence Brightening: The long term brightening of most stars, including the Sun, during the course of their stellar evolution.

Mass: A measure of the amount of material in an object, distinct from weight, which is influenced by the force of gravity.

Meridian: A great circle that passes through an observer's zenith and both celestial poles. Thus, a line running due north and south.

Meteor Shower: Numerous meteors that seem to radiate from a given point in the sky. Showers usually occur when the Earth passes through collections of material left in the path of a comet.

Meter: The basic metric unit of length.

Milky Way: The galaxy in which we reside. It appears as a diffuse band of light that encircles the sky. It is composed of millions of stars and nebulae.

Morning Star: A planet which rises in the east before Sunrise, and is then obscured with the approach of morning twilight.

Nautical Mile: The average length of an arc on the Earth's surface that crosses an angle of one minute from the center of the Earth (a sixtieth of a degree).

Neap Tides: The less extreme tides that occur when the Moon is near the first and third quarter phases.

Nebula: A cloud of dust or gas in space.

Orbit: A closed path along which a body moves as it revolves about a point in space.

Partial Eclipse: An eclipse of the Moon or the Sun in which the object is not totally obscured.

more GLOSSARY

Penumbra: Portion of a shadow from which only part of the light source is occulted by an opaque body.

Penumbral Eclipse: An eclipse of the Moon in which the Moon merely passes through the penumbra of the Earth's shadow.

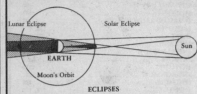

ECLIPSES

Perennial: Present at all times of the year. A plant which lives for many years.

Perigee: The point in the orbit of a body about the Earth, at which point it is positioned nearest the Earth.

Perihelion: The point in the orbit of a body about the Sun, at which it is positioned closest to the Sun.

pH: The relative acidity or alkalinity of a substance as measured on a scale from 0 (extreme acid) to 14 (extreme base). Pure water has a neutral pH of 7.0. The values represent the logarithm of the Hydrogen ion concentration.

Retrograde Motion: The apparent backward (Westward) motion along the ecliptic of an object as seen against the background of stars.

Right Ascension: Distance in hours, minutes and seconds, East along the celestial equator, from the first point of Aries.

Spring Tides: The most extreme tides produced when the Moon, Sun and Earth are aligned, hence at new and full Moons.

Stellar Evolution: The life cycle of a star. A star's change in size, pressure, luminosity, and structure.

Summer Solstice: The point on the ecliptic where the Sun appears farthest North of the equator. The first day of summer.

Sunspots: Regions of the Sun that appear dark because they are temporarily cooler than the rest of the Sun. Frequency of these spots occurs on an 11.2 year cycle. Last maximum year was 1979.

Superior Conjunction: A configuration of Mercury and Venus when they appear at the same degree of celestial longitude as the Sun, on its far side.

Synodic Period: The time required for a given planet to move from a configuration through a cycle ending back up at that configuration, i.e., New Moon to New Moon.

Syzygy: A configuration of any three celestial objects lined up as in conjunction or opposition.

Tide: The deformation of land, water and or atmospheric masses by the gravitational attraction of other celestial bodies.

Total Eclipse: An eclipse of the Sun where the Sun's face is completely obscured by the Moon. An eclipse of the Moon when the Moon is completely obscured within the umbra of the Earth's shadow.

Transit: The passage of a body across a given meridian.

Trine: Two planets in 120° relationship.

Twinkle: The apparent changes in the brightness and color of a star due to the motion of the Earth's atmosphere.

Umbra: The completely dark central portion of a shadow. The darker central portion of a Sunspot.

Universe: All of space that is occupied by matter and/or radiation.

Vernal Equinox: The point on the celestial equator where the Sun crosses it from south to north . One of two intersection points of the celestial equator and the ecliptic. This point is designated the First Point of Aries. The first day of spring.

Winter Solstice: A point on the ecliptic at which the Sun reaches its maximum distance south of the celestial equator. The first day of winter.

Zenith: The point directly overhead from the observer.

Zodiac: A band on the celestial sphere about 18° in latitude, centered on the ecliptic and along which all the planets, Moon and Sun appear to move across the sky during the course of the seasons. Twelve constellations: Aries, Taurus, Gemini, Cancer, Leo, Virgo, Libra, Scorpio, Sagittarius, Capricorn, Aquarius, and Pisces.

INDEX

222

Monthly Features

1984